*

A Contemporary Guide to Literary Terms

with Strategies for Writing Essays about Literature

THIRD EDITION

EDWIN J. BARTON and GLENDA A. HUDSON
California State University, Bakersfield

WADSWORTH
CENGAGE Learning™

Australia • Brazil • Japan • Korea • Mexico • Singapore • Spain • United Kingdom • United States

WADSWORTH
CENGAGE Learning

A Contemporary Guide to Literary Terms: with Strategies for Writing Essays about Literature, Third Edition

Edwin J. Barton and Glenda A. Hudson

Senior Publisher: Lyn Uhl

Publisher: Michael Rosenberg

Development Editor: Megan Garvey

Assistant Editor: Erin Bosco

Editorial Assistant: Rebecca Donahue

Marketing Manager: Melissa Holt

Marketing Coordinator: Brittany Blais

Marketing Communications Manager: Glenn McGibbon

Content Project Management: PreMediaGlobal

Art Director: Marissa Falco

Print Buyer: Betsy Donaghey

Rights Acquisition Specialist, Text: Shalice Shah-Caldwell

Production Service: PreMediaGlobal

Cover Designer: Hanh L. Luu

Compositor: PreMediaGlobal

For product information and technology assistance, contact us at **Cengage Learning Customer & Sales Support, 1-800-354-9706**

For permission to use material from this text or product, submit all requests online at **www.cengage.com/permissions**. Further permissions questions can be emailed to **permissionrequest@cengage.com.**

Library of Congress Control Number: 2010940625

ISBN-13: 978-1-111-34795-6

ISBN-10: 1-111-34795-6

Wadsworth
20 Channel Center Street
Boston, MA 02210
USA

Cengage Learning is a leading provider of customized learning solutions with office locations around the globe, including Singapore, the United Kingdom, Australia, Mexico, Brazil and Japan. Locate your local office at **international.cengage.com/region**

Cengage Learning products are represented in Canada by Nelson Education, Ltd.

For your course and learning solutions, visit **www.cengage.com**

Purchase any of our products at your local college store or at our preferred online store **www.cengagebrain.com**

Instructors: Please visit **login.cengage.com** and log in to access instructor-specific resources.

Printed in the United States of America
1 2 3 4 5 6 7 14 13 12 11 10

Contents

Preface

Whether you are an English major in an upper-level literature seminar or a nonmajor taking a required introductory course, or whether you are a graduate student studying foreign languages or a nonstudent reading for pleasure, your reading of literature can be immeasurably enriched with a deeper knowledge of literary terms and techniques. The discovery and identification of elements and approaches in drama, fiction, and poetry can bring a whole new level of enjoyment to any work of literature, and yet, without a guide to these literary conventions, many readers miss out. This brief yet comprehensive guide can give today's students—and general readers—the tools they need to understand and appreciate literature of all types.

The idea for the text originated with our students, who indicated that they needed a handbook to literature that provided advice in a concise, specific, and user-friendly format. They also wanted a text that offered basic definitions, helpful descriptions, and expanded examples (not merely references) from a wide range of literature, both classic and multicultural. With these needs in mind, we have created a practical handbook that provides cogent descriptions of traditional and contemporary literary terms without overburdening readers with excessive detail.

The definitions frequently incorporate stimulating discussion of how the original meaning of a term has evolved. The examples seek to clarify the meaning and use of terms in practical criticism. To promote further study, we have cross-referenced entries and descriptions. In many entries, references to authorities on terminology are provided. In addition, a list of secondary sources used in the entries is included at the end of the guide.

NEW TO THE THIRD EDITION

Drawing on the wide array of valuable suggestions provided by reviewers, instructors, and students, we have added new entries and made improvements to existing entries in the new edition. In every instance, we have insisted on the initial intent of this glossary, which was to provide students and instructors with clear definitions of literary terms and useful examples from both traditional and contemporary literature.

The third edition of *A Contemporary Guide to Literary Terms* incorporates important features:

- new entries for Antihero, Burlesque, Biographical Criticism, Ecocriticism, Fairy Tale, Folk Tale, Postcolonialism, and Sublime
- revised entries, when appropriate
- a new sample essay in the writing section comparing Shakespeare's *Hamlet* to Miller's *Death of A Salesman*
- a fully updated glossary, updated to reflect changes in MLA format

WIDE RANGE OF ILLUSTRATIVE MATERIAL

A Contemporary Guide to Literary Terms, Third Edition, encompasses a wide range of illuminating extended examples from a variety of literary genres (fiction, poetry, drama, and nonfiction prose) and film. These examples have been selected for both their familiarity and accessibility to readers from diverse backgrounds and age groups. The examples from film, combined with extracts from more traditional works, seek to involve readers in the critical process of reading and to encourage analysis of both high and popular culture.

ABUNDANT EXAMPLES OF PRACTICAL CRITICISM

A unique feature of the *Guide* is that it offers examples of practical criticism to illustrate the literary terms and to make individual entries useful for classroom discussion. No other literary handbook or glossary performs this task at length and with such detail. The text does not favor any individual approach to the study of literary works. Instead, it strives to orient students to all methods of contemporary criticism and to provide the groundwork to enable them to resist rigid or reductive approaches and to make their own choices. Thus, a major goal of this book is to introduce students to the diversity of literature and to the richness of critical approaches and contemporary literary theory available to them.

STRATEGIES FOR WRITING ESSAYS ABOUT LITERATURE

A Contemporary Guide to Literary Terms includes a second section entitled "Strategies for Writing Essays about Literature." This section includes six annotated student essays (five analytical and one research). We provide a background narrative for the first five essays, describing challenges faced by student writers in composing their essays and strategies for solving them. The background essays are intended as brief case studies on the process of writing a literary essay from start to finish. In addition, we include sections on Advice for Essay Examinations, Avoiding Plagiarism, A Brief Guide to Documenting Sources, and Grammar, Punctuation, and Style.

SUGGESTED USES FOR *A CONTEMPORARY GUIDE TO LITERARY TERMS*

We suggest that *A Contemporary Guide to Literary Terms* be used as a required reference for all introduction to literature courses, as well as courses that combine the studies of literature and composition. The book is intended to aid instructors in explaining basic literary definitions and the premises of contemporary critical approaches. By providing both instructors and students with a practical resource, we seek to help them avoid unnecessary repetition of basic definitions and concepts, so that they may devote more class time to discussing specific texts and to improving student writing.

The guide may also be used as a required supplementary text for intermediate and upper-level literature courses, especially those serving general studies students as well as literature majors. In addition, it will serve as a reference book for students in interdisciplinary courses, providing users with a basic literary background and acquaintance with contemporary theory.

ACKNOWLEDGMENTS

We are indebted to the superb advice and warm encouragement of our new editors at Cengage Learning, Michael Rosenberg, Publisher; and Megan Garvey, Development Editor. Monica Ayuso, Steven Carter, Lorna Clymer, Kim Flachmann, Michael Flachmann, Solomon Iyasere, Victor Lasseter, Jeff Mason, Merry Pawlowski, and Andrew Troup, our colleagues at California State University, Bakersfield, offered invaluable insights for the entries. We also thank the reviewers for their recommendations for revising this guide: J. David Moton, Bakersfield College; Jesse T. Airaudi, Baylor University (TX); Larry D. Griffin, Dyersburg State Community College (TN); Ilona Ilinitch Law, University of South Carolina-Aiken; Ilene Rubenstein, California State University-Northridge; P.C. Scheponik, Montgomery County Community College (PA); Richard J. Schrader, Boston College (MA); Marguerite Tassi, University of Nebraska at Kearney; and Linda Van der Wal, Grand Canyon University (AZ). Above all, we wish to express our gratitude to our students at California State University for their interest, participation, and enthusiasm.

E.J.B.
G.A.H.

How to Use the Guide

Principal Literary Terms

Capital letters in boldface **(PARODY; SETTING)** designate the principal literary terms; individual entries for these terms are presented in alphabetical order. At the end of most entries, other entries are cross-referenced or recommended for additional information (see **MYTH**; see **DECONSTRUCTION** and **CULTURAL CRITICISM**).

Related Terms

Lowercase letters in boldface appearing in the body of an entry **(comedy of manners; crosscutting)** designate other literary terms that are briefly discussed **(burlesque** under **MOCK HEROIC; spondee** under **METER**).

Published Works

Italicized titles (*Pride and Prejudice; The Color Purple*) designate published works and films. Dates of publication are indicated for all works discussed in the entries. Italics are also employed to distinguish words and phrases in languages other than English.

Indexes

Both principal literary terms and related terms are listed in an index at the end of the guide. A list of all works used as examples is offered in a separate index.

.

List of Secondary Sources

Abelove, Henry, et al., eds. *The Lesbian and Gay Studies Reader*. New York: Routledge, 1993.

Abrams, M. H. *The Correspondent Breeze: Essays on English Romanticism*. New York: Norton, 1984.

Auerbach, Erich. *Mimesis: The Representation of Reality in Western Literature*. Trans. Willard R. Trask. Princeton: Princeton UP, 1953.

Baker, Jr., Houston A. "Generational Shifts and the Recent Criticism of Afro-American Literature." *Black American Literature Forum* 15, 1 (1981): 3–21.

Barthes, Roland. *S/Z*. Trans. Richard Miller. New York: Hill, 1974.

Brooks, Cleanth. *The Well Wrought Urn: Studies in the Structure of Poetry*. New York: Harcourt, 1975.

Corbett, Edward. *Classical Rhetoric for the Modern Student*. 2nd ed. New York: Oxford UP, 1971.

Culler, Jonathan. *On Deconstruction*. Ithaca: Cornell UP, 1982.

Eliot, T. S. "Hamlet and His Problems." *The Sacred Wood: Essays on Poetry and Criticism*. London: Methuen, 1920.

———. "Tradition and the Individual Talent." *Selected Essays*. New York: Harcourt, 1950; 1978. 3–11.

Empson, William. *Seven Types of Ambiguity*. 3rd ed. London: Chatto, 1953.

Fish, Stanley. *Is There a Text in This Class!* Cambridge: Harvard UP, 1980.

Frye, Northrop. *Anatomy of Criticism: Four Essays*. Princeton: Princeton UP, 1957.

Gates, Jr., Henry Louis. *The Signifying Monkey: A Theory of Afro-American Literary Criticism*. Oxford: Oxford UP, 1988.

Greenblatt, Stephen. *Renaissance Self-Fashioning*. Chicago: U of Chicago P, 1980.

Hassan, Ihab. "Pluralism in Postmodern Perspective." *The Postmodern Turn: Essays in Postmodern Theory and Culture*. Columbus: Ohio State UP, 1987. 167–187.

Jagose, Annamarie. *Queer Theory: An Introduction*. New York: New York UP, 1996.

Jameson, Frederic. *The Political Unconscious*. Ithaca: Cornell UP, 1981.

Jung, Carl. *Archetypes and the Collective Unconscious*. Vol. 9 of *The Collected Works*. 20 vols. Princeton: Princeton UP, 1968.

Leal, Luis, and Pepe Barron. "Chicano Literature: An Overview." *Three American Literatures*. Ed. Houston A. Baker, Jr. New York: PMLA, 1982. 9–32.

Lewis, C. S. *Allegory of Love*. Oxford: Oxford UP, 1936.

Olsen, Tillie. *Silences*. New York: Delacorte, 1965.

Paredes, Raymund A. "The Evolution of Chicano Literature." *Three American Literatures*. Ed. Houston A. Baker, Jr. New York: PMLA, 1982. 33–79.

Propp, Vladimir. *Morphology of the Folktale*. 2nd ed. Austin: U of Texas P, 1968.

Ransom, John Crowe. *The World's Body*. Baton Rouge: Louisiana State UP, 1968.

Rich, Adrienne. *On Lies, Secrets, and Silence: Selected Prose, 1966–1978*. New York: Norton, 1979.

Saussure, Ferdinand de. *Course in General Linguistics*. Trans. Charles Bally. New York: Philosophical Library, 1959.

Sedgwick, Eve Kosofsky. *Epistemology of the Closet*. Berkeley: U of California P, 1992.

Showalter, Elaine. *A Literature of Their Own*. Princeton: Princeton UP, 1977.

Smith, Barbara Herrnstein. *Contingencies of Value: Alternative Perspectives for Critical Theory*. Cambridge: Harvard UP, 1988.

Terrell, Carroll. *A Companion to the Cantos of Ezra Pound*. Orono: National Poetry Foundation, 1984.

Tey, Diana Rebolledo, and Eliana S. Rivero, eds. "Introduction." *Infinite Divisions: An Anthology of Chicana Literature*. Tucson: U of Arizona P, 1993. 1–33.

Wellek, Rene. "The Concept of Romanticism in Literary History." *Concepts of Criticism*. Ed. Stephen Nichols. New Haven: Yale UP, 1963.

William K. Wimsatt. *The Verbal Icon: Studies in the Meaning of Poetry*. Lexington: U of Kentucky P, 1963.

PART I

*

Glossary

A

ABSTRACT LANGUAGE

The word *abstract* derives from the Latin *abstractus*, which means "removed from." The term is conventionally employed to describe ideas and words that are removed from material reality. In speaking of language or diction, conventional linguists employ the term *abstract* to identify words that are used to refer to concepts rather than concrete or physical reality. Whereas words such as *girl, forest*, and *stone* are commonly used to refer to persons, places, and objects, words such as *love, peace*, and *steadfastness* are more often employed to express ideas or emotions. In Wordsworth's sonnet entitled "London, 1802" (published in 1807), for example, the speaker addresses himself to the soul of John Milton and pleads for the restoration of the qualities of greatness associated with a bygone era:

> . . . We are selfish men;
> Oh! raise us up, return to us again;
> And give us manners, virtue, freedom, power.

Rather than pleading with the ghost of Milton to give his countrymen quantities of material goods, Wordsworth calls on him to bestow the more abstract qualities of "virtue, freedom, power."

Some critics and commentators have found recourse to using the term *abstract art* to describe works that are blatantly nonreferential: that is to say, they are works of art that do not refer to conventional expressions of persons, places, or things in the physical world. In early twentieth-century painting, the **abstract expressionists** eschewed the pictorial genres of portraits and landscapes; instead, they worked with arrangements of shapes and colors, geometric and nongeometric designs. These abstract expressionists sought to strip their medium down to basics. The first steps were to remove the **mimetic** and **narrative** elements from their art. Their paintings tell no story and do not seek to imitate conventional representations of concrete reality. Similarly, some modern poets seem to choose and arrange words primarily for their sound values. In "Bantams in Pine-Woods" (1923), for instance, Wallace Stevens begins his poem, which is about the relationship between the poet and the world he observes, with a rather curious couplet:

> Chieftan Iffucan of Azcan in caftan
> Of tan with henna hackles, halt!

Dictionary meanings for most of the words in this couplet could be found and construed into a descriptive address to a rooster. However, the excessive alliteration in these lines suggests that Stevens is more interested in the aural effects of these words than he is in their referential meaning; that is to say, these lines are abstract in the sense that they do not seek to form a mental picture of an actual bantam in a real forest of pines but rather to call attention to the agency of sound and the relations between sounds in the lines. The arrangement and repetition of sounds are the message of the poem, since they do not seek to represent a concrete reality. Indeed, one of the points of Stevens's poetry is precisely that poets cannot represent the concrete world objectively or accurately because their thoughts and feelings create abstractions. See **CONCRETE LANGUAGE, MIMESIS** and **NARRATIVE POINT OF VIEW**.

ABSURD, THE

The phrase *the absurd* derives from the Latin *absurdus*, meaning "discordant"; the term is often employed by **existentialist philosophers** to describe a kind of spiritual alienation: feeling "out of tune" with the universe in which one exists. According to some existentialist thinkers, this sense of alienation or disharmony proceeds from a loss of faith in such traditional metaphysical concepts as a rationally ordered universe directed by a benevolent deity. With this loss of faith in a transcendent power, human beings may come to perceive their lives as meaningless and themselves as helpless in the face of a vast nothingness.

The **literature of the absurd** is most prominently represented in the works of several modern playwrights—Samuel Beckett, Eugene Ionesco, Edward Albee, and Harold Pinter—as well as the French thinkers and writers Jean-Paul Sartre and Albert Camus. Camus's novel entitled *The Stranger* (1942) reports the experiences of its hero (or antihero), Meursault, whose name means "death wish." Having learned of his mother's death in an old-age home, Meursault finds that he is unable to feel the depth of his loss; instead, he indulges himself in sensual pleasures until he accidentally kills an Arab, stands for trial, and faces death by the guillotine. At the conclusion of the novel, Meursault contemplates his situation and discovers a kind of perverse consolation in his awareness of the absurd: "It was as if that great rush of anger had washed me clean, emptied me of hope, and gazing up at the dark sky spangled with its signs and stars, for the first time, the first, I laid my heart open to the benign indifference of the universe. To feel it so like myself, indeed, so brotherly, made me realize that I'd been happy, and that I was happy still." Thus, for Meursault, this awareness of the indifference of the universe brings relief, since he had worried that his own indifference to life was unjustified or morally wrong.

In many cases, the literature of the absurd sharpens the sense of a seemingly irrational existence (without inherent purpose or truth) by means of **gallows humor** and **black comedy** or **grotesque comedy**. In Joseph Heller's novel *Catch-22* (1961), for example, a military physician asks the protagonist, Yossarian, to pose as a dying soldier for an Italian-American family who have arrived too late to pay their last respects:

> "Giuseppe," the mother said.
> "Did you have a priest?" the brother wanted to know.
> "Yes," Yossarian lied, wincing again.
> "That's good," the brother decided. "Just as long as you're getting every-thing you've got coming to you. We came all the way from New York. We were afraid we wouldn't get here in time."
> "In time for what?"
> "In time to see you before you died."
> "What difference would it make?"
> "We didn't want you to die by yourself."
> "What difference would it make?"
> "He must be getting delirious," the brother said. "He keeps saying the same thing over and over again."
> "That's really funny," the old man replied. "All the time I thought his name was Giuseppe, and now I find out his name is Yossarian. That's really very funny."

The ironic comedy of the situation serves both to undercut and make more poignant the suggestion that even the love of one's family can make no difference to a dying man.

In the **theater of the absurd**, the audience is confronted with seemingly unintelligible plots and characters who speak and behave irrationally. In Beckett's play *Waiting for Godot* (1955), for instance, the protagonists seek to amuse themselves with aimless conversation and meaningless activity while waiting, without much hope, for the appearance of Godot, whose very name suggests an absent deity. Another representative example of the theater of the absurd may be found in Tom Stoppard's tragic farce *Rosencrantz and Guildenstern Are Dead* (1966), which was made into a film of the same name in 1990. The title characters find themselves trapped in a play, Shakespeare's *Hamlet*, that calls for them to be put to death. Their situation is absurd in the sense that their thoughts and actions are meaningless in the context of predetermined fate. See **EXPRESSIONISM**.

AESTHETICS/AESTHETICISM/AESTHETIC MOVEMENT

The word *aesthetics* derives from the Greek *aisthetikos*, which translates as "pertaining to sense perception." Modern literary critics have tended to use the term when referring to perceptions of beauty or the beautiful, but aesthetics may also be associated with the notion of good taste. That is to say, one who perceives or judges beauty finely may be said to have an aesthetic sense. The term is also employed to describe a writer's theory of or approach to artistic expression.

In the late nineteenth century, proponents of **Aestheticism** in France associated themselves with the phrase *"l'art pour l'art"* (art for art's sake), proclaiming that the pursuit of the beautiful had little or nothing to do with practical purpose or moral instruction. In this regard, they were influenced by critical statements of Edgar Allan Poe, who asserted in his essay "The Poetic Principle" (1850), "I would define, in brief, the Poetry of words as *The Rhythmical Creation of Beauty*. Its sole arbiter is Taste. With the Intellect or with the Conscience, it has only collateral relations. Unless incidentally, it has no concern whatever either with Duty or with Truth."

The **Aesthetic Movement** is associated not only with French poets and novelists such as Baudelaire, Gautier, Mallarmé, and Flaubert but also with English writers such as Swinburne, Wilde, Symons, and Yeats. The English aestheticists also tended to hold up the creation and contemplation of beauty as the sole reasons for and measures of art. One of the early examples of this aesthetic credo may be found in the concluding lines of John Keats's poem "Ode on a Grecian Urn" (1820):

"Beauty is truth, truth beauty,"—that is all
Ye know on earth, and all ye need know.

One of the most lucid and famous expressions of Aestheticism comes in the conclusion of Walter Pater's study entitled *Studies in the History of the Renaissance* (1873): "Of this wisdom, the poetic passion, the desire of beauty, the love of art for art's sake, has most; for art comes to you professing frankly to give nothing but the highest quality to your moments as they pass, and simply for those moments' sake."

A number of contemporary theorists have objected to Aestheticism on the grounds that it urges an ahistorical appreciation of literature: that is, the tendency to place art outside of the forces and processes of history. See **MARXIST CRITICISM**; see also **NEW CRITICISM/FORMALISM**, and **NEW HISTORICISM**.

AFFECTIVE FALLACY

As described by W. K. Wimsatt and Monroe C. Beardsley in an essay reprinted in *The Verbal Icon* (1954), the affective fallacy is "a confusion between the poem and its *results* (what it *is* and what it *does*)." For instance, a reader may judge a literary work by the emotional effect it elicits in him or her. This sort of appreciation, according to Wimsatt and Beardsley, is limited because it relies on impressions rather than analysis of technical devices such as diction, syntax, imagery, and tone. According to the **New Critics** of the mid-twentieth century, relying merely on feelings about a work of literature may lead readers to embrace a kind of relativism, in which there are no critical opinions but only a variety of arbitrary responses.

Although the New Critics strenuously warned against the dangers of affective readings and urged their students to concentrate on the text (specifically its internal and external forms), a contemporary school of criticism devoted to studying **reader-response** has challenged the notion of the affective fallacy. Reader-response critics such as Stanley Fish have argued that all readings are arbitrary and that reliance on affective responses is no more fallacious than reliance on New Critical methods. See **NEW CRITICISM/FORMALISM** and **READER-RESPONSE CRITICISM**.

ALLEGORY

An allegory is a work of art intending to be meaningful on at least two levels of understanding: typically, a literal level and an abstract (e.g., moral) level. The term derives from the Greek *allegorein*, meaning "to speak in other terms." Literary critics tend to use allegory in referring to a narrative poem, a play, or a work of prose fiction that bears meaning on both a **literal** and a **figurative** or **moral** level.

In **Christian allegories**, for instance, characters' journeys may be appreciated not only as their physical progress through time and space (literal level) but also as their spiritual progress or moral development (figurative level) toward heaven and salvation. **Allegorical characters** are often **personifications** of qualities, concepts, or types. For example, in Hawthorne's "Young Goodman Brown" (1835), the protagonist's wife is named Faith; her name may be appreciated on at least two levels. Near the beginning of the story, Young Goodman Brown starts a journey to meet with an elder traveler, who may be thought to represent the Devil or Satan. Upon Goodman Brown's arrival, the elder traveler asks why he is late for their appointment. Goodman Brown replies, "Faith kept me back a while." In a literal sense, this response suggests that Brown was physically detained by his wife. On the figurative level, however, some readers may infer that Hawthorne plays on the concept that faith in God, or our friends and family, enables us to resist the lure of evil.

Goodman Brown journeys from the familiar surroundings of his town to unfamiliar parts of the dark forest. In a literal sense, he moves from a community organized around a central meeting place or church to a wilderness. On a figurative or allegorical level, he abandons his moral and spiritual center for the chaos of the spiritual darkness.

In **political allegories**, such as George Orwell's *Animal Farm* (1945), the characters and actions of a work may be understood to represent the author's interpretation of political or historical figures and events. In **allegories of ideas**, such as Jonathan Swift's *Gulliver's Travels* (1726), characters and actions may serve to comment on philosophical principles or belief systems.

Other traditional works of literature employing allegorical plots, themes, characters, and settings include **morality plays**, such as *Everyman* (c. 1509-1519), and religious works, such as John Bunyan's *Pilgrim's Progress* (1678-1684). Dante's

Divine Comedy (c. 1314) is a typological allegory, which may be understood on at least four levels: literal (concrete), allegorical (moral), tropological (figurative), and anagogical (spiritual).

More contemporary examples include such films as the so-called *Star Wars* trilogy (1977-1983) and *Monty Python and the Holy Grail* (Terry Gilliam, 1975). In the former, Luke Skywalker and Princess Leia belong to a rebel group opposed to the ruling Empire. On the figurative level, these two groups clearly represent the forces of good and evil in the universe. Indeed, the characters often refer to "the force," a universal energy source that may be tapped for either benevolent or destructive purposes. With his dark apparel, helmet and cloak, and machine-like breathing, Darth Vader is a blatantly allegorical character representing evil. He belongs to "the dark side." His name would seem to be a play on the words "dark," "death," "invader," and, perhaps most tellingly, "father." The plot of the *Star Wars* films concerns itself principally with the spiritual development of Luke Skywalker. With the help of spiritual advisors such as Obi-Wan Kenobi and Yoda, Luke acquires the strength, discipline, and maturity to resist the temptation of the "dark side." In the end, the forces of good conquer the forces of evil, and Luke even manages to save Darth Vader's soul.

Monty Python and the Holy Grail satirizes the allegorical elements associated with Arthurian legends. The film plays on a knowledge of these allegories in several ways. In an obvious way, the characters of the film mock the spiritual qualities of courage, honor, and chastity represented literally and figuratively by the knights of the round table, because the knights in the Monty Python version prove to be cowardly, deceitful, and lecherous. See **PERSONIFICATION**.

ALLITERATION

Alliteration is the repetition of sound in poetry or prose. This repetition may come at the beginning, middle, or end of words. Although some critics wish to limit the use of the term to describe only the repetition of consonants or only the repetition of sounds in approximate rhymes, this broader definition is more serviceable. There are two types of alliteration: **consonance**, which designates the repetition of consonant sounds, and **assonance**, which refers to the repetition of vowel sounds.

A passage from Coleridge's "The Rime of the Ancient Mariner" (1798) offers several examples of consonance:

> The fair breeze blew,
> the white foam flew,
> The furrow followed free;
> We were the first that ever burst
> Into that silent sea.

In these lines, Coleridge employs consonance for several purposes: to slow the pace of the lines, to create a dramatic tone, and, perhaps above all, to give pleasure to those who read aloud.

Consonance can likewise be used to great effect in prose, as the beginning of Poe's "The Fall of the House of Usher" (1839) illustrates: "During the whole of a dull, dark, and soundless day in the autumn of the year, when the clouds hung oppressively low in the heavens. . . ." The repetition of the *d, 1,* and *h* sounds slows the pace of the phrases and thereby gives an oppressively melancholy tone to the exposition.

The opening lines of Wallace Stevens's "Sunday Morning" (1923) offer several examples of assonance:

> Complacencies of the peignoir, and late
> Coffee and oranges in a sunny chair,
> And the green freedom of a cockatoo . . .

The repetition of the long *a* sounds in the first line may convey the sense of comfort the woman feels lingering over breakfast in her dressing gown, whereas the repetition of the long *e* sounds in the third line may suggest the unfettered pleasure of the cockatoo.

In some cases, writers may employ both consonance and assonance to bind words and phrases, as Cathy Song does in her poem entitled "Lost Sister" (1983):

> In China,
> Even the peasants
> Named their first daughters
> Jade—
> the stone that in the far fields
> could moisten the dry season,
> could make men move mountains
> for the healing green of the inner hills
> glistening like slices of winter melon.

The alliteration in these lines gives a rhythmic feel to the free verse poem. See **CONSONANT SOUNDS** and **FREE VERSE**.

ALLUSION

An allusion is an indirect or inexplicit reference by one text to another text, to a historical occurrence, or to myths and legends. A direct allusion refers to a historical, mythic, or legendary person, place, or activity by name. An inexplicit allusion relies on associations that only those readers who are familiar with history, myth, and legends may notice.

In Act 4 of Shakespeare's *Antony and Cleopatra* (1606-1607), Antony believes he has been betrayed by Cleopatra and angrily proclaims,

> The shirt of Nessus is upon me; teach me,
> Alcides, thou mine ancestor, thy rage.
> Let me lodge Lichus on the horns o' th' moon,

And with those hands, that grasp'd the heaviest club,
Subdue my worthiest self. (4.12.43-47)

The term *allusion* derives from the Latin verb *alludere*, which means "to play with." In this case, Antony plays with a reference to Greek mythology; that is to say, although he relies on knowledge of the myth to be understood, he alters the meaning of the myth to suit his own circumstances. He compares himself to the mythic hero Heracles (also known as Hercules), a descendent of Alcaeus (thus the reference to the familial line known as Alcides). Nessus was a centaur who attempted to rape Heracles's wife, Deianeira. Having been mortally wounded by Heracles, who punished him for his crime with a poisoned arrow, Nessus gave to Deianeira a sample of his blood, which he claimed would enable her to win back Heracles's love should he ever cease to love her. When Heracles later fell in love with Iole, Deianeira sought to reclaim him by sending him a garment smeared with the blood of Nessus. Far from making Heracles love her, the garment smeared with poisoned blood drove Heracles mad with rage. Antony alludes to this myth by comparing his situation to Heracles's; he believes he has been harmed by his lover, Cleopatra, when she was supposed to be helping him.

In some cases, authors allude to works of literature by contemporaries; such is the case with Lorraine Hansberry's *Raisin in the Sun* (1959), the very title of which alludes to Langston Hughes's poem "Dream Deferred" (1951):

What happens to a dream deferred?
Does it dry up
Like a raisin in the sun?
Or fester like a sore—

And then run?
Does it stink like rotten meat?
Or crust and sugar over—
Like a syrupy sweet?

Maybe it just sags
Like a heavy load.

Or does it explode?

Hansberry uses this allusion to place her play about an urban black family, whose dream it is to move into a suburban, largely white neighborhood, in the context of the larger historical pursuit of equality for blacks in America. See **INTERTEXTUALITY**.

AMBIGUITY

The word *ambiguity* is defined as "susceptibility to multiple interpretations": that is to say, ambiguity leads to uncertainty about meaning or intention. Prior to the twentieth century, literary critics used the term to describe either a stylistic flaw or an ingenious play on multiple meanings of a word, a passage, or an idea. Writing that was unintentionally difficult to comprehend was considered ambiguous in a negative sense. By the mid-twentieth century, deliberate ambiguity, in which the author intentionally opens his or her work to various kinds and levels of interpretation, was noted by many of the New Critics as a mark of masterful artistry. This latter sense of the term was promoted by William Empson in his study entitled *Seven Types of Ambiguity* (1930). As an example of his third kind of ambiguity, Empson quotes a passage from Samuel Johnson's "The Vanity of Human Wishes" (1749) in which the speaker describes the situation of the aging man who prays for a long life but finds his later years plagued by problems and persons he cannot control:

> The watchful Guests still hint the last Offence,
> The Daughter's Petulance, the Son's Expence;
> Improve his heady Rage with treacherous Skill,
> And mould his Passions till they make his Will.

In punning on the word *heady*, Johnson uses ambiguity to positive effect. As Empson points out, "heady" may refer to "head of the family" or the sense that his problems with his daughter and son will soon "come to a head." These interpretations, of course, supplement the more obvious meanings of "heady Rage": the faults of his son and daughter are making this father's head ache or are driving him insane with anger. Likewise, the word *Will* may be interpreted as meaning either "desire" or "a legal document bequeathing wealth and possessions." That is to say, on the one hand, the daughter's bad temper and the son's expensive tastes combine to frustrate the father, so that the children can have their way and make their father's "Will" their own; on the other hand, their behavior serves to make him ill with "Rage," thus hastening his death and his children's control of his fortune through his "Will." The multiple possibilities of interpretations for these words and phrases, according to Empson, demonstrate the range of Johnson's wit, since he is able to make all the meanings "dovetail" with the central themes of the poem: the ways in which human wishes show themselves to be "vain," which is itself a pun on words (*vain* in the sense of immodest and *vain* in the sense of useless).

The Colombian writer Gabriel García Márquez employs ambiguity throughout his story "A Very Old Man with Enormous Wings" (1955). When the inhabitants of a small village find an old man with wings, they begin to speculate about his identity: some believe he is a shipwrecked sailor; others insist that he is an angel sent from heaven. The evidence for the latter interpretation is ambiguous: those who go to him seeking cures for their physical problems do find themselves altered, but in ways they did not expect:

> . . . the few miracles attributed to the angel showed a certain mental disorder, like the blind man who didn't recover his sight but grew three new teeth, or the paralytic who didn't get to walk but almost won the lottery, and the leper whose sores sprouted sunflowers.

The ambiguous identity of the very old man is never settled. At the end of the story, one of the villagers raises the possibility that the old man never existed at all:

> Elisenda let out a sigh of relief, for herself and for him, when she saw him pass over the last of the houses, holding himself up in some way with the risky flapping of a senile vulture. She kept watching him until it was no longer possible for her to see him, because then he was no longer an annoyance in her life but an imaginary dot on the horizon of the sea.

García Márquez's use of ambiguity deliberately raises the whole problem of interpretation by suggesting that meaning is always somewhat uncertain. See **INTERPRETATION/MEANING** and **NEW CRITICISM/ FORMALISM**.

AMERICAN LITERARY PERIODS

Although contemporary literary historians are hesitant about assigning periods and dates to American literary history, most scholars and anthologists of American literature consent to a general outline: Early American literature from the first Puritan settlements in New England to the events leading up to the Revolutionary War (early 1600s to 1770s); the Early National or Federal period from the beginnings of the Revolution to the formation of the Transcendentalist Club in Boston (1770s to 1830s); the American Romantic period from the beginnings of American Transcendentalism to the end of the American Civil War (1830s to 1865); the period of American Realism and Naturalism from the conclusion of the Civil War to the turn of the century (1865 to the early 1900s); the period of American Modernism from the early part of the twentieth century to the decade immediately following World War II; and what has come to be called the period of Postmodernism (1960s to present).

Colonial Period

The Early American or Colonial period is largely characterized by literature of a religious nature. William Bradford's *Of Plymouth Plantation* and John Winthrop's *Journal*, both of which were written in the early 1600s, relate the stories of the Separatist and Puritan flight from religious corruption and intolerance in the Old World and of their desire for religious freedom in the New World. Both journals draw on Old Testament characters and events to express the meaning of their experiences, in which they see themselves as latter-day Israelites, the new chosen people of God, making their exodus from a land of persecution to a second Promised Land. In a sermon entitled "A Model of Christian Charity," Winthrop concludes his vision of a Christian community in covenant with God by alluding to *Matthew* 5.14-15:

> We shall find that the God of Israel is among us, when ten of us shall be able to resist a thousand of our enemies; when He shall make us a praise and glory that men shall say of succeeding plantations, "the Lord make it like that of New England." For we must consider that we shall be as a city upon a hill. The eyes of all people are upon us, so that if we shall deal falsely with our God in this work we have undertaken, and so cause Him to withdraw His present help from us, we shall be made a story and a by-word through the world.

Likewise, Christian poets Anne Bradstreet and Edward Taylor use their verses to praise God and acknowledge his sovereignty and grace. As an epitaph for her deceased grandson Simon, Bradstreet writes,

> No sooner came, but gone, and fall'n asleep.
> Acquaintance short, yet parting caused us weep;
> Three flowers, two scarcely blown, the last i' th' bud,
> Cropped by th' Almighty's hand, yet is He good.
> With dreadful awe before Him let's be mute,
> Such was His will, but why, let's not dispute,
> With humble hearts and mouths put in the dust,
> Let's say He's merciful as well as just.

In this way, Bradstreet seeks to find comfort in the notion that the death was God's will and that God's absolute sovereignty in human affairs is not only justified but also benevolent. This same theme is central to Jonathan Edwards's sermon "Sinners in the Hands of an Angry God":

> The God that holds you over the pit of hell, much as one holds a spider or some loathsome insect over the fire, abhors you, and is dreadfully provoked. His wrath towards you burns like fire; He looks upon you as worthy of nothing else but to be cast into the fire; He is of purer eyes than to bear to have you in His sight; you are ten thousand times more abominable in His eyes than the most hateful venomous serpent is in ours. You have offended Him infinitely more than ever stubborn rebel did his prince; and yet it is nothing but His hand that holds you from falling into the fire every moment.

Other important works of this period include Mary Rowlandson's captivity narrative and the poetry of African-American Phillis Wheatley.

Early National Period

The American brand of Calvinist theology, which dominates the literature of the Colonial period, gives way in the decades leading up to the American Revolution to ideals and beliefs born of what Thomas Paine calls "the age of reason": deism, democracy, and the American dream. In the first chapter of *The Age of*

Reason (1793), Paine offers a "profession of faith" that succinctly sums up the relation between deism (belief in the existence of one God based on the evidence of reason and nature) and democracy (a form of government in which power is vested in the people):

> I believe in one God, and no more, and I hope for happiness beyond this life. I believe in the equality of man, and I believe that religious duties consist in doing justice, loving mercy, and endeavouring to make our fellow creatures happy. But, lest it should be supposed that I believe many other things in addition to these, I shall, in the progress of this work, declare things I do not believe, and my reasons for not believing them. I do not believe in the creed professed by the Jewish church, by the Roman church, by the Greek church, by the Turkish church, by the Protestant church, nor by any church that I know of. My own mind is my own church.

The note of individualism struck in the last line of this passage aligns Paine with one of the towering figures of the period, Benjamin Franklin, whose *Autobiography* is among the most important and influential works in American literature. In the opening chapter, Franklin writes:

> Having emerg'd from the Poverty and Obscurity in which I was born and bred, to a State of Affluence and some Degree of Reputation in the World, and having gone so far thro' with a considerable Share of Felicity, the conducting Means I made use of, which, with the Blessing of God, so well succeeded, my Posterity may like to know, as they may find some of them suitable to their own Situations, and therefore fit to be imitated.

Thus, Franklin creates the notion of the "Great American Dream," in which an individual, through hard work, thrift, ingenuity, and moral uprightness, can rise from "rags to riches." Other important works of this period include *The Federalist Papers* of James Madison and Alexander Hamilton, the poetry of the Connecticut Wits, and the slave narratives of Frederick Douglass and other African-Americans.

Romantic Period

The period of American Romanticism, which is sometimes called the American Renaissance, is notable for the influence of European Romanticism on American literature, the introduction of transcendentalist thought, and the writing of what Nathaniel Hawthorne called "blasted allegories." Perhaps the most important influence of European Romanticism is found in the notion that nature and natural processes can be used to reflect, express, or refine human emotions. William Cullen Bryant's "Thanatopsis" (1821), though written prior to 1830, is nevertheless a representative expression of this idea in American literature:

> To him who in the love of Nature holds
> Communion with her visible forms, she speaks
> A various language; for his gayer hours

She has a voice of gladness, and a smile
And eloquence of beauty, and she glides
Into his darker musings, with a mild
And gentle sympathy, that steals away
Their sharpness, ere he is aware.

Likewise, in the poetry of Walt Whitman, nature and natural processes "speak" to him, often providing **epiphanies** (moments of profound insight), as in "Out of the Cradle Endlessly Rocking" (1859):

The boy ecstatic, with his bare feet the waves, with his hair the atmosphere dallying,
The love in the heart long pent, now loose, now at last tumultuously bursting,
The aria's meaning, the ears, the soul, swiftly depositing,
The strange tears down the cheeks coursing,
The colloquy there, the trio, each uttering,
The undertone, the savage old mother incessantly crying,
The boy's soul's questions sullenly timing, some drown'd secret hissing,
To the outsetting bard.

In this case, "the savage old mother," the sea, teaches the boy, "the outsetting bard," that death is part of the process of nature. The "drown'd secret hissing" of the sea is the repeated word: "Death, death, death, death, death."

American transcendentalists, too, were influenced by European Romantics, especially Samuel Taylor Coleridge, whose *Biographia Literaria* (1817) touts the power of imaginative faculties and intuition. American **Transcendentalism** also drew on Platonic philosophy, which insists that reality exists in the realm of ideas rather than in the physical world, and Eastern religions, which vaunt the spiritual over the material. This type of idealism was rejected by another group of American Romantics who have been called antitranscendentalists. The works of Nathaniel Hawthorne, Herman Melville, and Emily Dickinson often draw upon the history and theology of Puritanism in America, but they undermine the absolutism of Puritan allegories by introducing ambiguities and epistemological doubts. In the chapter of Melville's *Moby-Dick* (1851) entitled "The Doubloon," for instance, several of the sailors seek to interpret the inscriptions on a coin nailed to the mast by Captain Ahab. Each sailor's interpretation is so radically different from the others that the character Pip remarks, "I look, you look, he looks; we look, ye look, they look. . . . And I, you, and he; and we, ye, and they are all bats." Unlike the transcendentalists, who imagine that the human soul can seek for and reach ultimate truths, Melville raises questions about human epistemology (the study of what we know and how we know it) that suggest that human beings are forever blind to truth because they project their own preoccupations on to whatever they behold. Other important works of this period include the writings of Washington Irving, the novels of James Fenimore Cooper, the short fiction of Edgar Allen Poe, and the nonfiction prose of protofeminist Margaret Fuller.

Period of Realism and Naturalism

The period of American **Realism** was, in part, a reaction against certain types of Romanticism that were thought too ethereal and sentimental to deal with the pragmatic realities of a world hardened by rapid advances in technology, rampant materialism, and radical skepticism. Mark Twain's *The Adventures of Huckleberry Finn* (1885), William Dean Howells's *The Rise of Silas Lapham* (1885), and Henry James's *The Ambassadors* (1903) are representative of this period in which American literature was often critical of cultural pretensions and moral hypocrisies of America and Americans. In this period as well, the works of American Naturalism emerged. The basic tenet of **Naturalism** was that far from possessing the freedom of will imagined by the transcendentalists, men and women were determined by forces beyond their control: nature, heredity, and social environment. Stephen Crane's *The Red Badge of Courage* (1894), Frank Norris's *McTeague* (1899), and Theodore Dreiser's *Sister Carrie* (1900) are representative examples of Naturalist works of fiction, many of which were influenced by ideas associated with social Darwinism. Other important works of this period include the novels of Edith Wharton, the regional fiction of Sarah Orne Jewett and Kate Chopin, and both the short and long fiction of Jack London.

Modernist Period

For many American writers of the Modernist period, the crucial historical event was World War I, after which the old notions of religion, honor, the progress of civilization, and the improvability of man no longer seemed tenable. Several of the so-called High Modernists believed that civilization and civilized man existed only in fragments: enduring myths, classical literature, and pockets of history and culture. In their major works of poetry, Ezra Pound and T. S. Eliot juxtapose fragments of high culture with a fallen, mechanistic, and spiritless modern world. American **Modernism** is also noted for producing great technical innovations in writing. The experimental techniques of Gertrude Stein and William Faulkner in prose fiction and those of Pound in his *Cantos* and Eliot in *The Waste Land* are among the best examples. Other important works of this period include the poetry of Edwin Arlington Robinson, Robert Frost, and Wallace Stevens and the prose fiction of F. Scott Fitzgerald, Ernest Hemingway, and Willa Cather.

Postmodern Period

The **Postmodern** period in American literature is often associated with the social and political upheaval of the late 1960s, but, in some ways, it began with the so-called confessional poets (Robert Lowell, John Berryman, Sylvia Plath) and Beat Generation writers (Allan Ginsberg, Jack Kerouac, William Burroughs), many of whom were writing in the 1950s. Although it is not easily classified, **postmodern** literature is generally characterized by a predilection for parody of classical themes and genres, a delight in experimenting with self-reflexive styles, and a penchant for the absurd (see **POSTMODERNISM**). Representative works of this period include the plays of Edward Albee, the poetry of Robert Duncan and Jack Spicer, and the novels of John Barth, Thomas Pynchon, and Don Delillo. See **MODERNISM**, **NATURALISM**, **POSTMODERNISM**, **REALISM**, **ROMANTICISM**, and **TRANSCENDENTALISM**.

ANALOGY

An analogy is a comparison between persons, places, objects, or ideas for the purpose of explanation. The term derives from the Greek *analogos*, which means "proportionate"; thus an analogy is distinguishable by its fourfold structure or proportionate ratio. In his *Poetics*, Aristotle (384–322 B.C.) states that a metaphorical analogy is present "whenever there are four terms so related that the second (B) is to the first (A), as the fourth (D) is to the third (C)." Ezra Pound's short poem entitled "In a Station of the Metro" (1916) offers an example:

> The apparition of these faces in the crowd,
> Petals on a wet, black bough.

Pound compares the appearance of a few striking faces (A) in a subway station filled with people (B) to the striking contrast of bright flowers (C) against the background of "a wet, black bough" (D).

In prose, analogies are commonly employed to show similarity between persons, objects, or concepts, usually to clarify or justify a point. In *A Vindication of the Rights of Woman* (1792), Mary Wollenstonecraft offers a direct analogy, in the form of a simile, between women and flowers:

> The conduct and manners of women, in fact, evidently prove that their minds are not in a healthy state; for, like the flowers which are planted in too rich a soil, strength and usefulness are sacrificed to beauty; and the flaunting leaves, after having pleased a fastidious eye, fade, disregarded on the stalk, long before the season when they ought to have arrived at maturity.

Through this analogy, Wollenstonecraft clarifies her point about what she calls the "false system of education" given to females in her society: like some flowers, they are trained to be frail and beautiful rather than hearty and useful.

In his "Letter from Birmingham Jail" (1963), Martin Luther King, Jr., employs several allusions as analogies to justify his methods of calling attention to the need for civil rights for black Americans:

> But though I was initially disappointed at being categorized as an extremist, as I continued to think about the matter I gradually gained a measure of satisfaction from the label. Was not Jesus an extremist for love . . . Was not Amos an extremist for justice . . . Was not Paul an extremist for the Christian gospel . . . Was not Martin Luther an extremist . . . And John Bunyan . . . And Abraham Lincoln . . . And Thomas Jefferson. . . .

Through these analogies, King compares the justifications for his cause to those of Biblical figures, Protestant reformers, and widely admired American presidents.

ANTIHERO

An antihero in literature is a main character who is bereft of the qualities such as honor, bravery, and virtue associated with a classic hero or protagonist; likewise, an antihero's actions, deeds, or experiences are not those of a noble character in a tragedy, for instance, who suffers a downfall that inspires pity and fear in the audience. Although antiheroes can be found in earlier periods of literature, they are more prominent in modern literature, particularly the literature following World War I and World War II. In many ways, the preponderance of antiheroes in modern fiction and drama reflects skepticism about or loss of faith in traditional heroes and the qualities that make them heroic.

In Albert Camus's *The Stranger* (1942), the main character, called Meursault, is a kind of existential antihero in the sense that his life or existence is seemingly without meaning or purpose. In the beginning of the novel, the news of his mother's death has no effect on him; indeed, he shows little affect under any circumstances. Later in the plot, Meursault kills an Arab for no discernible reason. The first-person retrospective description of the act makes it appear almost involuntary:

> It seemed that the sky had opened above me to rain with fire. All my being gripped me, and I tensed my hand on the revolver. The trigger gave way; I felt the burnished underbelly of the butt, and then it was, in the brightness of the dry and deafening moment, that everything commenced. I was shaking with sweat and sun. I understood that I had destroyed the equilibrium of the day, the exceptional silence of the strand where I had once been content. And then I put four more bullets into the inert body, which absorbed them without movement. And they were like four sharp knocks on the door of misfortune.

Nowhere in this narration is there any suggestion of heroic motive or even justification for the killing. There is no sense of honor or courage in the shooting, or of good triumphing over evil. Near the end of the novel, after Meursault has been sentenced to death, he thinks about his execution:

> [It was] as if this great rage had purged me of evil, made me void of hope; all at once the night was charged with signs and stars; I opened myself for the first time to the tender indifference of the universe; that it felt as I did, like a brother ultimately, and I sensed that I had been restored to happiness and to life once more. And for everything to be complete, so that I could truly feel less alone, I desired that there be a huge crowd of spectators at my execution to welcome me with shrieks of loathing.

Meursault appreciates that his actions are neither heroic nor malicious; he is an antihero who wishes his execution to be greeted with expressions of hatred, if only to give it some semblance of meaning.

Another sort of antihero is presented by Arthur Miller in his play *Death of a Salesman* (1949). The main character of this tragedy is Willy Loman, a man whose name suggests that he is not of noble birth or in any sense aristocratic, unlike the more traditional protagonists in Shakespearean tragedies, such as *Hamlet*, for example. Nevertheless, Miller makes a case in his essay "Tragedy and the Common Man" (1949) for a different, more modern tragic hero, who is not a great figure in the classic way of a noble prince such as Hamlet, but who is nevertheless a tragic figure in that he tries, at least, "to evaluate himself justly" and "to achieve his humanity." Despite Miller's protestations, Willy Loman is generally considered to be more of an antihero than a hero. In the "Requiem" of the play, after Willy has committed suicide, his neighbor and friend Charley offers a brief eulogy:

> Nobody dast blame this man. You don't understand. Willy was a salesman. And for a salesman there is no rock bottom to the life. He don't put a bolt to a nut, he don't tell you the law or give you medicine. He's a man way out there in the blue, riding on a smile and a shoeshine. And when they start not smiling back—that's an earthquake. And then you get yourself a couple of spots on your hat, and you're finished. Nobody dast blame this man. A salesman is got to dream, boy. It comes with the territory.

As Charley's remarks explain, Willy never achieved anything tangible. He only had his dreams, which he did not achieve either. Nor does Willy ever fully "evaluate himself justly." Unlike, Sophocles's Oedipus, for instance, who comes to recognize the terrible truth about his identity and his fate, Willy never faces the truth. As Willy's elder son, Biff, responds to Charley's eulogy, "Charley, the man didn't know who he was." In this way, Willy seems more nearly an antihero than a hero. See **NARRATIVE POINT OF VIEW**, **PROTAGONIST**, and **TRAGEDY**.

ANTAGONIST

The word *antagonist* derives from the Greek *antagonizesthai*, which means "to struggle against." The term is most often used to designate the main adversary of the hero or protagonist, or a character with whom the protagonist comes into conflict, although an antagonist is not necessarily a villain.

In Shakespeare's *Hamlet* (1601), Hamlet identifies his uncle, Claudius, as both the antagonist of the play and the villain after learning about Claudius's murder of Hamlet the elder:

> O villain, villain, smiling, damned villain!
> My tables—meet it is I set it down

That one may smile, and smile, and be a villain!
At least I am sure it may be so in Denmark.
So, uncle, there you are. . . . (1.5.106-110)

As Hamlet suggests in these lines, the antagonist may appear to be benevolent by
hiding behind a false mask, but he or she is usually revealed as a villain by work's
end. Such is certainly the case in Joyce Carol Oates's story "Where Are You
Going, Where Have You Been?" (1970). The protagonist of this story is a teenager named Connie, who is seduced and intimidated by a character named
Arnold Friend (A. Friend or an old friend), who appears to be a young man of
her age. Over the course of the action, however, she comes to see not only his
otherness but also his malicious intent:

> "Connie, don't fool around with me. I mean—I mean, don't fool
> around," he said, shaking his head. He laughed incredulously. He placed
> his sunglasses on top of his head, carefully, as if he were indeed wearing
> a wig and brought the stems down behind his ears. Connie stared at
> him, another wave of dizziness and fear rising in her so that for a
> moment he wasn't even in focus but was just a blur standing there
> against his gold car, and she had the idea that he had driven up the
> driveway all right but had come from nowhere before that and
> belonged nowhere and that everything about him and even about the
> music that was so familiar to her was only half real.

In this passage, Connie comes to realize that Arnold has disguised himself to look
like a peer and comported himself to seem like a friend. But his true identity is
alien to her, and his real motive is evil. The protagonist's recognition of or confrontation with the antagonist often marks the climax of the plot. See **PLOT**
and **PROTAGONIST**.

APOSTROPHE

The word *apostrophe* derives from the Greek verb *apostrephein*, meaning "to turn
away." In literary criticism, apostrophe is a term used to describe a digression (a
verbal act of "turning away" from the audience) by a speaker, a narrator, or a
character to address an absent or imaginary person, a real or imagined object or
process, or an abstract quality. In those cases where the speaker addresses an
absent or deceased person, the apostrophe often suggests a desire to restore the
missing or lost figure to existence. In the cases where a speaker addresses an
object, a process, or a quality, the apostrophe often serves to personify that to
which it turns its attention.

John Milton's poem "To Mr. Lawrence" (1673) begins with an apostrophe to
Edward Lawrence, an absent friend with whom he desires to meet and converse:

Lawrence, of virtuous father virtuous son,
Now that the fields are dank, and ways are mire,

> Where shall we sometimes meet, and by the fire
> Help waste a sullen day. . . .

The apostrophe creates the illusion of a speaker addressing a present rather than an absent friend.

A passage from Frederick Douglass's *Narrative of the Life of Frederick Douglass, An American Slave* (1845) offers an example of an apostrophe addressed to an object. He addresses a number of ships sailing through Chesapeake Bay and compares their seeming freedom with his slavery:

> You are loosened from your moorings, and are free; I am fast in my chains and am a slave! You move merrily before the gentle gale, and I sadly before the bloody whip!

The ships are seemingly personified by the comparison, as though they can appreciate their freedom and "move merrily" before the wind.

Charlotte Smith's sonnet "To Fortitude" (1784) apostrophizes an abstract quality:

> Nymph of the rock! whose dauntless spirit braves
> The beating storm, and bitter winds that howl
> Round thy cold breast; and hear'st the bursting waves
> And the deep thunder with unshaken soul; Oh come!

The apostrophe serves to personify fortitude by referring to it as a brave and unshaken "nymph of the rock."

Elizabeth Bishop's story "In the Village" (1953) includes an apostrophe to the quality of a mother's voice: "Oh, beautiful sound, strike again." With this apostrophe, the speaker addresses a specific quality, but in doing so she expresses a desire to bring her mother back to life. See **PERSONIFICATION**.

ARCHETYPE

The term *archetype* derives from the Greek *arkhetupos*, meaning "first moulded as a pattern." In common usage, the word is synonymous with prototype: the original model. In literary criticism, the word is most often used to refer to characters, plots, themes, and images that recur throughout the history of literature, both oral and written. These archetypes are recognized as designs or patterns.

Proponents of **archetypal criticism** often draw on the work of psychoanalyst Carl Jung and literary critic Northrop Frye. In the early twentieth century, Jung posited the theory of a "collective unconscious," which he described as a kind of racial memory or primitive instinct that all humans share. This collective unconscious manifests itself in our responses to "primordial images." In *The Archetypes and the Collective Unconscious* (1959), Jung suggests that archetypal images and processes have been passed down through the ages in the form of universal mythologies: "All the mythologized processes of nature, such as summer and winter, the phases of the moon, the rainy seasons, and so forth, are in no sense allegories of these objective occurrences; rather they are symbolic expressions of the inner, unconscious drama of the psyche which becomes accessible to man's consciousness by way of projection—that is, mirrored in the events of nature." In other words, our mythological and literary associations with the seasons, for example, were born out of primitive responses to natural processes; thus, we tend to associate spring with feelings of exuberance and renewal, whereas autumn is often associated with more somber emotions.

Northrop Frye developed an archetypal approach to literature in his *Anatomy of Criticism* (1957). Among other ideas, Frye asserted a correspondence between the four seasons and four of the principal genres of literature: spring with comedy, summer with romance, fall with tragedy, and winter with irony. The images and associations in the opening stanzas of John Keats's poem "La Belle Dame Sans Merci" (1820) may be considered as examples of Frye's archetypal critique:

> O, what can ail thee, knight-at-arms,
>   Alone and palely loitering?
> The sedge has wither'd from the lake,
>   And no birds sing.
>
> O, what can ail thee, knight-at-arms,
>   So haggard and so woe-begone?
> The squirrel's granary is full,
>   And the harvest's done.

An archetypal critic might suggest that the speaker in Keats's poem deliberately associates the "haggard" and "woe-begone" condition of the knight-at-arms with the late fall or early winter, in which the "sedge has wither'd from the lake, / And no birds sing," to make more poignant this expression of a human emotion or state of being. A Jungian critic might comment that Keats projects the knight-at-arms's feelings upon the natural surroundings, whereas Frye might claim that the two are made to correspond to re-create either the "mythos of fall," which he associates with tragedy, or the "mythos of winter," which he associates with irony.

Archetypal critics have sought to catalogue some of the more common archetypes: natural elements (earth, wind, fire, and water); colors (red, green, blue, black, and white); numbers (three, four, and seven); characters (mother and father figures, heroes, soul mates, witches, and wise old men); settings (gardens and deserts); motifs (creation, destruction, and regeneration myths); and plots (the ritualized tales of quest, initiation, and sacrifice). The various stories of Christ's birth, life, and death, for instance, engage a wide range of archetypes. The Virgin Mary may be understood as the archetypal Good Mother, who is associated with birth and protection. Each of the Magi may be thought to represent the archetype of the wise old man possessing divine knowledge or intuition. Christ's baptism in the river foreshadows death and rebirth; His forty days in the wilderness suggest the archetypal desert of spiritual dryness; His death on the cross reenacts the motif of the sacrificial scapegoat. Finally, the number three is perhaps the clearest example of an archetype, symbolizing the spiritual unity of the Holy Trinity. Other specific examples of archetypes include water (related to birth and resurrection, fertility, death, and the unconscious mind), the sun (related to creative energy, the father principle, and the passage of time and life), and types of male figures (including the wise old man, the hero, and the trickster).

Alice Munro's "Wild Swans" (1978), which is a story of initiation, offers examples of archetypes employed in a contemporary literary work. A teenager named Rose goes on a train journey from a small town in Canada to the city of Toronto. On her trip, she encounters a man dressed like a minister who initiates her to the world of adult sexuality. During the course of the story, then, she undergoes separation (leaving her hometown), transformation (sexual initiation), and return. A description of the scenery Rose views through the train window suggests the motif of transformation to adulthood, which is a variation of the rebirth archetype:

> She went on looking out the window at the spring morning. There was no snow left down here. The trees and the bushes seemed to have a paler bark than they did at home. Even the sunlight looked different. It was as different from home, here, as the coast of the Mediterranean would be, or the valley of California.

For archetypal critics, the difference in physical landscape suggests the transformation in Rose's psychic landscape; she will return home a different person. Moreover, spring is the season associated with transformation and rebirth. Even the protagonist's name, Rose, and the title of the story, "Wild Swans," are suggestive of archetypes associated with rebirth, violent passion, rape, and metamorphosis. See **MYTH**.

ASIDE

An aside is a speech or a remark, made by a character on stage, which is by convention heard only by the audience and not by the other characters. This dramatic technique works explicitly to develop a relationship between a character and an audience. A dramatic analogue to the novel's representation of interior thought, an aside may be used for either dramatic or comic effect. But it nearly always serves the purpose of creating tension between private and public discourse: what the character offering the aside says in "private" to the audience, and what he or she says in "public" to the other characters.

Among the most famous asides in drama are those offered by Iago in Shakespeare's *Othello* (1602). In Act 2, for example, Iago pretends to be a good-natured ironist in his conversation with Desdemona and Cassio. But in his aside he reveals his malicious intention to exploit them for his own purposes:

> [Aside] He takes her by the palm. Ay, well said, whisper. With as little a web as this I will ensnare as great a fly as Cassio. Ay, smile upon her, do;

I will give thee in thine own courtship. You say true; 'tis so, indeed. If
such tricks as these strip you out of your lieutenantry, it had been better
you had not kiss'd your three fingers so oft, which now again you are
most apt to play the sir in. . . . (2.1.166-175)

While he feigns his loyalty and goodwill to the other characters, Iago secretly
plans to make the innocent friendship of Desdemona and Cassio look like an
affair to Othello, Desdemona's husband. Thus, the gap between Iago's outward
mask—the honest and trustworthy counselor—and his true intentions—to use
Cassio and Desdemona to make Othello jealous—are revealed in his aside.

The beginning of a scene in Peter Shaffer's *Amadeus* (1980) provides a contemporary example. The setting is the Palace of Schonbrunn, where the
Emperor Joseph is in his music room, with his court musicians, awaiting the
arrival of Wolfgang Amadeus Mozart:

JOSEPH: Fetes and fireworks, gentlemen! Mozart is here! He's waiting below!

ALL: Majesty!

JOSEPH: Je suis follement impatient! [I am madly impatient!]

SALIERI: [To audience] The Emperor Joseph the Second of Austria. Son of Maria
Theresa. Brother of Marie Antoinette. Adorer of music—provided
that it made no demands upon the royal brain. [To the EMPEROR,
deferentially] Majesty, I have written a little march in Mozart's honor.
May I play it as he comes in?

In his aside to the audience, Salieri reveals his private opinion of the Emperor,
which contrasts with the deferential tone of his public discourse with the Emperor.
See **DRAMATIC MONOLOGUE** and **SOLILOQUY**.

AUTHOR/*AUTEUR*

The word *author* derives from the Latin verb *augere*, meaning "to create or
increase." In common parlance, an author is one who writes or composes a
book, as Aristotle is the author of *Poetics*, William Shakespeare is the author of
Hamlet, or Toni Morrison is the author of *Beloved*. The traditional associations of
the term, however, have come under scrutiny in contemporary literary theory.
Whereas author was conventionally associated with concepts of authority, creativity, and individual genius, contemporary theorists have questioned whether
any of these notions are valid. The concept of authority can be traced to ancient
and medieval scholars who accepted the interpretations of theology, science, and
moral philosophy set down by men whom they considered knowers or indisput-
able sources. The notion of the author as creator developed through the romantic idea of a writer as one whose imagination gave birth to original ideas and
images. The notion of the author as an individual genius reached its zenith in
the late nineteenth and early twentieth centuries, when the mind of the literary

artist was thought to be superior to and alienated from that of the common crowd.

Contemporary theorists have extended the skepticism of modernist critics who questioned the concept of authority by noting the errors and ignorance of the ancient and medieval knowers, as well as those of more modern "authorities": e.g., Galileo's repudiation of Aristotelian and Copernican world views; Einstein's critique of Newtonian physics. The idea of originality has been interrogated by critics such as Harold Bloom, whose theory of "the anxiety of influence" asserts that literary artists seek to disguise their lack of originality by denying or attacking those writers who have influenced their thinking. Above all, contemporary critics have attacked the concept of the writer as an individual genius, an autonomous subject whose mind and work transcend the historical, social, economic, and political contexts of his or her age. Unlike the **New Critics**, who sought to remove a text from biographical and historical contexts, contemporary theorists seek to discover the ways in which both the author and his or her work are products of cultural and political processes. Moreover, **reader-response** theorists have suggested that the meaning of a text is created as much by readers as by its putative author.

Auteur is the French word for "author." *Auteurism* is a theory or critical stance that developed out of film studies in France after the Second World War. Rather than view a film as a collaborative effort, proponents of *auteurism* tend to see it as the rendering of the artistic vision of the director, whom they refer to as the *auteur* of the film. Critics of *auteur* theories often cite the crucial roles of screenplay writers, cinematographers, and producers—not to mention actors, camera operators, film editors, and so on—to argue against the glorification of the director.

In critiquing the body of work (or *oeuvre*) of a director, *auteur* theorists seek to examine each film largely in the context of the *auteur's* other films or in the context of films made by other celebrated *auteurs*. Thus, for example, each film directed by Alfred Hitchcock (or as *auteur* theorists might say, each Alfred Hitchcock film) may be studied by comparing it to other films directed by Hitchcock in order to note similarities and differences, recurrent themes and cinematic devices, and evidence of artistic development or change. Some critics have noticed Hitchcock's penchant for plots in which the protagonist, wrongly accused of a crime, must flee from both the police and the real criminal to prove his innocence. Adherents to *auteurism* might call this a recurring motif of Hitchcock's *oeuvre*. The director of a contemporary *film noir* may be considered an *auteur* whose art is worthy of comparison with other classic works of the film noir genre.

Auteurs of the "golden age of Hollywood" include Hitchcock, D. W. Griffith, Orson Welles, and John Ford. European directors who are sometimes studied as *auteurs* include François Truffaut, Bernardo Bertolucci, and Jean-Luc Godard. Contemporary directors such as Francis Ford Coppola, Woody Allen, and Martin Scorsese are treated as *auteurs* by some film critics. See **FILM NOIR, NEW CRITICISM/FORMALISM, PROTAGONIST**, and **READER-RESPONSE CRITICISM**.

B

BALLAD

The word *ballad* is most often employed to describe a narrative poem composed in short stanzas. The term derives from a medieval French word meaning "dancing song," which suggests the popular or folk origins of this oral form. Indeed, the typical **ballad stanza**, a quatrain (four lines) with an *abab* or *abcb* rhyme scheme, is adapted to both dancing and singing. Common types include popular ballads, short ballads, and hymns.

Popular ballads tell a story embodying folk wisdom or depicting heroic adventures. They often present a dramatic story involving conflict and the death of the protagonist or the speaker. The closing stanzas of the anonymous ballad "Johnie Armstrong" (sixteenth century) offer an example:

Then like a mad man Johnie laid about,	a
And like a mad man then fought he,	b
Until a false Scot came Johnie behind,	c
And run him through the fair body.	d

Saying, "Fight on, my merry men all,
And see that none of you be ta'en;
For I will stand by and bleed but awhile,
And then will I come and fight again."

News then was brought to young Johnie Armstrong,
And as he stood by his nurse's knee,
Who vowed if e'er he lived for to be a man,
Of the treacherous Scots revenged he'd be.

Like many ballads, this one betrays an **iambic** rhythm (a pattern in which an unstressed syllable is followed by a stressed syllable). The lines are end-stopped (punctuated) to give emphasis to the terminal rhymes.

In a **long ballad stanza**, all four lines are **tetrameter** (four metrical feet). This is the verse form employed in the anonymous ballad of "Bonny Barbara Allan" (sixteenth century):

> He turned his face unto the wall,
>> And death was with him dealing:
> "Adieu, adieu, my dear friends all,
>> And be kind to Barbara Allan."

The last two lines in the stanza serve as a **refrain**, which is a common feature of ballads.

In the **short ballad stanza**, lines 1, 2, and 4 are **trimeter** (three metrical feet), while only line 3 is tetrameter. This is the verse form employed by Langston Hughes in "Sylvester's Dying Bed" (1959):

> Sweet gals was a-moanin'
> "Sylvester's gonna die!"
> And a hundred pretty mamas
> Bowed their heads to cry.

In the **hymn stanza**, the lines alternate between tetrameter and trimeter. This is the form employed by Isaac Watts in his hymn "Our God, Our Help" (1719):

> Our God, our help in ages past,
>> Our hope for years to come.
> Our shelter from the stormy blast,
>> And our eternal home.

The hymn stanza is also employed in many of Emily Bronte's poems, including "Ah! why, because the dazzling sun" (1846):

> Ah! why, because the dazzling sun
> Restored my earth to joy
> Have you departed, everyone,
> And left a desert sky?

See **CAESURA/ENJAMBEMENT, METER, QUATRAIN, REFRAIN**, and **RHYME**.

BATHOS/PATHOS

The tenn *bathos* derives from the Greek word meaning "depth." It refers to a fall from an elevated height to the level of the trivial or absurd. Bathos is used effectively in Jane Austen's *Northanger Abbey* (1818). The heroine, Catherine Morland, is an avid reader of Gothic novels and expects her life to be like that of characters in the novels. On her first night at Northanger Abbey, she finds a black chest in her bedchamber and anticipates with horror that it will contain the memoirs of an unfortunate young woman trapped there in the past: "She shuddered, tossed about in her bed, and envied every quiet sleeper. . . . Hollow murmurs seemed to creep along the gallery, and more than once her blood was chilled by the sound of distant moans." When Catherine awakes the next morning and inspects the contents, she discovers, much to her chagrin, that the chest contains nothing more than a laundry list: "She felt humbled to the dust. . . . Nothing could now be clearer than the absurdity of her recent fancies. To suppose that a manuscript of many generations past could have remained undiscovered in a room such as that, so modern, so habitable!—or that she should be the first to possess the skill of unlocking a cabinet, the key of which was open to all!" The passage is bathetic because what Catherine presumes to be a profound and horrifying discovery turns out to be a comic anticlimax.

Pathos, on the other hand, which derives from a Greek verb meaning "to suffer," denotes an experience of truly profound spiritual loss, emotional anguish, or physical wounding. Emily Dickinson's poem 258 expresses the pathos of spiritual and emotional pain:

> There's a certain Slant of light,
> Winter Afternoons—
> That oppresses like the Heft
> Of Cathedral Tunes—
>
> Heavenly Hurt, it gives us—
> We can find no scar,
> But internal difference,
> Where the Meanings, are—
>
> None may teach it—Any—
> 'Tis the Seal Despair—
> An imperial affliction
> Sent us of the Air—
>
> When it comes, the Landscape listens—
> Shadows—hold their breath—
> When it goes, 'tis like the Distance
> On the look of Death—

As these lines suggest, the experience of pathos is not only profoundly hurtful but also of long duration; it is sometimes invisible but, nonetheless, palpable. In literature, a moment of true pathos commands the attention, respect, and sympathy of the audience, whereas the bathetic crosses the line over to the maudlin, the absurd, or even the ridiculous.

BILDUNGSROMAN

The German word *Bildungsroman* literally means "development novel." Literary critics tend to use the term interchangeably with **apprenticeship** or **coming-of-age novel**, a work of fiction presenting the development of a protagonist from childhood or adolescence to maturity.

Charles Dickens's *The Personal History and Experience of David Copperfield* (1850), a semiautobiographical novel, is among the most familiar examples of the *Bildungsroman* in English. The book begins with a chapter entitled "I am

Born" and ends with "A Last Retrospect," in which the narrator (who is also the protagonist) sees himself on a "journey along the road of life."

J. D. Salinger's *The Catcher in the Rye* (1951), which is itself a kind of *Bildungsroman*, satirizes the typical nineteenth-century apprenticeship novel in its opening passage:

> If you really want to hear about it, the first thing you'll probably want to know is where I was born, and what my lousy childhood was like, and how my parents were occupied and all before they had me, and all that David Copperfield kind of crap, but I don't feel like going into it, if you want to know the truth.

Nevertheless, Salinger's protagonist, Holden Caulfield, undergoes a transformation from innocence to experience, as his comments in the final chapter of the novel suggest: "That's the whole trouble. You can't ever find a place that's nice and peaceful, because there isn't any."

Other examples of the *Bildungsroman* include Mark Twain's *The Adventures of Huckleberry Finn* (1884), and Ralph Ellison's *Invisible Man* (1952). Charlotte Bronte's *Jane Eyre* (1847) is an example of a *Bildungsroman* written by a woman, of which there were few since this is traditionally a male genre. The protagonists of apprenticeship novels often serve as **first-person narrators**. Their point of view is frequently retrospective, enabling the author to play on the ironic gap between the experienced narrator's view of his or her formerly naive attitudes, as for example in Ellison's *Invisible Man:*

> It goes a long way back, some twenty years. All my life I had been looking for something, and everywhere I turned someone tried to tell me what it was. I accepted their answers too, though they were often in contradiction and even self-contradictory. I was naive. I was looking for myself and asking everyone except myself questions which I, and only I, could answer. It took me a long time and much painful boomeranging of my expectations to achieve a realization everyone else appears to have been born with: That I am nobody but myself. But first I had to discover that I am an invisible man!

Although the protagonist in a *Bildungsroman* usually acquires a new awareness of the ways of the world, he or she often decides to take up a position somewhat outside the societal norm. Such is the case with Jane Eyre, who exclaims in Bronte's novel, "School rules, school duties, school habits and notions, and voices and faces, and costumes, and preferences, and antipathies: such was what I knew of existence. And now I felt that it was not enough. I tired of the routine of eight years in one afternoon. I desired liberty; for liberty I gasped; for liberty I uttered a prayer; it seemed scattered on the wind then faintly blowing." Similarly, Huck Finn declares in the closing lines of Twain's novel, "But I reckon I got to light out for the Territory ahead of the rest, because Aunt Sally she's going to adopt me and sivilize me and I can't stand it. I been there before." The nature of development portrayed in a *Bildungsroman* naturally changes over time; that is to say, the definition of a successful development depends on the social norms of the day. See **NARRATIVE POINT OF VIEW**.

BIOGRAPHICAL CRITICISM

Biographical criticism is a term used to describe interpretations of literature based on the life of the author of a work. In these interpretations, aspects or details of the author's life are used to shed light on characters, events, settings, and moods of a work of literature. In considering Jane Austen's *Persuasion* (1818), a biographical critic might point out that two of Austen's brothers had high-ranking positions in Nelson's navy, and that Austen reflected her knowledge of the profession in her closely observed descriptions of naval officers in the novel. In Charles Dickens's *Great Expectations* (1861), a biographical critic might explore the author's childhood and show how his miserable experience working in a blacking factory and shame over his father being imprisoned for debt color the experiences of the young Pip. And in Alice Walker's *The Color Purple* (1982), a biographical critic might consider Walker's upbringing under Jim Crow laws in rural Georgia of the 1940s and 1950s, and how it affects her perception of characters and circumstances in the novel. New Critics or formalist critics have challenged biographical criticism for what they judge to be the "biographical fallacy"; that is to say, they criticize biographical critics for interpreting the work only through the author's life and for paying insufficient attention to the form of a work and its universal artistic genius. See **NEW CRITICISM**.

BLANK VERSE

The term *blank verse* serves to describe unrhymed lines of **iambic pentameter**: that is, in the strictest sense, lines of verse with five metrical feet, in which the stress falls on the second syllable of the foot. Irregular blank verse contains nine to fourteen syllables per line.

Because blank verse is the form that comes nearest to the natural rhythms of English, it has been widely used in each of the major subgenres of poetry: dramatic, epic, and lyric verse. Each of Shakespeare's plays offers examples of blank verse employed in a drama. In Act 1, scene 1, of *Twelfth Night* (1601), for instance, Duke Orsini expresses his desire to love and be loved:

> If music be the food of love, play on,
> Give me excess of it; that, surfeiting,
> The appetite may sicken and so die.
> That strain again! It had a dying fall;
> O, it came o'er my ear like the sweet sound
> That breathes upon a bank of violets,
> Stealing and giving odour! Enough, no more;

'Tis not so sweet now as it was before.
O spirit of love, how quick and fresh art thou!

In this passage, Shakespeare uses blank verse for the purpose of exposition: the lines set the context of this romantic comedy by suggesting the duke's emotional state. Only a very few of the lines in this passage are perfectly iambic: that is, having two-syllable feet in which the second syllable receives more emphasis than the first when one speaks the line in a normal voice.

```
   u     /    u / u  /  u /u  /
That breathes upon a bank of violets
```

Nevertheless, the majority of lines are pentameter, and the variations allow Shakespeare to control the pace through **caesura** (pauses created by punctuation or changes in rhythm) and **enjambement** (allowing one line to run over into the next). Although the words "more" and "before" rhyme, the passage does not employ a pattern of rhyming.

Book IV of Milton's *Paradise Lost* (1667), in which Satan ponders repentance of his evil ways, offers an example of blank verse employed in an epic poem:

```
u  /  u  /   u  /  u  /   u  /
But say I could repent, and could obtain,
u  /  u  /   u  /  u  /   u  /
By act of grace, my former state; how soon
Would height recall high thoughts, how soon unsay
What feigned submission swore! Ease would recant
Vows made in pain, as violent and void;
For never can true reconcilement grow
Where wounds of deadly hate have pierced so deep:
```

Since Milton does not need to concern himself with rhyming these lines, he is able to make lines ebb and flow largely through his use of caesura, enjambement, and **anaphora** (repetition of words at the beginning of sentences and clauses): "how soon / Would height recall high thoughts, how soon unsay / What feigned submission swore! Ease would recant / Vows made in pain. . . ."

Elizabeth Bishop's "Poem" (1976) offers an example of blank verse employed in a lyric poem. The speaker recalls a small town in Nova Scotia, of which she is reminded by a sketch collected by a former resident:

I never knew him. We both knew this place,
apparently, this literal small backwater,
Looked at it long enough to memorize it,
our years apart. How strange. And it's still loved,
or its memory is (it must have changed a lot).
Our visions coincided—"visions" is
too serious a word—our looks, two looks:
art "coping from life" and life itself,
life and memory of it so compressed
they've turned into each other. Which is which?

The blank verse suits this poem of meditation. The lines seem natural in their starting and stopping, as though recording the actual process of thought. Nevertheless, the poem has both a rhythm and a form. See **CAESURA/ENJAMBE-MENT** and **METER**.

BURLESQUE

Burlesque is a French word meaning "comical" that derives from the Italian *bur-lesco*, the root of which means "joke." In literature, a burlesque is a comic or satiric imitation of other literary works, themes, subgenres, styles, and conventions. Some critics have sought to distinguish between high and low forms of burlesque by referring to all types of parody as high burlesque and all forms of travesty as low burlesque.

In general, a parody seeks to imitate a form or a subject in a way that shows respect for the original. Alexander Pope's *The Rape of the Lock* (1712), subtitled "A Herio-Comical Poem," begins by invoking a muse and employs many other conventions of a traditional epic poem such as Homer's *The Iliad* (eighth century B.C.):

> What dire Offence from am'rous Causes springs,
> What mighty Contests rise from trivial Things,
> I sing—This Verse to Caryll, Muse is due;
> This, ev'n Belinda may vouchsafe to view:
> Slight is the Subject, but not so the Praise,
> If She inspire, and He approve my Lays. (1-6)

As these lines explain, unlike the subject of *The Iliad*, the Trojan War, which was precipitated by the abduction of a queen, the "Contest" that is the subject of this poem arises "from trivial Things," in this case, the theft of a lock of Belinda's hair; moreover, the "Subject" of the poem is "Slight," which means it is of little import or is less profound than a truly heroic poem. For this reason, a parody such as Pope's *The Rape of the Lock* is often called a mock epic or mock-heroic poem. A more contemporary example of a parody is Joseph Heller's novel *Catch-22* (1961), which is also a mock epic with *The Iliad* as its original. Whereas the stated argument of *The Iliad* is the wrath of Achilles at the beginning of the Trojan War, the subject of *Catch-22* is the angst of the protagonist, Yossarian, who is obliged to fly combat missions during World War II. Whereas the situations of the main characters would seem to be similar, the subject of Heller's novel is in many ways an inversion of the theme in Homer's epic poem. For instance, Achilles refuses to join the battle on principle because Agamemnon, the leader of the Greek army, has appropriated his mistress, not because he is afraid to fight. Yossarian, on the other hand, refuses to fly bombing missions because he is an admitted coward who fears his death is imminent. The similarities and differences between these two protagonists become explicit in the parody when Yossarian states formally his refusal to fly any more missions and "marches backward with his gun on his hip," leading one of his superiors to quip, "Who does he think he is—Achilles?"

Unlike a parody, a travesty either deliberately makes a shambles of the original or degrades the original through ridicule of its themes and conventions. Miguel Cervantes's *Don Quixote* (1605), for example, is a travesty of medieval romances, which the protagonist of Cervantes's romance reads with passion and attempts to relive. Cervantes makes clear from the start that his book is to be understood as a burlesque, for instead of describing his hero and his equipage as enviable and majestic, he draws his protagonist as pitiable and penurious:

> In a certain corner of la Mancha, the name of which I do not choose to
> remember, there lately lived one of those country gentlemen, who
> adorn their halls with a rusty lance and worm-eaten target, and ride
> forth on the skeleton of a horse, to course with a sort of a starved
> greyhound. (Tobias Smollett, trans.)

As Cervantes's travesty of a romance continues, Don Quixote involves himself, not in heroic deeds of valor, but in delusional quests such as tilting his lance at a windmill that he imagines to be a great monster.

The play within the play in William Shakespeare's *A Midsummer Night's Dream* (1595-1596) is an example of a travesty that descends to farce. The so-called "rude mechanicals," Bottom and his fellow guild members, attempt to put on a stage version of Ovid's "Pyramus and Thisbe" in celebration of the marriage of Theseus, the Duke of Athens, to Hippolyta. On the wedding night, Philostrate, the master of revels, warns Theseus that the play is farcical. When Theseus questions him about the description of the mechanicals' play as "A tedious brief scene of young Pyramus / And his love Thisby; very tragical mirth" (5.1.56-57), Philostrate responds,

> A play there is, my lord, some ten words long,
> Which is as brief as I have known a play;
> But by ten words, my lord, it is too long,
> Which makes it tedious. For in all the play
> There is not one word apt, one player fitted.
> And tragical, my noble lord, it is,
> For Pyramus therein doth kill himself.
> Which when I saw rehearsed, I must confess,
> Made mine eyes water, but more merry tears
> The passion of loud laughter never shed. (5.1.61-70)

The oxymoron "tragical mirth" suggests that the original tragic tale of "Pyramus and Thisbe" becomes in the hands of Bottom and his friends an object of mirth and laughter. In the final scene of this farce, for instance, Bottom, who portrays Pyramus, melodramatically commits suicide, only to rise to his feet a few moments later and step out of character to address the audience.

A more contemporary example is Anthony Hecht's "The Dover Bitch" (1968), which is a travesty of Mathew Arnold's celebrated poem "Dover Beach" (1867). The theme in Arnold's poem is a perceived ebbing of "the sea of faith" in God and religion, which the speaker characterizes as a profound loss. The presumed interlocutor or addressee in the poem is a loved one, whom many scholars believe to be Arnold's wife. "Dover Beach" ends with an assertion that, given the waning of faith in divinity, human love and friendship become greater necessities:

Ah, love, let us be true
To one another! For the world, which seems
To lie before us like a land of dreams,
So various, so beautiful, so new,
Hath really neither joy, nor love, nor light,
Nor certitude, nor peace, nor help for pain;

Hecht's travesty seemingly ignores the theme of "Dover Beach" altogether. Instead, the speaker sets the scene of Arnold and "this girl" standing above the cliffs of Dover, then imagines that the girl is rather bored by what Arnold is saying and can think only of "what his whiskers would feel like / On the back of her neck." Indeed, the speaker in "The Dover Bitch" goes on to suggest that Arnold's interlocutor is a somewhat coarse and licentious woman. She is reported to have uttered "one or two unprintable things," and the speaker admits to being in her company now and then for "drinks" and to "give her a good time." In short, Hecht's poem derives its comic effects largely by trivializing Arnold's serious persona and deflating the penchant of his poetry to take a philosophical turn by creating a very modern addressee who bears little or no similarity to the original.

Examples of burlesques in film include Mel Brooks's *Blazing Saddles* (1974), which lampoons the themes and conventions of classic American westerns, and *Rosencrantz and Guildenstern Are Dead* (1990), a film based on Tom Stoppard's play by the same name, which is itself a travesty of *Hamlet*. See **COMEDY** and **PARODY**.

C

CAESURA/ENJAMBEMENT

The word *caesura* derives from the Latin verb *caedere*, meaning "to cut off." Literary critics use the term to refer to any break or pause in a line of poetry. In common usage, caesuras are pauses marked by punctuation. The following lines from Keats's "Ode to a Nightingale" (1820) offer four examples:

Was it a vision, or a waking dream?
Fled is that music:—Do I wake or sleep?

The comma after "vision" and the colon/dash following "music" are **internal caesuras**; the question marks at the ends of the lines are **terminal caesuras**. The duration of pauses determines the strength of caesuras. Periods, question marks, and exclamation points indicate strong caesuras. Colons, semicolons, and dashes are moderately strong; commas are relatively brief.

When a caesura occurs at the end of a line, the line is end-stopped. When no caesura occurs at the end of a line, so that one line runs over to the next line, the poet has enjambed the lines. The word **enjambement** derives from the Old French verb *enjamber*, which means "to straddle." In verse, the running-on of one line to the next, without caesura at the end of the first line, makes the lines enjambed. The following lines from Louise Erdrich's "Jacklight" (1984) offer an example:

It is their turn now,
their turn to follow us. Listen,
they put down their equipment.
It is useless in the tall brush.
And now they take the first steps, not knowing
how deep the woods are and lightless.
How deep the woods are.

The third, fourth, sixth, and seventh lines of this excerpt are strongly end-stopped. Only the fifth and sixth lines are enjambed. With enjambement, the poet signals that the reader is to read through the end of one line and on to the next. Since no pause is apparent at the end of the fifth line, Erdrich has clearly intended the enjambement of these lines. In many cases, a poet will use an internal caesura to set up the enjambement of lines. Thus, in Erdrich's poem, the caesura after "steps" helps to prepare her audience to read through the end of the line to the beginning of the next. Since many twentieth-century poets use punctuation unconventionally, when they use it at all, readers may not know which lines are end-stopped and which are enjambed.

Other poets use caesuras in unconventional ways to achieve visual and sound effects. The first two stanzas of Emily Dickinson's "'Tis so appalling—it exhilirates" (written 1861; published 1935) provide several examples:

> 'Tis so appalling—it exhilirates—
> So over Horror, it half Captivates—
> The Soul stares after it, secure—
> A Sepulchre, fears frost, no more—
>
> To scan a Ghost, is faint—
> But grappling, conquers it—
> How easy, Torment, now—
> Suspense kept sawing so—

Dickinson's eccentric use of dashes is sometimes very effective. In the first line of the excerpt, she isolates "it exhilirates" to emphasize the extent of the "Horror." In the fourth line, Dickinson uses a comma between the subject and the verb to isolate the alliterative phrase "fears frost." A similar effect is achieved by dividing lines five and six with internal caesuras, both of which slow down the lines and emphasize the alliteration of "Ghost" and "grappling." See **ALLITERATION**.

CANON

The word *canon* derives from the Greek *kanon*, meaning "a measuring line, rule." For Christians, *canon* has two important significations: "a body of laws of a church" and "a list of books of the Holy Scripture officially accepted as genuine." This latter meaning of *canon* has been imported by literary historians and scholars to refer to a largely unofficial list of literary works having lasting cultural and educational value. It also refers to the "official" body of work of a single writer, for example, the Shakespeare canon, the Austen canon. The question of "the canon," which remains largely unresolved, has become one of the most contentious and divisive debates in higher education.

Until recently, it was generally accepted that the measuring lines or rules for selection were artistic merit and durability. Durability was thought to mean not only that a work had survived in the educated public's opinion but also that it had proved so profound and engaging as to be timeless in its appeal. Artistic merit was to be measured by comparison with other canonical works as well as by originality. These assumptions form the basis for T. S. Eliot's observations in his essay entitled "Tradition and the Individual Talent" (1917):

> The existing monuments [of literature] form an ideal order among themselves, which is modified by the introduction of the new (the really new) work of art among them. The existing order is complete before the new work arrives; for in order to persist after the supervention of novelty, the whole existing order must be, if ever so slightly, altered; and so the relation, proportions, values of each work of art toward the whole are readjusted; and this is conformity between the old and the new. Whoever has approved this idea of order, of the form of European, of English literature will not find it preposterous that the past should be altered by the present as much as the present is directed by the past. And the poet who is aware of this will be aware of great difficulties and responsibilities.

The canon was, for Eliot, a flexible and shifting order in the sense that the monumental works, self-selected by their own excellence, were great and rich enough to survive alteration and adjustment, and sufficiently accommodating to admit new works to their tradition.

In the last few decades, several challenges to the traditional canon have been mounted by those who believe that the old order needs to be altered more radically. Some have accused the traditional canon of elitism for excluding works of common or popular culture; others have claimed that the old order is dominated by European authors and patriarchal (or male-oriented) values that tend to marginalize minority cultures and perspectives. Barbara Herrnstein Smith suggests in her essay entitled "Contingencies of Value" (1983) that the canon has been "managed" by interested parties for the purpose of sustaining their own beliefs and authority:

> What is commonly referred to as "the test of time" . . . is not, as the figure implies, an impersonal and impartial mechanism; for the cultural institutions through which it operates (schools, libraries, theaters, museums, publishing and printing houses, editorial boards, prize-awarding commissions, state censors, etc.) are, of course, all managed by persons (who, by definition, are those with cultural power and commonly other forms of power as well), and since the texts that are selected and preserved by "time" will always tend to be those which "fit" (and, indeed, have often been designed to fit) their characteristic needs, interests, resources, and purposes, that testing mechanism has its own built-in partialities accumulated in and thus intensified by time.

Based on these beliefs, a number of critics, historians, and activists have called for multicultural curricula that would not be bound by the traditional canon and its notions of value.

CARPE DIEM

The term *carpe diem* is a Latin phrase meaning "seize the day." The philosophy of *carpe diem* asserts the notion that since life is short, one must make the most of one's youth. This motif became very popular in the love poetry of the seventeenth century. It is traditionally a male **trope** (a figure of speech involving a turn or change of meaning), in which a male speaker engages in seduction of a known or imagined female. Edmund Waller's "Go Lovely Rose" (1645) is an example of a lyric poem that expresses this theme:

> Small is the worth
> Of beauty from the light retired;
>   Bid her come forth,
> Suffer herself to be desired,
>   And not blush so to be admired.
>
>   Then die, that she
> The common fate of all things rare
>   May read in thee:
> How small a part of time they share,
>   That are so wondrous sweet and fair.

Waller's poem employs one of the traditional metaphors of the *carpe diem* theme: namely, to compare the beauty of a young woman to the short-lived existence of a flower. Robert Herrick picks up on this same motif in "To the Virgins, to Make Much of Time" (1648):

> Gather ye rosebuds while ye may,
>   Old time is still a-flying;
> And this same flower that smiles to-day
>   To-morrow will be dying.

In many cases, lyrics expressing the *carpe diem* motif appear to be poems of seduction. The notion that time is precious is often expressed by contrasting imagery of the sun's rapid course through the sky with literary figures describing the immeasurable length of eternity after death. Such is the case in one of the most famous of *carpe diem* lyrics, Andrew Marvell's "To His Coy Mistress" (1681).

Several women poets have written lyrics in imitation of and response to the masculine tradition of *carpe diem* poetry. The opening lines of Edna St. Vincent Millay's "Never May the Fruit Be Plucked" (1923) illustrate one type of response:

> Never, never may the fruit be plucked from the bough
> And gathered into barrels.
> He that would eat of love must eat it where it hangs.

In these lines, the speaker seems to address the male seducer, warning against treating female sexuality as a possession to be hoarded.

CHARACTER

Literary critics most often use the term *character* to refer to a fictional person in a narrative or dramatic work of literature. Generally speaking, characters are created and revealed by three means: exposition, action, and dialogue.

The opening paragraph of Joyce Carol Oates's "Where Are You Going, Where Have You Been?" (1970) offers an example of **characterization** achieved by an **omniscient narrator** through exposition:

> Her name was Connie. She was fifteen and she had a quick nervous giggling habit of craning her neck to glance into mirrors or checking other people's faces to make sure her own was all right. Her mother, who noticed everything and who hadn't much reason any longer to look at her own face, always scolded Connie about it. "Stop gawking at yourself, who are you? You think you're so pretty?" she would say. Connie would raise her eyebrows at the familiar complaints and look right through her mother, into a shadowy vision of herself as she was right at that moment: she knew she was pretty, and that was everything. Her mother had been pretty once too, if you could believe those old snapshots in the album, but now her looks were gone and that was why she was always after Connie.

Oates creates a context for the whole of her story by revealing Connie's adolescent vanity and self-absorption through direct descriptions of her habits and thoughts.

In Mark Twain's *The Adventures of Huckleberry Finn* (1884), the passage in which Huck manages to fake his own death provides an example of character revealed through action:

> I took the axe and smashed in the door—I beat it and hacked it considerable, a-doing it. I fetched the pig in and took him back nearly to the table and hacked into his throat with the ax, and laid him down on the ground to bleed. . . . Well, next I took an old sack and put a lot of big rocks in it,—all I could drag—and I started it from the pig and dragged it to the door and through the woods down to the river and dumped it in, and down it sunk, out of sight. You could easy see that something had been dragged over the ground.

This description of Huck's actions enables the reader to appreciate his hardihood, intelligence, and resourcefulness.

In Arthur Miller's *Death of a Salesman* (1949), one of Willy Loman's conversations with his wife, Linda, offers an example of characterization revealed through dialogue:

> WILLY: I'm fat. I'm very foolish to look at, Linda. I didn't tell you, but Christmas time I happened to be calling on F. H. Stewarts, and a salesman I know, as I was going in to see the buyer I heard him say something about—walrus. And I—I cracked him right across the face. I won't take that. I simply will not take that. But they do laugh at me. I know that.

Throughout this speech, Miller reveals Willy's deep-seated self-consciousness and lack of confidence in himself.

Some critics insist on a distinction first made by E. M. Forster in *Aspects of the Novel* (1927) between levels of characterization: **flat** and **round**. A **flat character** is often a kind of caricature or a stereotypical figure, one who expresses a single quality or idea. Flat characters are commonplace in allegories, frequently representing notions of good and evil. In any event, flat characters are one-dimensional, meaning that they do not develop or change in the course of a narrative or a dramatic work.

Charles Dickens is often celebrated for his vast gallery of flat characters. One such is the indomitably grim and severe figure of Miss Murdstone in *David Copperfield* (1850):

> It was Miss Murdstone who was arrived, and a gloomy-looking lady she was; dark . . . with very heavy eyebrows, nearly meeting over her large nose, as if being disabled by the wrongs of her sex from wearing whiskers, she had carried them to that account. She brought with her two uncompromising hard black boxes, with her initials on the lids in hard brass nails. When she paid the coachman she took her money out of a hard steel purse, and she kept the purse in a very jail of a bag which hung upon her arm by a heavy chain, and shut up like a bite. I had never, at that time, seen such a metallic lady altogether as Miss Murdstone was.

With typical exaggeration and blatant repetition, Dickens's portrait of this heartless and "metallic" lady includes not only heavy-handed descriptions of her person and the accoutrements of her luggage and purse but also the explicit associations of her very name.

Whereas a flat character is one-dimensional, a **round character** may prove to be at least two-dimensional or more fully developed psychologically. The characterization of Edna Pontellier in Kate Chopin's *The Awakening* (1899) offers an example:

> Mrs. Pontellier's eyes were quick and bright; they were a yellowish brown, about the color of her hair. She had a way of turning them swiftly upon an object and holding them there as if lost in some inward maze of contemplation or thought.
> Her eyebrows were a shade darker than her hair. They were thick and almost horizontal emphasizing the depth of her eyes. She was rather handsome than beautiful. Her face was captivating by reason of a certain frankness of expression and a contradictory subtle play of features.

Both the suggestion of an "inward maze of contemplation" and the indication of "a contradictory subtle play of features" foreshadow the complexity of character that contributes to one of Chopin's important themes: namely, Edna's ambivalence about her desires and her obligations.

In the late nineteenth and early twentieth centuries, modernist writers attempted to create or reveal character by means of presenting interior thoughts and feelings. The techniques they employed are generally appreciated under the concepts of **interior monologue** and **stream of consciousness**. See **DIALOGUE, MODERNISM, NARRATIVE POINT OF VIEW, PLOT**, and **STREAM OF CONSCIOUSNESS**.

CHORUS

The term *chorus* derives from the Greek word *khoros*, meaning "dance or band of dancers and singers." In ancient Greek festivals, a chorus was literally a group that sang in verse while performing a dance or ritualized movements. In classic Greek drama, the chorus serves the function of representing the community and its traditions and values. It comments on the action of the play as well as on the likely consequences of the action. Such is the case in Aeschylus's *Agamemnon* (fifth century B.C.), for instance, when near the end of the tragedy, the chorus confronts Aegisthus (whose lover, Clytemnestra, has killed her husband, Agamemnon), accuses him of cowardice, and warns of the consequences of treachery and revenge:

CHORUS:
But why, why then, you coward, could you not have slain
Your man yourself? Why must it be his wife who killed,
To curse the country and the gods within the ground?
Oh, can Orestes live, be somewhere in sunlight still?
Shall fate grown gracious ever bring him back again
In strength of hand to overwhelm these murderers?

In this way, the chorus not only makes judgment on the action but also foretells the result: namely, that Orestes, Agamemnon's son, will seek to avenge his father's murder.

The chorus appears in an attenuated form in some of Shakespeare's plays. The prologue to *Romeo and Juliet* (1595), for example, is delivered by a chorus who serve to set the scene and summarize the tragic plot and its consequences:

Two households, both alike in dignity,
In fair Verona, where we lay our scene,
From ancient grudge break to new mutiny,
Where civil blood makes civil hands unclean,
From forth the fatal loins of these two foes
A pair of star-cross'd lovers take their life. . . . (lines 1-6)

Along with its reduced role, the chorus was also reduced in size, often falling to one **chorus-character** or **choral character**. Nevertheless, in most instances, this chorus-character still retained the functions of commentator and soothsayer. In Jean Anouilh's *Antigone* (1943), for instance, the chorus is represented by a single character:

CHORUS:
. . . Antigone is young. She would much rather live than die. But there is no help for it. When you are on the side of the gods against the tyrant, of Man against the State, of purity against corruption—when, in short, your name is Antigone, there is only one part you can play; and she will have to play hers through to the end. Mind you, Antigone doesn't know all these things about herself. I know them because it is my business to know them. That's what a Greek Chorus is for. . . .

This choral figure in Anouilh's play offers a twentieth-century view of the limitations placed on the protagonist in classic Greek tragedy. This voice is clearly more individual and less sober than those of choruses in Greek tragedies.

CLASSICISM

As is the case with many general terms, *classicism* has been used by critics in a wide variety of ways. In its most familiar sense, *classicism* is associated with a knowledge of and predilection for the literature, philosophy, art, and aesthetic tastes of the ancient Greek and Roman cultures. As a critical term, *classicism* describes the espousal and teaching of art embodying the virtues ascribed to these cultures: simplicity, clarity, balance, unity, reason, and integrity. The works commonly associated with *classicism* are often noted for their ethical appeal and their concern with moral behavior.

In literary criticism, classicism has a long tradition: from Aristotle's *Poetics* of the fourth century B.C. to the critical prose of Ezra Pound and T. S. Eliot in the first half of the twentieth century. In his *Poetics*, Aristotle focuses his attention on the general principles of dramatic construction: that is, the shapes, forms, manners, and purposes of poetry and drama. In a representative passage, Aristotle names plot, character, thought, and diction as the four principal parts of tragedy. He then goes on to focus on the first of these, plot, which he believes more important than the rest:

> Now that we have defined these terms, let us discuss what kind of process the arrangement of incidents must be, since this is the first and most important element of tragedy. We have posited that tragedy is a complete and whole action having a proper magnitude. For it is possible for something to be whole and yet not have any considerable magnitude. To be a whole is to have a beginning and a middle and an end. . . . It is necessary, therefore, that well-constructed plots not begin by chance, anywhere, nor end anywhere, but that they conform to the distinctions made above.

These dicta are typical of Aristotle's concern for **unity of action** ("complete and whole action"), integrity ("whole action having a proper magnitude"), and logic ("well-constructed plots [that do] not begin by chance").

The principles of classicism became the foundation for the literary forms and conventions of Elizabethan writers such as Sir Philip Sidney, whose essay *The Defence of Poetry* (1595) suggests his affinities with the literature of both ancient Greek and Latin writers. Sidney's brand of classicism, however, is closer to that of the Latin poet Horace than to that of Aristotle. *The Defence of Poetry* places great importance on the moral, civic, and didactic responsibilities of the poet: "So that, the end of all earthly learning being virtuous action, those skills, that most serve to bring forth that, have most just title to be prince over all the rest. Wherein we can show the poet's nobleness, by setting him before his other competitors, among whom as the principal challengers step forth the moral philosophers. . . ."

Neoclassicism

In the Neoclassical period of English literature, the classicism of Dryden, Pope, and Johnson is both pronounced and overt. In Pope's poem *An Essay on Criticism* (1711), for instance, he makes explicit reference to the ancient Greeks and their principles of artistic expression and criticism:

> Those rules of old discovered, not devised,
> Are Nature still, but Nature methodized;
> Nature, like liberty, is but restrained
> By the same laws which first herself ordained.
> Hear how learn'd Greece her useful rules indites,
> When to repress and when indulge our flights. . . .

In making reference to "Nature," Pope suggests that the poet should imitate natural order. According to Pope, the natural order to be imitated is that which we know through reason and science: that is to say, both form and content should take as their models the laws of nature apprehended through study. Pope's lines also advocate balance and restraint in both poetry and criticism, qualities that would come under attack by the English Romantics who succeeded the Neoclassicists.

A resurgence of classicism was brought about in the twentieth century by T. S. Eliot and Ezra Pound, among others. In his essay "Tradition and the Individual Talent" (1917), T. S. Eliot offers a modernist attitude towards classicism:

> [Tradition] cannot be inherited, and if you want it you must obtain it
> by great labor. It involves, in the first place, the historical sense, which
> we may call nearly indispensable to anyone who would continue to be a
> poet beyond his twenty-fifth year; and the historical sense involves a
> perception, not only of the pastness of the past, but of its presence. . . .
> No poet, no artist of any art, has his complete meaning alone. His sig-
> nificance, his appreciation is the appreciation of his relation to the dead
> poets and artists. You cannot value him alone; you must set him, for
> contrast and comparison, among the dead. I mean this as a principle of
> aesthetic, not merely historical, criticism.

For Eliot, then, classicism must be sustained or revived by familiarity with the traditional canon and judgments based on an awareness of how works of the classic tradition continue to inform contemporary literature and culture. See **CANON**.

COMEDY

The term *comedy* is most often applied to plays and films in which the protagonist or protagonists overcome adversity to reach a successful conclusion. The word *comedy* derives from Greek roots meaning "a singer in the revels." The tone or mood of a comedy is generally lighter than that of a tragedy. This is particularly true of the *commedia* of the Middle Ages, which indulges in farce. However, some comedies are very serious and poignant. Dante's *Divine Comedy* (c. 1314), for example, conceives of comedy as a rising from adversity to prosperity.

One of the most familiar subgenres in literature and film is the **romantic comedy**. This kind of comedy usually focuses attention on one or more pairs of lovers who typically must endure a series of humorous trials and tribulations before living happily ever after. In the first act and scene of Shakespeare's *A Midsummer Night's Dream* (1595-1596), the words of Lysander, whose love for Hermia is opposed by **Hermia's father**, foreshadow the complications of the plot:

> Ay me! for aught that I could ever read,
> Could ever hear by tale or history,
> The course of true love never did run smooth . . .

In the course of *A Midsummer Night's Dream*, the jealous Oberon, king of the fairies, and his mischievous assistant, Puck, employ a magic potion to make unsuited couples fall in love with each other. By the end of the play, however, the spells are lifted, enabling the true lovers to reunite. In the conclusion, Puck comments on the fantastic quality of the play's movement from chaos to order:

> If we shadows have offended,
> Think but this, and all is mended,
> That you have but slumb'red here
> While these visions did appear. (5.1.423-426)

Such plots abound in the romantic comedies of the golden age of Hollywood. In *My Favorite Wife* (Garson Kanin, 1940), for example, the male lead, believing his first wife to be killed in a shipwreck, marries a woman whom he does not love. At the start of his second honeymoon, his first wife miraculously reappears on the scene. In the course of the film, the hero decides to forsake his second wife in order to renew his love for his first wife, only to discover that she has lived for several years with another man on a deserted island. The conclusion of the film presents a pleasurable symmetry, since the hero, having overcome his jealousy, winds up seeking to annul his second marriage in court before the same judge who granted him a death certificate for his first wife, enabling him to wed the second. As in several of Shakespeare's romantic comedies, no obstacles to love and harmony seem too great to surmount in Hollywood's plots. More recent examples of this film genre include *When Harry Met Sally* (Rob Reiner, 1989) and *Sleepless in Seattle* (Nora Ephron, 1992).

One of the conventions of the romantic comedy is the disguised lover, as is represented by the character of Rosalind, the daughter of a Duke, in Shakespeare's *As You Like It* (1599). She is forced to flee the court by her uncle, who has usurped her father's position. Deciding to seek her father in the forest of Arden, Rosalind disguises herself as a boy. On reaching the forest, she is reunited with her lover, Orlando, who fails to recognize her. By maintaining her disguise, Rosalind comes to learn the true depth of Orlando's love for her. In the end, the rightful Duke is restored, and the lovers are set to be married. The motif of the disguised woman who becomes privy to the secret thoughts and feelings of her lover has often been repeated. The tables are turned in the contemporary film *Tootsie* (Sydney Pollack, 1982), where the male lover adopts a female disguise; nevertheless, the basic conventions of the genre remain intact.

Like romantic comedy, the **comedy of manners**, which is characterized by satirical portrayal of lifestyles and conditions of society, examines the course of love and the ways of lovers. However, the comedy of manners is usually more realistic, eschewing the use of fairies, magic, and other elements of the fantastic. Moreover, the comedy of manners is more scathing in its criticism than romantic comedy.

Unlike the lovers in romantic comedy, the lovers in a comedy of manners face obstacles of their own making. In Shakespeare's *Love's Labour's Lost* (1595), for instance, a king and three of his courtiers forswear the company of women in order to pursue a program of religious and scholarly contemplation. However, when a princess and her three ladies in waiting appear on the scene, the noble intentions of the gentlemen begin to falter. A similar reversal of feelings occurs in *Much Ado About Nothing* (1598), in which Beatrice and Benedick begin the play as archenemies who cannot resist trading insults:

BEATRICE: I wonder that you will still be talking, Signior Benedick; nobody marks you.

BENEDICK: What, my dear Lady Disdain! Are you yet living?

BEATRICE: Is it possible disdain should die while she hath such meet food to feed it as Signior Benedick? Courtesy itself must convert to disdain if you come in her presence. (1.1.116-123)

In the course of events, however, these two discover a playful love hiding beneath their superficial contempt for one another:

BENEDICK: A miracle! here's our own hands against our ears. Come. I will have thee; but, by this light, I take thee for pity.

BEATRICE: I would not deny you; but, by this good day, I yield upon great persuasion; and partly to save your life, for I was told you were in a consumption.

BENEDICK: I will stop your mouth. [Kissing her.] (5.4.91-97)

The lasting appeal of this kind of comedy is evidenced by the success of the 1994 film version of the play, directed by Kenneth Branagh.

The comedy of manners underwent a period of high development during the English Restoration of the late seventeenth century, at the hands of playwrights such as Congreve, Wycherley, and Etherege. Their plays seek to satirize moral pretensions and hypocrisy by lampooning the dress, manners, and speech of fops, would-be wits, lecherous moralizers, and absurdly jealous husbands. This type of **satiric comedy** revels in exposing the hypocritical conventions and ridiculous artificialities of high society, relying heavily on wit, word play, and rhetorical flourishes. Oscar Wilde's *The Importance of Being Earnest* (1895), a more modern example of this brand of the comedy of manners, offers a multitude of examples of verbal wit used to poke fun at social and moral pretensions. In Act 2, the protagonist visits his ward at his country home but pretends to be the wicked brother he has invented as his alter ego:

CECILY: . . . You, I see from your card, are Uncle Jack's brother, my cousin Ernest, my wicked cousin Ernest.

ALGERNON: Oh! I am not really wicked at all, cousin Cecily. You mustn't think that I am wicked.

CECILY: If you are not, then you have certainly been deceiving us all in a very inexcusable manner. I hope you have not been leading a double life, pretending to be wicked and being really good all the time. That would be hypocrisy.

Whereas the comedy of manners often seems to delight in the faults and foibles of humanity, satiric comedy seeks to act as a scourge and a corrective by treating the vain and the foolish with high sarcasm. See **THE ABSURD** and **SATIRE**.

CONCEIT

The word *conceit* derives from the Latin verb *concipere*, meaning "to take to oneself, or to take into the mind." As this derivation suggests, conceits are characteristic means of expression that reflect habits of thought and perception: the ways in which one conceives, perceives, thinks about, or "takes in" the world of objects and ideas. Thus, in speaking of the conceits an author employs in a literary work, critics often refer to characteristic diction, syntax, or figures of speech that represent the author's cast of mind or way of seeing and understanding. Conceits also reflect a culture's characteristic ways of conceiving of reality.

Emily Dickinson's poetry, for instance, expresses a delight in personifying or objectifying abstractions:

Because I could not stop for Death—
He kindly stopped for me—
The Carriage held but just Ourselves—
And Immortality.

(1890)

Dickinson personifies "Death" as a "kindly" carriage driver and "Immortality" as a fellow passenger in this carriage bound for eternity. While personification and objectification of abstractions are common devices among poets, Dickinson's unusual characterizations are often shockingly original and idiosyncratic: "My Life had stood—a Loaded Gun—"; "Remorse—is Memory—awake— / Her Parties all astir—", or "After great pain, a formal feeling comes— / The Nerves sit ceremonious, like Tombs—." Such conceits may be said to represent Dickinson's unusual means of conceiving of human existence and feelings. Morever, these conceits reflect the lasting influence of Calvinist theology in nineteenth-century New England culture. The personifications of concepts of guilt, death, and immortality are elaborate versions of Protestant allegorical figures.

In some ways, Dickinson's innovative figures of speech are reminiscent of the **metaphysical conceits** associated with English poets of the seventeenth century, such as John Donne, George Herbert, Richard Crashaw, and Abraham Cowley. These poets and others are noted for their original and surprising comparisons. Perhaps the most famous of these is found in John Donne's "A Valediction: Forbidding Mourning" (1633), in which he employs an extended metaphor comparing two lovers to twin legs of a compass used to draw a circle. Addressing the relationship of two souls, his lover's and his own, the speaker in Donne's poem insists that

> If they be two, they are two so
>   As stiff twin compasses are two:
> Thy soul, the fixed foot, makes no show
>   To move, but doth, if the other do;
>
> And though it in the center sit,
>   Yet when the other far doth roam,
> It leans, and hearkens after it,
>   And grows erect, as that comes home.
>
> Such wilt thou be to me, who must,
>   Like the other foot, obliquely run;
> Thy firmness makes my circle just,
>   And makes me end where I begun.

This comparison is metaphysical in the sense that it suggests an analogy between the invisible relations between two souls and the visible relations between the two feet of the compass; the analogy is unusual in that love is compared to a mathematician's tool rather than some object or process in nature.

Not all conceits are fresh or original. The love sonnets of the fourteenth-century Italian poet Francis Petrarch employ a number of figures that were no doubt innovative in their day:

> Upon the breeze she spread her golden hair
> that in a thousand gentle knots was turned,
> and the sweet light beyond all measure burned
> in eyes where now that radiance is rare . . .
>   (circa 1327; trans. Anthony Mortimer, 1977)

In this passage, Petrarch compares (directly or indirectly) the brightness of his lover's eyes to the radiance of the sun. Such exaggerated comparisons are part of the charm of Petrarch's verse. Moreover, they express a shift from the cultural dominance of Christianity to a growing secularism; prior to Petrarch's time, such exaggerated comparisons were usually reserved for praise of religious figures such as the Virgin Mary. By the sixteenth century, however, Petrarchan conceits had become worn by use. Nevertheless, many English poets continued to employ such hackneyed formulas as those manifested in a sonnet by Henry Constable:

> My lady's presence makes the roses red
> Because to see her lips they blush for shame.
> The lily's leaves, for envy, pale became.

And her white hands in them this envy bred.
The marigold the leaves abroad doth spread
Because the sun's and her power is the same.

(1594)

Lines like these inspired Shakespeare to write a sonnet satirizing the traditional Petrarchan conceits of beauty and love:

My mistress' eyes are nothing like the sun;
Coral is far more red than her lips' red;
If snow be white, why then her breasts are dun;
If hairs be wires, black wires grow on her head.

(1609)

Thus, as Shakespeare's sonnet suggests, even the most elaborate and unusual conceits can become tired clichés through overuse. See **ANALOGY**, **HYPERBOLE**, and **PERSONIFICATION**.

CONCRETE LANGUAGE

The word *concrete* derives from the Latin verb *concrescere*, meaning "to grow together, harden." In discussing diction, it is useful to oppose concrete language with **abstract language**. Whereas abstract words such as *love, peace*, and *steadfastness* are used to express ideas or emotions, concrete diction is used to refer to particular persons, places, and objects: *girl, forest, stone*. Concrete language names or describes the perceptible and material world; that is to say, concrete diction appeals to or engages the senses.

Gerard Manley Hopkins's "Pied Beauty" (1918) offers an example of concrete diction in poetry:

Glory be to God for dappled things—
    For skies of couple-colour as a brinded cow;
        For rose-moles all in stipple upon trout that swim;
Fresh-firecoal chestnut-falls; finches' wings;
    Landscape plotted and pierced—fold, fallow, and plough;
        And all trades, their gear and tackle and trim.

Hopkins clearly revels in language that appeals to the visual sense. These lines offer specific, material examples of "dappled things."

The opening lines of Gary Soto's "History" (1977) offer another example of concrete diction:

Grandma lit the stove.
Morning sunlight
Lengthened in spears
Across the linoleum floor.
Wrapped in a shawl,

> Her eyes small
> With sleep,
> She sliced papas,
> Pounded chiles
> With a stone
> Bought from Guadalajara.

Instead of describing his subject as an early riser, Soto uses a language of specificity and sensory appeal: "Her eyes small / With sleep." Likewise, rather than merely indicating that she prepared food, the speaker describes her activities in concrete terms: "She sliced papas, / Pounded chiles / With a stone. . . ."

The differences between abstract and concrete language are also observable in prose. The opening chapter of Thomas Hardy's *The Return of the Native* (1878) describes Egdon Heath as "a thing majestic without severity, impressive without showiness, emphatic in its admonitions, grand in its simplicity." The language of this description is abstract, attributing to the landscape qualities that are not tangible. By contrast, the following excerpt from Mark Twain's *The Adventures of Huckleberry Finn* (1884) manifests Huck's pleasure in the material objects he finds in an abandoned house floating down the Mississippi River:

> We got an old tin lantern, and a butcher-knife without any handle, and
> a bran-new Barlow knife worth two bits in any store, and a lot of tallow
> candles, and a tin candlestick, and a gourd, and a tin cup, and a ratty old
> bed-quilt off the bed, and a reticule of needles and pins and beeswax
> and buttons and thread and all such truck in it, and a hatchet and some
> nails, and fish-line as thick as my little finger, with some monstrous
> hooks on it, and a roll of buckskin, and a leather dog-collar, and a
> horse-shoe. . . .

In *Wide Sargasso Sea* (1966), Jean Rhys employs concrete diction to describe a garden in Jamaica:

> Underneath the tree ferns, tall as forest ferns, the light was green.
> Orchids flourished out of reach or for some reason not to be touched.
> One was snaky looking, another like an octopus with long thin brown
> tentacles bare of leaves hanging from a twisted root. Twice a year the
> octopus orchid flowered—then not an inch of tentacle showed. It was a
> bell-shaped mass of white, mauve, deep purple, wonderful to see.

As these passages demonstrate, concrete language serves to engage the senses, whereas abstract language proves more suitable to analysis and commentary. See **ABSTRACT LANGUAGE**.

CONSONANT SOUNDS

Significant repetition of consonant sounds produces five kinds of effects: **resonance**, **exhaustion**, **liquidity**, **plosiveness**, and **harshness**.

Resonance is the quality of duration produced by nasals—such as *n, m, ng*—and fricatives—such as *z, v,* and a voiced *s* (as in raise)—as well as a voiced *th* (as in them). For instance, the duration of final sounds in *curt* and *curve,* or *mass* and *maze,* or *sob* and *song* may be compared. Resonating words tend to resound throughout the line. They can be used to create harmony or dissonance. W. B. Yeats employs a series of resonant consonants in "Byzantium" (1932):

> Night resonance recedes, night-walker's song
> After great cathedral gong

The resonance of these consonants serves to convey the receding sound of a gong.

Exhaustion connotes a tone of weariness or languor that is created by voiceless fricatives, alone or in combination: *h, f,* the voiceless *s* (as in *mass*), *sh* (as in *mush*), and the voiceless *th* (as in *mouth*). The length of exhaustive consonants, if grouped together, forces the reader to pause in order to take a breath. Anne Bradstreet uses a series of exhaustives in "Here Follows Some Verses upon the Burning of Our House July 10th, 1666" (1867):

> My pleasantest things in ashes lie,
> And them behold no more shall I.
> Under thy roof no guest shall sit
> Nor at thy table eat a bit.
> No pleasant tale shall e'er be told,
> Nor things recounted done of old.
> No candle e'er shall shine in thee,
> Nor bridgroom's voice e'er heard shall be.

Liquidity is the quality of smoothness or suavity that results from using liquid consonants and semivowels: *l, r, w, y,* as in the words *low, ray, way,* and *yew.* Derek Walcott is explicit about his delight in liquid consonant sounds in the opening of his poem "A Sea-Chantey" (1964):

> Anguilla, Adina,
> Antigua, Cannelles,
> Andreuille, all the *l*'s,
> Voyelles, of the liquid Antilles,
> The names tremble like needles
> Of anchored frigates,
> Yachts tranquil as lilies,
> In ports of calm coral.

These liquid sounds are particularly smooth when they seem to span two syllables: "Antilles" and "lilies." Liquids are also sensuous, as in the following lines from Tennyson's "The Lotos-Eaters" (1832):

> Music that gentlier on the spirit lies,
> Than tired eyelids upon tired eyes;
> Music that brings sweet sleep down from the blissful skies

Plosiveness and **harshness**, the qualities of sounds that jar the nerves or grate against the ear, occur when certain hard consonants are employed repetitively. These consonants include stops—such as *b, p, t, d, g,* and *k*—as well as ch and /'. These consonants sound hard and restrained. Shakespeare uses nearly all of these in the famous storm scene of *King Lear* (1605-1606):

> Blow, winds, and crack your cheeks! rage! blow!
> You cataracts and hurricanoes, spout
> Till you have drenched our steeples, drowned the cocks! (3.2.1-3)

The consonants g and *k* are particularly harsh when they begin or end a word. Seamus Heaney exploits the effects of these harsh consonants in the beginning of his poem "Digging" (1965):

> Between my finger and my thumb
> The squat pen rests; snug as a gun.

> Under my window, a clean rasping sound
> When the spade sinks into gravelly ground:
> My father digging. . . .

Heaney uses these harsh consonants to imitate the sounds of digging with a spade. See **ALLITERATION**.

COUPLET

Strictly defined, a couplet consists of two lines of verse forming a discrete unit of meaning. However, the term is more commonly used to denote any two lines of rhymed poetry: a **rhyming couplet**. Among the most familiar examples of this verse form are the rhyming couplets that conclude Shakespeare's sonnets.

> If this be error and upon me proved,
> I never writ, nor no man ever loved. (Sonnet CXVI)

> And yet, by heaven, I think my love as rare
> As any she belied with false compare. (Sonnet CXXIX)

Shakespeare employs the couplet to sum up or comment upon the themes or arguments presented in the first twelve lines of the sonnet. The couplet is well suited to these functions because it gives a sense of being both balanced and self-contained.

The **heroic couplet** consists of two lines of rhymed iambic pentameter. Unlike a Shakespearean sonnet, which employs only one couplet at the end of the poem, heroic verse consists entirely of heroic couplets. Chaucer uses heroic couplets for most of *The Canterbury Tales* (c. 1390):

> Whan that Aprill with his shoures soote
> That droghte of March hath perced to the roote,
> And bathed every veyne in swich licour
> Of which vertu engendred is the flour;

Whan Zephirus eek with his sweete breeth
Inspired hath in every holt and heeth
The tendre croppes, and the yonge sonne
Hath in the Ram his halfe cours yronne,
And smale foweles maken melodye,
That slepen al the nyght with open eye—
So priketh hem nature in hir corages—
Thanne longen folk to goon on pilgrimages. . . .

In the seventeenth and eighteenth centuries, heroic verse became the dominant form of English poetry. John Dryden, Samuel Johnson, and Alexander Pope, to name a few principals, all found the heroic couplet an appropriate form for the classical rhetoric and logical development of their poetry. Pope's *An Essay on Man* (1732-1734) is a representative example of heroic verse used to construct and express rational arguments. Indeed, Pope's avowed purpose in this poem, echoing Milton's statement of purpose in *Paradise Lost* (1667), is to "vindicate the ways of God to man":

Respecting man, whatever wrong we call,
May, must be right, as relative to all.
In human works, though labored on with pain,
A thousand movements scarce one purpose gain;
In God's, one single can its end produce;
Yet serves to second too some other use.
So man, who here seems principal alone,
Perhaps acts second to some sphere unknown,
Touches some wheel, or verges to some goal;
'Tis but a part we see, and not a whole.

In this passage, the heroic couplet serves to give a sense of balance to Pope's assertion of the distinctions between man's limited knowledge and God's infinite understanding. These couplets likewise seem to convey a tone of certainty and authority, which may be thought to contribute to Pope's ethical appeal.

An excerpt from Wole Soyinka's "The Apotheosis of Major Doe" (1988) offers a contemporary example of couplets used to great effect:

Flown on flags, graced by diplomatic corps
We consecrate the nightmare, kiss a nation's sore.

To mask the real, the world is turned a stage,
A rampant play of symbols masks a people's rage.

Soyinka employs couplets to emphasize the terminal rhymes, which themselves drive home the poet's juxtaposition of the symbolic forms and the actual states of colonialism and military rule in Africa.

COURTLY LOVE

The courtly love tradition is commonly thought to have originated with the troubadours: traveling singers and poets who flourished during the twelfth

century in Provence (a region in the south of France). The songs and poems of
the troubadours were characterized by protestations of love and infatuation,
which may have developed as secularized versions of the songs of praise dedi-
cated to the Virgin Mary. In any event, the courtly love tradition is based on a
philosophy of love that persisted through the Middle Ages. C. S. Lewis describes
the nature of this philosophy in *The Allegory of Love* (1936):

> The sentiment, of course is love, but love of a highly specialized sort,
> whose characteristics may be enumerated as Humility, Courtesy, Adul-
> tery, and the Religion of Love. The lover is always abject. Obedience to
> his lady's lightest wish, however whimsical, and silent acquiescence to her
> rebukes, however unjust, are the only virtues he dares claim. There is a
> service of love closely modelled on the service which a feudal vassal owes
> to his lord. The lover is the lady's "man." He addresses her as *midons*,
> which etymologically represents not "my lady" but "my lord." The
> whole attitude has been rightly described as "a feudalisation of love."

The characteristics of humility and courtesy are often associated with the code of
chivalry, but they are also a development from expressions of religious feeling.
Having figuratively placed his lady upon a pedestal, the lover often worships
her from afar, both because he considers himself unworthy of her attention and
because she is often married or promised to another man. His infatuation is so
great that he often succumbs to sighing, moaning, and weeping over his
wretched state as an emotionally abused lover. Indeed, the courtly lover may
even offer to die for love. Such is the case with the hero of Chaucer's *Troilus
and Cressida* (1385). Urged on by Pandar, Troilus reveals the pangs of love that
wound him:

> Troilus heaved a deep and mournful sigh,
> And said to him, "Perhaps it may be best
> If with your friendly wish I should comply,
> And tear my secret from my aching breast,
> Though well I know you can bring me no rest.
> But lest you think I have no trust in thee,
> I'll tell thee, friend, just how it stands with me.
>
> 'Lo, Love, against which he who most defendeth
> Himself, the more thereby his effort faileth,
> This Love so far his rule o'er me extendeth,
> That now my heart to death a straight course saileth!
> Love-longing over me so deep prevaileth,
> That here to die for Love were greater joy
> Than be both King of Greece and King of Troy. . . ."
>
> (trans. George P. Krapp)

The incidence of adultery in stories, poems, and plays that take up courtly
love motifs may seem to contradict the idea of spiritualized love. However, sexual relations between the lovers are often treated as sins necessary for ultimate

redemption and receiving grace. Moreover, adultery is treated as a kind of refined behavior because it is usually limited to the upper classes, and as justified behavior because it gives expression to authentic passions that are largely absent from arranged marriages. Perhaps the most familiar example of adulterous courtly love is found in the Arthurian legends. The consummated love affair of Launcelot and Guinevere, as told by Sir Thomas Malory in Le *Morte D'Arthur* (1485), offers evidence of many aspects of the tradition of courtly love. In Chapter IX, Launcelot goes to visit Guinevere, Arthur's wife, who has taken to a nunnery to atone for her sinful love. Although she commands Launcelot to "forsake [her] company" and to "take . . . a wife, and live with her with joy and bliss," he refuses to be untrue to their love:

> Now, sweet madam, said Sir Launcelot, would ye that I should now return to my country, and there to wed a lady? Nay, madam, wit you well that shall I never do, for I shall never be so false to you of that I have promised; but the same destiny ye have taken you to, I will take me unto, for to please Jesu, and ever for you I cast me specially to pray.

For Launcelot, to forswear his promise of love to Guinevere would be to taint his code of honor; in the way of the courtly lover, he would rather suffer in isolation.

In the modern age, James Joyce offers a subtle satire of the courtly love tradition in "Araby" (1914) with his narrator's first-person retrospective account of his first infatuation:

> Her name sprang to my lips at moments in strange prayers and praises which I myself did not understand. My eyes were often full of tears (I could not tell why) and at times a flood from my heart seemed to pour itself out into my bosom. I thought little of the future. I did not know whether I would ever speak to her or not or, if I spoke to her, how I could tell her of my confused adoration. But my body was like a harp and her words and gestures were like fingers running upon the wires.

Joyce plays on the overly emotional and worshipful infatuation of a boy whose notions of love have been acquired by reading romantic fiction. He fancies himself a knight on a quest, bound to the courtly tradition of Platonic love.

Some contemporary critics have come to view the courtly love tradition as an idealization of women that served in part to disempower them in the world. See **FEMINIST CRITICISM** and **PLATONIC**.

CULTURAL CRITICISM

In recent years, programs in cultural studies have sought to broaden the focus of the humanities in general (and English departments in particular) from the study of works of literature and other approved books to an interdisciplinary analysis of cultural "texts." Cultural critics define a "text" as any discursive or signifying practice: that is, any object or process that may be read or interpreted as representing a culture's system of beliefs, values, hierarchies, or laws. These texts include all cultural artifacts, practices, institutions, and phenomena: works of literature, marriage rituals, prisons, and soap operas. According to proponents of cultural studies, such texts may be read and analyzed in terms of their relation to the dominant and competing cultural ideologies (belief systems). For instance, examining marriage rituals of a particular time and place might reveal the cultural expectations of men and women, as well as the ratios of power and prestige between them. Such analyses may influence the ways in which readers interpret literary texts in which marriage is an important goal, motivation, theme, or element of plot. Likewise, a study of access to literacy in nineteenth-century America might reveal why women, lower-class males, and people of color rarely became authors. A passage from Tillie Olsen's *Silences* (1965) offers an example of the relationship between culture and literary production in a discussion of the increasing number of women writers in the twentieth century:

> In this second century, we [women] have access to areas of work and of life experience previously denied; higher education; longer stronger lives; for the first time in human history, freedom from compulsory childbearing; freer bodies and attitudes toward sexuality; a beginning of technological easing of household tasks; and—of greatest importance to those like myself who come from generations of illiterate women—increasing literacy, and higher degrees of it. Each one of these is a vast gain.

This type of cultural examination might also serve to explain the ways in which women are generally represented (or not represented) in nineteenth-century American fiction.

The term *cultural criticism* embraces a number of approaches to literary texts, all of which attempt to analyze works of literature by seeing them in their historical and cultural contexts rather than as works of art in isolation. Moreover, in many but not all cases, advocates of cultural studies seek to analyze Western culture in ways that reveal subtly oppressive practices and largely unconscious belief systems attendant to and maintained by capitalist economies. For instance, in addition to discussing Conrad's *Heart of Darkness* (1902) as a novel that employs innovative narrative techniques and syntactic devices to give a new dimension to the archetypal motifs of initiation, death, and rebirth, cultural critics have focused on the practices of European imperialists, the relations between races in Africa, and the ways in which ivory came to be valued as a commodity. See **ETHNIC STUDIES, FEMINIST CRITICISM, MARXIST CRITICISM,** and **NEW HISTORICISM**.

D

DECONSTRUCTION

Deconstruction is a theory and a practice of reading that enables one to question seemingly stable and thoroughgoing interpretations of a text. As an approach to literature, deconstruction works as both an extension and a critique of **hermeneutics** (the science of **interpretation** or the ways of understanding) of the **New Critics**, who seek to examine the logical structure and patterns of **imagery** in a work of literature in order to discover its **unity** of construction and meaning. Deconstructive theorists such as Jacques Derrida insist that the notion of a unified work is illusory, and that the meaning of a text is always indeterminate. The reasons for this indeterminacy are many, but most of them are related to what deconstructive theorists see as the problems of language: namely, that the relationships between words and concepts are arbitrary (see **Semiotics**) and that, therefore, a literary text, which is necessarily written or spoken in language, cannot match up with reality except in arbitrary and questionable ways. Ultimately, like the New Critics before them, deconstructive theorists assert that language can refer only to itself; as Derrida has put it, "There is nothing outside the text." In other words, language cannot reach to or represent reality. Thus, all attempts to discover (or argue) reality and truth through language are subject to challenge.

Although New Critics were skeptical about the relationship between literature and reality, they tended to support the idea that successful literary works have a discernible form, an intrinsic unity, and a logical structure. Deconstructive theorists assert that such notions of structure and unity in a text are problematic and misleading because they are based largely on readings adhering to binary logic, which seeks to understand by noting oppositions. Moreover, unlike New Critical interpretations, deconstructive readings do not attempt to resolve or explain away the contradictions between the apparent oppositions in works of literature. For example, deconstructive analysis may be used to explore unresolved contradictions in and competing interpretations of Emily Dickinson's "The difference between Despair" (1914):

The difference between Despair
And Fear—is like the One

> Between the instant of a Wreck—
> And when the Wreck has been—
>
> The Mind is smooth—no Motion—
> Contented as the Eye
> Upon the Forehead of a Bust—
> That knows—it cannot see—

The explicit binary opposition in this poem is "The difference between Despair / And Fear." However, several other oppositions are implied: mind/heart or intellect/emotion; contentment/agitation; knowing/uncertainty.

Although the poem appears to be concerned with explaining the "difference" between despair and fear, a proponent of deconstructive theory might argue that the poem demonstrates the inherent problem of language, which Derrida sums up in a word of his own invention, *différance*, a pun on the French words for difference and deference. According to Derrida, words never achieve a meaning that is fully present and confirmable; their only meaning is negative, in the sense that they are not the same as other words. Thus, the word "fear," for instance, is meaningful only because it is not tear, sear, leer, or any other word, including "despair." Another way of understanding this concept of *différance* is to consider the experience of using a dictionary. In looking up the meaning of a word, one finds only other words, whose meanings are explained by other words, so that the meaning of the first word is constantly deferred or postponed. That is to say, one never reaches the original, ultimate, or absolute meaning.

In turning to Dickinson's poem, the deconstructive reader might begin by noting a hierarchy among the oppositions set up in the poem. For instance, "Despair" is clearly privileged in the sense that "Fear" receives far less attention and no description, even though the poem begins by implying that the "difference" will be examined from both sides. Therefore, despair is treated as a positive presence, a known feeling, whereas fear can only be appreciated negatively as an absence because it is defined only as lacking the qualities associated with despair. Moreover, in privileging despair over fear, the poem also seems to privilege intellectual detachment over emotional involvement. The entire second stanza suggests a controlled superiority achieved by disdaining emotional wreckage and attaining a state of indifference. The simile of the "Bust" associates this indifference with a realm of art that is both removed from and superior to the realm of human emotion.

Having exposed this privileging of one set of concepts over another set, the deconstructive reader might proceed to overturn this hierarchy by demonstrating the uncertainty of the text. One of the seemingly small inconsistencies in the text is the confusing parallelism of the first stanza. According to its grammatical scheme, despair is associated with "the instant of a Wreck," since they both come first in their respective parts of the analogy, and fear is associated with "when the Wreck has been." If the logical structure of the stanza is understood in this way, then despair must be understood as the emotion attending the sudden occurrence of "a Wreck," and fear must be understood as the controlling emotion in the aftermath. In this sense, it is fear that makes the mind smooth and contented, perhaps because the mind is too shocked or overwhelmed to think. Thus, the difference between the words "despair" and "fear"—a difference posited by the speaker in the beginning of the poem—is uncertain because the qualities associated with despair might just as easily be associated with fear.

Rather than worry about this indeterminacy, proponents of deconstruction revel in infinite play of significance. They do not seek to destroy or discredit a work so much as to discover how a text problematizes (finds contradictions or barriers to understanding), critiques, and dismantles itself. Reading, for the deconstructive critic, is not a search for ultimate truth but a continual discovery and rediscovery of a pluralism of competing truths that cannot be ranked in any sort of hierarchy. See **FEMINIST CRITICISM, INTERPRETATION/ MEANING**, and **NEW CRITICISM/FORMALISM**.

DIALOGUE

In literary criticism, *dialogue* is commonly defined as any written form of conversation between two or more speakers. Dialogue generally serves two main purposes: to advance the plot and to reveal character.

Jean Rhys's *Wide Sargasso Sea* (1966) offers an example of dialogue that is employed to advance the plot and give insight into character. A high-spirited exchange between newlyweds Antoinette and Edward Rochester, and a servant named Amelie, not only dramatizes the rivalry between Antoinette and Amelie but also announces the departure of another key character and foreshadows a sexual encounter between Amelie and Edward.

> "Finish quickly," said Antoinette, "and go and tell Christophine I want to see her."
> Amelie rested her hands on the broom handle. "Christophine is going," she said.
> "Going?" repeated Antoinette.
> "Yes, going," said Amelie. "Christophine don't like this sweet honeymoon house." Turning round she saw me and laughed loudly. "Your husban' look like he see zombie. Must be tired of the sweet honeymoon too."
> Antoinette jumped out of bed and slapped her face.
> "I hit you back white cockroach, I hit you back," said Amelie. And she did.
> Antoinette gripped her hair. Amelie, whose teeth were bared, seemed to be trying to bite.
> "Antoinette, for God's sake," I said from the doorway.
> She swung round, very pale. Amelie buried her face in her hands and pretended to sob, but I could see her watching me through her fingers.
> "Go away, child," I said.
> "You call her child," said Antoinette. "She is older than the devil himself, and the devil is not more cruel."

In *The Homecoming* (1965), Harold Pinter uses a dialogue between Teddy and Lenny, two brothers reunited after six years, to reveal character and to portend the turn of events:

TEDDY: How are you?

LENNY: Well, just sleeping a bit restlessly, that's all. Tonight, anyway.

TEDDY: Bad dreams?

LENNY: No, I wouldn't say I was dreaming. It's not exactly a dream. It's just that something keeps waking me up. Some kind of tick.

TEDDY: A tick?

LENNY: Yes.

TEDDY: Well, what is it?

LENNY: I don't know. *Pause.*

TEDDY: Have you got a clock in your room?

LENNY: Yes.

TEDDY: Well, maybe it's the clock.

LENNY: Yes, could be, I suppose.

Pause·

> Well, if it's the clock, I'd better do something about it. Stifle it in some way, or something.

From this dialogue, the audience discerns the detachment and aloofness of Teddy, as well as Lenny's tendency toward violence. Moreover, the dialogue advances plot because it reveals the lack of communication between the members of this family, and how the resulting tension sets in motion the train of events which lead to Lenny's making shocking passes at Teddy's wife.

DICTION

When used as a literary term, *diction* refers to the kinds or levels of language employed in a work. For instance, literary critics sometimes seek to distinguish between **abstract** and **concrete language**, **soft** and **hard diction**, and **formal** and **informal diction**.

Excerpts from William Wordsworth's "Ode: Intimations of Immortality from Recollections of Early Childhood" (1807) and Gerard Manley Hopkins's "God's Grandeur" (1918) illustrate the difference between **soft** and **hard diction** in poetry:

> Ye blessed Creatures, I have heard the call
>   Ye to each other make; I see
> The heavens laugh with you in your jubilee;
>   My heart is at your festival,
>   My head hath its coronal,

The fulness of your bliss, I feel—I feel it all.

★ ★ ★ ★ ★ ★ ★ ★ ★ ★

The world is charged with the grandeur of God.
  It will flame out, like shining from shook foil;
  It gathers to a greatness, like the ooze of oil
Crushed. Why do men then now not reck his rod?
Generations have trod, have trod, have trod;
  And all is seared with trade; bleared, smeared with toil;
  And wears man's smudge and shares man's smell: the soil
Is bare now, nor can foot feel, being shod.

In the first passage, which is an excerpt from Wordsworth's poem, the words and phrases are often abstract—"The fulness of your bliss"—and the images are vague —"My heart is at your festival." Moreover, the diction is soft in another sense: namely, that Wordsworth eschews the use of diction marked by hard sounds, which give emphasis and texture to the lines. By contrast, the excerpt from Hopkins's poem is replete with concrete diction and images: "like the ooze of oil" and "smeared with toil." Likewise, the diction is hard in its sound, giving emphasis through repetition of consonants.

The distinction between **formal** and **informal diction** is often more sub-tle; indeed, it may prove more useful to delineate three levels of diction: high, middle, and low. A passage from Edgar Allan Poe's "The Cask of Amontillado" (1846) offers an example of high diction:

> The thousand injuries of Fortunato I had borne as best I could, but when he ventured upon insult, I vowed revenge. You, who so well know the nature of my soul, will not suppose, however, that I gave utterance to a threat. At length I would be avenged; this was a point definitively settled—but the very definitiveness with which it was resolved, precluded the idea of risk. It must not only punish, but punish with impunity. A wrong is unredressed when retribution overtakes its redresser.

Poe's diction in this passage is both formal and highly latinate: "ventured," "utterance," "definitiveness," "precluded," "impunity."

The following excerpt from James Joyce's "Eveline" (1914), which describes the protagonist's relationship with her father, offers an example of middle diction:

> He said she used to squander the money, that she had no head, that he wasn't going to give her his hard-earned money to throw about the streets, and much more, for he was usually fairly bad of a Saturday night. In the end he would give her the money and ask her had she any intention of buying Sunday's dinner. Then she had to rush out as quickly as she could and do her marketing, holding her black leather purse tightly in her hand as she elbowed her way through the crowds and returning home late under her load of provisions.

In general, the diction in this excerpt is quite plain, even colloquial in the use of the phrases "she had no head"; "he was usually fairly bad of a Saturday night"; and "she elbowed her way." However, this low diction is interspersed with words such as "squander," "intention," and "provisions," all of which partake of the more literary diction of the high style. On the whole, Joyce uses a middle diction in this passage.

By contrast, Alice Walker employs low diction to great effect in the following excerpt from *The Color Purple* (1982):

> Pretty soon it be time for Shug to go. She sing every week-end now at Harpo's. He make right smart money off of her, and she make some too. Plus she gitting strong again and stout. First night or two her songs come out good but a little weak, now she belt them out. Folks out in the yard hear her with no trouble. She and Swain sound real good together. She sing, he pick his box. It nice at Harpo's.

Words and phrases such as "right smart," "gitting," "come out good," "folks," and "real good" partake of colloquial diction. See **ABSTRACT LANGUAGE**, **CONCRETE LANGUAGE**, and **CONSONANT SOUNDS**.

DOPPELGÄNGER

Doppelgänger is a German word that literally means "double walker"; it is commonly used to refer to a ghostly shadow-self or alter ego. In literature, the deliberate doubling of characters who are mirror images of one another creates *doppelgängers*. In Edgar Allan Poe's story "William Wilson," for example, the narrator, who calls himself William Wilson, encounters at boarding school another student with the same name; moreover, the narrator observes that this other William Wilson is remarkably similar to himself in person and manner:

> His cue, which was to perfect an imitation of myself, lay both in words and inactions; and most admirably did he play his part. My dress it was an easy matter to copy; my gait and general manner were, without difficulty, appropriated; in spite of his constitutional defect, even my voice did not escape him. My louder tones were, of course, unattempted, but then the key, it was identical; and his singular whisper, it grew the very echo of my own.

As the story goes on, the reader comes to recognize the other William Wilson as the narrator's shadow-self and conscience. At the end of the story, after his alter ego has revealed him to be a cheat at cards, the narrator confronts his *doppelgänger* in a room with a large mirror and kills him. At this moment, he recognizes this shadow-self as a reflection of himself:

> It was Wilson; but he spoke no longer in a whisper, and I could have fancied that I myself was speaking while he said:
>   "You have conquered, and I yield. Yet, henceforward art thou also dead—dead to the World, to Heaven and to Hope! In me didst thou

exist—and, in my death, see by this image, which is thine own, how utterly thou hast murdered thyself."

This revelation explains why, as the narrator notes at the beginning of the story, the other boys at the school are unaccountably blind to the rivalry between the two Wilsons: only the narrator is capable of seeing his doppelganger.

This notion of the *doppelgänger* as a secret-self provides the context for Joseph Conrad's tale "The Secret Sharer," in which the narrator is a ship captain who comes to harbor an escaped murderer with whom he sympathizes. After inviting this escapee aboard his ship and providing him with clothes, the narrator engages him in a conversation about his history and observes that

> The shadowy, dark head, like mine, seemed to nod imperceptibly above the ghostly gray of my sleeping suit. It was, in the night, as though I had been faced by my own reflection in the depths of a somber and immense mirror.

Likewise, at the end of the story, after hiding his ghostly self and then enabling him to escape overboard, the narrator notes,

> Walking to the taffrail, I was in time to make out, on the very edge of a darkness thrown by a towering black mass like the very gateway of Erebus—yes, I was in time to catch an evanescent glimpse of my white hat left behind to mark the spot where the secret sharer of my cabin and of my thoughts, as though he were my second self, had lowered himself into the water to take his punishment: a free man, a proud swimmer striking out for a new destiny.

The suggestions that this swimmer is the narrator's "second self" and "secret sharer" confirm that Conrad intends him to serve as the captain's *doppelgänger*.

Other works of fiction that prominently employ *doppelgängers* include Charlotte Bronte's *Jane Eyre* (Jane and Bertha Rochester), Emily Bronte's *Wuthering Heights* (Cathy and Heathcliff), and Vladimir Nabokov's *Lolita* (Humbert Humbert and Clare Quilty). The *doppelgänger* motif has also proved popular in film, most famously in the films of Alfred Hitchcock, whose *Shadow of a Doubt*, *Strangers on a Train*, *North by Northwest*, *Vertigo*, and *Psycho* all play on the notion of ghostly double walkers or shadow-selves.

DRAMA

The word *drama* derives from the Greek word *drao*, meaning "to do." The genre of drama may be divided into various subgenres, including **comedy**, **tragedy**, and **comedy of manners**. Classical drama was first performed by the ancient Greeks and Romans, often in connection with religious events or festivals. Playwrights from these periods include Aeschylus, Sophocles, and Seneca. During the medieval period, the church staged plays to teach the lessons of the Bible. These plays evolved into mystery plays and miracle and morality dramas (for example, the plays of the Chester cycle and Everyman [c. 1509-1519]) that were supported by trade and religious guilds and staged on wagons that traveled from town to town. Often allegorical in nature, morality plays depicted personifications of abstract qualities (such as Fellowship, Knowledge, and Death) and offered a **parable** about the vanity of life.

In the Renaissance, playwrights combined formal elements from drama of antiquity with traditions from medieval drama (such as comic features). Plays from this period may be subdivided into such groups as the *revenge tragedies, nationalistic chronicle plays*, and *romantic comedies*. Playwrights of the Renaissance include William Shakespeare, Ben Jonson, and John Chapman. During the Restoration period, heroic tragedies and comedies of manners satirizing contemporary society became popular. Major playwrights include Dryden, Congreve, Aphra Behn, Etherege, and Wycherly. Many of the comedies of manners depicted the wit, bawdiness, cynicism, and amorality of life in the court in London. In the eighteenth century, sentimental comedy, domestic tragedy, and genteel comedies of manners were frequently performed on stage, including works by Sheridan and Goldsmith. During the major part of the nineteenth century, melodrama was popular on the stage. Late in the century, comedies of manners by such playwrights as Oscar Wilde and serious social drama by such playwrights as George Bernard Shaw predominated. In the twentieth century, serious social drama by Arthur Miller, John Osborne, and Lorraine Hansberry flourished. Other forms of drama—for example, the **absurdist plays** of Samuel Beckett and Harold Pinter and the **symbolic**, **expressionistic plays** of Eugene O'Neill and Tennessee Williams—also evolved.

DRAMATIC MONOLOGUE

A *dramatic monologue* is a special kind of **lyric** poem in which the speaker reveals his or her character through an extended speech or a one-way dialogue. Unlike a **soliloquy**, a dramatic monologue is not addressed to the audience; instead, the reader is placed in the position of overhearing the speaker's monologue or dialogue with another whose words are not revealed. Since the monologue captures a critical moment in a character's life, it can reveal change or growth, revelation or epiphany, or renewed commitment to an ingrained perspective. **Setting** is also a dimension of the dramatic monologue as it develops a context for the speaker's attitudes.

Robert Browning's "Soliloquy of the Spanish Cloister" (1842) is a dramatic monologue in which we overhear a monk expressing his secret feelings about one of his "brothers in Christ":

> Gr-r-r—there go, my heart's abhorrence!
>   Water your damned flower-pots, do!
> If hate killed men, Brother Lawrence,
>   God's blood, would not mine kill you!

What? your myrtle-bush wants trimming?
Oh, that rose has prior claims—
Needs its leaden vase filled brimming?
Hell dry you up with its flames!

In overhearing the speaker's thoughts about Brother Lawrence, we learn that he must play the hypocrite, pretending to be courteous and charitable to his fellow monk while secretly desiring to express his hatred through some outward sign, action, or words.

By contrast, Browning's "My Last Duchess" (1842) presents one side of an imagined conversation between the Duke of Ferrara and an emissary of the Count of Tyrol, who has come to see him about the terms of engagement and marriage between the duke and the count's daughter. In the midst of their talk, the duke pulls aside a curtain revealing a portrait of his former wife:

Will't please you sit and look at her? I said
"Fra Pandolf" by design, for never read
Strangers like you that pictured countenance,
The depth and passion of its earnest glance,
But to myself they turned (since none puts by
The curtain I have drawn for you, but I)
And seemed as they would ask me,
If they durst, How such a glance came there; so, not the first
Are you to turn and ask thus. Sir, 'twas not
Her husband's presence only, called that spot
Of joy into the Duchess' cheek. . . .

The duke's conversation suggests his possessive attitude toward his former wife (only he is allowed to reveal her likeness in the portrait) and his jealousy (he believes "that spot / Of joy" in her cheek was elicited by men other than himself).

Louise Erdrich's "Windigo" (1984), a lyric presentation of a Chippewa legend, is a contemporary example of the dramatic monologue:

You knew I was coming for you, little one,
when the kettle jumped into the fire.
Towels flapped on the hooks,
And the dog crept off, groaning,
to the deepest part of the woods.

In the hackles of the dry brush a thin laughter started up.
Mother scolded the food warm and smooth in the pot
And called you to eat.
But I spoke in the cold trees:
New *one, I* have come for you, child hide and lie still.

In this poem, the windigo, a demon of winter who consumes human flesh, is overheard speaking to a young girl. See **ASIDE**, **LYRIC**, and **SOLILOQUY**.

E

ECOCRITICISM

The term *ecocriticism* is a linguistic blend of ecology and literary criticism. Briefly defined, ecocriticism is an effort to merge environmental concerns with literary studies and practice. The proximate roots of ecocriticism can be found in the poetry of the English Romantics and in the nature writings of late nineteenth century and early twentieth century non-fiction prose, most notably in Henry David Thoreau's *Walden* (1854).

The English Romantic poets were great admirers of the natural world for at least two reasons. First, they found nature to be aesthetically pleasing, especially with regard to its "organic unity"—what might be called today the interconnectedness or interdependence of the natural environment. The second reason these Romantics appreciated nature was that it was a source of inspiration for their art, as well as a means of expressing their thoughts and feelings: that is to say, they used the external landscape of nature to give body to the internal landscape of their hearts and minds. William Wordsworth's sonnet "The World is Too Much with Us" (1807) provides an example of the Romantics' attitude toward nature:

> The world is too much with us; late and soon,
> Getting and spending, we lay waste our powers:
> Little we see in nature that is ours;
> We have given our hearts away, a sordid boon!
> This Sea that bares her bosom to the moon;
> The winds that will be howling at all hours,
> And are up-gathered now like sleeping flowers;
> For this, for everything, we are out of tune;
> It moves us not.—Great God! I'd rather be
> A Pagan suckled in a creed outworn;
> So might I, standing on this pleasant lea,
> Have glimpses that would make me less forlorn;
> Have sight of Proteus rising from the sea;
> Or hear old Triton blow his wreathed horn.

Wordsworth's sonnet was written in the early nineteenth century and reflects the progress of the Industrial Revolution in England. One of the effects of growing industrialization of the English economy was that it promoted consumerism—the "getting and spending" to which Wordsworth refers. Another effect of this industrial economy was the waning of agriculture and of the rhythms and emotions associated with living off the land. Wordsworth's poem suggests that an obsession with "getting and spending" has caused consumers to become "out of tune" with nature because they have "given [their] hearts away." In the sestet of the sonnet, Wordsworth indignantly proclaims that he would prefer to be a "Pagan" rather than lose his emotional and spiritual relation with nature. The pagans to whom he alludes are pantheists, who believe that all of nature is possessed of deities: the wind, the sea, the sun, the trees, and so on. Ecocriticism generally agrees with the notions suggested by this poem that both capitalism and Christianity are unfavorable and even ruinous to nature or the natural environment: the first because it conceives of nature as a commodity and the second because it promotes the idea that God gave man dominion over the earth and all its creatures.

In *Walden*, Thoreau follows the example of his mentor Ralph Waldo Emerson in refusing to appreciate nature only at the level of commodity. In his essay entitled "Nature" (1836), Emerson distinguishes between "the stick of timber of the wood-cutter" and "the tree of the poet." The first perception arises from seeing nature as something that can be made into a commodity or product; the second perception sees nature as a source of inspiration and of aesthetic beauty. Thoreau's two-year sojourn in the woods near Walden pond inspired him to contemplate and write about living life "deliberately," a word he uses as a multi-layered pun, meaning not only "carefully" and "slowly" but also "consciously" and "intentionally." For Thoreau this way of living requires a harmonious relation with the natural world and a preference for conservation rather than consumerism. In the first chapter of *Walden*, "Economy," Thoreau makes a distinction between the necessities of existence and the superfluities of extravagances:

> By the words, necessary of life, I mean whatever, of all that man obtains by his own exertions, has been from the first, or from long use has become, so important to human life that few, if any, whether from savageness, or poverty, or philosophy, ever attempt to do without it. To many creatures there is in this sense but one necessary of life, Food. To the bison of the prairie it is a few inches of palatable grass, with water to drink; unless he seeks the Shelter of the forest of the mountain's shadow. None of the brute creation requires more than Food and Shelter. The necessaries of life for man in this climate may, accurately enough, be distributed under the several heads of Food, Shelter, Clothing, and Fuel.

Later in the same chapter, Thoreau clarifies the meaning of economy:

> When a man is warmed by the several modes which I have described, what does he want next? Surely not more warmth of the same kind, as

> more and richer food, larger and more splendid houses, finer and more
> abundant clothing, more numerous incessant and hotter fires, and the
> like. When one has obtained those things which are necessary to life,
> there is another alternative than to obtain the superfluities . . .

Thoreau's later advice to "simplify, simplify, simplify" suggests not only that one
should conserve natural resources but also that one should practice true and reasonable "economy" by using only what one needs.

Examples of ecocriticism with regard to classic literature might include reading James Fenimore Cooper's historical romances with a focus on the descriptions of ecological disasters, such as the extinction of the passenger pigeon,
rather than on the romantic adventures of an archetypal American woodsman
and hunter. Likewise, one may read Herman Melville's *Moby-Dick* (1851) with
a focus on the horrors of the whaling industry rather than the monomaniacal
revenge of Captain Ahab.

Of the twentieth-century books that have influenced ecocriticism, the
most famous is Rachel Carson's *Silent Spring* (1962), which offers detailed
accounts of the pernicious and often deadly effects of DDT and other forms
of pollution. Some proponents of ecocriticism have sought to merge with proponents of other critical movements—feminists and Native Americans, for
example—to suggest a more widespread and systematic abuse of both natural and
cultural environments. See **FEMINIST CRITICISM**, **ROMANTICISM**, and
TRANSCENDENTALISM.

EIGHTEENTH-CENTURY PERIOD
(IN ENGLISH LITERATURE)

The eighteenth-century period is divided by many literary critics into two major
eras: the Augustan period and the Age of Sensibility.

The Augustan period refers to the period from 1700 to 1745 (the year after
the death of Alexander Pope). The term *Augustan* derives from the original age
in antiquity, that is, the age of such writers as Virgil, Horace, and Ovid during
the reign of the Roman Emperor Augustus (27 B.C. to A.D. 14). Eighteenth-
century writers such as Pope, John Dryden, and Jonathan Swift imitated the literary forms and ideals, including moderation, reason, order, and clarity of the
Roman Augustans. Daniel Defoe, one of the first English novelists, also wrote
during the Augustan period, but his work represents popular rather than classical
writing. Pope exalts neoclassical ideals in *Moral Essays: Of the Use of Riches* (1731):

> Consult the Genius of the Place in all,
> That tells the Waters or to rise or fall,
> Or helps the ambitious Hill the Heav'ns to scale,
> Or scoops in circling Theatres the Vale,
> Calls in the Country, catches op'ning Glades,
> Joins willing Woods, and varies Shades from Shades,

> Now breaks, or now directs, th' intending Lines,
> Paints as you plant, and, as you work, Designs.
>   Still follow Sense, of ev'ry Art the Soul,
> Parts answ'ring Parts shall slide into a Whole.
> Spontaneous Beauties all around advance,
> Start ev'n from Difficulty, strike, from Chance;
> Nature shall join you; Time shall make it grow
> A Work to wonder at—perhaps a Stow. (57-70)

Pope uses rhetorical schemes (*parallelism, chiasmus, climax*) and the balance of heroic couplets to convey the notion of how one should consult the natural features, contours, and beauties of an estate before improving it with artifice. Thus, Pope implies that in landscaping as in writing poetry, one must "Still follow Sense, of ev'ry Art the Soul"; then "Parts answ'ring Parts shall slide into a Whole."

The Age of Sensibility encompasses the second half of the eighteenth century, from 1745 until approximately 1784 (the death of Samuel Johnson). Johnson is a significant figure in this period because of his influence over his contemporaries, including James Boswell, Oliver Goldsmith, and Edmund Burke. During this time, radical new ideas about culture and literature evolved. In particular, there was a departure from neoclassical qualities of reason, intellect, and moderation and a focus on intuition, empathy, and feeling. This focus on intuition, empathy, and feeling gave rise to the development of literature of sensibility. Representative writers of this type of literature include Samuel Richardson, Henry Mackenzie, and Laurence Sterne. As a representative author of the Age of Sensibility, Goldsmith offers a nostalgic vision of his childhood in "The Deserted Village" (1770). His depiction of an idyllic natural world is a protest against the depopulation of the countryside in the second half of the eighteenth century, tyrannical landlords, and the effect of the city on the peasants:

> Sweet smiling village, loveliest of the lawn,
> Thy sports are fled, and all thy charms withdrawn;
> Amidst thy bowers the tyrant's hand is seen,
> And desolation saddens all thy green:
> Only one master grasps the whole domain,
> And half a village stints thy smiling plain.
> No more thy glassy brook reflects the day,
> But choked with sedges, works its weedy way.
> Along thy glades, a solitary guest,
> The hollow sounding bittern guards its nest;
> Amidst thy desert walks the lapwing flies,
> And tires their echoes with unvaried cries.
> Sunk are thy bowers in shapeless ruin all,
> And the long grass o'ertops the mouldering wall,
> And trembling, shrinking from the spoiler's hand,
> Far, far away thy children leave the land. (34-50)

Goldsmith's meditative mood looks forward to the vision of the natural world in such Romantic poems as Wordsworth's "Michael." Like Wordsworth, Goldsmith stresses the need for the poet to be a teacher. See **CLASSICISM**, **ROMANTICISM**.

ELEGY

The word *elegy* derives from the Greek *elegos*, meaning "lament." Most critics use the term *elegy* to describe a meditative poem lamenting a death. Elegies typically contain a pattern of loss and consolation and a discussion of the transitory nature of all things.

In its classical form, an elegy is written in elegiac meter: alternating hexameter (six feet) and pentameter (five feet) lines. However, this form gave way in English to the elegiac stanza: four lines of iambic pentameter with an *abab* rhyme scheme. One of the most famous examples of the latter is Thomas Gray's "Elegy Written in a Country Church-Yard" (1751). A brief excerpt reveals some of its standard features:

> Beneath those rugged elms, that yew-tree's shade,
> Where heaves the turf in many a mould'ring heap,
> Each in his narrow cell for ever laid,
> The rude Forefathers of the hamlet sleep.
>
> The breezy call of incense-blooming Morn,
> The swallow twitt'ring from the straw-built shed,
> The cock's shrill clarion, or the echoing horn,
> No more shall rouse them from their lowly bed.
>
> And no more the blazing hearth shall burn,
> Or busy housewife ply her evening care:
> No children run to lisp their sire's return,
> Or climb his knees the envied kiss to share.

Gray's elegy is characterized by its meditative tone lamenting the dead's loss of the simple pleasures of nature, home, and family.

John Milton's "Lycidas" (1638) is an example of the pastoral elegy, in which the speaker casts the deceased loved one in the role of a shepherd who has been insufficiently mourned. Drawing on conventions of the classical elegies of Virgil, the speaker in elegies such as Milton's usually invokes the muse of poetry, describes a scene of mourning or a procession of mourners, offers a meditative digression on the cruelty of fate, and finds consolation in thinking that the death of the friend or loved one was meant to be. The speaker often expresses grief in an exaggerated fashion, employing imagery of nature in mourning to heighten the emotional quality of the lamentation, as is exemplified in the following passage from "Lycidas":

> But, oh! the heavy change, now thou art gone,
> Now thou art gone, and never must return!
> Thee, Shepherd, thee the woods, and desert caves,

With wild thyme and the gadding vine o'ergrown,
And all their echoes, mourn,
The willows, and the hazel copses green,
Shall now no more be seen,
Fanning their joyous leaves to thy soft lays.

Derek Walcott's "Elegy" (1969) for Che Guevara, the Argentine revolutionary who played an important role in the Cuban revolution of the late 1950s, is a contemporary example of the form:

Our hammock swung between Americas,
we miss you, Liberty. Che's
bullet-riddled body falls,
and those who cried, the Republic must first die
to be reborn, are dead,
the freeborn citizen's ballot in the head.
Still, everybody wants to go to bed
with Miss America. And, if there's no bread,
let them eat cherry pie.

But the old choice of running, howling, wounded
wolf-deep in her woods,
while the white papers snow on
genocide is gone;
no face can hide
its public, private pain,
wincing, already statued.

Although Walcott's elegy offers a pointedly political slant on the death of a hero, it nevertheless adheres to some of the formulas of the traditional elegy, such as the deliberate exaggeration of equating Che's death with the death of "Liberty." Moreover, the idea that the mourning for the dead one is both private and public is very much in line with the tenor of elegiac poems throughout the history of the subgenre. See **METER** and **PASTORAL**.

ENGLISH LITERARY PERIODS

See **OLD ENGLISH PERIOD, MIDDLE ENGLISH PERIOD, RENAISSANCE PERIOD, RESTORATION PERIOD, EIGHTEENTH-CENTURY PERIOD, ROMANTICISM, VICTORIAN PERIOD, MODERNISM,** and **POSTMODERNISM.**

EPIC

An *epic* is defined as a long narrative poem "celebrating episodes of a people's heroic tradition." An epic can be a poem that is wholly mythic in origin or, as the

American poet Ezra Pound has described it, "a poem including history," specifically the history of a people or a race. In many cases, it is a mixture of myth and history.

Characteristics present in most epics include the hero (who epitomizes significant qualities of the culture), the setting (which often covers a vast extent of space), heroic elements (such as battles and warfare), use of the supernatural, and elevation of language.

Many critics distinguish between two kinds of epics: the **traditional** (or **folk) epic** and the **literary** (or **art) epic**. The **traditional epic**, which may have been originally an oral or anonymous poem, typically focuses on the adventures of a hero who is important to or representative of a nation; such is the case for example in Homer's *The Odyssey* (eighth century B.C.) in which the narrative describes the wanderings of the Greek war hero Odysseus:

> Sing in me, Muse, and through me tell the story
> of that man skilled in all ways of contending,
> the wanderer, harried for years on end,
> after he plundered the stronghold
> on the proud height of Troy.
>
> He saw the townlands
> and learned the minds of many distant men,
> and weathered many bitter nights and days
> in his deep heart at sea, while he fought only
> to save his life, to bring his shipmates home.
> But not by will nor valor could he save them,
> for their own recklessness destroyed them all.
>
> (trans. Robert Fitzgerald)

As is often the case in folk epics, the problems of the hero in *The Odyssey* are caused or exacerbated by the wills and whims of deities. Odysseus's ten years of wandering, for instance, result in part from ill will borne against him by Poseidon, god of the sea, who seeks revenge for his son Polyphemus (a cyclops), who was made blind by Odysseus.

Traditional epics such as Homer's *The Iliad* (eighth century B.C.) give evidence of certain formulae. They often begin with the argument or a statement of theme:

> Anger be now your song immortal one,
> Akhilleus' anger, doomed and ruinous,
> that caused the Akhaians loss on bitter loss
> and crowded brave souls in the undergloom,
> leaving so many dead men—carrion
> for dogs and birds; and the will of Zeus was done.
> Begin it when the two men first contending
> broke with one another—the Lord Marshal
> Agamemnon, Atreus' son, and Prince Akhilleus.

Thus, the theme of *The Iliad* is "the wrath of Achilles," who, feeling himself ill-treated by Agamemnon, has withdrawn from the field during the Trojan War.

He later returns when he learns of the death of his friend Patroclus. The poem begins *in medias res:* that is, in the middle of the action. Once again, the gods are involved in the death and suffering; indeed, they take sides in the war and sometimes aid their favorites in battle. Other formulae include epic catalogues of warriors, long speeches, and epic **similes** or **epithets**.

The **literary** or **art epic** is a conscious imitation of a folk epic. The most famous of these is Virgil's *Aeneid* (first century B.C.), which is clearly an imitation of the Homeric epics discussed above. Whereas Homer's epics tell the tales of the tribe of the Greeks, Virgil's *Aeneid* tells the story of the founding of Rome by Aeneas. Later literary epics often focused on the Christian tradition and the Christian God; such is the case in Dante's *Divine Comedy* (early fourteenth century) in which the poet himself journeys through hell, purgatory, and heaven (often with Virgil as his guide both literally and figuratively) in order to understand the ways of God. Milton's *Paradise Lost* (1667), which draws heavily on Virgil's poem, seeks to "justify the ways of God to men" by telling the Christian tale of the Garden of Eden:

> Of Man's First Disobedience, and the Fruit
> Of that Forbidden Tree, whose mortal taste
> Brought Death into the World, and all our woe,
> With loss of Eden, till one greater Man
> Restore us, and regain the blissful Seat,
> Sing Heav'nly Muse, that on the secret top
> Of Oreb, or of Sinai, didst inspire
> That shepherd, who first taught the chosen Seed,
> In the Beginning how the Heav'ns and the Earth
> Rose out of chaos. . . .

Although some English Romantic poets (William Blake, for example), the Victorian poet Elizabeth Barrett Browning (*Aurora Leigh*, 1856), and certain nineteenth-century American poets (Whitman and Longfellow, among others) wrote epic poems, the form fell largely out of use until the twentieth century. Both Ezra Pound and James Joyce decided to imitate Homer's *The Odyssey* and "make it new." In his series of poems entitled *The Cantos* (1930-1969), which begins with an Old English rendition of Book XI of *The Odyssey*, Pound juxtaposes ancient, medieval, and modern sources (both mythic and historical) from diverse cultures to offer a world history of "pockets of civilization." In his novel *Ulysses* (1922), Joyce imitates the structure and conventions of the books of *The Odyssey* in rendering one day in the life of a representative modern man, a Dubliner named Leopold Bloom.

The epic is by no means a form particular to Western literature. The *Ramayana* and the *Mahabharata* are two ancient Hindu epics, the former, like *The Iliad*, having to do with a great war. Nigerian novelist Chinua Achebe's *Things Fall Apart* (1958) is a contemporary example of a work that employs many elements of the traditional epic:

> Okonkwo was well known throughout the nine villages and even
> beyond. His fame rested on solid personal achievements. As a young man
> of eighteen he had brought honor to his village by throwing Amalinze the

Cat. Amalinze was the great wrestler who for seven years was unbeaten, from Umuofia to Mbaino. He was called the Cat because his back would never touch the earth. It was this man that Okonkwo threw in a fight which the old men agreed was one of the fiercest since the founder of their town engaged a spirit of the wild for seven days and seven nights.

This opening paragraph of the novel focuses attention on "episodes of a people's heroic tradition," particularly the courageous exploits of Okonkwo and the legendary encounters of "the founder of their town." See **EPITHET**, **MODERNISM**, and **SIMILE**.

EPIGRAM

The general definition of *epigram* is any terse, witty, pointed statement. In literary criticism, the term is commonly used to describe a short poem notable for its concision of statement, pithiness, and wit. The word *epigram* derives from the Greek *epos* and *graphein*, meaning "to write on." Indeed, for the ancient Greeks and Romans, epigram meant simply an inscription, often one that served as an epitaph for the dead.

Using the work of the Latin epigrammist Martial as a model, the English poet Ben Jonson wrote a series of epigrams, some of which were meant to serve the original purpose of epitaphs. One such is his poem entitled "On My First Daughter" (1616):

Here lies, to each her parents' ruth,
Mary, the daughter of their youth;
Yet, all heaven's gifts being heaven's due,
It makes the father less to rue.
At six months' end she parted hence
With safety of her innocence;
Whose soul heaven's Queen (whose name she bears),
In comfort of her mother's tears
Hath placed amongst her virgin train;
Where, while that severed doth remain,
This grave partakes the fleshly birth;
Which cover lightly, gentle earth.

The Mexican poet Octavio Paz offers a contemporary example of this form in his "Epitaph for an Old Woman" (1968):

They buried her in the family tomb
and in the depth the dust
of what was once her husband
                           trembled:
joy for the living
                is sorrow for the dead.

Jonson was likewise adept at fashioning epigrams of pointed, satiric wit, such as his poem addressed "To Fool or Knave" (1616):

Thy praise or dispraise is to me alike;
One doth not stroke me, nor the other strike.

Epigrams do not always take the form of verse; one may fairly call a pithy statement in prose an epigram. The Victorian writer Oscar Wilde was famous for his epigrammatic wit, which he sprinkled liberally among his plays, poems, stories, letters, and conversation. In his play entitled *Lady Windermere's Fan* (1892), for instance, he writes, "Experience is the name everyone gives to their mistakes." Dorothy Parker acknowledges her debt to Wilde in a well-known epigram of her own from "A Pig's Eye View of Literature" (1937):

If, with the literate, I am
Impelled to try an epigram,
I never seek to take the credit;
We all assume that Oscar said it.

In addition to Parker, Mark Twain remains one of American literature's most famous epigrammatic wits. In his novel *Pudd'nhead Wilson* (1894), Twain observes, "Few things are harder to put up with than the annoyance of a good example."

EPIPHANY

The word *epiphany* derives from the Greek verb *epiphainein*, meaning "to show or to manifest." In its religious sense, an epiphany refers to the appearance or manifestation of a deity; thus, some Christian denominations celebrate the sixth of January to commemorate the showing forth of the Christ-child to the Magi in Bethlehem. The secular meaning of *epiphany* is "a sudden flash of recognition."

Although the concept of epiphany is clearly present in English Romantic poetry (e.g., Wordsworth's *The Prelude*, 1850), the word came into prominence as a literary term through its use in the writings of James Joyce. An early draft of *A Portrait of the Artist as a Young Man* (1915), then titled *Stephen Hero*, explains Joyce's use of the word:

By an epiphany he meant a sudden spiritual manifestation, whether in the vulgarity of speech or of gesture or in a memorable phase of the mind itself. He believed that it was for the man of letters to record these epiphanies with extreme care, seeing that they themselves are the most delicate and evanescent of moments.

One of the most famous epiphanies in Joyce's fiction is that of the protagonist, Gabriel Conroy, in the final story of *Dubliners* (1914), entitled "The Dead."

Having listened to his wife's passionate description of a former lover whom she believes "died for [her]," Gabriel comes to see himself and his situation in a sudden flash of insight and understanding:

> Gabriel felt humiliated by the failure of his irony and by the evocation of this figure from the dead, a boy in the gasworks. While he had been full of memories of their secret life together, full of tenderness and joy and desire, she had been comparing him in her mind with another. A shameful consciousness of his own person assailed him. He saw himself as a ludicrous figure, acting as a pennyboy for his aunts, a nervous well-meaning sentimentalist, orating to vulgarians and idealising his own clownish lusts, the pitiable fatuous fellow he had caught a glimpse of in the mirror.

In a sense, the mirror reveals Gabriel to himself, as if for the first time. But his epiphany reveals more than his appearance; it manifests his essential self, his nature, his desires, his foolishness, and his delusions.

The Brazilian writer Clarice Lispector explores epiphanic experiences throughout her fiction. In "The Message" (1964), for example, two adolescents experience a revelation at a mysterious, sphinx-like house:

> They looked at the house like tiny children standing at the bottom of a flight of stairs. . . . Dumbfounded, in an extreme union of fear and respect and paleness, in the presence of truth. Naked anguish had taken a leap and landed before them—not even as familiar as the word they had become accustomed to using. Simply an enormous house, rustic, with no neck, only that ancient might.
>
> I am that very thing you have been looking for all this time, the large house said.

The house makes the boy and girl aware of their ignorance of life and creates in them an anxiety about the future. Their epiphany signals the end of their childhood.

EPISTOLARY NOVEL

The term *epistolary* is an adjectival form of *epistle*, which was traditionally a name for a formal letter; thus, in an epistolary novel, the narrative is conveyed by means of letters from one character to another.

Samuel Richardson's *Pamela* (1740-1741) and *Clarissa* (1748-1749) are perhaps the most famous epistolary novels in English. In the latter, the story is told by means of letters between the protagonist, Clarissa Harlowe, and Anna Howe, her friend and confidante, as well as a correspondence between Richard Lovelace, Clarissa's suitor, and his friend John Belford. In this way, readers may come to appreciate plots and themes of the novel from several points of view, as well as acquire insights into the psychology and motives of characters. Much of the dramatic tension in epistolary novels derives from the characters' attempts to interpret the epistles of their correspondents and their desires to make their own intentions understood by means of letter writing. These problems of interpretation and intention are raised in *Clarissa* by a letter from Belford to Lovelace. Having gone to call on Clarissa on Lovelace's behalf, Belford is placed in the awkward position of being asked to read aloud to her one of his letters from Lovelace:

> Having mentioned the outrageous letter you had written to me on this occasion, she asked if I had that letter about me?
>
> I owned I had.
>
> She wished to see it.
>
> This puzzled me horribly: for you must needs think that most of the free things which, among us rakes, pass for wit, and spirit, must be shocking stuff to the ears or eyes of persons of delicacy of that sex: and then such an air of levity runs through thy most serious letters, such a false bravery, endeavouring to carry off ludicrously the subjects that most affect thee; that those letters are generally the least fit to be seen, which ought to be most to thy credit.

Such misunderstandings of the purpose and tone of correspondence contribute to the dramatic tension of epistolary novels.

Other well-known examples of the epistolary novel include *Shamela* (1741), Fielding's parody of *Pamela*; Burney's *Evelina* (1778); and Smollett's *Humphry Clinker* (1778). Although the genre largely disappeared after the eighteenth century, letters were still employed to great effect in nineteenth-century novels such as Jane Austen's *Pride and Prejudice* (1814).

Alice Walker's *The Color Purple* (1982) is a contemporary revival of the epistolary form, in which the narrative is carried forth by means of the protagonist's letters to God and her correspondence with her sister. In the opening chapter, Celie heeds her father's warning that "You better not never tell nobody [about her forced incest] but God" by addressing a letter:

> Dear God,
>
> I am fourteen years old . . . I have always been a good girl. Maybe you can give me a sign letting me know what is happening to me.

Near the middle of the novel, Celie begins to read a series of letters from her sister Nettie, from whom she has been forcibly separated:

> Dear Celie,
>
> I wrote a letter to you almost every day on the ship coming to Africa. But by the time we docked I was so down, I tore them into little pieces and dropped them into the water. Albert is not going to let you have my letters and so what use is there in writing them. That's the way I felt when I tore them up and sent them to you on the waves. But now I feel different.

In this way, we are permitted access to the thoughts and feelings of the sisters through their letters.

EPITHET

Broadly defined, an *epithet* is an adjective or adjective phrase that expresses a characteristic quality of the noun it modifies: a babbling brook or a swelling sea, for instance. In some cases, an epithet becomes synonymous with a noun. As a literary term, however, *epithet* is more often used to denote a particularly striking adjective or adjective phrase. John Milton's "Il Penseroso" (1645) employs a number of epithets:

> Thus, Night, oft see me in thy pale career,
> Till *civil-suited morn* appear
>
> ★ ★ ★ ★ ★ ★ ★ ★ ★ ★
>
> And the waters murmuring
> With such consort as they keep
> Entice the *dewy-feathered sleep*   (italics added)

Indeed, near the end of the poem, Milton piles epithet upon epithet to characterize the temperament and surroundings of *il penseroso* (the pensive one):

> But let my due feet never fail
> To walk the *studious cloister's pale*,
> And love the *high embowed roof*,
> With *antic pillars* massy proof,
> And *storied windows* richly dight,
> Casting a *dim religious light*.
> There let the *pealing organ* blow,
> To the *full-voiced choir* below . . .   (italics added)

Milton's model for many of these adjectival constructions was no doubt the **Homeric epithet**. Unlike the epithets in Milton's poem, the Homeric epithets in *The Odyssey* and *The Iliad* (eighth century B.C.) are repeated so often that they seem to be synonymous with the character or natural process they describe: "rosy-fingered dawn," "wine-dark sea," "the sound-minded Telemachus," "the bright-eyed goddess Athene," "Odysseus of many wiles."

In Old English, epithets take the form of **kennings**. Kennings are repeated phrases such as *hwael-weg*, which means "whale path" and becomes in Old English poetry a stock figure of speech for *sea*.

Joy Harjo, a Creek Indian poet, employs epithets in her poem entitled "Vision" (1983):

> Bright horses rolled over over
> And over the dusking sky.

American Indian poetry often includes epithets such as "bright horses" and "the dusking sky," many of which emphasize the importance of natural elements and processes.

ETHNIC STUDIES

The term *ethnic studies* is associated with the cultural history and artistic production of those who belong to ethnic minority groups. In many ways, the growth of ethnic studies of literature and culture has been parallel to the development of women's studies and **feminist criticism**: both movements have sought to expand the **canon** of literature to recognize and include works by underrepresented groups, and each has striven to raise awareness of problems with the stereotyping, oppression, and marginalization of these groups in Western cultures. In recent decades, two ethnic literatures and critical traditions have come into particular prominence: African-American studies and Chicano/a studies.

African-American Studies

In "Generational Shifts and the Recent Criticism of Afro-American Literature" (1981), Houston A. Baker, Jr., describes three stages of Afro-American literary criticism. The first stage, which Baker associates with "integrationist poetics," was represented in the first half of the twentieth century by scholars who sought to collect, edit, publish, and promote the works of African-American writers largely for the purpose of gaining acceptance from the (White) literary and scholarly establishment. In the 1950s and early 1960s, many Afro-American writers and critics looked upon their literature and scholarship as means of achieving equality through integration with White society. This early scholarly approach urged the assimilation of "Negro" writing into the canon of American literature, wherein it would be judged according to the traditional standards of literary criticism.

The stage that Baker associates with "romantic Marxism" and the "Black Aesthetic" came into its own in the mid to late 1960s, which were the years of ascendancy for the Black Power movement. Far from seeking to assimilate Black literature into the tradition of (White) American culture, the "Black Arts Movement" proposed a revolutionary approach focusing on cultural achievements of Black writers, artists, and musicians, most particularly as they grew out of struggles against economic, political, and social oppression. This stage was characterized, as Baker suggests, by literature of protest and identity politics, as represented by the poetry of Amiri Baraka (LeRoi Jones), the prose of Stokely Carmichael, and the criticism of Stephen Henderson.

Since the mid 1970s, the most prominent figures in African-American criticism have focused their efforts on developing poststructural theories of African-American literature and history. This stage, which has been called the "Reconstruction of Instruction," was initiated by a 1977 seminar at Yale on "Afro-American Literature and Course Design" and the publication of a volume entitled *Afro-American Literature: The Reconstruction of Instruction* (1978), edited by Robert Stepto and Dexter Fisher. Seeking an alternative to what they considered overly simplistic sociological and political approaches, theorists such as Stepto and Henry Louis Gates, Jr., have turned their attention away from extraliterary matters of politics and sociology and toward the history and practice of African-American literature. For his part, Gates has developed an approach that sees individual works of literature in the context of a Black tradition of language and literature. In "Criticism in the Jungle" (1984), Gates calls for African-American criticism to "derive principles . . . from the black tradition itself, as defined in the idiom of critical theory but also in the idiom which constitutes the 'language of blackness,' the signifying difference which makes the black tradition our very own." In other words, the course he recommends to critics of African-American literature is twofold: first, to work through the emerging post-structural theories of language and literature for the purpose of discovering a series of frameworks or methods, and, second, to study the genres and types of the Black tradition (myths, folktales, autobiographies, songs, poems, and novels, along with themes, characters, and plots) and the uses of language that are unique to the Black tradition (idiomatic expressions, recurring metaphors, and other figures of speech and syntax).

More recently, several women writers and critics, inspired by the works of Zora Neale Hurston, have brought a feminist perspective to African-American theory and practice. Alice Walker has called for a "womanist" appreciation of the tradition of Black literature; Barbara Smith has urged critics and scholars to explore the connections between Black women's lives and their own unique forms of artistic expression; and bell hooks has insisted that African-American theory recognize the differences in class among African-Americans and their cultural practices.

Chicano/a Studies

The words *Chicano* and *Chicana* were originally used to designate Americans (male and female, respectively) with Mexican parents. The term *Chicano/a studies* describes a variety of approaches to exploring the culture and identity of Americans with Mexican ancestry. Like African-American studies, Chicano/a studies came into prominence through the identity politics and social protest movement of the 1960s and 1970s. According to Luis Leal and Pepe Barron's "Chicano Literature: An Overview" (1982), the "desire to establish a separate identity has resulted in a literature that reflects a unique culture and possesses characteristics that differentiate it from other literatures." Leal and Barron explain that Chicano/a literature is generally characterized by pride in Aztec/Indian heritage, protest against socioeconomic oppression, and experimentation with bilingualism (Spanish and English).

An emerging literature, Chicano/a writing encompasses historical, social, and universal themes. The origins of Chicano/a literature, according to Leal and Barron, are found in Spanish ballads, romances, pastorals, and folktales brought to Mexico by explorers. These *corridas, romances, pastorelas*, and *cuentos* were adapted by Mexicans for their own purposes. After the Mexican Revolution of 1913-1915, Mexicans began to employ these popular forms as a means of social protest. In this way, they came to develop a group consciousness. This political consciousness, as Leal and Barron explain, was transformed by Mexicans living in the American Southwest in the 1940s into a separate ethnic consciousness; that is to say, these Mexican-Americans saw themselves as people of

Mexican heritage living in America. This emerging Pachuco (later Chicano) culture gave rise to a literature of identity that sought to explore its roots in Aztec folklore or Indian heritage, as well as a literature of confrontation that protested against the economic oppression and social exclusion of Mexican-Americans. The latter often focuses attention on the plight of itinerant farm workers and life in the barrios of Southwestern cities. Both Chicano traditions have produced experimental literature that seeks to fuse Spanish and English language, as well as Mexican and American cultures. Contemporary Chicano authors include Rudolpho Anaya, Luis Valdez, and Gary Soto.

Chicano literary works started to flourish in the 1960s and 1970s, and in the beginning male authors were the most recognized. Indeed, early publications by Chicana authors highlighted their anxiety about being silenced by their male counterparts. Chicana publications started to appear in the 1970s and began to thrive in the 1980s. In the main, Chicana authors explore forms of oppression and strategies of survival, probe social and political themes, and search for personal identity in their heritage. According to Alicia Gaspar de Alba, the Chicana writer "is the keeper of the culture, keeper of the memories, the rituals, the stories, the superstitions, the language, the imagery of her Mexican heritage." Contemporary Chicana authors include Sandra Cisneros, Helena Maria Viramontes, and Denise Chavez.

Other areas of ethnic studies include Native American (American Indian) studies and Asian-American studies. Contemporary Native American authors include N. Scott Momaday, Louise Erdrich, and Joy Harjo. Contemporary Asian-American authors include Maxine Hong Kingston, David Henry Hwang, and Amy Tan. See **CANON** and **FEMINIST CRITICISM**.

EXPRESSIONISM

The term *expressionism* refers to both a period and a style of art. Art and literary historians agree that the expressionists were most prominent in Europe during the First World War. In painting as in literature, expressionists sought to represent emotions or emotional states rather than represent or imitate reality. In many cases, the emotions expressed are those of angst, fear, anger, confusion, and bitterness. Edvard Munch's "The Scream" (1893), which presents a distorted, almost cartoon-like figure with its hands clasped to the sides of its head and its mouth open wide to scream, epitomizes the expressionist mode of the visual arts.

In literature, expressionism derives from the belief that any objective attempt to depict the emotional reality of a character will fail. As a result, expressionists reject attempts to create realism and instead use the grotesque, bizarre, and idiosyncratic to portray characters. Likewise, there is a heavy reliance on **symbolism** to help represent subjective reality.

For many commentators and historians, the work that epitomizes literary expressionism is Franz Kafka's short story "The Metamorphosis" (1916). In this passage from the beginning of the story, Kafka expresses the protagonist's psychological state through a shockingly exaggerated physical metamorphosis:

> As Gregor Samsa awoke one morning from uneasy dreams he found himself transformed in his bed into a gigantic insect. He was lying on his hard, as it were armor-plated, back and when he lifted his head a little he could see his dome-like brown belly divided into stiff arched segments on top of which the bed quilt could hardly keep in position and was about to slide off completely. His numerous legs, which were pitifully thin compared to the rest of his bulk, waved helplessly before his eyes.

Having eschewed more subtly figurative modes of revealing character, Kafka expresses Gregor Samsa's fear and self-hatred by literally transforming him into a helpless and loathsome creature.

With the notable exceptions of Kafka and a few others, most of the successful expressionists in literature were dramatists: the Swedish August Strindberg, the German Bertolt Brecht, and the Americans Eugene O'Neill and Tennessee Williams. The plays of these and others associated with expressionist theater are often characterized by emotionally intense, nightmarish scenes; bizarre, seemingly incoherent dialogue; distorted, dreamlike settings; and violently expressive styles of acting.

In film, the classics of German expressionism include *The Cabinet of Dr. Caligari* (Robert Wiene, 1919) and *Nosferatu* [F. W. Murnau, 1922), which is an early example of the vampire film genre. More contemporary examples of expressionist film include some of the flashback scenes in *The Crow* (Alex Proyas, 1994) and the wildly exaggerated (comic) acting style of Jim Carrey in *The Mask* (Charles Russell, 1994).

✳

F

FABLE

A *fable* is a brief tale, in either prose or verse, that offers a moral lesson. Some critics like to distinguish fables, which often feature animal characters, from **parables** and **allegories**, which more often employ human characters.

Perhaps the most famous representatives of this genre are the *Fables* of Aesop (c. 620-560 B.C.). In "The Hare and the Tortoise," for example, the story of a race between the speedy but overconfident hare and the slow but steady tortoise is told. During the course of the race, the hare, believing she can easily outstrip her rival with a burst of speed at the end, decides to take a nap, while the tortoise plods on with determination. Having overslept, the hare awakens suddenly and races to the finish line, only to find that the tortoise has already reached the goal. Thus, the moral of the fable is "slow and steady wins the race."

Other notable examples of this genre include the works of the French writer La Fontaine; the Russian fabulist (composer of fables) Krylov; the Englishman Rudyard Kipling, author of *The Jungle Book* (1894); and the American Joel Chandler Harris, who wrote the Uncle Remus stories. George Orwell's *Animal Farm* (1945) is a celebrated example of a modern fable that serves the purpose of political satire. Many of the Disney animated features are fables. *The Lion King* (1994), for instance, teaches the importance of responsibility and courage through the adventures of a lion cub who grows up to take his birthright as king of the jungle. See **ALLEGORY** and **PARABLE**.

FAIRY TALE

The term *fairy tale* became part of the English language in the eighteenth century and is French in origin. The French writer Madame d'Aulnoy published a book in 1698 entitled *Contes des fées* (*Tales of the Fairies*). This book was reprinted on numerous occasions over the next fifty years and is probably responsible for the term *fairy tale*. Fairy tales can be hundreds, even thousands of years old. Many were transmitted orally from generation to generation until they were collected by such individuals as Charles Perrault and the Grimm brothers. They were originally told to entertain adults at work and at play, and that is why some variants are replete with violence and sexual innuendo and situations. Later on, editors and collectors often purged the salacious elements and added morals to the fairy tales to make them suitable for children.

Fairy tales belong to the genre of the **folk tale**. A fairy tale is usually characterized as being about magic or about spells or marvelous incidents, although it does not have to be about fairies. It often begins with the phrase "once upon a time," deals with good versus evil, and uses such fundamental figures as beautiful princesses, brave heroes, wicked stepmothers or witches, wise fairy godmothers, and animals with the power of speech. Examples include "Cinderella," "Snow White," "Hansel and Gretel," and "Jack the Giant killer." Fairy tales often come in an array of versions. For example, multitudinous versions of the Cinderella myth exist, but the most popular is that of Charles Perrault. While the tale is probably about one thousand years old, the earliest English version of the Cinderella story is Robert Samber's translation (1729) of Perrault's tale first published in his *Histoires ou contes du Temps Passé* (1697). Another popular variant is that of the Grimm brothers, who revised and published a set of folktales entitled *Kinder und Hausmärchen* (1812), which included the tale "Ash Girl" or "Ashputtel." In some versions of the fairy tale, Cinderella is gentle and mild, but in others she is capable of being vicious and vengeful. Perrault's version of the fairy tale alters the heroine of the tale collected and presented by the Grimms. The tough, wily, perceptive, and active Cinderella of Grimm mutates to the shy, docile, self-devaluing, passive heroine of Perrault's version. Furthermore, Cinderella's treatment of her ugly sisters is completely dissimilar in the two versions. In Perrault's tale, Cinderella submissively forgives her sisters for their cruelty and jealousy, accommodates them in the palace, and marries them off to two nobles of the court. In contrasting fashion, in the German story, Cinderella does not make allowances for her sisters; pigeons peck out their eyes, and so they are punished for their cruelty with blindness. See **FOLK TALE**.

FEMINIST CRITICISM

Feminist theory is a term that embraces a wide variety of approaches to the questions of women's place and power in culture and society. But most of these approaches are allied by their critical analysis of patriarchal (male-dominated) and phallocentric (male-centered) institutions and practices, and their interests in promoting women's issues and concerns. Feminist theories often draw on key concepts of **deconstruction**, **new historicism**, **psychoanalysis**, and **Marxism**, developing and adapting them to the purposes of *gynocriticism*, a term coined by Elaine Showalter to describe approaches to literature attuned to the perspectives of women.

Theories of Gynocriticism

In her study entitled *A Literature of Their Own: British Women Novelists from Bronte to Lessing* (1977), Showalter delineates the history and tendencies of "the female tradition" in British literature:

> First, there is a prolonged phase of *imitation* of the prevailing modes of the dominant tradition, and *internalization* of its standards of art and its view on social roles. Second, there is a phase of *protest* against these standards and values, and *advocacy* of minority rights and values, including a demand for autonomy. Finally, there is a phase of *self-discovery*, a turning inward freed from some of the dependency of opposition, a search for identity. An appropriate terminology for women writers is to call these stages, *Feminine, Feminist*, and *Female*.

Although Showalter is concerned particularly with British novelists, her outline is descriptive of women's literature in general. The "*imitation* of prevailing modes of the dominant tradition" and "*internalization* of . . . its view on social roles" associated with the first phase are generally descriptive of Mary Wollstonecraft's *A Vindication of the Rights of Woman* (1792), which employed the eighteenth-century form of reasoned argument to critique a "a false system of education" for women and urged reforms aimed at making women "affectionate wives and rational mothers." The phase of "*protest*" and "*advocacy* of minority rights and values" is well represented by Virginia Woolf's *A Room of One's Own* (1929), in which Woolf protests women's oppressive material conditions and woefully insufficient educational opportunities by imagining the thwarted genius of "Shakespeare's sister." In "Professions for Women" (1949), she advocates "killing the Angel in the House": that is, the stereotype of female perfection who proved "utterly unselfish" and "sacrificed herself daily." The final or *Female* phase is exemplified by Adrienne Rich in "When We Dead Awaken: Writing as Re-Vision" (1971):

> Re-vision—the act of looking back, of seeing with fresh eyes, of entering an old text from a new critical direction—is for women more than a chapter in cultural history; it is an act of survival. Until we can understand the assumptions in which we are drenched we cannot know ourselves. And this drive to self-knowledge, for women, is more than a search for identity; it is part of our refusal of the self-destructiveness of male-dominated society.

Practices of Awareness and Self-Discovery

Two of the important practices in feminist critique or revision are raising awareness of the ways in which women (or images of women) are oppressed, demonized, or marginalized, and discovering motifs of female awakenings or processes of self-discovery. A feminist reading of Theodore Roethke's "My Papa's Waltz" (1948) offers an example of the former practice:

> The whiskey on your breath
> Could make a small boy dizzy;

But I hung on like death:
Such waltzing was not easy.

We romped until the pans
Slid from the kitchen shelf;
My mother's countenance
Could not unfrown itself.

The hand that held my wrist
Was battered on one knuckle;
At every step you missed
My right ear scraped a buckle.

You beat time on my head
With a palm caked hard by dirt,
Then waltzed me off to bed
Still clinging to your shirt.

Although this poem is usually characterized as a mostly fond remembrance of a father, a feminist approach might offer a number of criticisms of the portrayal of women. First of all, the mother is marginalized in the poem: that is to say, she stands on the margins of the central activity of the poem: papa's waltz. Moreover, when she is mentioned, the mother is characterized in a negative way: she not only frowns but proves incapable of changing her expression. Her objections are silent and passive; she seems to have neither will nor power to alter the situation. Her protest is no more effective than that of the pans that "slid from the kitchen shelf." Indeed, the organization of the stanza seems to imply that the association between the pans falling and the mother's frowning is not coincidental. The kitchen is her particular if limited sphere; she neither approves of nor joins in the fun because of her concern with cooking utensils. By contrast, the father, affectionately called Papa, is imaged as a free-willed, active, and dominating character. Although some of the speaker's description might be considered slightly damning or ambivalent, the poem as a whole seems to value the memory of Papa, his "palm caked hard by dirt," and his rough-and-tumble waltzing; mother, on the other hand, remains forever static with her frowning "countenance."

A passage from "The Story of An Hour" (1894) by Kate Chopin (an author whose work was overlooked until it was rediscovered and revisioned by women scholars) lends itself to a brief analysis of the motif of female awakening. The protagonist, Mrs. Mallard, who is considered to be an invalid because of her "heart trouble," learns from a report that her husband has been killed in a train accident. In order to cope with this news, Mrs. Mallard retreats to her room, where she gazes out the window at the sky:

She was young, with a fair, calm face, whose lines bespoke repression and even a certain strength. But now there was a dull stare in her eyes, whose gaze was fixed away off yonder on one of those patches of blue sky. It was not a glance of reflection, but rather indicated a suspension of intelligent thought.

There was something coming to her and she was waiting for it, fearfully. What was it? She did not know; it was too subtle and elusive to name. But she felt it, creeping out of the sky, reaching toward her through the sounds, the scent, the color that filled the sky.

Now her bosom rose and fell tumultuously. She was beginning to recognize this thing that was approaching to possess her, and she was striving to beat it back with her will—as powerless as her two white slender hands would have been.

When she abandoned herself a little whispered word escaped her slightly parted lips. She said it over and over under her breath: "free, free, free!" The vacant stare and the look of terror that had followed it went from her eyes. They stayed keen and bright. Her pulses beat fast, and the coursing blood warmed and relaxed every inch of her body.

She did not stop to ask if it were or were not a monstrous joy that held her. A clear and exalted perception enabled her to dismiss the suggestion as trivial.

The passage presents three levels of awakening—physical, mental, and spiritual—which are nevertheless interrelated. Despite evidence of "repression," the lines on Mrs. Mallard's face indicate "a certain strength" that she rediscovers as "her pulses beat fast, and the coursing blood warmed and relaxed every inch of her body." This latter excerpt suggests that Mrs. Mallard's "heart trouble" was caused by the very repression from which she now feels freed. The "suspension of intelligent thought" betokens a change in her ways of knowing. To appreciate the "something" that proves "too subtle and elusive to name," she must engage the kind of intuitive understanding attuned to "the sounds, the scents, the color that filled the air." Only in this way can she achieve the "clear and exalted perception" that enables her to dismiss guilty questions about whether "it were or were not a monstrous joy that held her." This joy proceeds from the spiritual sense of freedom that overcomes her "terror." Thus, the reader witnesses the triumph of her body over the allegations of weakness, of her intuitive powers over guilty thoughts, and of freedom over repression. As Mrs. Mallard later whispers to herself, she is free in "body and soul" of patriarchal oppression, at least until she discovers that she has been the victim of a false report. When she sees her husband coming through the front door of the house, she collapses and dies. The story ends ironically, with the doctors' determination that Mrs. Mallard died of "heart disease—of joy that kills." Having awakened to her "exalted perception" and sense of freedom, she refuses to return to the repressed life she had formerly led. Moreover, the text problematizes (finds contradictions or barriers to understanding) and overturns the stereotypical binary oppositions that feminist theory associates with patriarchy: male/female; strength/weakness; reason/intuition; activity/passivity; and independence/dependence.

European and Anglo-American Feminism

Many feminist theorists have been influenced by the works of Europeans Hélène Cixous, Luce Irigaray, and Julia Kristeva, all of whom are concerned with questions of language. Both Cixous and Irigaray encourage women to "write their bodies": that is, for Cixous, to express their unconscious feelings and desires and, for Irigaray, to express the pleasure of their bodies. Kristeva encourages a kind of writing that expresses the human experience prior to acquisition of language, in a stage of development including prenatal gestation which she calls "the semiotic register." Unlike male psychoanalysts and linguists in the tradition of Sigmund Freud and Jacques Lacan, whom they accuse of phallogocentrism (placing male sexuality and male systems of power at the center of all theories), all three women give significant value to the figure of the mother and the relations between mother and child. Moreover, each of these theories challenges traditional philosophies of language and suggests alternatives to or departures from male perspectives and male-centered logic.

One of the crucial distinctions for feminists is that between sex (which is determined by biology) and gender (which is a cultural construct). Anglo-American feminists have given particular attention to experiential and autobiographical writing in order to examine the nature of the female subjectivity: that is, women's thoughts and feelings about themselves rather than fictional renderings or images conferred on them by male writers. Such writings often serve to deconstruct gender stereotypes and received notions about women's roles in human history. See **CULTURAL CRITICISM, DECONSTRUCTION,** and **PSYCHOANALYTIC THEORY AND CRITICISM**.

FIGURATIVE LANGUAGE

Literary critics use the term *figurative language* to refer to both **figures of speech** (tropes) and **rhetorical schemes** (syntactic figures). Common figures of speech include **metaphor, simile, metonymy, personification,** and **synecdoche. Anaphora, antithesis, parallelism, chiasmus,** and **climax** are among the classic rhetorical schemes.

The term *trope* derives from the Greek word *tropos,* meaning "a turn." Tropes are figures of speech that change the literal meaning of a word by turning it toward another word or concept. In a passage from Emily Bronte's *Wuthering Heights* (1847), for instance, Catherine Earnshaw contrasts her love for the two men in her life:

> My love for Linton is like the foliage in the woods; time will change it, I'm well aware, as winter changes the trees—My love for Heathcliff resembles the eternal rocks beneath: —a source of little visible delight, but necessary.

By means of tropes (in this case, two similes), the word "love," which is literally a feeling, is turned toward concrete objects—"foliage" and "rocks"—in order to express a distinction between two kinds of love.

Syntactic figures involve the structure, word order, or phrasing of lines of poetry or sentences and paragraphs of prose. A passage from Pope's *Essay on Man* (1733) offers at least two examples.

All nature is but art, unknown to thee;
All chance, direction, which thou canst not see;
All discord, harmony, not understood;
All partial evil, universal good. . . .

The most obvious syntactic device in these lines is the use of *all* at the beginning of each line; this rhetorical scheme is called *anaphora*. Pope also uses the same sentence pattern in each line: subject, linking verb (or ellipsis), subject complement, and adjective phrase. This kind of syntactic repetition is called **parallelism**, which gives balance and continuity to the lines.

For definitions and examples of common figures of speech, see individual entries: e.g., **METAPHOR**. For definitions and examples of classic syntactic formulas, see **RHETORIC/RHETORICAL SCHEMES**.

FILM EDITING

The phrase *film editing* refers to selection and arrangement of shots and camera techniques. These techniques are employed to create specific effects: a sense of continuity, a lapse of time, a jarring incongruity, to name but a few.

Shots

Shot is a term used to describe any operation of a camera. **Close-ups** are camera shots that magnify the subject or object of attention; **middle-range shots** seem to place the viewer in the same room with the subject or object; **long shots** are taken at a noticeable distance. At the end of *Sunset Boulevard* (Billy Wilder, 1950), former silent screen star Norma Desmond (played by Gloria Swanson) announces to her director that she is ready for her close-up, at which point she moves toward the camera as it moves toward her, revealing both her grotesque attempts to hide her age and her distorted sense of reality. Several of the important scenes in *Crimes of the Heart* (Bruce Beresford, 1986) involve shots of the three McGrath sisters (played by Sissy Spacek, Diane Keaton, and Jessica Lange) sitting around a kitchen table discussing their lives. The long shot at the end of *Raiders of the Lost Ark* (Steven Spielberg, 1981) draws the camera away from the wooden crate holding the Lost Ark of the Covenant to reveal the extent of the massive warehouse, full of similar wooden crates, in which the Ark will be stored and (by implication) hidden.

Film directors and editors combine groups of shots to create scenes and sequences. A **scene** generally focuses on action in a single setting, for example, a love scene in a bedroom. A **sequence** often involves a group of related scenes that form an intelligible whole. In *My Brilliant Career* (Gillian Armstrong, 1979), for instance, a sequence showing the heroine's cosmetic transformation from wild adolescent to refined adult involves varied scenes featuring particular shots of her hands. The first scene of the sequence shows Sybylla being served breakfast wearing a face mask and gloves; she uses her ghoulish appearance to frighten a servant. In the second scene, Sybylla softens her hands in lemon water, while a servant counts strokes as she brushes Sybylla's hair. In the third scene, the elegantly dressed heroine sits and reads in an orchard; her gloved hands turn the pages of a book. A man hands her a bouquet, which she accepts and then defiantly hurls into a pond. In *Bullitt* (Peter Yates, 1968), the famous car chase sequence, which involves a series of related shots, extends from the hills of downtown San Francisco to a gas station on the outskirts of the city, where it ends with an explosion.

Cuts

Shots, scenes, and sequences can be begun and ended by a number of editing techniques. The most basic of these techniques is the **cut**. A cut is simply an abrupt switch from one image to another. In presenting a scene with dialogue, for instance, a director may employ a series of cuts from one speaker to the next, using different cameras or shots. Likewise, a director may employ a cut to signal the end of a scene or a sequence of shots. **Crosscutting** is a means of juxtaposing (presenting in rapid succession or side by side) two or more scenes or actions, often for the purposes of suggesting simultaneity or showing contrast. Perhaps the most famous use of crosscutting in film is that employed by Russian filmmaker Sergei Eisenstein in *Battleship Potemkin* (1925). In one sequence, Eisenstein crosscuts between shots of soldiers marching aggressively to disperse a crowd and shots of an unattended baby-carriage bouncing precariously down a long flight of steps. In doing so, Eisenstein seeks to juxtapose images of power and helplessness, violence and innocence. Crosscutting is also used effectively in one of the closing sequences of *Apocalypse Now* (Francis Ford Coppola, 1979), in which shots of Captain Willard (Martin Sheen) during his machete murder of a rogue colonel (Marlon Brando) are crosscut with shots of a ritual slaughter of cattle.

Transitions

Techniques for transitions between shots, scenes, and sequences include dissolves, fades, and irises-in or -out. A **dissolve** is a means of transition in which one image disappears as another image emerges. In the Danish classic *Day of Wrath* (Carl Theodor Dreyer, 1943), for instance, the image of a stake at which an accused woman is burned during the witchhunts in medieval Europe dissolves into an image of a cross. Not all dissolves are symbolic, however. In *Who's Afraid of Virginia Woolf* (Mike Nichols, *1966*), the image of George (Richard Burton) watching his wife (Elizabeth Taylor) speed away from a roadhouse parking lot in their station wagon dissolves into a shot of the station wagon hastily parked (in front of their house) with one door open and a signal light blinking. This dissolve suggests not only the passage of time but also George's recognition of Martha's intention to cheat on him. A **fade** involves the slow disappearance of a shot to a black screen, sometimes followed by the fade-in or slow emergence of a different image. One of the conventional uses of this technique in **film noir** (see entry) involves a scene in which the protagonist, often a private detective, loses consciousness (whether he is drugged or knocked on the head) and comes back to consciousness in a strange room. **Iris-in** and **iris-out** involve the progressive expansion or reduction of a screen image through the perspective of a widening or narrowing circle. This technique is employed to punctuate the stages of the confidence game plot in *The Sting* (George Roy Hill, 1973).

Panning and Tracking

Panning and **tracking** are camera techniques that involve movement. In the exposition or opening scene, a director may seek to establish the setting by having the camera move across the length of a city or a landscape. This panning of the physical setting is employed in James Bond films to signal the change of scene to an exotic or chic location: Rio de Janeiro or a volcanic range in Japan. Tracking, by contrast, involves the camera's moving along with the action, without any cuts. One of the most famous tracking shots occurs at the beginning of *A Touch of Evil* (Orson Welles, 1958), during which the camera moves along in a Mexican border town. This scene is alluded to in *The Player* (Robert Altman, 1992) during a tracking shot in which two film studio employees discuss Welles's technical genius. See **FILM NOIR**.

FILM NOIR

Film noir is a term used to describe a film genre most often associated with cinematic versions of detective and crime fiction. The phrase *film noir* literally means "dark film," which describes both the mood and the lighting of the typical examples. The signature scenes are usually urban and nocturnal, shot with stark contrast between light and darkness. The *chiaroscuro* ("clear/dark") effect of light and shade expresses visually the quest for clarity in a world obscured by deceit.

One archetypal plot involves a hard-boiled detective who is hired to solve a murder and find the truth about a crime involving a *femme fatale* (woman of fate or destruction) by whom he is seduced. In *The Maltese Falcon* (John Huston, 1941), for instance, a private detective named Sam Spade (Humphrey Bogart) is hired by a *femme fatale* (Mary Astor) to recover a valuable statuette. During the course of the film, Spade falls in love with his client, whom he nevertheless mistrusts. In the end, he discovers that she is implicated in two murders. Faced with a choice between love and justice, Spade decides to turn his client over to the police, after promising to wait for her release. Familiar variations of this plot include *Murder, My Sweet* (Edward Dymtryk, 1944) and *Chinatown* (Roman Polanski, 1974).

Another archetypal plot of the *film noir* tradition depicts the inevitable doom of illicit lovers who plot to kill the spouse who stands in their way. In *Double Indemnity* (Billy Wilder, 1944), for instance, a life insurance salesman named Walter Neff (Fred MacMurray) is involved in a plot by Phyllis Dietrichson (Barbara Stanwyck) to kill her husband and collect the insurance money. In the end, the lovers find cause to be suspicious and wind up shooting each other. A more recent reworking of this plot is recognizable in *Body Heat* (Lawrence Kasdan, 1981).

More than the plots themselves, examples of the *film noir* are recognizable by their style. The use of lighting is often especially stylized: an opened door throws a shaft of light upon a darkened room, revealing a corpse; a detective smokes a cigarette in his downtown office, alternately revealed and obscured by the flashing of a neon light through the blinds; a figure with a gun emerges from the shadows, shoots, and moves forward until a streetlamp illuminates his or her face. A contemporary example of film noir is *L.A. Confidential* (1997). See **FILM EDITING**.

FLASHBACK

Flashback is both a literary and a film technique in which chronological and sequential narrative is interrupted by the recollection of an image or a scene from the recent or distant past. One of the most common and effective uses of flashback consists of describing or presenting characters' memories of crucial moments in their lives so as to compare their former activities or conditions with their present situations. Such is the case in Arthur Miller's *Death of a Salesman* (1949), in which the aging protagonist, Willy Loman, experiences a series of extended flashbacks to a more innocent and hopeful period of his life. In the middle of Act I, Miller's stage directions instruct producers and directors of the play as to his intended means of signaling transitions from present to past.

> . . . Willy's form is dimly seen below in the darkened kitchen. He opens the refrigerator, searches in there, and takes out a bottle of milk. The apartment houses are fading out, and the entire house and surroundings become covered with leaves. Music insinuates itself as the leaves appear.

> WILLY: Just wanna be careful with those girls, Biff, that's all. Don't make any promises. No promises of any kind. Because a girl, y'know, they always believe what you tell 'em and you're very young, Biff, you're too young to be talking seriously to girls.

> Light rises on the kitchen. Willy, talking, shuts the refrigerator door and comes downstage to the kitchen table. He pours milk into a glass. He is totally immersed in himself, smiling faintly.

> WILLY: Too young entirely, Biff. You want to finish your schooling first. Then when you're all set, there'll be plenty of girls for a boy like you . . .

This flashback creates a dramatic juxtaposition as Willy, a tired and defeated man with two unmarried and unsuccessful grown-up sons, recalls his days as a young father of two teenage boys with seemingly great promise.

In film, a flashback scene is often signaled by a **fade**, a **dissolve**, or a rapid cut to the past. In the classic film *Citizen Kane* (1941), director Orson Welles employs this technique as a means of revealing the fictional biography of his protagonist, John Foster Kane. A news reporter interviews a number of Kane's family, friends, and associates, all of whom recall portions of his life through flashbacks.

A more contemporary work of fiction that makes repeated use of flashbacks is Amy Tan's *The Joy Luck Club* (1989), in which the lives of four Chinese-American women and their daughters are presented through a series of recollected scenes. In one section, Waverly Jong is trying to explain her relationship with her mother, Lindo Jong. She begins by describing her in the present tense and then moves to a flashback:

> My mother knows how to hit a nerve. And the pain I feel is worse than any other kind of misery. Because what she does always comes as a shock, exactly like an electric jolt, that grounds itself permanently in my memory. I still remember the first time I felt it.
>
> I was ten years old. Even though I was young, I knew my ability to play chess was a gift. It was effortless, so easy. I could see things on the chessboard that other people could not. . . . And my mother loved to show me off, like one of my many trophies she polished. She used to discuss my games as if she had devised the strategies.

The flashbacks in this novel serve to show how the past influences the present in the relationships between the daughters and their mothers. See **FILM EDITING**.

FOLK TALE

The term *folk tale* means tale of the folk or of the ordinary people of a nation. Folk tales are usually brief, anonymous stories that articulate the attitudes, customs, and values of the common people. They constitute part of the folklore of a people, or the gathering of common knowledge, stories, habits, and ways of a people passed down orally through the ages. The folk of the past were usually illiterate, and therefore they transmitted tales from generation to generation until they were collected and/or edited. Fairy tales are a subgenre of folk tales, as are ballads, fables, legends, myths, riddles, and nursery rhymes. See **BALLAD**, **FABLE**, **FAIRY TALE**, and **MYTH**.

FORESHADOWING

Foreshadowing is a technique by which an author suggests or predicts an outcome of plot. In Shakespeare's *Romeo and Juliet* (1595), for instance, Juliet remarks as Romeo descends from her balcony,

> O God, I have an ill-divining soul!
> Methinks I see thee, now thou art below,
> As one dead in the bottom of a tomb (3.5.54-56)

These lines foreshadow the conclusion of the play when Juliet feigns death by taking a sleeping potion, only to awake in her tomb and find Romeo killed by his own hand.

Flannery O'Connor's "A Good Man Is Hard to Find" (1955) provides an example of ironic foreshadowing. In the beginning of the story, the grandmother employs scare tactics to achieve her ends; she desires to go to Tennessee to visit relations, but her son has decided to take the whole family on a Florida vacation:

> "Now look here, Bailey," she said, "see here, read this," and she stood with one hand on her thin hip and the other rattling the newspaper at his bald head. "Here this fellow calls himself The Misfit is aloose from the Federal Pen and headed toward Florida and you read here what it says he did to those people. Just you read it. I wouldn't take my children in any direction with a criminal like that aloose in it. I couldn't answer to my conscience if I did."

This dialogue foreshadows the climax of the story, during which the grandmother unwittingly takes her family in the precise direction of The Misfit, who instructs his henchmen to execute all save the grandmother, whom he kills himself.

FREE VERSE

Free verse is a broadly descriptive term for poetry that does not follow a regular metrical pattern or rhyme scheme. The nineteenth-century American poet Walt Whitman, whom the twentieth-century American poet Ezra Pound credited with "breaking the [iambic] pentameter," popularized free verse in poems such as "Song of Myself" (1855):

> Have you reckon'd a thousand acres much? have you reckon'd the earth much?
> Have you practis'd so long to learn to read?
> Have you felt so proud to get at the meaning of poems?
>
> Stop this day and night with me and you shall possess the origin of all poems,
> You shall possess the good of the earth and sun, (there are millions of suns left,)
> You shall no longer take things at second or third hand, nor look through the eyes of the dead, nor feed on the spectres in books,
> You shall not look through my eyes either, nor take things from me,
> You shall listen to all sides and filter them from your self.

Eschewing end rhymes, metrical patterns, and even similar line lengths, Whitman relies on syntactic schemes to give the feel of poetry to his lines.

Caribbean poet Kamau Brathwaite's poem entitled "Crab" (1983) offers a contemporary example of free verse:

> From this cramped hand
> crippled by candlelight
> a crab scuttles

its mail'd dragonish swords
its clenched armour
rattles the lame mango leaves

the sun burns the gravel drier
as it explores cliffs, lions of grasshopper voices
shrieking the trees' seas

Following the examples of modernist poets such as Ezra Pound, T. S. Eliot, and William Carlos Williams, contemporary poets have made free verse the most common of poetic "forms." See **METER**.

G

GENRE

The word *genre* derives from the Latin *generis*, meaning "kind." As a critical term, *genre* is commonly used to designate a category or a type of literature. The broader genres include works of **prose fiction** (novels and short stories), **poetry**, **drama**, and **nonfiction prose works** (essays). However, *genre* may be employed to describe more narrow categories: **epistolary novel**, **epic**, **lyric**, **comedy**, **tragedy**, **western**, **romance**, **detective novel**, **autobiography**, and others.

Prose Fiction

Works of prose fiction, novels and short stories, are usually written in standard paragraph form without any noticeable pattern of rhyme, meter, or lineation. Novels generally exceed 50,000 words, and they are often divided into chapters. They typically present characters and actions through both dialogue and description. Nathaniel Hawthorne's *The Scarlet Letter* (1850) and Harper Lee's *To Kill a Mockingbird* (1960) are generally representative of novels. In contrast to novels, short stories do not often exceed 30,000 words; with far less scope for development, shorter works of prose fiction require greater concision and pithiness. Edgar Allan Poe's "The Fall of the House of Usher" (1839) and Gabriel García Márquez's "A Very Old Man with Enormous Wings" (1955) are generally representative of short stories.

Poetry

Poems differ from works of prose fiction in that they are usually marked by patterns of meter, rhyme, or lineation. The majority of poems in English before the twentieth century betray some sort of rhythm (metrical pattern); many also employ repetition of sound (rhyming or alliteration). In the late nineteenth and twentieth centuries, many poets chose to write free verse, which need not employ either meter or rhyme but often uses a special lineation. That is to say, the lines are usually not incorporated into paragraph form but, instead, are arranged vertically to indicate pauses and transitions, or movement of thought. John Donne's "Holy Sonnet X: Death Be Not Proud" (1633), Robert Frost's "Mending Wall" (1914), and Sylvia Plath's "Daddy" (1965) are generally representative of poetry.

Drama

Dramatic works differ from works of prose fiction and poetry in that they are dominated by dialogue; moreover, most plays are meant to be performed by actors on a stage. Shakespeare's *Othello* (1604) and Lorraine Hansberry's *Raisin in the Sun* (1959) are generally representative of plays.

Nonfiction Prose

Nonfiction prose works may seek to argue or explain an issue or a concept, or they may be biographical or autobiographical. They are usually presented in paragraphs, and they often take the form of speeches, letters, essays, biographies, memoirs, textbooks, or works of science or history. *The Declaration of Independence* (1776), Charles Darwin's *The Descent of Man* (1871), Martin Luther King's "Letter from Birmingham City Jail" (1963), and Louis Menand's *The Metaphysical Club* (2001) are generally representative of nonfiction prose works.

Many critics find distinctions between genres useful in designing an approach to a literary work. Indeed, a loosely organized school of genre critics, influenced by the neo-Aristotelian critics or the Chicago School, flourished in the 1950s. Perhaps the most influential of these was Northrop Frye, who categorized all literature into four dominant genres or mythoi: comedy, romance, tragedy, and irony. See **ARCHETYPE**, **COMEDY**, **EPIC**, **EPISTOLARY NOVEL**, **LYRIC**, and **ROMANCE**.

GOTHIC

Originally a word used to describe generally the cultural characteristics of a medieval Germanic tribe (the Goths), the term *gothic* came to be more closely associated with an expressive style of building. Gothic architecture, which developed in Europe between the twelfth and sixteenth centuries, was characterized by pointed vaults and arches, steep roofs, stained-glass windows, and flying buttresses. The English Romantics of the late eighteenth and early nineteenth centuries came to think of this gothic style as both awe inspiring and mysterious.

This interest in the strangely beautiful and horribly thrilling gave rise to the gothic novel. Horace Walpole, whose *Castle of Otranto* was published in 1764, is often credited with inventing this genre. Although its characteristics are many and varied, the gothic novel usually seeks to create an atmosphere of lurking mystery and looming horror. In *The Italian* (1797), for instance, Ann Radcliffe employs descriptions that project onto the natural world the ominously Romantic qualities of gothic architecture:

> They soon after arrived at the tremendous pass, through which Ellena had approached the monastery, and whose horrors were considerably heightened at this dusky hour, for the moonlight fell only partially upon the deep barriers of the gorge, and frequently the precipice, with the road on its brow, was entirely shadowed by other cliffs and woody points that rose above it.

As this passage illustrates, Radcliffe's descriptions are subtly suggestive when compared to the more explicit and graphic horrors of gothic novels such as Matthew Lewis's *The Monk* (1796). In a famous scene of the latter, Ambrosio (the monk, or the Abbot, as he is called) silences a young woman by murder before she can tell the Inquisitors that he raped her:

> Quickened by her cries, the sound of foot-steps was heard approaching. The Abbot expected every moment to see the Inquisitors arrive. Antonia still resisted, and He now enforced her silence by means the most horrible and inhuman. He still grasped Matilda's dagger: without allowing himself a moment's reflection, He raised it, and plunged it twice in the bosom of Antonia! She shrieked, and sank upon the ground. The Monk endeavoured to bear her away with him, but She still embraced the pillar firmly. At that instant the light of approaching Torches flashed upon the Walls. Dreading a discovery, Ambrosio was compelled to abandon his Victim, and hastily fled back to the Vault, where He had left Matilda.

Daphne du Maurier's *Rebecca* (1938), which Alfred Hitchcock made into a film of the same name in 1940, offers a more contemporary example of the gothic novel. The perilously rocky scenery of the Cornish coast, the awe-inspiring architecture of the de Winter ancestral home, the brooding hero and naive heroine are typical gothic elements contributing to the mystery and suspense of the work. See **ROMANCE**.

H

HAMARTIA

Hamartia is a Greek word for "sin" or "error"; it derives from the verb *harmata-nein*, meaning "to err" or "to miss the mark." As Aristotle asserts in his *Poetics* (fourth century B.C.), the hero's reversal of fortune in classical tragedy usually results from mistaken judgment, weakness of character, or accident. In Sophocles's *Oedipus the King* (fourth century B.C.), for instance, the *hamartia* is Oedipus's pride or **hubris**. Angered by the crime (the murder of his predecessor, King Laius) that has provoked the gods to visit a plague upon his city, Oedipus vows to discover and punish the guilty party:

> Upon the murderer I invoke this curse—
> whether he is one man and all unknown,
> or one of many—may he wear out this life
> in misery to miserable doom!
> If with my knowledge he lives at my hearth
> I pray that I myself may feel my curse.

In this passage, Oedipus reveals his insolence and pride. For despite the warnings of the seer Teiresias, who knows the identity of the murderer, Oedipus pursues his investigation until he discovers that he unknowingly killed his father and married his mother.

During the Renaissance, *hamartia* evolved into the concept of a **tragic flaw** in character, which Shakespeare's protagonist ponders in a soliloquy in *Hamlet* (1601):

> So oft it chances in particular men
> That for some vicious mole of nature in them,
> As in their birth, wherein they are not guilty,
> (Since nature cannot choose his origin)
> By their o'ergrowth of some complexion,
> Oft breaking down the pales and forts of reason,
> Or by some habit that too much o'erleavens

The form of plausive manners, that these men,
Carrying, I say, the stamp of one defect,
Being nature's livery, or fortune's star,
Their virtues else, be they as pure as grace,
As infinite as man may undergo,
Shall in the general censure take corruption
From that particular fault. (1.4.23-36)

In other words, a noble and virtuous figure may come to a tragic end because of "one defect" resulting from an accident of nature, fate, or fortune. See **TRAGEDY**.

HYPERBOLE

Hyperbole is a Greek word, meaning "excess, or a throwing beyond." As a literary term, it is most often employed to describe a deliberate exaggeration. In Shakespeare's *Antony and Cleopatra* (1606-1607), for instance, Cleopatra's descriptions of Antony in Act 5, scene 2, are clearly hyperbolic:

His face was as the heav'ns, and therein stuck
A sun and moon, which kept their course and lighted
The little O, the earth . . .
His legs bestrid the ocean; his rear'd arm
Crested the world.

Cleopatra exaggerates the brightness of Antony's visage by comparing it to the lights of the sun and moon; likewise, in the second part of the excerpt, she compares him to a colossus. Such hyperbolic descriptions are not meant to be taken literally; they are expressive of feelings.

Robert Frost's poem "After Apple-Picking" (1916) offers a more contemporary example of hyperbole:

For I have had too much
Of apple-picking: I am overtired
Of the great harvest I myself desired.
There were ten thousand thousand fruit to touch,
Cherish in hand, lift down, and not let fall.

The speaker uses the deliberate exaggeration of "ten thousand thousand" to express his extreme weariness of both body and spirit.

$$*$$

I

IDEOLOGY

The word *ideology* is defined as "the body of ideas reflecting the social needs and aspirations of an individual, group, class, or culture." In common parlance, it is most often associated with a set of beliefs or abstract notions, especially doctrinaire political opinions. In **cultural criticism**, however, the term *ideology* is more often used to refer to a system of images and perceptions that influences both individuals and groups to adopt a manufactured view of reality and truth.

Marxist connotations of ideology have been particularly influential in literary theory. Among the principal concepts of Marxist critiques of culture is the necessity of analyzing the ways in which the human subject is formed and socialized in capitalist societies. According to Marxist critics of capitalist cultures, the ruling class has found it easier and more effective to employ mass media, for instance, rather than force or intimidation to subjugate the lower classes. In other words, the lower classes are more likely to accept their social positions when they internalize the view or perception of reality provided by books, newspapers, magazines, television, and films, along with the standard messages of institutions such as governments, schools, and churches, than they would if they were forcibly kept in their places by a military or police state. For Marxist theorists, then, ideology is both the set of images used to suppress class struggle and the system of beliefs promoted by these images.

Popular films such as Sylvester Stallone's *Rocky* movies of the 1970s and 1980s can be understood to serve an ideological purpose. The basic theme of these films is the rags-to-riches motif, in which the down-and-out prizefighter is afforded his chance for fame and riches. Through his hard work and sacrifice, both of which proceed from his decency, his humility, and his acceptance of American ideals, Rocky comes to live the American dream of success. Having achieved fame and fortune, Rocky rarely fails to attribute his success to God, country, and family. When he occasionally diverges from this adherence to conventional American ideology, the tension in the films' plots is resolved by his rediscovery of the truths or realities he has temporarily discarded or ignored. For a Marxist critic, this reification (treating of an abstract notion as if it were a material reality) of the American dream in the story of Rocky serves to strengthen the belief among audiences that economic disadvantage and deprivation result from the failure of the individual will and determination rather than an unfair system of economic opportunities and rewards. Moreover, the popularity of the *Rocky* sequels, whose predictability only increases their appeal, is attributable to their reinforcement of the ideological notions promoted by the original. See **CULTURAL CRITICISM** and **MARXIST CRITICISM**.

IMAGERY

Although some critics use the term interchangeably with *figurative language* (metaphors, metonyms, similes, and the like), *imagery* may also be employed more broadly to refer to any descriptions meant to appeal to the senses. The most familiar type of image is visual description, as in John Keats's "To Autumn" (1820):

> Season of mists and mellow fruitfulness,
>   Close bosom-friend of the maturing sun;
> Conspiring with him how to load and bless
>   With fruit the vines that round the thatch-eaves turn;
> To bend with apples the mossed cottage-trees,
>   And fill all fruit with ripeness to the core;
>   To swell the gourd, and plump the hazel shells
>   With a sweet kernel; to set budding more,
> And still more, later flowers for the bees,
> Until they think warm days will never cease,
>   For summer has o'er-brimmed their clammy cells.

In the first six lines of the stanza, Keats introduces the states of nature associated with autumn: "mellow fruitfulness" and "ripeness." In the last five lines, he employs imagery to offer a visual sense of this fruitfulness and ripeness: "To swell the gourd, and plump the hazel shells. . . ." In the last stanza of "To Autumn," Keats turns largely to sound imagery:

> Then in a wailful choir the small gnats mourn
>   Among the river sallows, borne aloft
>   Or sinking as the light wind lives or dies;
> And full-grown lambs loud bleat from hilly bourn;
>   Hedge crickets sing; and now with treble soft
>   The redbreast whistles from a garden-croft;
>   And gathering swallows twitter in the skies.

In order to associate a certain concept or quality with a character, setting, or action, a writer may develop a recognizable pattern of imagery. Such is the case in Laura Esquivel's *Like Water for Chocolate* (1992), when the protagonist is preparing a cake for her sister's wedding:

> Now she was afraid the same thing would happen again, for she was unable to concentrate on making the icing for the cake, no matter how

hard she tried. The whiteness of the granulated sugar frightened her. She felt powerless against it, feeling that at any moment the white color might seize her mind, dragging along those snow-white images from her childhood, May-time images of being taken all in white, to offer white flowers to the Virgin. She entered the church in a row of girls all dressed in white and approached the altar, which was covered with white candles and flowers, illuminated by a heavenly white light streaming through the stained-glass window of the white church.

The imagery of whiteness builds on associations with religion, innocence, and beauty, as well as the protagonist's fears.

Both examples suggest how imagery may be used to create texture and tone in writing. See **METAPHOR** and **SIMILE**.

IMPRESSIONISM

Impressionism is a broad term most often used to describe a subjective or highly personal style of writing. The word was borrowed from painting, where it distinguished a nineteenth-century school of painters who wished to offer an impression of a person, object, scene, or landscape rather than reproduce it to the standard of photographic "realism." Impressionist painters such as Claude Monet, Pierre Auguste Renoir, and Berthe Morisot, for instance, offer highly subjective and fleeting notions of gardens, meadows, or cathedrals—and their effects on the visual and tactile senses.

In the late nineteenth and early twentieth centuries, a number of novelists attempted to adapt this impressionist mode to literature. Virginia Woolf, whose work is often characterized as impressionist, employs a highly subjective style of description and narration in *To the Lighthouse* (1927). Two brief passages will serve as examples:

Now all the candles were lit up, and the faces on both sides of the table were brought nearer by the candle-light, and composed, as they had not been in the twilight, into a party round a table, for the night was now shut off by panes of glass, which, far from giving any accurate view of the outside world, rippled it so strangely that here, inside the room, seemed to be order and dry land; there, outside, a reflection in which things wavered and vanished, waterily.

★ ★ ★ ★ ★ ★ ★ ★ ★ ★

. . . [her eyes] seemed to go round the table unveiling each of these people, and their thoughts and their feelings, without effort, like a light stealing under water so that its ripples and the reeds in it and the minnows balancing themselves, and the sudden silent trout are all lit up hanging, trembling. So she saw them; she heard them; but whatever they said had also this quality, as if what they said was like the

> movement of a trout when, at the same time, one can see the ripple and
> the gravel, something to the right, something to the left; and the whole
> is held together; whereas in active life she would be netting and sepa-
> rating one thing from another. . . .

In the first passage, the scene is described by means of "a reflection in which
things wavered and vanished, waterily," like the way in which the subjects in
certain impressionist paintings seem to waver and vanish in light and color. The
second passage offers a sense of the subjectivity of the narrative point of view.
The impressions of Mrs. Ramsey, the central consciousness of the novel, are
not "netting and separating one thing from another" so as to render each one
distinctly; instead, her impressions render the scene "like a light stealing under
water."

INTERPRETATION/MEANING

The verb *interpret* derives from the Latin *interpretari*, meaning "to explain," and
the noun *interpres*, "a negotiator." Thus, **interpretation** is an act of both explanation and negotiation. In traditional literary criticism, the two parties between
which the interpreter acts as negotiator are the text and the reader. The interpreter attempts to negotiate between the two by explaining or translating the
meaning of the text for the reader. The word ***meaning*** derives from the Middle
English *menen*, "to intend." Thus, for some critics, meaning has been linked with
the author's intention. However, both the **New Critics** of the mid-twentieth
century and the poststructural theorists of the latter part of the century have
questioned both an author's ability to achieve his or her intention and a reader's
ability to divine it.

   Two of the primary difficulties in determining the meaning or meanings of a
text arise from the problems of subjectivity and **ideology**. Contemporary theorists assert that interpreters are unavoidably biased by their points of view or belief
systems, even when they consciously attempt to be objective and open-minded.
Meaning becomes a function of interpreters' ways of understanding. In the nineteenth century, the term **hermeneutics**, which derives from the Greek *herme-
neuein* (meaning "to unfold or interpret"), was increasingly associated with the
science of understanding known as **epistemology**, which attempts to study
what we know and how we know it. Drawing on this connection, some
twentieth-century critics and commentators came to believe that a given practice
of interpretation, known as *praxis* or *exegesis*, is largely determined by the interpreter's hermeneutics (theory of interpretation). Therefore, critics employing different theories of intepretation may arrive at different conclusions and offer
competing readings of a text.

   This problem of the theory determining the practice had led the contemporary
theorist Stanley Fish, most notably in *Is There a Text in This Class?* (1980), to shift
his focus away from the critic as negotiator or intermediary between the reader and
the text. Instead, Fish seeks to explore the direct attempts of readers to interpret or

translate the meaning of a text (see **Reader-Response Criticism**). Nevertheless, questions about the extent to which belief systems influence readers' interpretations remain. As Fish sees it, the meaning of a text depends not so much on the individual reader as on the "interpretive community" to which he or she belongs. Interpretive communities create meaning by influencing the strategies readers employ to understand texts. These strategies are shaped by both formal education and socialization. See **AMBIGUITY**, **IDEOLOGY**, **NEW CRITICISM/FORMALISM**, and **READER-RESPONSE CRITICISM**.

INTERTEXTUALITY

Intertextuality is a term used to describe the implicit and explicit relations between texts. Allusions and parodies are among the most direct examples of intertextuality. An **allusion** in a text quotes from or refers to another text, thereby bringing the meaning of each text to bear on the significance or appreciation of the other. Likewise, a **parody** may borrow the form or style of another text, as in the case of the **mock heroic**, which humorously imitates the epic form. In such cases, the significance of the parodic text may be said to depend on the text it imitates, but the parody may also forever change our attitude to the original.

T. S. Eliot's "The Love Song of J. Alfred Prufrock" (1917) offers many examples of intertextuality through allusion. In the course of the poem, the speaker reveals himself as a man who does not have the will or self-confidence to express his desires to women. Thus, he never moves beyond the role of companion: a suitable person to invite to tea.

> Should I, after tea and cakes and ices,
> Have the strength to force the moment to its crisis?
> But though I have wept and fasted, wept and prayed,
> Though I have seen my head (grown slightly bald) brought in upon
>   a platter,
> I am no prophet—and here's no matter;
> I have seen the moment of my greatness flicker,
> And I have seen the eternal Footman hold my coat, and snicker,
> And in short, I was afraid.

The allusion embodied in the "head . . . brought in upon a platter" suggests the intertextuality between Eliot's poem and the story of John the Baptist in the Bible (Matthew 14). John's execution and the presentation of his head upon a large dish before the court of Herod came about at the request of Salome, a dancer who so charmed Herod with her performance that he granted her any wish of her choice. Prufrock's belief that his fate has likewise been placed in the hands of a woman, with tragic results, helps to explain his fear and mistrust of women. Nevertheless, he admits the comparison with John is imperfect since he is "no prophet." The intertextuality of this passage suggests how texts can interpenetrate, expand, and alter one another.

Intertextuality describes not only the relations among literary works but also among cultural artifacts and processes. Sandra Cisneros's story "Barbie-Q" (1991), for instance, makes use of intertextuality between the story of two young girls growing up in a poor neighborhood in a major city and the copy for Barbie doll advertisements of the 1960s:

> Yours is the one with mean eyes and a ponytail. Striped swimsuit, sti-lettos, sunglasses, and gold hoop earrings. Mine is the one with bubble hair. Red swimsuit, stilettos, pearl earrings, and a wire stand. But that's all we can afford, besides one extra outfit apiece. Yours, "Red Flair," sophisticated A-line coatdress with a Jackie Kennedy pillbox hat, white gloves, handbag, and heels included. Mine, "Solo in the Spotlight," evening elegance in black glitter strapless gown with a puffy skirt at the bottom like a mermaid tail, formal-length gloves, pink chiffon scarf, and mike included.

The interweaving of two texts—one a fictional narrative, the other a product description—deepens the contrast between the girls' actual lives and their dreams of material success and glamour.

Examples of intertextuality in film include *The Kiss of the Spider Woman* (Hector Babenco, 1985; based on a play by Manuel Puig), in which two prison-ers in an Argentine jail—one a political prisoner, the other arrested for homosex-uality—interweave the narratives of their own lives with the latter prisoner's oral rendering of a Nazi propaganda film that he interprets as a movie about love and romance. *Play It Again Sam* (Herbert Ross, 1972; based on a play by Woody Allen) depicts the attempts of a divorced man to find romance by behaving like the Humphrey Bogart character in his favorite film, *Casablanca*. See **ALLU-SION**, **MOCK HEROIC**, and **PARODY**.

IRONY

The word *irony* derives from the Greek *eironeia*, meaning "feigned ignorance, dissembling." In ancient Greek comedy, one of the stock characters, the *eiron* ("a dissembler, one who says less than he thinks"), outwits other characters by deceiving them; he deliberately uses words that convey precisely the opposite meaning of his real thoughts, feelings, or intentions. The term is also commonly employed by critics to describe a situation in which the result of circumstances is the opposite of what might reasonably be expected. In most cases, irony involves a misunderstanding or a difference in understanding. For instance, one character may have superior knowledge or insight that is unknown or unavailable to another character. This gap in understanding creates irony, which can also be appreciated by the reader or audience.

Edgar Allan Poe's "The Cask of Amontillado" (1846) offers examples of several kinds of irony. The narrator, Montressor, begins the story by telling of his intention to seek revenge on a character ironically named Fortunato. Montressor invites

Fortunato to descend to his wine cellars, ostensibly to judge a pipe of Amontillado (sherry); his real intention, however, is to murder Fortunato. Poe's story is particularly rich in its use of **dramatic irony**, in which the reader shares with the narrator (or authorial voice) knowledge of a situation or intention unknown to one or more of the characters. For instance, as they stop to sample some of the wine in the cellar, Fortunato makes a strange gesticulation toward Montressor:

> I looked at him in surprise. He repeated the movement—a grotesque one.
> "You do not comprehend?" he said.
> "Not I," I replied.
> "Then you are not of the brotherhood."
> "How?"
> "You are not of the masons."
> "Yes, yes," I said; "yes, yes."
> "You! Impossible! A mason?"
> "A mason," I replied.
> "A sign," he said.
> "It is this," I answered, producing a trowel from beneath the folds of my *roquelaire*.
> "You jest," he exclaimed, recoiling a few paces. "But let us proceed to the Amontillado!"

When he asks for a sign that Montressor is a mason, he expects a secret gesture or code known only to the fraternal order of masons. Thus, when Montressor produces a trowel, which is used by actual stonemasons and bricklayers, Fortunato believes his host is merely jesting. The dramatic irony of this scene becomes clear when the reader discovers that Montressor has given Fortunato a very serious sign, indeed: namely that he intends to act as a mason by burying Fortunato alive behind a wall of stone and mortar.

Earlier in the story, Poe employs a kind of **verbal irony**, in which the meaning intended by a speaker differs from the meaning understood by one or more of the other characters. While descending the stairs to the cellars, Montressor expresses concern about Fortunato's fit of coughing and urges him to turn back. Fortunato exclaims, "Enough . . . the cough is a mere nothing; it will not kill me. I shall not die of a cough." Although Fortunato intends this exclamation as a simple exaggeration, Montressor takes pleasure in the verbal irony of the statement, replying, "True—true . . . and, indeed, I had no intention of alarming you unnecessarily; but you should use all proper caution."

One of the other common types of irony is **cosmic irony**, in which fate or destiny appears to play a cruel joke on human hopes. Thomas Hardy, whose novels make great use of cosmic irony, offers a more succinct example in his poem entitled "The Convergence of the Twain" (1914), about the ironic fate of a reputedly unsinkable ship called *The Titanic:*

> And as the smart ship grew
>   In stature, grace, and hue,
> In shadowy silent distance grew the Iceberg too.

> Alien they seemed to be:
> No mortal eye could see
> The intimate welding of their later history,
>
> Or sign that they were bent
> By paths coincident
> On being anon twin halves of one august event,
>
> Till the Spinner of the Years
> Said "Now!" And each one hears,
> And consummation comes, and jars two hemispheres.

As Hardy's lines suggest, the role of fate ("the Spinner of the Years") cannot be anticipated by humans ("No mortal eye could see") without divine or supernatural warning.

Tragic irony occurs when a noble character is undone by mistaken judgment, as in the case of Sophocles's *Oedipus the King* (see **Hamartia)**, or an innocent character is deceived by a villain who is aware of the irony of a situation, as in Shakespeare's *Macbeth* (1606). In the case of *Oedipus*, the king attempts to prove his noble character by seeking out his predecessor's murderer, only to discover that he is the guilty party. In contrast, works such as Indian writer R. K. Narayan's "Trail of the Green Blazer" (1972) produce a kind of **comic irony**. In the case of Narayan's story, an ignoble character, a pickpocket named Raju, is punished for attempting to do a good deed. Having discovered a present for a child (a toy balloon) in the pocketbook he has stolen from a man in a green jacket, Raju attempts to restore the wallet to its owner without his noticing. Ironically, the man in the green blazer catches Raju in the act and accuses him of thievery:

> Even before the Magistrate, Raju kept saying, "I was only trying to put back the purse." And everyone laughed. It became a stock joke in the police world. Raju's wife came to see him in jail and said, "You have brought shame on us," and wept.
>
> Raju replied indignantly, "Why? I was only trying to put it back." He served his term of eighteen months and came back into the world—not quite decided what he should do with himself. He told himself, "If ever I pick up something again, I shall make sure I don't have to put it back." For now he believed that God had gifted the likes of him with only one-way deftness. Those fingers were not meant to put anything back.

The comic irony in this passage results from the reversal of expectation: that is to say, the received idea that good deeds are rewarded and evil actions are punished is reversed. See **HAMARTIA**.

L

LYRIC

The word *lyric* derives from the Greek *lura*, meaning "lyre." The ancient Greeks made a distinction between poems or songs sung by a group (choric) and those sung by a solitary singer to the accompaniment of a lyre or harp (lyric). In general terms, a lyric is any relatively short poem in which a single speaker expresses an emotional state or process of thought. The Psalms of David in the Bible, for instance, which were reputedly sung with the accompaniment of a lyre, often present emotions brought on by David's contemplation of his relation to God:

> I am poured out like water, and all my bones are out of joint:
> my heart is like wax; it is melted in the midst of my bowels.
>
> My strength is dried up like a potsherd; and my tongue cleaveth
> to my jaws; and thou hast brought me into the dust of death.
>
> Psalm 22: 14-15

The speaker employs a number of physical images and comparisons to indicate his spiritual devastation.

Like many of the Romantics, Samuel Taylor Coleridge employs descriptions of external landscapes (in this case, the signs of weather in the sky) to express the speaker's emotional state in his poem entitled "Dejection: An Ode" (1802):

> For lo! the New-moon winter-bright!
>   And overspread with phantom light,
>   (With swimming phantom light o'erspread
>   But rimmed and circled by a silver thread)
> I see the old moon in her lap, foretelling
>   The coming-on of rain and squally blast.
> And oh! that even now the gust were swelling,
>   And the slant night-shower driving loud and fast!
> Those sounds which oft have raised me, whilst they awed,
>   And sent my soul abroad,

Might now perhaps their wonted impulse give,
Might startle this dull pain, and make it move and live!

As the latter part of this first section of Coleridge's poem suggests, the lyric poem is often a kind of meditation. It may be joyful or, as in this case, melancholy. The speaker ponders his dejection and theorizes that he might be startled out of his "dull pain" if the weather were to change suddenly to "rain and squally blast." All of this is offered in the first person, as though the poet were offering his thoughts and feelings at a given moment.

In contrast to Coleridge's poem, Christina Rossetti's poem "A Birthday" (1857) expresses feelings of great happiness:

My heart is like a singing bird
Whose nest is in a watered shoot:
My heart is like an apple-tree
Whose boughs are bent with thickset fruit;
My heart is like a rainbow shell
That paddles in a halcyon sea;
My heart is gladder than all these
Because my love is come to me.

Raise me a dais of silk and down;
Hang it with vair and purple dyes;
Carve it in doves, and pomegranates,
And peacocks with a hundred eyes;
Work it in gold and silver grapes,
In leaves and silver fleurs-de-lys;
Because the birthday of my life
Is come, my love is come to me.

The speaker of the poem uses images of nature's bounty and beauty in the first stanza, and of silk, fur, gold, and silver in the second, to describe her glad heart and artistic desires. The poem is very much a kind of song, as the first line suggests. See **PERSONA**.

M

MAGIC REALISM

Magic realism is a term used to describe the commingling of everyday reality with supernatural events. The two become so intertwined that strange, unearthly happenings become almost an accepted, even normal part of daily life. Magic realism was used originally to describe a postexpressionist style of painting in the 1920s. The term was changed to *magical realism* in the 1950s and employed to describe a major literary technique of Latin American writers, especially Jorge Luis Borges. The term is now used to describe the work of other Latin American authors, such as Jorge Amado, Isabel Allende, and Gabriel García Márquez, Mexican writer Laura Esquivel, German fiction writer Günter Grass, and English novelist John Fowles. In Amado's *The Two Deaths of Quincas Wateryell* (1961), the hero is believed to be dead but occasionally reappears inebriated in the marketplace or playing cards in the church courtyard. Near the end of the novel, the "dead" man even celebrates his birthday before he dies a second time:

> It looked as though it would be a night to remember. Quincas Wateryell was in splendid form. An unwonted enthusiasm took possession of the little group, making them feel as though that magic night, with the light of the full moon enveloping the mystery of Bahia, belonged to them alone. On the Street of the Pillory, couples hid in doorways that were centuries old; cats meowed on the rooftops; guitars played mournful serenades. It was a night of enchantment. Drumbeats throbbed in the distance, and Pillory Square resembled a fantastic stageset.

The realistic details of couples hiding in doorways, cats meowing, and guitars and drumbeats playing is seamlessly amalgamated with the mystery of the moonlit night, the "fantastic stageset" of the Square, and the magical appearance of the dead Quincas Wateryell enjoying life to the full. As a result, bizarre events, such as the revelry and debauchery of the dead man, seem part of ordinary life.

MALAPROPISM

The term *malapropism* derives from a character named Mrs. Malaprop in Richard Sheridan's play *The Rivals* (1775). Mrs. Malaprop, whose name derives from the French phrase *mal a propos* (meaning "not suited to the purpose"), is particularly notable in the play for her misapplication of words. Thus, a *malapropism* is a general term for the misuse of words, especially words that sound like other words. In Act 1, Scene 2 of Sheridan's play, Mrs. Malaprop's reply to Sir Anthony Absolute's question about how a lady should be educated provides numerous examples of malapropisms:

> Observe me, Sir Anthony,—I would by no means wish a daughter of mine to be a *progeny* of learning; I don't think so much learning becomes a young woman; for instance—I would never let her meddle with Greek, or Hebrew, or Algebra, or Simony, or Fluxions, or Paradoxes, or such inflammatory branches of learning . . . But, Sir Anthony, I would send her, at nine years old, in order to learn a little ingenuity and artifice.—Then, Sir, she should have a *supercilious* knowledge in accounts;—and as she grew up, I would have her instructed in geometry, that she might know something of the *contagious* countries;—but above all, Sir Anthony, she should be mistress of orthodoxy, that she might not mis-spell, and mis-pronounce words so shamefully as girls do; and likewise that she might *reprehend* the true meaning of what she is saying. (italics added)

The words italicized are but a few of the more obvious misapplications in this passage: Mrs. Malaprop mistakes "progeny" for prodigy, "supercilious" for superficial, "contagious" for contiguous, and "reprehend" for apprehend. By insisting, "above all," that a girl should learn to "reprehend the true meaning of what she is saying," Mrs. Malaprop says better than she knows. As for "Simony, or Fluxions, or Paradoxes, or such inflammatory branches of learning," perhaps only Mrs. Malaprop (or her creator) truly knows what it is she means (or doesn't mean) to say.

Malapropisms were by no means the invention of Sheridan. In Shakespeare's *A Midsummer Night's Dream*, for example, the characters referred to by Puck as "rude mechanicals" regularly misapply words. In their performance of *Pyramus and Thisbe*, given to celebrate the wedding of Theseus, the Duke of Athens, characters such as Bottom the weaver and Flute the bellows mender misuse language in a multiplicity of ways. In a speech bemoaning the presumed killing of Thisbe by a lion, Bottom (in the role of Pyramus) asks, "O, wherefore, Nature, didst thou lions frame? Since lion vile hath here deflow'r'd my dear." Bottom's mistaking the word "deflowered" for devoured is but one of his many malapropisms, all of which amuse the more sophisticated audience whose witty plays on words demonstrate that they are able to use language to their advantage, unlike Bottom and his friends, who are more often ill-used by language. See **PUN**.

MARXIST CRITICISM

Marxist theory is a broad term used to describe systems of thought deriving or developing from the writings of political economists Karl Marx and Friedrich Engels and their followers. Marxist literary theory generally adheres to the basic tenet of Marxist theory: that human consciousness should be understood in relation to political economy, class struggle, and **ideology**. As Terry Eagleton has shown, one of the clearest statements of Marx's approach is offered in the Preface to *A Contribution to the Critique of Political Economy (1859)*:

> In the social production of their life, men enter into definite relations that are indispensable and independent of their will, relations of production which correspond to a definite stage of development of their material productive forces. The sum total of these relations of production constitutes the economic structure of society, the real foundation, on which rises a legal and political superstructure and to which correspond definite forms of social consciousness. The mode of production of material life conditions the social, political and intellectual life process in general. It is not the consciousness of men that determines their being, but on the contrary, their social being that determines their consciousness.

In other words, the relations that men and women have to legal and political institutions are determined by their social status, which is determined by their economic roles (or situations) and the ways that they are encouraged to accept these roles (or situations). For this reason, Marxist critics tend to focus on the ideological function of literature: that is, the extent to which approved or classic literature has served historically to support or sustain the beliefs and the privileges of the ruling classes.

In his study entitled *The Political Unconscious: Narrative as a Socially Symbolic Act* (1981), the Marxist critic Frederic Jameson explains that although ideology operates largely on the unconscious level, readers may still detect it by focusing on the relation of literature to "the economic structure of society" or "the real foundation." In examining the use of the sea in literary **modernism**, for instance, Jameson remarks upon the following passage from Joseph Conrad's *Lord Jim* (1900), which describes the protagonist's presumed relation as an adventurous sailor to the economic structure of his society:

> His station was in the fore-top, and often from there he looked down, with the contempt of a man destined to shine in the midst of dangers, at the peaceful multitude of roofs cut in two by the brown tide of the stream, while scattered on the outskirts of the surrounding plain the factory chimneys rose perpendicular against a grimy sky, each like a slender pencil, and belching out smoke like a volcano.

According to Jameson, this passage reveals the protagonist's attempt to distance or remove himself from the fundamental reality of industrial economic structures and class divisions. As Jameson puts the case, Jim seeks to "step completely outside all three class terrains [the aristocracy or upper class, the bourgeoisie or middle class, and the proletariat or working class] and see them all equally, from over a great distance, as so much picturesque landscape." In this sense, Conrad's protagonist reveals his desire to ignore the effects of capitalism and the ideology that maintains its control over the political unconscious. See **CULTURAL CRITICISM**, **IDEOLOGY**, and **FEMINIST CRITICISM**.

METAPHOR

The word *metaphor* derives from the Greek verb *metapherein*, meaning "to transfer." Simply stated, a metaphor serves to transfer the sense of one word to another. Many literary critics choose to explain metaphors in terms of the two words from and to which meaning is transferred: namely, the tenor and the vehicle. The tenor is the subject of comparison, what is to be compared, and the vehicle is the means of comparison, what the subject is compared to or with. A poem by Emily Dickinson offers a useful example:

> "Hope" is the thing with feathers—
> That perches in the soul—
> And sings the tune without the words—
> And never stops—at all—
>
> And sweetest—in the gale—is heard—
> And sore must be the storm—
> That could abash the little Bird
> That kept so many warm—
>
> I've heard it in the chillest land—
> And on the strangest Sea—
> Yet, never, in Extremity,
> It asked a crumb—of Me.
>   (1861)

In the first line of the poem, the metaphor is implicit: the tenor is clearly identified as "Hope," but the vehicle (bird) is described only as "the thing with feathers." In the second stanza, the metaphor becomes **explicit** with the naming of the vehicle ("little Bird"). "Hope" is the subject of comparison, and "little Bird" is what the subject is compared to. According to Dickinson's metaphor, hope is something like a bird in the sense that it "never stops" comforting us, much as a bird seemingly "never stops" singing. This comparison between hope and a bird is maintained and developed throughout the poem, making it an **extended metaphor**.

The following passage from T. S. Eliot's "The Love Song of J. Alfred Prufrock" (1917) offers another example of an extended metaphor:

> The yellow fog that rubs its back upon the window-panes,
> The yellow smoke that rubs its muzzle upon the window-panes,

Licked its tongue into the corners of the evening,
Lingered upon the pools that stand in drains,
Let fall upon its back the soot that falls from chimneys,
Slipped by the terrace, made a sudden leap,
And seeing that it was a soft October night,
Curled once about the house, and fell asleep.

Throughout these lines, the tenor is "fog" or "smoke," and the vehicle is a cat. Thus, the fog "licked its tongue into the corners of the evening" and "curled once about the house, and fell asleep" in the way of a cat. This metaphor is related to **personification**.

Some poets delight in original and outlandish metaphors; John Donne's "Holy Sonnet XIV" (1633) offers several examples of unusual comparisons:

Batter my heart, three-personed God; for You
As yet but knock, breathe, shine, and seek to mend;
That I may rise and stand, o'erthrow me, and bend
Your force to break, blow, burn, and make me new.

Donne implicitly compares the Holy Trinity to a tinker (whose job it is to "knock, breathe, shine, and seek to mend" metal objects) and a blacksmith (whose profession calls for him "to break, blow, burn, and make . . . new"). Here the metaphors are also **conceits**.

Other poets employ more obvious and conventional metaphors, which can be just as effective and poignant. In his poem entitled "The Fist" (1976), the contemporary Caribbean poet Derek Walcott writes,

The fist clenched round my heart
loosens a little, and I gasp
brightness; but it tightens
again. When have I ever not loved
the pain of love?

In this metaphor, the tenor "pain of love" is compared to the vehicle "the fist clenched round my heart." See **CONCEIT**, **FIGURATIVE LANGUAGE**, **IMAGERY**, and **PERSONIFICATION**.

METER

The word *meter* derives from the Greek *metron*, meaning "measure, rule." In literary criticism, the term is most commonly used to refer to systems employed to measure the rhythm of poetry. Of the three principal systems of measurement, the most widely used is the **accentual-syllabic**, which attempts to mark the accented and unaccented sounds in a line of poetry, as well as the number of syllables.

The simplest way to approach the accentual-syllabic system of measurement is to begin by dividing a line of poetry into syllables and noting the relative stress given to each syllable. Generally speaking, monosyllabic nouns *(boy, girl, tree)*; monosyllabic verbs *(walk, see, breathe)*; and monosyllabic adjectives *(red, tall, old)* receive **emphasis** or **accent** when a line is read in a natural voice. That is to say, these are generally **stressed syllables**. Articles *(a, the)*; monosyllabic prepositions *(of, in, at)*; possessive pronouns *(my, his, their)*; and suffixes *(-est, -ing, -ed)* do not receive emphasis or accent. That is to say, they are generally **unstressed**. Monosyllabic conjunctions *(and, or)*; monosyllabic auxiliary verbs *(can, have, may)*; and "to be" verbs *(is, are, was, were)* are generally unstressed as well. Polysyllabic words *(trouble, inspire, nightingale)* require closer scrutiny to determine the relative stress or unstress of syllables; however, if the reader cannot determine the stressed syllables by ear, he or she may find the words in a dictionary and note which syllables are accented.

Metrical Pattern and Rhythm

In order to scan a line of poetry, readers should mark the stressed syllables with an accent "/" and the unstressed syllables with a "u". The following line from Shakespeare's "Sonnet XVIII" (1609) will serve for an example:

> u / u / u   /   u / u /
> So long as men can breathe or eyes can see

The line is marked by a pattern of alternating unstressed and stressed sounds. This pattern is called **iambic**; because it moves from unstressed to stressed, this rhythm is called a rising meter. Iambic meters are considered to be closest to the natural rhythms of English.

A line from Shakespeare's *Macbeth* (1606) offers an example of the opposite pattern:

> / u / u / u / u
> Double, double, toil and trouble

The line is marked by a pattern of stressed and unstressed syllables, which is called **trochaic**; because it moves from stressed to unstressed, this rhythm is called a falling meter.

A line from Ben Jonson's "A Celebration of Charis: Her Triumph" (1640) offers a three-syllable pattern:

> u   u /   u u / u u /
> Have you marked but the fall o' the snow

This pattern of two unstressed syllables followed by a stressed syllable is called **anapestic**; like iambic, this is a rising meter.

Thomas Hardy's "The Voice" (1914) employs this three-syllable pattern in reverse:

> / u u / u u / u u / u u
> Woman much missed how you call to me, call to me

This pattern of one stressed syllable followed by two unstressed syllables is called **dactylic**; like the trochaic rhythm, this is a falling meter. The examples of dactylic rhythms in English are rare.

In many cases, poets employ a substitution or variation in the rhythmic or metrical pattern. A line from Shakespeare's "Sonnet CXXX" (1609) offers an example:

```
u  /   u  /    /    /    /    u  u   /
If hairs be wires, black wires grow on her head
```

The first of the two variations from this dominantly iambic line occurs when Shakespeare uses two accented syllables consecutively. This pattern of two stressed syllables is called **spondaic**; that is to say, "black wires" forms a **spondee**. Spondees serve to slow down the pace of a line and to give emphasis to words and phrases.

A line from Shakespeare's "Sonnet XVIII" (1609) offers an example of consecutive unstressed syllables:

```
 u  / u  u  u  /    u  /  u   /
And often is his gold complexion dimmed
```

The second metrical foot of this line is made up of two unstressed syllables. This pattern is called **pyrrhic**; that is to say, these two syllables form a **pyrrhus**. Pyrrhic feet serve to speed the pace of a line.

Metrical Feet

Having determined the metrical pattern of a line, readers should measure the number of metrical feet and express that number according to the following designations:

One foot = monometer
Two feet = dimeter
Three feet = trimeter
Four feet = tetrameter
Five feet = pentameter
Six feet = hexameter
Seven feet = septameter
Eight feet = octameter

Two lines from Shakespeare's "Sonnet LXXIII" (1609) will serve as a first example:

```
 u   /   u   /  u   /    u  /   u  /
That time / of year / thou mayst / in me / behold
 u   /   u   /    u  /    u  /   u  /
When yel / low leaves, / or none, / or few, / do hang
```

These lines show a clear pattern of iambic feet; since each line has five iambs, this measure is called iambic pentameter. It is the most common meter of poetry written in English.

The opening lines of John Donne's "Song" (1630) offer an example of a different rhythm:

```
/   u    /  u  / u   /
Go and / catch a / falling / star

/    u   /  u  /   u    /
Get with / child a / mandrake / root
```

Although the last foot in each is shortened through catalexis (a deliberate omission of the last foot, which is common with falling rhythms in English), these lines show a pattern of trochaic feet. Including the truncated foot, each line has four feet; therefore, this rhythm is called trochaic tetrameter.

One of the famous examples of an anapestic rhythm is Byron's "The Destruction of Sennacherib" (1815):

```
u  u /  u u u   /    u  u  /  u u  /
The Assyr / ian came down / like the wolf / on the fold,

u   u /  u    u   /   u u /  u u  /
And his co / horts were gleam / ing in pur / ple and gold;

u   u  /  u  u  /   u u  /  u u /
And the sheen / of their spears / was like stars / on the sea
```

Despite the extra syllable in "Assyrian," all three lines show a clear pattern of anapestic rhythm; since each line has four feet, this pattern is called anapestic tetrameter.

Some poets employ a regular and consistent rhythm; such is the case in Margaret Walker's "Poppa Chicken" (1989):

```
/  u  /  u  /  u  /  u
Poppa / was a / sugah / daddy

/   u   u u  /
Pimping / in his prime;

/  u  /  u   /  u   /
All the / gals for / miles a / round

/   u  /  u   /
Walked to / Poppa's / time.

/  u  /  u  /   u    /
Poppa / Chicken / owned the / town,

/  u  /  u   /
Give his / women / hell;

/  u  /  u  /  u   /
All the / gals on / Poppa's / time

/  u  /  u   /
Said that / he was / swell.
```

Except for the slight variation in line two, these stanzas follow a pattern of alternating trochaic tetrameter and trochaic trimeter.

Most poems include lines that do not conform exactly to the dominant metrical patterns. Such lines, called irregular, often have too many or too few syllables to fit the pattern precisely. See **BLANK VERSE**, **FREE VERSE**, **RHYTHM**, and **RHYME**.

METONYMY

The word *metonymy* comes from the Greek *metonumia*, meaning "substitute naming." The term refers to a **figure of speech** in which one word or phrase is substituted for another with which it is closely associated. For example, one might use the word "crown" to refer to the king or queen of a nation because it is strongly associated with royalty.

The opening lines of William Wordsworth's "London, 1802" (published in 1807) offer several examples of metonymy:

> Milton! thou shouldst be living at this hour:
> England hath need of thee: she is a fen
> Of stagnant waters: altar, sword, and pen,
> Fireside, the heroic wealth of hall and bower,
> Have forfeited their ancient English dower
> Of inward happiness. . . .

In the third and fourth lines of the poem, "altar" is a metonym for religion; "sword" for the military; "pen" for literature; and "fireside" for domestic life.

Aurora Levins Morales employs a metonymic figure in her poem "Child of the Americas" (1986):

> I am new. History made me. My first language was spanglish.
> I was born at the crossroads
> and I am whole.

In this excerpt, "crossroads" is metonymic for the merging of cultures and languages.

MIDDLE ENGLISH PERIOD
(IN ENGLISH LITERATURE)

The Middle English period covers the time between the Norman Conquest in 1066, when French invaders created significant changes in the language and culture of England, and approximately 1500, when writers came to compose literature in distinctly modern English. Middle English blended the native language derived from Anglo-Saxon with Anglo-Norman elements of word order and vocabulary. The period between 1100 and 1350 is known as the Anglo-Norman period because of the prevalence of French language and culture. Works from this period include fean Jean de Meun's *Roman de la Rose* (c. 1250).

The second half of the fourteenth century is especially important in the Middle English period. Chaucer wrote his major works, including *The Canterbury Tales* (c. 1390), during this time. Other significant works include William Langland's religious and satirical poem *Piers Plowman* (1377-1386) and the anonymous chivalric romance *Sir Gawain and the Green Knight* (c. 1375). During the fifteenth century, Thomas Malory's prose epic, *Le Morte D'Arthur* (1485), was written, and many mystery dramas and miracle and morality plays, such as the plays of the Chester cycle and *Everyman* (c. 1509-1519), were composed and performed. The plays were supported by trade and religious guilds and staged on wagons that traveled from town to town. Often allegorical in nature, morality plays depicted personifications of abstract qualities (such as Fellowship, Knowledge, and Death) and offered a **parable** about the vanity of life.

Chaucer's "General Prologue" to *The Canterbury Tales* contains a characteristic Middle English description of a pilgrim referred to as the Wife of Bath:

> A good wif was there of beside Bathe,
> But she was somdel deef, and that was scathe.
> Of cloth-making she hadde swich an haunt,
> She passed hem of Ypres and of Gaunt.
> In all the parish, wif ne was there noon
> That to the offring before her sholde goon.
> And if there did, certeyn so wroth was she
> That she was out of alle charitee.

By employing **iambic pentameter**, Chaucer initiates the rhythmical scheme that was to predominate in English poetry. The lines have a conversational quality that is close to the rhythms of spoken English. Chaucer makes use of **irony** in the extract when he describes the proud and uncharitable Wife of Bath as a "worthy" woman.

MIMESIS

Mimesis is the Greek word for "imitation." In literary criticism, the term refers to writers' attempts to imitate or represent reality. The mimetic tradition has a long history, starting with Aristotle, who begins his *Poetics* (fourth century B.C.) by defining epic poetry and drama (among other forms) as imitations of action. In many ways, Aristotle's discussion of imitation serves as a response to Plato's *The Republic* and *The Ion*, in which Plato considers imitations and imitators to be too far removed from truth.

Perhaps the most famous modern book on the subject is Erich Auerbach's *Mimesis: The Representation of Reality in Western Literature* (1946). In the first chapter of his study, Auerbach introduces his readers to two traditions that heavily influenced European literature: the Homeric and the Old Testament. In discussing the former, he offers the example of Book 19 of Homer's *The Odyssey*, in which the protagonist, Odysseus, has returned home in disguise to his wife, Penelope, after a twenty-year absence, only to be recognized by his old nurse, Euryclea. The truth about Odysseus's identity comes home to her when she recognizes a scar upon his thigh while she is washing his feet as a gesture of hospitality to a stranger.

> So he spoke, and the old woman took a glittering basin
> That she used for washing feet; she poured in much water,
> The cold; then she transferred in the hot. Odysseus
> Was sitting by the hearth, and suddenly turned toward the darkness.
> For at once he was apprehensive in heart lest when she touched him
> She noticed his scar and the facts become apparent.
> She went near and was washing her master, and right away knew
> The scar which once a boar dealt him with its shining tusk
> When he had come to Parnassos to see Autolycus and his sons. . . .

As Auerbach notes, Homer's narration goes on in great detail about Odysseus's boyhood journey, a feast given in his honor, the hunt for the boar, his wound, his return to his parents, and more, before it resumes with the scene of Euryclea's recognition:

> The old woman took the scar in the palms of her hands and knew it
> As she touched it; she let the foot drop that she held,
> And his shin fell into the basin and the bronze clattered.
> It tipped back to one side and the water spilled out onto the ground.
> Both delight and pain gripped her mind, and her two eyes
> Filled with tears, and her resonant voice was held back.
> She touched Odysseus' chin and spoke to him:
> "Indeed you are Odysseus, dear child; not even I
> Knew you at first, till I had touched my master all over."

As Auerbach explains, the Homeric means of representing reality depends on "externalization of phenomena in terms perceptible to the senses":

> Here is the scar, which comes up in the course of the narrative; and
> Homer's feeling simply will not permit him to see it appear out of the
> darkness of an unilluminated past; it must be set in full light, and with it
> a portion of the hero's boyhood. . . . The basic impulse of the Homeric
> style [is] to represent phenomena in a fully externalized form, visible and
> palpable in all their parts, and completely fixed in their spatial and tem-
> poral relations. Nor do psychological processes receive any other treat-
> ment; here too nothing must remain hidden and unexpressed.

Auerbach contrasts this form of mimesis with that of the Biblical Old Testa-ment. He uses the story of the sacrifice of Isaac as an example:

> And it came to pass after these things, that God did tempt Abraham, and
> said unto him, Abraham; and he said, Behold, here I am.
>   And he said, Take now thy son, thine only son Isaac, whom thou
> lovest, and get thee into the land of Moriah; and offer him there for a
> burnt offering upon one of the mountains which I will tell thee of.

And Abraham rose up early in the morning, and saddled his ass, and took two of his young men with him, and Isaac his son, and clave the wood for the burnt offering, and rose up, and went unto the place of which God had told him.

As Auerbach notes, in contrast to the Homeric tradition of mimesis, the Biblical means of representation eschews close description of sensory details and psychological development:

... God gives his command, and the story itself begins ... it unrolls with no episodes in a few independent sentences whose syntactical connection is of the most rudimentary sort. In this atmosphere it is unthinkable that an implement, a landscape through which the travellers passed, the serving-men, or the ass, should be described, that their origin or descent or material or appearance or usefulness should be set forth in terms of praise; they do not even admit an adjective,· they are serving-men, ass, wood, and knife, and nothing else, without an epithet; they are there to serve the end which God has commanded; what in other respects they were, are, or will be, remains in darkness.

Thus, the representation of reality is not universal but varied according to culture, influences, and purposes. See **PLATONIC**.

MOCK HEROIC

The mock heroic (or **mock epic**) is a literary form that **lampoons** the motifs and conventions of the traditional epic by treating an insignificant or mundane action as though it were an heroic event. Perhaps the most famous example is Alexander Pope's *The Rape of the Lock* (1714). Pope announces his intention to use a mock heroic style in the opening lines of the poem:

What dire Offence from am'rous Causes springs,
What mighty Contests rise from trivial Things. . . .

In *The Rape of the Lock*, Pope lampoons an actual quarrel between the families of Robert (Lord) Petre and Arabella Fermor, which was instigated by Lord Petre's snipping off a lock of Miss Fermor's hair without obtaining her permission. Pope's treatment of the event and the ensuing quarrel is a deliberate travesty of a war epic, such as Homer's *The Iliad*. This mocking style is manifest in Pope's fictional description of the trivial offense, the cutting of the lock:

The Peer now spreads the glitt'ring Forfex wide,
T'inclose the Lock; now joins it, to divide.
Ev'n then, before the fatal Engine clos'd,
A wretched Sylph too fondly interpos'd;
Fate urg'd the Shears, and cut the Sylph in twain,
(But Airy Substance soon unites again)

The meeting Points the sacred Hairs dissever
From the fair Head, for ever and for ever!
    Then flash'd the living Lightning from her Eyes,
And Screams of Horror rend th'affrighted Skies.
Not louder Shrieks to pitying Heav'n are cast,
When Husbands or when Lap-dogs breathe their last,
Or when rich China Vessels, fall'n from high,
In glitt'ring Dust and painted Fragments lie!

Whereas Homer's war epic describes brutal killing and horrible carnage, Pope's poem uses the same high style to depict the snipping of a lock of hair. Whereas Homer writes about the participation of the Olympic gods in the slaughters of the Trojan War, Pope deals with a sylph (a fairy made of air) who is accidentally "cut . . . in twain" by a pair of scissors. Whereas Homer describes the pitiable cries of pain and lamentation uttered by those who witness comrades, friends, and loved ones slain in battle, Pope compares the "Screams of Horror" let loose by the offended lady to "Shrieks" attending the death of a lap-dog or the breaking of china. In short, Pope deliberately exaggerates the seriousness of trivial events so that his readers can appreciate his satirical stance.

A mock epic may be distinguished from a **travesty**, in which the subject matter of a specific work of literature (or a body of work) is treated in a grotesquely comic manner. Derek Walcott's play *The Joker of Seville* (1978) is a travesty of a number of literary works. In one passage, for instance, Walcott explicitly mocks Homer's *The Iliad* and *The Odyssey* through a speech by a character named Tisbea:

O what is more refreshing than this image of a sun-browned fishergirl with literary pretensions descending through the golden almond leaves, past the lecherous, gummed eyes of old trees bulging with amazement like those who watched Helen walk the battlements of Troy, even though books are hard to come by, and for me, Tisbea, to be that image? Yes, for this doe-eyed creature to come to this beach necklaced with the wreckage of a storm? This image would startle the world, O breasts forever firm in their principies! O little lipped door always locked to lechers! O plump inviolate little heart! I must remember to take this all down; every day I lose three metaphors through laziness! Yet if I were Nausicaa and there, sprawled on the crumpled satin of the beach at Tarragon . . . oh, that's too good, too good, I must remember it, no quill, no quill . . . What was it—if I were Nausicaa on the smooth beach, no, not smooth, was it smooth? Well, anyway, and there lying naked and sleek . . . Why did I bring up Nausicaa . . . I am not Nausicaa, that shell-gathering princess, I am humble Tisbea on the wrecked coast of New Tarragon and I am simply going to walk along this beach singing my innocent song when I encounter. . . .
    (Screams)
A man! Naked!

In the first part of the passage, Walcott has Tisbea compare herself to Helen of Troy and use in her speech travesties of **Homeric epithets**: "descending through the golden almond leaves, past the lecherous, gummed eyes of old trees bulging with amazement." In the latter part of the passage, Tisbea compares herself to Nausicaa, a chaste princess who finds the shipwrecked and naked Odysseus on the shores of her native land. Walcott deliberately employs **burlesque** humor in the bawdy references to "breasts forever firm in their principles" and the "little lipped door always locked to lechers." See **EPIC** and **EPITHET**.

MODERNISM

The term *modernism* is commonly employed by historians and critics to designate an international literary movement that flourished from the 1880s to the end of World War II and gave rise to radical experiments in literary technique. The central event for many of the "high" modernists—W. B. Yeats, Ezra Pound, H. D. (Hilda Doolittle), Gertrude Stein, T. S. Eliot, Wyndham Lewis, and Virginia Woolf, among others—was World War I, which signified for many artists and intellectuals a turning point in human history.

The horrors of the First World War (1914-1918), during which Britain, France, Germany, and Russia each suffered casualties of more than a million soldiers and civilians, served to deepen the loss of faith, carried over from the latter half of the nineteenth century, in the old orders of Western civilization. It was also during this period that artists, literary and otherwise, began to express both fascination with and alienation from the dramatic changes in human culture and technology brought on by the prewar buildup, World War I itself, and its aftermath. W. B. Yeats's poem "The Second Coming" (1919), for example, announces the dissolution of the old order of civilization and the birth of a new and barbaric age:

> Turning and turning in the widening gyre
> The falcon cannot hear the falconer;
> Things fall apart; the centre cannot hold;
> Mere anarchy is loosed upon the world,
> The blood-dimmed tide is loosed, and everywhere
> The ceremony of innocence is drowned;
> The best lack all conviction, while the worst
> Are full of passionate intensity.

Near the end of the poem, Yeats imagines an apocalyptic figure, with "[a] gaze blank and pitiless as the sun," heralding an end to the Christian era:

> The darkness drops again; but now I know
> That twenty centuries of stony sleep
> Were vexed to nightmare by a rocking cradle,
> And what rough beast, its hour come round at last,
> Slouches toward Bethlehem to be born?

In his poem entitled "Hugh Selwyn Mauberley" (1920), Ezra Pound mourns the loss of life in World War I and rails against the high cost of rescuing a decadent European culture:

> There died a myriad,
> And of the best, among them,
> For an old bitch gone in the teeth,
> For a botched civilization,
>
> Charm, smiling at the good mouth,
> Quick eyes gone under earth's lid,
> For two gross of broken statues,
> For a few thousand battered books.

In an earlier section of the poem, Pound deplores the commercialism of the new machine age, in which respect for quality and handcrafted beauty has given way to an obsession with quantity and speed of production:

> The age demanded an image
> Of its accelerated grimace,
> Something for the modern stage,
> Not, at any rate, an Attic grace;
>
> ★ ★ ★ ★ ★ ★ ★ ★ ★ ★
>
> The "age demanded" chiefly a mold in plaster,
> Made with no loss of time,
> A prose kinema, not, not assuredly, alabaster
> Or the "sculpture" of rhyme.
>
> ★ ★ ★ ★ ★ ★ ★ ★ ★ ★
>
> All things are a flowing
> Sage Heraclitus says;
> But a tawdry cheapness
> Shall outlast our day.

Pound's juxtaposition of ancient and modern worlds—the "Attic grace" of ancient Greek art and literature contrasted with the modern world's "image of its accelerated grimace"—is one of the signature techniques of "high" modernism. In James Joyce's novel *Ulysses* (1922), for instance, the characters and action may be understood to correspond, however loosely, to those of Homer's *The Odyssey* (eighth century B.C.). But instead of telling the tale of Odysseus's heroic exploits over the course of ten years at sea, Joyce describes the ups and downs of a middle-class and middle-aged Dubliner, Leopold Bloom, during the course of one day in June 1904. In doing so, Joyce seems to take up the challenge of Pound's modernist credo to "make it new": that is, to re-create history and literature from a modern perspective. For Joyce, Pound, and Eliot in particular, this meant flooding the past into the present by setting multiple allusions to earlier works of literature, history, philosophy, and art against a contemporary context of cultural decay and spiritual emptiness.

The modernists experimented with new styles and structures of poetry and prose. In many cases, they abandoned traditional rules of syntax and continuity, offering instead fragments and disordered narratives. Readers were expected to act as literary detectives capable of tracking down allusions and discovering hidden meanings in the relations between the parts. Moreover, human experience was often represented as nonlinear, relative, and subjective, as Woolf notes in *The Common Reader* (1925): "Life is not a series of gig lamps symmetrically arranged; life is a luminous halo, a semitransparent envelope surrounding us from the beginning of consciousness to the end." See **IMPRESSIONISM**, **POSTMODERNISM**, and **STREAM OF CONSCIOUSNESS**.

MOOD

In literary criticism, mood refers to the author's or the speaker's attitude toward the subject or theme of a work. The term *mood* is often used interchangeably with **tone** and **atmosphere**. Whereas mood is created by the attitude of the author or speaker to the subject, tone is more nearly the attitude of the author to the audience. Atmosphere differs from mood in the sense that it is usually created by the physical or emotional setting rather than the author's attitude toward the subject. Alfred Lord Tennyson's "Mariana" (1830) will serve as an example of both atmosphere and mood:

> With blackest moss the flower-pots
> Were thickly crusted, one and all;
> The rusted nails fell from the knots
> That held the pear to the gable-wall.
> The broken sheds loolc'd sad and strange:
> Unlifted was the clinking latch;
> Weeded and worn the ancient thatch
> Upon the lonely moated grange.
> She only said, "My life is dreary,
> He cometh not," she said;
> She said, "I am aweary, aweary,
> I would that I were dead!"

In this poem, the atmosphere is expressed in several ways. The imagery of "rusted nails," "broken sheds," and "lonely moated grange" all contribute to the atmosphere of desolation and despair. In addition, the consonance of the line "The broken sheds loolc'd sad and strange," with its striking use of exhaustive consonants suggests the speaker's mood of weariness. This mood is made explicit in the last four lines, which serve as a **refrain** throughout the poem. Tennyson's attitude toward Mariana's situation is implied by the use of sensuous and resonant **consonant sounds**, such as "Weeded and worn the ancient thatch / Upon the lonely moated grange." Like the poetry of the Pre-Raphaelites, with which this poem is often associated, Tennyson seems to find a strange beauty in ruin, whether physical or emotional.

The opening of Elizabeth Bowen's "The Demon Lover" (1945), in which the protagonist visits her home in the shell-shocked London of World War II, provides an example of atmosphere:

> Against the next batch of clouds, already piling up ink-dark, broken chimneys and parapets stood out. In her once familiar street, as in any unused channel, an unfamiliar queerness had silted up; a cat wove itself in and out of railings, but no human eye watched Mrs. Drover's return. Shifting some parcels under her arm, she slowly forced round her latchkey in an unwilling lock, then gave the door, which had warped, a push with her knee. Dead air came out to meet her as she went in.

The atmosphere of this exposition is clearly foreboding: the dark clouds, broken chimneys, unused street, solitary cat, not to mention the "dead air" that "came out to meet her as she went in," all prove ominous. See **CONSONANT SOUNDS**, **TONE**, and **VOICE**.

MYTH

A myth is a story of uncertain origin and authorship that seeks to explain processes of nature, the creation of the world and the human race, or traditional customs, political institutions, or religious rites. Myths explain such matters by means of narratives that depict the activities and intentions of deities or gods, from whom all processes and rituals are said to originate. These myths often survive long after the people of a nation or culture cease to believe in them. The term *myth* is sometimes used interchangeably with *legend*, but a legend is more often based on historical figures and events.

The ancient Greek myth of Persephone (or Kore) seeks to explain the natural phenomena of the seasons. According to the story, Persephone, while picking flowers in a meadow, was abducted by Hades and transported to the underworld to live as his queen. Having discovered her loss, Persephone's mother, Demeter, the goddess of the harvest, went to Zeus (king of the gods) to plead for her daughter's return. Zeus agreed to restore Persephone to the sunshine provided that she had not eaten anything while imprisoned in the underworld. Much to her sorrow, Demeter learned from Hades that her daughter had eaten some pomegranate seeds. Zeus, therefore, struck a compromise; for six months of the year, Persephone could roam above the earth, but for the other six, she must go below to live with Hades. Thus, during Persephone's tenure in the underworld, while Demeter mourns her absence, the fields and the vines wither and die (autumn and winter). But when Persephone returns, such is Demeter's joy that the seeds in the earth burst forth in blossom, flourish, and ripen (spring and summer).

In the first of his *Pisan Cantos* (1948), Ezra Pound alludes to the Australian aboriginal's myth of Wondjina:

> but Wanjina is, shall we say, Ouan Jin
> or the man with an education

and whose mouth was removed by his father
                    because he made too many *things*
whereby cluttered the bushman's baggage
vide the expedition of Frobenius' pupils about 1938
                              to Auss'ralia
Ouan Jin spoke and thereby created the named
                              thereby making clutter
the bane of men moving
and so his mouth was removed
as you will find it removed in his pictures

In the myth, according to Carroll Terrell's *A Companion to the Cantos of Ezra Pound* (1984), Wondjina (whose name Pound spells in two variant ways) was the son of the rainbow snake god, called Ungur, who "created the world by saying the names of things." But because Ungur wished for man to focus on the "vital processes and rituals" of life, he "closed [Wondjina's] mouth so that he could not speak," and thereby create clutter or distractions. Pound learned of this myth through the work of the German anthropologist Leo Frobenius.

Margaret Atwood's *Surfacing* (1972), in which the mysteries of childbirth are explained from the mother's perspective, offers an example of a contemporary myth by a woman:

But I bring with me from the distant past five nights ago the time-traveler, the primeval one who will have to learn, shape of a goldfish now in my belly, undergoing its watery changes. Word furrows potential already in its proto-brain, untraveled paths. No god and perhaps not real, even that is uncertain; I can't know yet, it's too early. But I assume it: if I die it dies, if I starve it starves with me. It might be the first one, the first true human; it must be born, allowed.

The narrator of this novel makes a journey into her own history, exploring strange memories and the primordial aspects of existence. See **ALLEGORY** and **EPIC**.

N

NARRATIVE POINT OF VIEW

A *narrative* is simply an account or a story related by a narrator, the teller of the story. All novels and short stories are narratives; likewise, poems that tell stories are called *narrative poems*. Writers of fiction, whether poetry or prose, may choose from a number of narrative points of view and types of narration. The point of view that an author chooses is intricately connected to the meaning he or she wishes to convey.

Literary critics use the phrase *point of view* to designate the scope and vantage of narration: that is, the nature of the narrator's relation to and the range of the narrator's knowledge of the characters and events of a narrative.

First-person Point of View

In a first-person point of view, an author usually restricts the narrator's scope to what he or she might reasonably be expected to experience first-hand, guess or infer from speech and actions, and learn from other characters or sources.

A narrator's vantage often depends on whether he or she is central or peripheral to the plot. In some cases, the narrator is also the protagonist, or *central* character, of the work. In Charles Dickens's *Great Expectations* (1861), for instance, the protagonist, called Pip, tells his own story in the first person. Since Pip narrates the story of his childhood and late youth from the vantage of mature adulthood, his tale is a retrospective narration: "My sister, Mrs. Joe Gargery, was more than twenty years older than I, and had established a great reputation with herself and the neighbors because she had brought me up 'by hand.' Having at that time to find out for myself what the expression meant, and knowing her to have a hard and heavy hand, and to be much in the habit of laying it upon her husband as well as upon me, I supposed that Joe Gargery and I were both brought up by hand."

Authors often employ this kind of narration to make the reader aware of an ironic gap between the thoughts and feelings of the protagonist as character and the experience and judgment of the protagonist as narrator. Such is the case in

Ralph Ellison's *Invisible Man* (1952): "All my life I had been looking for something, and everywhere I turned someone tried to tell me what it was. I accepted their answers too, though they were often in contradiction and even self-contradictory. I was naive."

F. Scott Fitzgerald's *The Great Gatsby* (1925) offers an example of a first-person narrator who is more *peripheral* to the action of a novel. Near the middle of the novel, Nick (the narrator) admits to his ignorance of the details of Gatsby's second romance with Daisy: "It was a halt, too, in my association with his affairs. For several weeks I didn't see him or hear his voice on the phone . . . but finally went over to his house one Sunday afternoon." In first-person narrations such as this, questions about the narrator's knowledge and credibility become crucial to understanding the work.

When the credibility of the narration is deliberately called into question, the teller of a tale is considered an unreliable narrator. Such is the case with Marlow in Joseph Conrad's *Heart of Darkness* (1902). Near the beginning of his story, Marlow admits that his recollection and understanding of events is "not very clear." In the film *Apocalypse Now* (1979), which is loosely based on Conrad's novel, director Francis Ford Coppola attempts to imitate this technique by offering snatches of firstperson narration in voice-over.

Chief Bromden, the Columbia Indian who tells his story in Ken Kesey's *One Flew Over the Cuckoo's Nest* (1962), is a clear example of an unreliable narrator: "I been silent so long now it's gonna roar out of me like floodwaters and you think the guy telling this is ranting and raving my God; you think this is too horrible to have really happened, this is too awful to be the truth! But, please. It's still hard for me to have a clear mind thinking on it. But it's the truth even if it didn't happen."

Second-person Point of View

The second-person narrative is rare; however, it is employed in some works of fiction. Jamaica Kincaid's "Girl" (1978), in which a mother offers advice to her daughter, offers an example:

> . . . this is how to love a man, and if this doesn't work there are other ways, and if they don't work don't feel too bad about giving up; this is how to spit up in the air if you feel like it, and this is how to move quick so that it doesn't fall on you; this is how to make ends meet; always squeeze bread to make sure it's fresh; *but what if the baker won't let me feel the bread*, you mean to say that after all you are really going to be the kind of woman who the baker won't let near the bread?

In the case of this illustration, the second-person point of view serves to make the narrative sound like a set of generic instructions based on received wisdom.

Third-person Point of View

Third-person points of view are generally distinguished according to two types: omniscient and limited. An **omniscient third-person narrator** knows everything about characters' actions, thoughts, and feelings, whereas a **limited third-person**

narrator tends to focus attention on the perceptions, thoughts, and feelings of a single character.

Some **omniscient narrators** prove to be **intrusive** in that they offer opinions about characters and actions. An early passage from Jane Austen's *Pride and Prejudice* (1813) offers a case in point: "Mr. Bennet was so odd a mixture of quick parts, sarcastic humour, reserve, and caprice, that the experience of three and twenty years had been insufficient to make his wife understand his character. Her mind was less difficult to develop. She was a woman of mean understanding, little information, and uncertain temper." The narrator's comments about Mrs. Bennet are particularly intrusive in that they *tell* the reader what to think of her.

Objective third-person narrators tend to *show* the characters and action without comment rather than *tell* the reader what to think. Raymond Carver's "Popular Mechanics" (1981) employs an objective narrator. At the end of a story reporting the break-up of a marriage, the narrator describes a potentially gruesome scene in a shockingly impersonal way:

> She would have it, this baby. She grabbed for the baby's other arm. She caught the baby around the wrist and leaned back.
>
> But he would not let go. He felt the baby slipping out of his hands and he pulled back very hard.
>
> In this manner, the issue was decided.

In reporting this scene, the narrative voice seems detached and unmoved, as though he or she is concerned only with reporting the facts. This mode of narration enables an author to maintain distance from the characters and action.

In film, a director may employ an **omniscient point of view**, in which the camera enables us to view the action through various characters. The opening scene of Francis Ford Coppola's *The Godfather* (1973), for instance, employs an omniscient point of view; it allows the audience to view a wedding from the perspectives of several characters. Woody Allen's *Hannah and Her Sisters* (1986) offers another example of an omniscient view.

A **third-person limited point of view** provides an author with both the aesthetic distance of the third-person narration and the focus of character available in first-person narrations. In Bobbie Ann Mason's "Shiloh" (1982), the narrative is offered in the third person, yet by filtering the passage through the perceptions and consciousness of the protagonist, Leroy Moffitt, Mason manages to present the characters and action through the focus of a single character:

> Leroy takes a lungful of smoke and closes his eyes as Norma Jean's words sink in. He tries to focus on the fact that thirty-five hundred soldiers died on the grounds around him. He can only think of that war as a board game with plastic soldiers. Leroy almost smiles as he compares the Confederates' daring attack on the Union camps with Virgil Mathis's raid on the bowling alley. General Grant, drunk and furious, shoved the Southerners back to Corinth, where Mabel and Jet Beasley were married years later, when Mabel was still thin and good-looking. The next day, Mabel and Jet visited the battleground, and then Norma

Jean was born, and then she married Leroy and they had a baby, which they lost, and now Leroy and Norma Jean are here at the same battleground. Leroy knows he is leaving out a lot. He is leaving out the insides of history. History was always just names and dates to him. It occurs to him that building a house out of logs is similarly empty—too simple. And the real inner workings of a marriage, like most of history, have escaped him.

Alfred Hitchcock's film *Rear Window* (1954) employs a **limited point of view** in the sense that the audience views the characters and actions through the eyes of the protagonist, who watches his neighbors through the rear window of his apartment. In several scenes, Hitchcock's direction makes viewers aware that their perceptions are limited by a frame as well. See **PERSONA**, **TONE**, and **VOICE**.

NATURALISM

Literary critics commonly use the term *naturalism* to describe the philosophy of determinism that informs or underlies some of the novels written in France, Russia, and the United States during the latter half of the nineteenth century. The basic premise of naturalism is that the thoughts, emotions, and actions of men and women are determined by forces beyond their control: nature, heredity, and social forces. Novelists working on the assumptions of naturalism attempted to achieve objectivity by presenting characters and actions with scientific realism that avoided moral judgment.

The extent of the naturalists' pessimism about human behavior depended on the type of determinism to which they subscribed. According to *hard determinism*, the thoughts, emotions, and activities of human beings were almost thoroughly determined by external forces and circumstances. Those writers who favored *soft determinism*, however, conceded that men and women could exercise free will.

Stephen Crane's *The Red Badge of Courage* (1895) is an example of a naturalistic novel informed by soft determinism. At the beginning of the novel, the protagonist, Henry Fleming, joins the Union forces in the American Civil War but fears that he may prove a coward during battle:

A little panic-fear grew in his mind. As his imagination went forward to a fight, he saw hideous possibilities. He contemplated the lurking menaces of the future, and failed in an effort to see himself standing stoutly in the midst of them. He recalled the visions of broken-beaded glory, but in the shadow of the impending tumult he suspected them to be impossible pictures.

He sprang from the bunk and began to pace nervously to and fro. "Good Lord, what's th' matter with me?" he said aloud.

He felt that in this crisis his laws of life were useless. Whatever he had learned of himself was here of no avail. He saw that he would again be obliged to experiment as he had in early youth. He must accumulate information of himself, and meanwhile he was resolved to remain close upon his guard lest those qualities of which he knew nothing should everlastingly disgrace him. . . .

Henry worries that his actions will be determined by his base nature—his fears and his instinct for self-preservation—rather than by his desire to be steadfast, dutiful, and courageous. In a later passage, Crane suggests that even Henry's desires for glory are determined, if not by nature then by his social training. Henry becomes aware of the agency of societal codes when a tattered comrade begins to question him about his actions after he flees the battle line in terror:

> The simple questions of the tattered man had been knife thrusts to him. They asserted a society that probes pitilessly at secrets until all is apparent. His late companion's chance persistency made him feel that he should not keep his crime concealed in his bosom. It was sure to be brought plain by one of those arrows which cloud the air and are constantly pricking, discovering, proclaiming those things which are willed to be forever hidden from this agency. It was not within the power of vigilance.

The passage suggests that free will is liable to be overcome by the determining forces of social training and practices, from which unbearable feelings such as guilt arise in the hearts and minds of human beings. Yet throughout the novel, Crane at least raises the possibility of human will overcoming (if only in part) both natural and social determinism.

By contrast, the hard determinism of Frank Norris's *McTeague* (1899) offers little faith in the possibility or efficacy of free will. Early on in the novel, the protagonist, a dimwitted and unlicensed dentist named McTeague, takes advantage of a female patient's unconsciousness and acts according to his animal passions in kissing her. Having described McTeague's actions, the narrator seeks to explain what impelled them:

> Below the fine fabric of all that good in him ran the foul stream of hereditary evil, like a sewer. The vices and sins of his father and of his father's father, to the third and fourth and fifth hundreth generation, tainted him. The evil of an entire race flowed in his veins. Why should it be? He did not desire it. Was he to blame?

In this way, Norris introduces the idea that his protagonist, despite any desire or will to resist, is thoroughly determined by sexual impulse and hereditary evil. In this sense, he is not even a moral animal, since he cannot overcome what determines him. Thus, in some senses, he may not be subject to accusation or blame.

Other writers associated with naturalism include the French novelists Emile Zola and Gustave Flaubert; and Americans Jack London, Theodore Dreiser, and John Dos Passos. See **REALISM**.

NEW CRITICISM/FORMALISM

New Criticism is a term used to describe a variety of approaches to literature, many of which were inspired by the critical prose of T. S. Eliot (see **Classicism** and **Objective Correlative**) and I. E. Richards after World War I and developed by the practical examples of John Crowe Ransom, Robert Penn Warren, Allen Tate, and Cleanth Brooks (among many others) after World War II; the adjective "new" is, therefore, misleading. However, New Critical ideas and methods did bring about radical change in literary scholarship and teaching in the 1930s and 1940s. Previous scholars tended to focus their attention on biography and history, seeing literature as a reflection of the author's life and the time in which he or she lived. The New Critics sought to shift the focus to the text itself by studying it in isolation from biographical and historical information. The practical result of this attention to the literary text was a new reliance on "close readings" to determine both the external form (e.g., sonnet, ballad, or ode) and the internal forms (structure of arguments and patterns of figurative language) of a literary work. For these reasons, New Critical approaches are sometimes called **formalist** critiques.

Logical Structure and Local Texture

In *The World's Body* (1938), John Crowe Ransom asserts that a literary critic must look beneath external forms to discover internal forms, which he calls the logical structure and local texture of a work. By *logical structure*, he means the forms in which the arguments or concepts of a poem (to take the genre favored by formalists) are presented. *Local texture* is the phrase Ransom uses to describe the patterns of metaphors and images. Shakespeare's "Sonnet LXXIII" (1609) lends itself to this type of formalist reading:

> That time of year thou mayst in me behold
> When yellow leaves, or none, or few, do hang
> Upon those boughs which shake against the cold,
> Bare ruined choirs, where late the sweet birds sang.
> In me thou see'st the twilight of such day
> As after sunset fadeth in the west,
> Which by and by black night doth take away,
> Death's second self, that seals up all in rest.
> In me thou see'st the glowing of such fire
> That on the ashes of his youth doth lie,
> As the death-bed whereon it must expire,
> Consumed with that which it was nourished by.
>   This thou perceiv'st, which makes thy love more strong,
> To love that well which thou must leave ere long.

The external form of the poem is that of an **English** (or **Shakespearean**) **sonnet**: three **quatrains** (groups of four lines), each of which is marked by a strong **caesura** (pauses, often marked by punctuation) and a **couplet** (a pair of matched lines) with a rhyme scheme of *abab cdcd efef gg*. Upon closer reading, however, a formalist critic would note internal forms as well. The logical structure of the poem becomes apparent in the form of three principal comparisons between the speaker and natural processes, followed by a concluding statement. Thus, the logical structure corresponds to the external form of the English sonnet. Moreover, each of the comparisons relates to concepts of time: time of year, time of day, and time that it takes a spent fire to go out. These likewise give a kind of structural unity to the argument or theme of the poem.

The specific metaphors and images that make up the local texture of this sonnet include the three comparisons. In the first quatrain, the speaker compares his time of life to the late autumn or early winter of the year, "When yellow leaves, or none, or few, do hang / Upon those boughs." However, he also compares the boughs of trees, "where late the sweet birds sang," to "bare ruined choirs." As with the dominant metaphor of this section, this one makes a comparison between the natural world—a tree in which birds no longer sing—and the human sphere—a church choir stall in which people no longer sing. These metaphors correspond well, as a formalist might point out, with the logical structure or argument of the poem, which concerns itself with various concepts of loss and absence: loss of youth, loss of leaves, absence of warmth, absence of sound, and so on. A formalist critic would perhaps go on to observe that the other sections of the poem proceed in similar fashion both structurally and metaphorically, until the couplet. The last two lines present an ironic statement: namely, that one's love of life grows stronger as one's time runs out. This couplet helps to explain the logical structure of the argument in which the dominant metaphors of the three quatrains suggest decreasing measurements of time: autumn, sunset, and the expiration of a fire without fuel. The speaker is aware that the end of his life is growing near, and he recognizes that this awareness makes him value life all the more.

Close Reading and the Poetry of Paradox

In *The Well Wrought Urn* (1947), Cleanth Brooks offers close readings of a number of poems to demonstrate that "well-wrought" poetry is marked by its use of paradox. For Brooks, the job of the critic is to explain how paradoxes make a poem deliberately difficult and, at the same time, serve to resolve and unify the poem's structure and theme. Near the beginning of the book, Brooks offers a reading of William Wordsworth's sonnet "It is a Beauteous Evening" (1807):

> It is a beauteous evening, calm and free,
> The holy time is quiet as a Nun
> Breathless with adoration; the broad sun
> Is sinking down in its tranquillity;
> The gentleness of heaven broods o'er the Sea:
> Listen! the mighty Being is awake,
> And doth with his eternal motion make
> A sound like thunder—everlastingly.

Dear Child! dear Girl! that walkest with me here,
If thou appear untouched by solemn thought,
Thy nature is not therefore less divine:
Thou liest in Abraham's bosom, all the year,
And worship'st at the Temple's inner shrine,
God being with thee when we know it not.

According to Brooks, the principal paradox in this poem centers on the girl with whom the speaker is walking. In the octave, the speaker seeks to inspire the girl to appreciate the "beauteous evening," to become as worshipful of nature as the evening itself, which is "quiet as a Nun / Breathless with adoration." In the beginning of the sestet, the speaker admits that the girl "appear[s] untouched by solemn thought" about the holiness and beauty of the night. Nevertheless, he insists at the end of the poem that she "worship[s] at the Temple's inner shrine."

As Brooks sees it, the central paradox of the poem concerns the girl, who is described as worshipful even though she seems "untouched by solemn thought." Brooks resolves this paradox by explaining that "she is filled with an unconscious sympathy for all of nature, not merely the grandiose and the solemn." That is to say, she is in tune with nature even when she is not consciously worshipping it. Indeed, the last line of the sonnet suggests this resolution: "God being with thee when we know it not." As Brooks goes on to explain, poetry should and must work through paradox, and not just in argument but also through imagery:

> T. S. Eliot has commented upon "that perpetual slight alteration of language, words perpetually juxtaposed in new and sudden combinations," which occurs in poetry. It is perpetual; it cannot be kept out of the poem; it can only be directed and controlled. The tendency of science is necessarily to stabilize terms, to freeze them into strict denotations; the poet's tendency is by contrast disruptive. . . . To take a very simple example, consider the adjectives in the first lines of Wordsworth's evening sonnet: beauteous, calm, free, holy, quiet, breathless. The juxtapositions are hardly startling; and yet notice this: the evening is like a nun breathless with adoration. The adjective "breathless" suggests tremendous excitement; and yet the evening is not only quiet but calm. There is no final contradiction here, to be sure; it is that kind of calm and that kind of excitement, and the two states may well occur together. But the poet has no one term. Even if he had a polysyllabic technical term, the term would not provide the solution for his problem. He must work by contradiction and qualification.

This passage is representative of New Criticism in several ways: in its appeal to the critical prose of T. S. Eliot; in its effort to note the differences between poetry and science; in its close attention to the language of the poem; in its intention both to problematize (find contradictions or barriers to understanding) and to resolve seeming contradictions; in its claim that skillful poets can direct and control language. This final claim, that great authors maintain an authoritative command of signs and significations, has come under attack in recent decades by poststructural theories of language and literature. See **BIOGRAPHICAL CRITICISM, CLASSICISM, DECONSTRUCTION, NEW HISTORICISM, OBJECTIVE CORRELATIVE**, and **STRUCTURALISM/ POSTSTRUCTURALISM**.

NEW HISTORICISM

New Historicism is a term used to describe widely varied practices of reading that have been developed in reaction to both **New Criticism** and **Poststructuralism**. That is to say, New Historicists react against the tendency of the formalist New Critics to read literary texts in isolation from historical, biographical, and cultural contexts, and the tendency of poststructuralist theories to rely on both Marxist critiques of capitalist society and rigid notions of social determinism. Instead, New Historicists seek to explore the complex relations between literature and culture, in which authors and their works show themselves to be, in some senses, bound by social codes and conventions, while they prove, in other ways, to subvert or undercut the dominant beliefs of their societies. In developing cultural contexts, New Historicists examine "marginal" texts: products of mass culture such as newspapers, magazines, advertisements, popular fiction, popular music, and films, as well as novels, poems, plays, diaries, and other writings by women, people of color, writers in colonized countries, and writers in Third World nations.

In the introduction to his book entitled *Renaissance Self-Fashioning* (1980), Stephen Greenblatt, who invented the term *New Historicism*, describes his multifaceted approach to reading literature and culture. He begins by enumerating three representative functions of literature. For New Historicists, works of literature may manifest the thoughts and actions of an author, the social conventions and dominant beliefs of an era or a culture, and criticisms of these conventions and beliefs. As Greenblatt explains, these three functions may be seen to overlap with and complement one another:

> Literature functions within this system in three interlocking ways: as a manifestation of the concrete behavior of its particular author, as itself the expression of the codes by which behavior is shaped, and as a reflection upon those codes. The interpretive practice that I have attempted to exemplify in the essays that follow must concern itself with all three of these functions. If interpretation limits itself to the behavior of the author, it becomes literary biography (in either a conventionally historical or psychological mode) and risks losing a sense of the larger networks of meaning in which both the author and his works participate. If, alternatively, literature is viewed exclusively as the expression of social rules and instructions, it risks being absorbed entirely into an ideological superstructure. . . . Finally, if literature is seen only as a detached reflection upon the prevailing behavioral codes, a view from a safe distance, we drastically diminish our grasp of art's concrete functions

in relation to individuals and to institutions, both of which shrink into an obligatory "historical background" that adds little to our understanding. We drift back toward a conception of art as addressed to a timeless, cultureless, universal human essence or, alternatively as a self-regarding, autonomous, closed system—in either case, art as opposed to social life.

In other words, New Historicists are critical of "old" historical approaches that tended to employ historical contexts only as a background to an author's work. For New Historicists, neither artists nor their art can be divorced or regarded in isolation from history and culture. Thus, what Greenblatt proposes is an approach that discovers interconnections among a written text, the life and behavior of its author, and the belief systems of his or her culture.

In a chapter of *Renaissance Self-Fashioning* entitled "The Improvisation of Power," for instance, Greenblatt reads Shakespeare's *Othello* (1602) as a text that may be understood in the context of European colonialism, the Protestant Reformation, and Shakespeare's experience in Elizabethan theater. All three are noticeable in the character, language, and attitude displayed by Iago as he first hatches his plot to deceive Othello by leading him to believe his lieutenant, Cassio (whose position Iago envies), is carrying on a sexual affair with Desdemona, Othello's wife:

> Cassio's a proper man, let me see now,
> To get his place, and to plume up my will,
> In double knavery . . . how, how? . . . let's see,
> After some time, to abuse Othello's ear
> That he is too familiar with his wife:
> He has a person and a smooth dispose,
> To be suspected, fram'd to make women false:
> The Moor is of a free and open nature,
> That thinks men honest that but seem to be so:
> And will as tenderly be led by the nose . . .
> As asses are.
> I ha't, it is engender'd; Hell and night
> Must bring this monstrous birth to the world's light.
> (1.3.390–402)

Greenblatt reads this passage as a revelation of Iago's ability to improvise, to think on his feet and manipulate situations to his advantage: "A double knavery . . . how, how? . . . let's see, / After some time, to abuse Othello's ear / That he is too familiar with his wife." Greenblatt sees a connection between this "ability to effect a divorce . . . between the tongue and the heart" and the ability of European colonialists to transform themselves and their belief systems in order to serve their lusts for power. In order to deceive and conquer the natives of the New World, for example, colonialists had to disguise their true intentions and justify their actions by creating fictions about both themselves and their victims.

Greenblatt also associates this ability to improvise with Shakespeare's genius for entering the psychology of diverse characters, a talent necessary both to the playwright and the actor, vocations with which he was equally familiar. Iago, himself, is capable of understanding Othello's weaknesses: "The Moor is of a free and open nature / That thinks men / honest that but seem to be so: / And will as tenderly be led by the nose . . . / As asses are." By putting himself in Othello's place and empathizing with Othello's nature, Iago ensures the success of his plot. In addition, Greenblatt finds in Iago's plan to concoct an alleged affair between Cassio and Desdemona a reflection of the Protestant Reformation's tendency to express sin in terms of sexual lusts and bodily functions. His own plot is "engender'd; Hell and night / Must bring this monstrous birth to the world's light." Thus, as even this short excerpt from the play suggests, *Othello* may be read to express, reflect, and interconnect matters of history, biography, and religious belief, all of which are of interest to the New Historicists. See **MARXIST CRITICISM, NEW CRITICISM/FORMALISM,** and **STRUCTURALISM/POSTSTRUCTURALISM.**

NOVEL

A novel is an extended prose narrative. The word *novel* derives from the Italian word for a realistic tale of the medieval period—*novella*. The word *roman* is also used in several languages for the novel (for example, the German *Bildungsroman* or novel of development). *Roman* is clearly connected to "romance," and the novel is rooted in romance. Most literary critics distinguish between two kinds of prose fiction: the novel, which is more often based on observation of life, and the romance, which is more often the product of fancy than observation. That is to say, a novel concerns itself primarily with the real or actual world, while the romance presents a blend of reality and fantasy. The earliest novels in English literature are often considered to be Aphra Behn's *Oroonoko* (1678) and Defoe's *Moll Flanders* (1722); however, the antecedents of the novel can be traced back much farther. Important influences on the novel include Arthurian romance (for example, Mallory's fifteenth-century *Le Morte D'Arthur*), Boccaccio's novella collection *De Cameron* (1348), Cervantes's satirical romance *Don Quixote* (1605), Marie-Madeleine de Lafayette's prose narrative *La Princesse de Cleves* (1678), and Bunyan's **allegory** *The Pilgrim's Progress* (1678-1684).

The genre of the novel can be divided into numerous subgenres such as the *picaresque novel*, the novel of sensibility, the epistolary novel, the gothic novel, the psychological novel, the realistic novel, the romance, the regional novel, the historical novel, and the social novel. The picaresque novel is derived from the Spanish word *picaro* meaning "rogue." It describes travels and adventures of characters and is usually episodic in form. Examples include Defoe's *Moll Flanders* (1722) and Smollett's *Humphry Clinker* (1771). The *novel of sensibility* or *sentimental novel* was especially popular in the second half of the eighteenth century. The term *sensibility* referred to refinement of feeling. It was associated with virtue and benevolence. Shedding tears, especially in response to the suffering of others, was regarded as a benevolent act. Mackenzie's *The Man of Feeling* (1771) and Sterne's *A Sentimental Journey* (1768) exemplify this subgenre. The excesses of sentimentality are satirized by Jane Austen in *Sense and Sensibility* (1811). The *psychological novel* is sometimes referred to as the *novel of character* and deals primarily with the motives and workings of the minds of characters. Richardson's *Pamela* (1740) and *Clarissa* (1747–1748) are often regarded as some of the earliest novels of character. The *regional novel* usually includes elements of local color. In other words, it incorporates descriptions of the setting and local customs of the region. Hardy's Wessex novels, including *Far from the Madding Crowd* (1869) and *The Return of the Native* (1874), and Willa Cather's Nebraska novels, including *O Pioneers!* (1913) and *My Antonia* (1918), exemplify the regional novel. The *historical novel* uses real-life settings, events, and individuals and makes them an integral part of the work in that they directly affect the characters and plot in the novel. Sir Walter Scott's *Waverley* (1814) and Dickens's *A Tale of Two Cities* (1859) serve as examples of this group of novels. The *social novel* encompasses works of fiction dealing specifically with social issues often for the purpose of promoting reform. Examples include Dickens's *Hard Times* (1837), Upton Sinclair's *The Jungle* (1906), and John Steinbeck's *The Grapes of Wrath* (1939). See **ALLEGORY**, **BILDUNGSROMAN**, **EPISTOLARY NOVEL**, **GOTHIC**, **REALISM**, and **ROMANCE**.

※

O

OBJECTIVE CORRELATIVE

Objective correlative is a term used by T. S. Eliot in his essay "Hamlet and His Problems" (1920) to describe "a set of objects, a situation, a chain of events which shall be the formula of [a] particular emotion, such that when the external facts, which must terminate in sensory experience, are given, the emotion is immediately evoked." In other words, in order to produce a particular emotional effect, a writer must try to find images, circumstances, and incidents universally associated with that particular emotion. This method is objective in the sense that it is impersonal; indeed, the ideal of the objective correlative appealed to the **New Critics**, who often held up Eliot as a model, precisely because it tries to expunge subjective elements from poetry. The writer does not express his or her personal emotions; instead, he or she employs objects, situations, and events that correlate to emotional experiences. A passage from Eliot's "Preludes" (1917) will serve as an example:

> The winter evening settles down
> With smell of steaks in passageways.
> Six o'clock.
> The burnt-out ends of smoky days.
> And now a gusty shower wraps
> The grimy scraps
> Of withered leaves about your feet
> And newspapers from vacant lots;
> The showers beat
> On broken blinds and chimney-pots,
> And at the corner of the street
> A lonely cab-horse steams and stamps.
> And then the lighting of the lamps.

The "set of objects" includes the "grimy scraps of withered leaves"; the "newspapers from vacant lots"; and the "broken blinds and chimneypots." The "situation" is a "winter evening" in an urban setting. The "chain of events" includes "the smell of steaks in passageways" (at "six o'clock"); the coming of "a gusty shower"; the appearance of "a lonely cab-horse" that "steams and stamps"; and finally "the lighting of the lamps" at nightfall. All of these contribute to the evocation of a particular emotional complex: a mixture of boredom, disgust, loneliness, and despair. See **NEW CRITICISM/FORMALISM**.

ODE

An ode was originally a form of dramatic poetry employed in ancient Greek plays. The words were spoken by a chorus with the accompaniment of music. This choric ode was recognizable for its three parts: the **strophe**, during which the singers moved together in one direction on the stage; the **antistrophe**, during which the chorus moved together in the opposite direction; and the **epode**, during which they stood still.

In English poetry, an ode is a type of lyric poem, spoken by a single voice. The ode is typically marked by its serious tone, exalted theme, dignified language, and imaginative thought. Critics generally acknowledge three types of ode: the **Pindaric ode**, the **Horatian ode**, and the **irregular ode**. The Pindaric ode retains some of the formal trappings of the choric ode: alternating strophes and antistrophes in which the stanza form is of the same pattern, and epodes, in which the stanza form changes. Three excerpts from William Collins's "Ode to Fear" (1747) will serve as examples:

[STROPHE]

Thou, to whom the World unknown
With all its shadowy Shapes is shown;
Who see'st appall'd th' unreal Scene,
While Fancy lifts the Veil between:
    Ah Fear! Ah frantic Fear!
    I see, I see Thee near.
I know thy hurried Step, thy haggard Eye!
Like Thee I start, like Thee disorder'd fly . . .

★ ★ ★ ★ ★ ★ ★ ★ ★ ★

EPODE

In earliest Greece to Thee with partial Choice,
    The Grief-full Muse addrest her infant Tongue;
The Maids and Matrons, on her awful Voice,
    Silent and pale in wild Amazement hung.

Yet He, the Bard who first invok'd thy Name,
    Disdain'd in Marathon its Pow'r to fell;
For not alone he nurs'd the Poet's flame,
    But reach'd from Virtue's Hand the Patriot's Steel.

★ ★ ★ ★ ★ ★ ★ ★ ★ ★

ANTISTROPHE

Thou who such weary Lengths hast past,
Where wilt thou rest, mad Nymph, at last?
Say, wilt thou shroud in haunted Cell,
Where gloomy Rape and Murder dwell?
   Or, in some hollow'd Seat,
   'Gainst which the big Waves beat,
Hear drowning Sea-men's cries in Tempests brought!
Dark Pow'r, with shudd'ring meek submitted Thought. . . .

The first excerpt, which comes from the strophe (untitled by Collins), and the third excerpt, which belongs to the antistrophe, are alike in stanza form: each is made up of a series of rhyming couplets, beginning with lines of **tetrameter** (four feet), moving to **trimeter** (three feet) in the fifth and sixth lines, and settling into **pentameter** (five feet) by the seventh and eighth lines. In the epode, however, Collins's ode employs **quatrains** (four-lined stanzas) with alternating rhyme, and the rhythm is **iambic pentameter** throughout.

The **Horatian ode** employs only one stanza type. A stanza of John Keats's "Ode on a Grecian Urn" (1819) will serve as an example:

Heard melodies are sweet, but those unheard
   Are sweeter; therefore, ye soft pipes, play on;
Not to the sensual ear, but, more endeared,
   Pipe to the spirit ditties of no tone;
Fair youth, beneath the trees, thou canst not leave
   Thy song, nor ever can those trees be bare;
     Bold lover, never, never canst thou kiss,
Though winning near the goal—yet, do not grieve;
     She cannot fade, though thou hast not thy bliss,
     Forever wilt thou love, and she be fair!

The stanza is made up wholly of pentameter lines and has a rhyme scheme of *ababcdecde*.

The **irregular ode** provides a poet with much more license. The stanzas may include lines of varying line lengths, and the stanzas themselves may be of differing length with diverse metrical and rhyming patterns. Two verse paragraphs from Cesare Pavese's "Encounter" (1943) illustrate the difference:

These hard hills which have made my body,
and whose many memories still shake me so, have revealed the miracle—
this she who does not know I love her and cannot understand her.

I encountered her one evening: a brighter presence
in the unsteady starlight, in the summer haze.

The smell of those hills was around me, everywhere,
a feeling deeper than shadow, a voice at once purer
and harsher, a voice of vanished seasons.
                    (trans. William Arrowsmith)

The first verse paragraph is made up of three lines, the second of five. The rhyming is sporadic. Nevertheless, the poem is characterized by the serious tone, dignified language, and imaginative thought associated with an ode. See **METER**.

OEDIPUS/ELECTRA COMPLEX

Oedipus complex is a psychoanalytic term, employed by Sigmund Freud, for a child's erotic attraction to the parent of the opposite sex and resentment toward (or jealousy of) the parent of the same sex. Freud named the complex after the protagonist in legend, immortalized in Sophocles's tragedy *Oedipus the King* (fourth century B.C.), who unwittingly kills his father and marries his mother.

In the classic case of the Oedipal stage of human psychological development, according to Freud, a boy between the ages of three and six comes to desire the exclusive love of his mother and to resent the interference or perceived rivalry of his father. The female equivalent is sometimes called the Electra complex, after the protagonist in the legend (and Sophocles's play *Electra*) who comes to hate her mother (and stepfather) but remains faithful to the memory of her father, whom they murdered.

For Freud, the Oedipus complex helps to explain the psychological compulsions of fathers and mothers and sisters and brothers, as well as other relatives and surrogates. In normal development, according to Freud, the feelings associated with the Oedipal stage are soon repressed. When they are extended or prolonged, however, they can prove dangerous and destructive.

In analyzing literature, some critics employ concepts and theories of psychoanalysis as means to interpretation. Ernest Jones, for instance, has offered a Freudian reading of Shakespeare's *Hamlet* (1601). According to Jones's interpretation, Hamlet's hesitance to avenge his father's murder by killing his uncle, Claudius, results from an unconscious identification with Claudius. That is to say, to kill Claudius would be to punish him for doing precisely what Hamlet himself unconsciously desires to do: namely, kill his father and marry his mother.

Several of Sylvia Plath's poems lend themselves to Freudian concepts of the Electra complex. An excerpt from her poem entitled "Daddy" (1965) provides a case in point:

> You stand at the blackboard, daddy,
> In the picture I have of you,
> A cleft in your chin instead of your foot
> But no less a devil for that, no not
> Any less the black man who
>
> Bit my pretty red heart in two.
> I was ten when they buried you.
> At twenty I tried to die
> And get back, back, back to you.
> I thought even the bones would do.

But they pulled me out of the sack,
And they stuck me together with glue.
And then I knew what to do.
I made a model of you.
A man in black with a Meinkampf look

And a love of the rack and the screw.
And I said I do, I do.
So daddy, I'm finally through. . . .

These lines suggest a female speaker whose latent desire for the love and approval of her father is mixed with anger and resentment about his premature death: "I was ten when they buried you. / At twenty I tried to die / And get back, back, back to you." The persona of the poem has even tried to resurrect her father (symbolically) by marrying a kind of perverse surrogate father: "I made a model of you, / A man in black with a Meinkampf look / And a love of the rack and screw. / And I said I do, I do."

The concepts and theories associated with the Oedipus complex have proved influential for both writers and film directors. The films of Alfred Hitchcock, for instance, are often blatantly Freudian in character and theme. Near the end of *Psycho* (1960), for instance, a psychiatrist seeks to explain why Norman Bates killed Marion Crane. According to the psychiatrist, Norman's problems began after his father died. Norman and his mother began to live "as though there was no one else in the world." But, some ten years later, Mrs. Bates took a lover; Norman was so jealous and enraged that he killed both the lover and his mother. Such was his guilt over the matricide that he stole her corpse from her coffin, treated it with embalming fluid, and kept it in his house, sometimes propping it in a chair to pretend that she was still alive. According to the psychiatrist, who interprets these events, Norman goes so far as to give half of his psychic life to his mother's personality and presumed wishes. That is the reason for Norman's murder of Marion; part of him desires her, but the part of his psyche dominated by his guilt about his mother becomes jealous and vengeful. See **PERSONA** and **PSYCHOANALYTIC THEORY AND CRITICISM**.

OLD ENGLISH PERIOD (IN ENGLISH LITERATURE)

The **Old English** or **Anglo-Saxon** period covers the time from the invasion of England by Teutonie tribes (Saxons, Angles, Jutes) in the first half of the fifth century to the conquest of England in 1066 by the Norman French and William the Conqueror. In the early part of the period, the invading tribes often drove out the native Britons, who moved to Wales and Cornwall in the far west. The Anglo-Saxons (whose name collectively refers to all the invaders) were eventually converted to Christianity after the arrival of St. Augustine in Canterbury in 597. Christianity established literacy in Anglo-Saxon culture, and the Anglo-Saxons began to develop a written literature (much of the previous literature had been in the oral tradition). Other tribes—in particular, Vikings from Scandinavia—invaded England during the eighth to the tenth centuries. They too settled in the lands they plundered and eventually came to adopt Christianity.

During the Old English period, a great tradition of culture and learning in monasteries evolved. Monks wrote and translated Latin texts, but they began writing in vernacular Anglo-Saxon or Old English in approximately 700. Works written in Anglo-Saxon include heroic legends such as "Widsith" and "Waldere," elegiac laments such as "Deor" and "The Seafarer," and theological works such as Aelfric's homilies and Wulfstan's *Sermo Lupi*. The works of the period deal principally with religious stories and also with tales of bygone events before Christian conversion. The ninth-century monarch King Alfred is also an important figure in the period since he translated a number of Latin works into Old English and initiated the Anglo-Saxon Chronicle (a yearly record of major events in England).

One of the most famous works of the period is the anonymous ***epic*** poem *Beowulf* (eighth century). In this work, the poet describes the glory of kings and tribes of the past:

> Hwaet we Gar-Dena   in gear-dagum
> theod-cyninga   thrym gefrunon
> hu da aethelingas ellen fremedon.
>   Oft Scyld Scefing   scethena threatum,
> monegum maegthum   meodo-setla ofteah;
> egsode Eorle,   syddan aerest weard
> feasceaft funden;   he theas frofre gebad:
> weox under wolcnum,   weord-myndum thah,
> odthaet him aeghwylc   thara ymb-sittendra
> ofer hron-rade hyran scolde,
> gmban gyldan: thet waes god cyning!

> (Listen, we have heard of the glory of the kings
> of the Spear danes in days gone by,
> how the princes performed valorous deeds.
> Scyld Scefing often took away the mead benches
> From the troops of his enemies, many tribes.
> He terrified the Heruli after he was first found destitute.
> He experienced solace in respect of that.
> He flourished on earth, he thrived with honor,
> Until each of the surrounding tribes
> over the whale's riding place
> should obey him and pay tribute. That was a good king!)

This opening of the poem contains typical Old English stylistic features such as the use of formal style, rhetorical flourishes, and figurative phrases. For instance, the poet uses a **kenning** or decorative phrase instead of a commonplace noun, as in "whale's riding place" for the ocean. Other important features of Anglo-Saxon poetry include the hard **caesura** or pause in the middle of each line and the heavy use of **consonance**, both of which create a distinctive Old English rhythm. See **EPIC, EPITHET**.

ONOMATOPOEIA

Onomatopoeia is the use of words whose sounds suggest their meanings: hiss, pop, slam, sizzle. Edgar Allan Poe's "The Bells" (1827) offers a number of examples of the ways in which onomatopoeia may be used to draw attention to sound in poetry. The echoing and resonance of sound is most striking in the third section of this poem, where Poe describes "loud alarum bells":

> How they clang, and clash, and roar!
>   What a horror they outpour
> On the bosom of the palpitating air!
>   Yet the ear, it fully knows
>   By the twanging
>   And the clanging,
>   How the danger ebbs and flows;
> Yet the ear distinctly tells,
>   In the jangling
>   And the wrangling,
>   How the danger sinks and swells,
> By the sinking or the swelling in the anger of the bells—
>   Of the bells,—
>   Of the bells, bells, bells, bells,
>   Bells, bells, bells—
> In the clamor and the clangor of the bells!

Poe's explicit reference to the ways in which the ear "fully knows" and "distinctly tells" encourages us to hear not only the meaningful sounds of "clanging" and "twanging" or "jangling" and "wrangling" but also the auditory distinctions between "sinking" and "swelling."

In his poem entitled "Digging" (1965), the contemporary Irish poet Seamus Heaney uses onomatopoeic language in a more subtle way:

> Under my window, a clean rasping sound
> When the spade sinks into the gravelly ground:
> My father digging. . . .

Those readers who will attune their ears to listen for onomatopoeic language will hear the sound of digging in "rasping" and "gravelly." Near the end of the poem, Heaney employs onomatopoeia to make even finer distinctions:

> Nicking and slicing neatly, heaving sods
> Over his shoulder, going down and down
> For the good turf. Digging.

The difference between the techniques of "nicking" and "slicing" can be heard in the sound of the words themselves.

OXYMORON

An *oxymoron* is a figure of speech in which opposite or contradictory ideas or terms are combined. The Greek word *oxymoron* derives from roots literally meaning "sharp-foolish"; a familiar oxymoron is the word *sophomore*, which means "wise fool."

In the first act of Shakespeare's *Romeo and Juliet* (1595), Romeo employs a number of oxymoronic phrases to describe his contradictory feelings of love:

> Why then, O brawling love! O loving hate!
> O any thing, of nothing first create!
> O heavy lightness! serious vanity!
> Mis-shapen chaos of well-seeming forms!
> Feather of lead, bright smoke, cold fire, sick health!
> Still-waking sleep, that is not what it is!
> This love feel I, that feel no love in this.
> Dost thou not laugh? (1.1.176-183)

A passage from Seamus Heaney's "Elegy for a Still-born Child" (1969) offers more contemporary examples:

> On lonely journeys, I think of it all,
> Birth of death, exhumation of burial,
>
> A wreath of small clothes, a memorial pram,
> And parents reaching for a phantom limb.

The oxymorons in this excerpt include "birth of death" and "exhumation of burial": the former suggests the beginning of the end, while the latter registers a revelation to the mind ("to exhume" also means "to bring to light" and "to recall") of the closure represented by burial. Thus, death is the birth of another form of existence, and burial brings to mind death's finality. These conflicting thoughts and emotions arise from the fact of a still-born child, who is born dead.

✳

P

PARABLE

A *parable* can be defined as both "a simple story illustrating a moral or religious lesson" and "an obscure or enigmatic saying." In many cases, the lessons offered by parables prove to be simple and enigmatic at the same time. The term derives from the Greek verb *paraballein*, meaning "to set beside or compare"; the method of comparison usually involves an **analogy** and often takes the form of an **allegory**. However, a parable differs from an allegory in that the analogies between the literal and moral (or spiritual) levels of a parable operate point for point, whereas the analogies between the two levels in an allegory are often more occasional.

Among the most familiar examples are the Christian parables. In order that the multitudes might see, hear, and understand, Christ offers in his parables analogies between everyday activities (daily life) and the ways to enter the kingdom of heaven (spiritual life). Matthew 13 presents the parable of the good seed:

> The kingdom of heaven is likened unto a man which sowed good seed
> in his field: But while men slept, his enemy came and sowed tares
> among the wheat, and went his way. But when the blade was sprung
> up, and brought forth fruit, then appeared the tares also. So the servants
> of the householder came and said unto him, Sir, didst not thou sow
> good seed in thy field? from whence then hath it tares? He said unto
> them, An enemy hath done this. The servants said unto him, Wilt thou
> then that we go and gather them up? But he said, Nay; lest while ye
> gather up the tares, ye root up also the wheat with them. Let both grow
> together until the harvest: and in the time of harvest I will say to the
> reapers, Gather ye together first the tares, and bind them in bundles to
> burn them: but gather the wheat into my barn. (24-30)

This is the literal level of daily life in the parable, which Jesus goes on to compare with the allegorical level of spiritual life:

> He that soweth the good seed is the Son of man: The field is the world;
> the good seed are the children of the kingdom; but the tares are

gathered and burned in the fire; so shall it be in the end of this world; and the reapers are the angels. As therefore the tares are gathered and burned in the fire; so shall it be in the end of this world. The Son of man shall send forth his angels, and they shall gather out of his kingdom all things that offend, and them which do iniquity; And shall cast them into a furnace of fire; there shall be wailing and gnashing of teeth. Then shall the righteous shine forth as the sun in the kingdom of their Father, Who hath ears to hear, let him hear. (37-43)

Thus, the harvest is likened to the day of judgment, the good seed to the righteous, and the tares to the wicked. Moreover, the parable seeks to explain why God allows the wicked to live and roam the earth, suggesting that they shall be sorted and punished in the end. This is the moral or lesson of the parable.

The stories of Czechoslovakian writer Franz Kafka often take the form of parables. In "The Bucket-Rider" (1919), for instance, Kafka draws on an actual occurrence: the coal shortage of the winter of 1916 in Prague. On the literal level, Kafka's story is about an everyday activity, the search for heating fuel, albeit during an extraordinary period of shortage. Yet, in typical fashion, Kafka introduces an element of absurdly comic exaggeration. The protagonist rides his bucket to the coaldealer's to prove his need:

> "Coaldealer!" I cry in a voice burned hollow by the frost and muffled
> in the cloud made by my breath, "please, coaldealer, give me a little coal.
> My bucket is so light that I can ride on it. Be kind. When I can I'll pay
> you."
>   The dealer puts his hand to his ear. "Do I hear rightly?" he throws
> the question over his shoulder to his wife. "Do I hear rightly? A
> customer."
>   "I hear nothing," says his wife, breathing in and out peacefully
> while she knits on, her back pleasantly warmed by the heat.

The coaldealer's wife is deaf to the protagonist's pleas, a circumstance that may be interpreted in at least two ways: she is literally deaf and cannot hear his begging, or she is spiritually deaf in that she cannot feel for his need and will not answer his call for charity. Kafka emphasizes this latter, allegorical sense of the story in the conclusion:

> She sees nothing and hears nothing; but all the same she loosens her
> apron strings and waves her apron to waft me away. She succeeds,
> unluckily. My bucket has all the virtues of a good steed except powers
> of resistance, which it has not; it is too light; a woman's apron can make
> it fly through the air.
>   "You bad woman!" I shout back, while she, turning into the shop,
> half contemptuous, half reassured, flourishes her fist in the air. "You bad
> woman! I begged you for a shovelful of the worst coal and you would
> not give it me." And with that I ascend into the regions of the ice
> mountains and am lost for ever.

The literal winter described at the end of the parable is analogous to the cold-heartedness of the coaldealer's wife, who represents human greed, meanness, and indifference in the modern world. Like the multitudes Christ describes, who know nothing of the mysteries of the kingdom of heaven, the coaldealer's wife "sees nothing and hears nothing" belonging to the great chain of human relations. See **ALLEGORY** and **ANALOGY**.

PARADOX

A paradox is a seemingly contradictory or absurd statement that is nevertheless true or sensible. The term derives from the Greek *paradoxon*, meaning "beyond opinion"; indeed, a paradox often calls for the teasing out of thought rather than merely projecting familiar ideas.

The work of the English metaphysical poets of the seventeenth century relies heavily on paradox. The sestet of John Donne's "Holy Sonnet XIV" (1633), in which the speaker pleads for God's help, offers an example:

> Yet dearly I love You, and would be loved fain,
> But am betrothed unto Your enemy:
> Divorce me, untie or break that knot again,
> Take me to You, imprison me, for I,
> Except You enthrall me, never shall be free,
> Nor ever chaste, except You ravish me.

The closing couplet presents two paradoxical concepts: that the speaker "never shall be free" unless he is "enthralled" to God, and that the speaker can never be "chaste" unless he is "ravish[ed]" by God. The implications that enslavement sets one free or that physical violence leaves one undefiled appear to be insupportable. But by teasing out these seemingly absurd propositions, readers may discover at least two senses in which each statement, though a paradox, is nevertheless true to its concept.

First of all, the words "enthrall," "free," "chaste," and "ravish" all have more than one meaning. Second, the context of this poem's argument is seventeenth-century Christian theology. The verb to enthrall does mean "to enslave," but it also means "to hold under strong influence; to enchant or fascinate." In this latter sense, the speaker may be asking God to exert a strong influence over him in order to free him from the influence of the "enemy." Moreover, the word free can mean "having liberty; independent," but it also means "not restricted by anything except its own limitations or nature," which may imply that the speaker is asking only for free will. Likewise, chaste means "not indulging in unlawful sexual intercourse," but the meaning of the word in this context would seem to be closer to "free from obscenity; pure in thought and act." Finally, the word ravish means not only "to seize and carry away by violence and force" but also "to fill with great joy or delight." In these contexts, Donne's paradoxical statements seem more sensible than absurd.

A section of Gwendolyn Brooks's A *Street in Bronzeville* (1945) entitled simply "the mother" offers a more contemporary example of a paradox. In the beginning of the poem, the speaker admits that "Abortions will not let you forget. / You remember the children you got that you did not get." The apparent contradiction of having "got" what "you did not get" may be resolved by recognizing that "got" means to have "come into the state of having (anything)"—in this case being pregnant—but that "get" can also mean "to beget or give birth to." Thus, the mother was in a state of having without giving birth to a child. In a later passage, the mother attempts to justify, or at least explain, her actions to her unborn children:

> If I stole your births and your names,
> Your straight baby tears and your games,
> Your stilted or lovely loves, your tumults, your marriages, aches,
>   and your deaths,
> If I poisoned the beginnings of your breaths,
> Believe that even in my deliberateness I was not deliberate.

The statement that in her "deliberateness" she "was not deliberate" seems illogical; however, since deliberateness means "due attention to arguments for and against" and deliberate as an adjective means "done on purpose," the speaker may be trying to distinguish between her decision (carefully considered) and her intent (not by design or with malice). As Brooks's poem goes on to suggest, such paradoxes enable a poet to say what cannot be said:

> Though why should I whine,
> Whine that the crime was other than mine?—
> Since anyhow you are dead.
> Or rather, or instead,
> You were never made.
> But that too, I am afraid,
> Is faulty: oh, what shall I say, how is the truth to be said?

Paradoxical figures can also be employed for humorous effect. The nineteenth-century Anglo-Irish poet and playwright Oscar Wilde became well known for his witty paradoxes: "I can resist everything except temptation" (*Lady Windermere's Fan*, 1892).

PARODY

Parodies are humorous imitations or burlesques (broadly or lewdly comic renderings) of ideas, styles, characters, or plots in other works of literature. Although humorous in tone, a parody often engages in serious criticism of some defect in style or mishandling of theme; however, it may serve the purpose of expressing good-humored admiration rather than satiric critique.

In *Through the Looking-Glass* (1872), Lewis Carroll parodies the following excerpt from William Wordsworth's "Resolution and Independence" (1807):

A gentle answer did the old Man make,
In courteous speech which forth he slowly drew:
And him with further words I thus bespake,
"What occupation do you there pursue?
This is a lonesome place for one like you."
Ere he replied, a flash of mild surprise
Broke from the sable orbs of his yet-vivid eyes.

          ★ ★ ★ ★ ★ ★ ★ ★ ★ ★

He told, that to these waters he had come
To gather leeches, being old and poor:
Employment hazardous and wearisome!
And he had many hardships to endure:
From pond to pond he roamed, from moor to moor;
Housing, with God's good help, by choice or chance;
And in this way he gained an honest maintenance.

          ★ ★ ★ ★ ★ ★ ★ ★ ★ ★

My former thoughts returned: the fear that kills;
And hope that is unwilling to be fed;
Cold, pain, and labor, and all fleshly ills;
And mighty Poets in their misery dead.
—Perplexed and longing to be comforted,
My question eagerly did I renew,
"How is it that you live, and what is it you do?"

Carroll, perhaps finding these lines somewhat maudlin and mawkish, burlesques them in "The White Knight's Song: Haddock's Eyes or the Aged Aged Man or Ways and Means or A-sitting on a Gate":

I'll tell thee everything I can;
There's little to relate,
I saw an aged, aged man,
A-sitting on a gate.
"Who are you, aged man?" I said.
"And how is it you live?"
And his answer trickled through my head
Like water through a sieve.

He said, "I look for butterflies
That sleep among the wheat;
I make them into mutton-pies,
And sell them in the street.
"I sell them unto men," he said,
"Who sail on stormy seas;
And that's the way I get my bread—
A trifle, if you please."

But I was thinking of a plan
To dye one's whiskers green,
And always use so large a fan
That it could not be seen.
So, having no reply to give
To what the old man said,
I cried, "Come, tell me how you live!"
And thumped him on the head.

Ezra Pound's parody of the poems in A. E. Housman's *A Shropshire Lad* (1896) offers a modern example. The poem entitled "With Rue My Heart Is Laden" is representative of the general drift of Housman's verse:

With rue my heart is laden
For golden friends I had,
For many a rose-lipt maiden
And many a lightfoot lad.

By brooks too broad for leaping
The lightfoot boys are laid;
The rose-lipt girls are sleeping
In fields where roses fade.R

In his parody, "Mr. Housman's Message" (1909), Pound critiques not only the shopworn theme but also the diction, rhyming, and versification:

O woe, woe,
People are born and die,
We also shall be dead pretty soon
Therefore let us act as if we were
                    dead already.

The bird sits on the hawthorn tree
But he dies also, presently.
Some lads get hung, and some get shot.
Woeful is this human lot.
                    Woe! woe, etcetera. . ..

London is a woeful place,
Shropshire is much pleasanter.
Then let us smile a little space
Upon fond nature's morbid grace.
                    Oh, Woe, woe, woe, etcetera. . . .

Pound's parody points up Housman's obsession with death, his use of natural imagery to support the idea of the transience of existence, and the recourse to commonplace rhymes ("shot" and "lot"; "place," "space," and "grace"). See **SATIRE**.

PASTORAL

The word *pastoral* derives from the Latin verb *pascere*, meaning "to graze." Literary critics use the term *pastoral* to refer to a number of poetic types, including the pastoral romance, pastoral lyric, pastoral drama, and pastoral elegy. All of these types evolved from the ancient Greek and Latin pastoral poems, such as the *Idylls* of Theocritus (c. 308-240 B.C.) and the *Eclogues* of Virgil (70-19 B.C.), which idealize life in the country.

Sir Philip Sidney's *Arcadia* (1590), a pastoral romance written largely in prose, includes an **eclogue** (a singing match between two shepherds):

STREPHON: Ye goatherd gods, that love the grassy mountains,
                 Ye nymphs which haunt the springs in pleasant valleys,
                 Ye satyrs joyed with free and quiet forests,
                 Vouchsafe your silent ears to plaining music,
                 Which to my woes gives still an early morning,
                 And draws the dolor on till weary evening.

KLAIUS: O Mercury, foregoer to the evening,
              O heavenly huntress of the savage mountains,
              O lovely star, entitled of the morning,
              While that my voice doth fill these woeful valleys,
              Vouchsafe your silent ears to plaining music,
              Which oft hath Echo tried in secret forests . . .

Christopher Marlowe's "The Passionate Shepherd to His Love" (1599) is an example of a pastoral lyric, a single voice employing pastoral imagery in a song-like poem:

Come live with me and be my love,
And we will all the pleasures prove
That valleys, groves, hills, and fields,
Woods, or steepy mountain yields.

And we will sit upon the rocks,
Seeing the shepherds feed their flocks,
By shallow rivers to whose falls
Melodious birds sing madrigals. . . .

Like the ancient pastorals, Marlowe's poem enumerates the pleasures of rustic life.

Shakespeare's As *You Like It* (1599) manifests many of the traditional elements of the pastoral drama. In the opening speech of Act 2, Duke Senior contrasts the authentic world of nature with the artificial world of the court:

Hath not old custom made this life more sweet
Than that of painted pomp? Are not these woods
More free from peril than the envious court?

And this our life, exempt from public haunt,
Finds tongues in trees, books in the running brooks,
Sermons in stones, and good in everything. (1.1.2-17)

One of the familiar conceits of the pastoral is clearly presented at the end of this excerpt: namely, that the natural world offers both moral and existential lessons.

Thomas Kinsella's "A Country Walk" (1962) adheres to many of the pastoral conventions, as the following passage illustrates:

Sick of the piercing company of women
I swung the gate shut with a furious sigh,
Rammed trembling hands in pockets and drew in
A breath of river air. A rook's wet wing
Cuffed abruptly upward through the drizzle.

On either hand dead trunks in drapes of creeper,
Strangled softly by horse mushroom, writhed
In vanished passion, broken down like sponge.
I walked their hushed stations, passion dying,
Each slow footfall a drop of peace returning.

The narrator revels in the peace and solitude of the countryside. The natural beauty calms and revives him. For an example of the pastoral elegy, see **ELEGY**. See also **CONCEIT**.

PATHETIC FALLACY

Victorian critic John Ruskin employed the term *pathetic fallacy* to describe figures of speech that assign human emotions to inanimate objects. Ruskin offers an example and commentary in *Modern Painters*, Vol.3 (1856):

They rowed her in across the rolling foam—
The cruel, crawling foam.

Ruskin argues that "the foam is not cruel, neither does it crawl. The state of mind which attributes to it these characteristics of a living creature is one in which reason is unhinged by grief. All violent feelings have the same effect. They produce in us a falseness in all our impressions of external things, which I would generally characterize as the 'pathetic fallacy.'"

In many ways, what Ruskin calls the pathetic fallacy is merely an exaggerated or melodramatic personification. Tennyson's *In Memoriam* (1850) offers an example:

Though Nature, red in tooth and claw
With ravine, shrieked against his creed.

Nature possesses neither teeth nor claws, nor does it shriek. The narrator of the poem is anguished about the doubt cast on the existence of a benevolent deity by the revolutionary scientific findings of the early Victorian period. In despair, he assigns human feelings of indifference and even malevolence to Nature.

PERSONA

Persona, the Latin word for "a mask, especially one worn by an actor," is often employed as a synonym for *character;* thus, in many plays, the *dramatis personae* or characters are introduced with a list of names and descriptions. In discussions of prose fiction and poetry, however, the term *persona* has a more specialized meaning. In discussing a novel or a story, critics sometimes use the term *persona* to designate the role or function of a narrator. In some cases, this persona seems to be nearly indistinguishable from the author; some of the intrusive narrators of eighteenth-century English fiction fall into this category. A brief passage from Henry Fielding's *Tom Jones* (1749) will serve as an example:

> Reader, I think proper, before we proceed any farther together, to acquaint thee that I intend to digress through this whole history as often as I see occasion; of which I am myself a better judge than any pitiful critic whatever. And here I must desire all those critics to mind their own business, and not to intermeddle with affairs or works which no ways concern them; for till they produce the authority by which they are constituted judges, I shall not plead to their jurisdiction.

Although Fielding seems to address the reader directly, he does so in the persona of a headstrong, querulous, and much-offended literary artist. Nevertheless, his address is certainly more direct than that of most nineteenth- and twentieth-century novelists.

The opening of Mark Twain's *The Adventures of Huckleberry Finn* (1884) reveals a narrator who, though clearly not the author himself, likewise serves as a kind of mask behind which the author can safely and humorously express some of his opinions:

> You don't know about me, without you have read a book by the name of "The Adventures of Tom Sawyer," but that ain't no matter. That book was made by Mr. Mark Twain, and he told the truth, mainly. There was things which he stretched, but mainly he told the truth. That is nothing. I never seen anybody bullied, one time or another, without it was Aunt Polly, or the widow, or maybe Mary. Aunt Polly—Tom's Aunt Polly, she is—and Mary, and the Widow Douglas, is all told about in that book—which is mostly a true book; with some stretchers, as I said before.

Twain's use of Huck as a persona gives him a voice for some of his beliefs while simultaneously providing him with some distance from the narration and some cover from the more savagely satirical passages in the novel.

In discussing poetry, some critics use the term *persona* to refer to the speaker of the poem. Some poets are obvious in their use of personas. Such is the case in Randall Jarrell's "The Death of the Ball Turret Gunner" (1945):

> From my mother's sleep I fell into the State,
> And I hunched in its belly till my wet fur froze.
> Six miles from earth, loosed from its dream of life,
> I woke to black flak and the nightmare fighters.
> When I died they washed me out of the turret with a hose.

Jarrell adopts the persona of a young man killed in World War II to make a statement about the relation between a military state and its people.

The first two stanzas of Gwendolyn Brooks's poem "The Crazy Woman" (1960) offer a more contemporary example of a persona in a poem:

> I shall not sing a May song.
> A May song should be gay.
> I'll wait until November
> And sing a song of gray.

> I'll wait until November.
> That is the time for me
> I'll go out in the frosty dark
> And sing most terribly.

Brooks adopts a persona who has known unhappiness and loss to sing this ballad about the difference between the gay songs of May and the terrible songs of November. See **NARRATIVE POINT OF VIEW**.

PERSONIFICATION

Personification is a **figure of speech** in which an object, an idea, or a quality is represented as a person. The Greek word for this figure is *prosopopoeia*, which derives from a verb meaning "to make a dramatic character."

Personification can take the form of an explicit comparison, as in the case of Robert Frost's simile in his poem entitled "Birches" (1916):

> You may see their trunks arching in the woods
> Years afterwards, trailing their leaves on the ground
> Like girls on hands and knees that throw their hair
> Before them over their heads to dry in the sun.

In this example of *prosopopoeia*, the birches' bent trunks are like girls on their hands and knees, and the leaves are like their hair.

More commonly, personification is metaphorical, as in Shakespeare's series of figures in "Sonnet XXXIII" (1609):

> Full many a glorious morning have I seen
> Flatter the mountain-tops with sovereign eye,

Kissing with golden face the meadows green,
Gilding pale streams with heavenly alchemy.

Shakespeare gives the morning an "eye" with which to flatter; a "face" with which to kiss; and an alchemist's pseudo-science with which to gild.

Personification is a particularly common figure among the English poets of the seventeenth and eighteenth centuries. Near the beginning of *The Dunciad* (1728), for instance, Alexander Pope personifies an idea or concept:

Poetic Justice, with her lifted scale,
Where, in nice balance, truth with gold she weighs,
And solid pudding against empty praise.

Pope plays on the familiar personification of justice as a blind woman holding scales.

Personification is a familiar **trope** (a "turn" of phrase or a figure of speech that alters the meaning of a word or concept) in many cultures, as the following lines from a translation, entitled "After Twenty Years" (1979), of a poem by the Arabic poet Fadwa Tuquan suggest:

Here the moon
Sells its face every night,
For a dagger, a candle, a braid of rain.

★ ★ ★ ★ ★ ★ ★ ★ ★ ★

Here the foot prints stop;
Here the moon was in labour.

In the first excerpt, the moon is personified as a prostitute; in the second part, the moon is personified as a mother giving birth.

PLATONIC

Literary critics use the term *Platonic* to refer to any work that appears to draw on the idealistic philosophy of Plato (c. 427-347 B.C.) or his followers. Platonic idealism privileges abstract concepts of perfection over concrete objects, which are necessarily imperfect imitations of ideals. In his philosophy, Plato makes a distinction between the sensible world (appreciable through the senses) and the realm of universal forms (appreciable through spiritual contemplation). He offers a similar distinction between two kinds of love: the lower of the two is merely sensual and temporary, whereas the higher form develops from a process of idealization (spiritual exaltation), such that it ultimately proves to be absolute and eternal. Plato also introduces the doctrine of reminiscence, which posits a spiritual existence before birth.

The Sensible and Ideal Worlds

In Book X of Plato's *The Republic*, a dialogue between Socrates and Glaucon helps to delineate the differences between the realm of the sensible and the realm of the universal, as well as Plato's general attitude toward art. In this dialogue, Socrates takes for his argument the example of the differences between the ideal bed, a bed made by a carpenter, and a painting of a bed:

> Beds, then are of three kinds, there are three artists who superintend them: God, the maker of the bed, and the painter?
>
> Yes, there are three of them.
>
> God, whether from choice or from necessity, made one bed in nature and one only; two or more such beds neither ever have been nor ever will be made by God.
>
> Why is that?
>
> Because even if He had made but two, a third would still appear behind them of which they again both possessed the form, and that would be the real bed and not the two others.
>
> Very true, he said.
>
> God knows this, I suppose, and He desired to be the real maker of a real bed, not a kind of maker of a kind of bed, and therefore He created a bed which is essentially and by nature one only.
>
> So it seems.
>
> Shall we, then, speak of Him as the natural author or maker of the bed?
>
> Yes, he replied; inasmuch as by the natural process of creation, He is the author of this and of all other things.
>
> And what shall we say of the carpenter—is not he also the maker of a bed?
>
> Yes.
>
> But would you call the painter an artificer and maker?
>
> Certainly not.
>
> Yet if he is not the maker, what is he in relation to the bed?
>
> I think, he said, that we may fairly designate him as the imitator of that which the others make.

In the world of universal forms, we may contemplate *the* ideal bed (the original and authentic idea of a bed) made by God. In the temporal world of the senses, we can perceive *a* bed made by a carpenter. Thrice removed from the ideal bed, we arrive at a painting of a bed, which is merely the imitation of "that which others have made."

Platonic Love

In *Phaedrus*, Plato examines the question of the nature of love through a dialogue between Socrates and Phaedrus. Near the beginning of this dialogue, Socrates attempts to make a distinction between the lower form of love, which proceeds from desire of pleasure, and a higher form of love, which aspires toward good and right:

> Let us note that in every one of us there are two guiding and ruling principles which lead us whither they will; one is the natural desire of

pleasure, the other is an acquired opinion which aspires after the best; and these two are sometimes in harmony and then again at war, and sometimes the one, sometimes the other conquers. When opinion by the help of reason leads us to the best, the conquering principle is called temperance; but when desire, which is devoid of reason, rules in us and drags us to pleasure, that power of misrule is called excess.

Thus, the higher form, or spiritual love, develops through moral reason rather than desire of pleasure; for this reason, the higher love is permanent and true, whereas the desire of pleasure is fickle and illusory. It is this Platonic doctrine which in part inspired the tradition of **courtly love**. In contemporary parlance, Platonic love is synonymous with love not consummated sexually.

The Doctrine of Reminiscence

Another Platonic idea that has proved influential in literature, especially among the English Romantics, is the doctrine of reminiscence: a theory proposing that the soul exists before the body, and that it is imbued with true knowledge, the memory of which fades as one grows out of childhood. In his "Ode: Intimations of Immortality from Recollections of Early Childhood" (1807), William Wordsworth draws explicitly (as his headnote explains) on the idea of "a pre-existent state":

> Our birth is but a sleep and a forgetting:
> The Soul that rises with us, our life's star,
>   Hath had elsewhere its setting,
>   And cometh from afar:
>   Not in entire forgetfulness,
>   And not in utter nakedness,
> But trailing clouds of glory do we come
>   From God, who is our home:
> Heaven lies about us in our infancy!
> Shades of the prison-house begin to close
>   Upon the growing Boy,
> But He beholds the light, and whence it flows,
>   He sees it in his joy;
> The Youth, who daily farther from the east
>   Must travel, still is Nature's Priest,
>   And by the vision splendid
>   Is on his way attended;
> At length the Man perceives it die away,
> And fade into the light of common day.

The attempt to escape "the prison-house" of life by making contact with that lost spiritual "elsewhere" is a recurring subject in English Romantic poetry. See **COURTLY LOVE**, **MIMESIS**, and **ROMANTICISM**.

PLOT

The term *plot* is commonly employed to refer to the actions and incidents of a narrative or a dramatic work; however, the plot of a work of literature may be distinguished from the work itself in the sense that appreciating the plot of a story or a play requires some understanding of motives and causes that create or drive the incidents and actions. To appreciate the plot of Shakespeare's *Hamlet* (1601), for instance, one must understand the motives behind Claudius's action and Hamlet's inaction.

In his *Poetics* (fourth century B.C.), Aristotle places great emphasis on plot (meaning a dramatic plot), which he begins by defining as "the arrangement of incidents." According to Aristotle, in order to be unified, a dramatic plot must have a clear beginning, middle, and end. It must not begin merely by chance or end arbitrarily; moreover, the middle should develop from the beginning and lead to the end. In order to be whole, the plot should have "a proper magnitude": that is to say, the plot should be neither too short to command attention to its beauty nor too long to allow contemplation of the whole. Aristotle goes on to distinguish between simple and complex plots. In a simple plot, the protagonist's change of fortune occurs "without Reversal of situation and without Recognition," whereas in the complex plot, the change in fortune "is accompanied by such Reversal, or by Recognition, or by both." The reversal of situation is referred to by the Greek word **peripety;** the word **anagnorisis** designates the moment of recognition. According to Aristotle, the most effective tragic plots are those in which the reversal of situation and the moment of recognition coincide.

One of the most familiar ways to identify elements of plot is to divide it into stages: **exposition, rising action, climax, falling action,** and **dénouement.** The exposition sets the scene (time and place) and provides the context for the action. In *Hamlet*, for instance, Claudius helps to delineate the context of the play in his opening speech:

> Though yet of Hamlet our dear brother's death
> The memory be green, and that it us befitted
> To bear our hearts in grief, and our whole kingdom
> To be contracted in one brow of woe,
> Yet so far hath discretion fought with nature
> That we with wisest sorrow think on him,
> Together with remembrance of ourselves.
> Therefore our sometime sister, now our queen,
> The imperial jointress to this warlike state,
> Have we, as 'twere, with a defeated joy,
> With an auspicious, and a dropping eye,
> With mirth in funeral, and with dirge in marriage,
> In equal scale weighing delight and dole,
> Taken to wife. . . (1.2.1-14)

The audience learns from this part of the **exposition** that King Hamlet has died, that his brother has succeeded to the throne and married the former king's wife, and that the people grieve for their fallen leader. The audience also learns that the people must be prepared to fight enemies who perceive their nation to be weakened.

The **rising action** often begins with a complication. In the case of *Hamlet*, the complication arrives in the form of the dead king's ghost:

> . . . Now, Hamlet, hear:
> 'Tis given out that, sleeping in my orchard,
> a serpent stung me, so the whole ear of Denmark
> Is by a forged process of my death
> Rankly abus'd; but know, thou noble youth,
> The serpent that did sting thy father's life
> Now wears his crown. (1.5.34–39)

The complication that initiates the rising action is the ghost's telling Hamlet of Claudius's fratricide. From this point until the climax, the protagonist (Hamlet) largely controls the action of the play.

The **climax** of a play often involves a turning point or crisis, from which no return seems possible. In *Hamlet*, the turning points would seem to come with the play within the play, through which Claudius becomes aware of Hamlet's knowledge of the former king's murder, with Hamlet's decision not to kill Claudius while he is praying, and with Hamlet's murder of Polonius. In effect, Hamlet allows Claudius (the antagonist) to take control of the falling action. In the **falling action**, which forces a resolution, Claudius plots the murder of Hamlet, not once but twice. In the first attempt, Claudius sends Hamlet to England with a letter commanding the receiver to kill the Prince of Denmark:

> And, England, if my love thou hold'st at aught—
> As my great power thereof may give thee sense,
> Since yet thy cicatrice looks raw and red
> After the Danish sword, and thy free awe
> Pays homage to us—thou mayst not coldly set
> Our sovereign process, which imports at full,
> By letters congruing to that effect,
> The present death of Hamlet. Do it, England,
> For like the hectic in my blood he rages,
> And thou must cure me. Till I know 'tis done,
> Howe'er my haps, my joys were ne'er begun. (4.3.58–68)

The last third or quarter of a tragic plot often involves a catastrophe, which sometimes includes the death of the protagonist. In *Hamlet*, the Prince of Denmark dies after killing Claudius. However, many critics use the word *dénouement*, which means "unknotting," to describe this stage of a plot, during which some mystery is solved or some problem is understood or resolved. In many cases, the plot unknots itself.

The plot may also contain one or more **subplots**, plots that are subordinate to the main plot of a drama. In *Hamlet*, for instance, the words and actions of

Laertes and Fortinbras are subplots that are meant to be compared and contrasted with the main plot. See **TRAGEDY**.

POETRY

The word *poetry* derives from the Greek verb *poiein*, meaning "to make." Thus, the poet is a "maker" or creator of verses, rhythms, and images. The origins of poetry are unknown, but many scholars suspect that it grew out of ancient tribal rituals that involved rhythmic chanting or singing. In the modern ages, the word *poetry* has been most familiarly used to distinguish rhythmic or metrical verse from prose (novels, stories, essays, letters, histories, biographies). One obvious distinction is that most poetry looks different on the page than a prose work because it is lineated according to metrical units or units of meaning rather than the paragraph form of prose. Other differences between poetry and prose have to do with the way poetry serves to delight a reader. According to Ezra Pound, a poet can "charge" his verse in three ways: through *phanopoeia* (imagery), *melopoeia* (sound effects), or *logopoeia* (word play). Although prose works may employ any or all of these as well, poetry generally uses them with greater intensity and concision. Works of poetry are often characterized by dense and multilayered figures of speech (**metaphor, simile, metonymy, synecdoche, and personification**). Sound effects employed by poets include **rhythm, meter, rhyme,** and **alliteration**, as well as recurring syntactical schemes (**anaphora, chiasmus, parallelism, antithesis,** and **climax**). *Logopoeia* usually involves plays on words that sound similar or have multiple meanings (**puns**) or words and phrases that have different shades of meaning in different contexts (connotative and denotative meanings, for example). Thus, a poet may seek to delight through imaginative figures, rhythmic and repetitive sounds, or exercise of wit.

Literary historians and scholars have long classified poetry into three general types: **epic, dramatic, lyric**. **Epic** poems, such as Homer's *The Odyssey*, Milton's *Paradise Lost*, and Pound's *The Cantos*, are usually long narrative works that tell the story of a people or the history of an important event. **Dramatic** poetry is most often found in a play, such as Shakespeare's *Hamlet* or *A Midsummer Night's Dream*, where it is spoken by different characters. A **lyric** poem, by contrast to both others, is usually a relatively short poem spoken by a single voice and expressing a particular emotional state or process of thought. Examples include Shakespeare's sonnets, the odes of the English Romantic poets, the poetry of Americans Emily Dickinson, Robert Frost, and Langston Hughes, and most of the contemporary poems currently anthologized.

Historically, poetry in English begins with Anglo-Saxon verse, which is highly alliterative and is marked by a strong **caesura** or rhythmical break in the middle of the line. In the Middle English period, Geoffrey Chaucer perfected the use of iambic pentameter and rhyming couplets in his long narrative poem *The Canterbury Tales*. In the Renaissance in England, the dominant forms are dramatic poetry (e.g., the plays of Shakespeare, Jonson, and Marlowe) and love lyrics (e.g., the shorter poems of Sydney, Campion, Donne, and Herrick). John Milton returned to the epic form in *Paradise Lost* and *Paradise Found*. The English poets of the Restoration (Swift, Pope, Johnson) specialized in satiric verse, often set in heroic couplets marked by witty plays on words and rhetorical schemes. The poetry of the English Romantics (Wordsworth, Coleridge, and Shelley) and Victorians is largely lyric verse, although Robert Browning invented a form later called the **dramatic monologue**. In the twentieth century, poetry in both England and America turned more and more to free verse, which eschews strict metrical, rhythmic, and rhyming patterns. See **DRAMATIC MONO-LOGUE, EPIC, FIGURATIVE LANGUAGE, FREE VERSE, LYRIC, METAPHOR, METER, RHYME, RHYTHM**, and **SONNET**.

POSTCOLONIALISM/POSTCOLONIAL STUDIES AND THEORY

The term *postcolonial* describes a period of time after "imperial" nations have ceased to rule or dominate "subaltern" cultures. Postcolonial studies seek to define and explore the structures and effects of colonial rule; these studies focus primarily on colonies in Africa, Asia, South America, and the Caribbean that were once ruled by European nations. Postcolonial theory is a multi-disciplinary (historical, philosophical, political, and sociological) analysis of the epistemology (way of thinking or means of knowing) that served to justify and sustain imperial subjection of colonies, as well as an attempt to reverse the impe-rial/subaltern power structure.

The book often credited with launching postcolonial theory is Edward Said's *Orientalism* (1978), in which he employs the concept of "cultural imperial-ism" to express the epistemology, the motives, and the practice of colonialism. The phrase "cultural imperialism" generally describes the assumptions of intellec-tual and cultural superiority that characterized imperialist nations and their atti-tudes toward their colonies. In particular, Said theorizes about the assumptions of the Occident (Western peoples) in their dealings with the Orient (Eastern peo-ples). This example of cultural imperialism and others have been clarified for many postcolonial theorists and scholars by the use of the word "subaltern" by Gayatri Chakrovorty Spivak. The roots of the word are *sub* (meaning "inferior") and *alter* meaning "other"). Thus, the word subaltern is suggestive of an attitude of superiority on the part of imperialists toward those inferior "others" (that is, racially different) whom they have colonized.

Postcolonial literature typically portrays the effects of colonial rule on post-colonial cultures and peoples; one of the recurring themes in postcolonial litera-ture is the relegation and/or suppression of "native" languages. For instance, in Chinua Achebe's novel *Things Fall Apart* (1958), there is a cultural clash in the second half of the novel between a lower Nigerian tribe to which the protago-nist, Okonkwo, has retreated and a group of Christian missionaries from

England. The missionaries manage to convert some of the outcasts and low-standing members of the clan of Mbanta by teaching them to read and write, as well as by attacking the logic of the tribal laws and taboos that have determined their status and plights. In doing so, the Christians, with their sovereign deity and sacred written text, manage to overwhelm for some, including Okonkwo's son, a culture based on the unwritten history of the clan, with which the stories and legends of their oral language are inextricably entwined. There is a second way in which the question of language is foregrounded in the novel: namely, in the prevalent use of Igbo words in the narration as a way of suggesting that English is insufficiently subtle or complex to convey the intricacies of tribal language and culture. Both uses of language, as a theme and a cultural artifact, serve to undercut the assumptions of W. B. Yeats's "The Second Coming" (1921), from which the novel takes its title. Unlike the poem by Yeats, which envisions the end of an enlightened Christian era and the beginning of savage anarchy, Achebe's novel suggests that Christians and Christianity are the anarchic agents that serve to undercut, if not obliterate, a long-standing culture based on kinship.

Another work of postcolonial literature that explicitly alludes to the Western canon is Derek Walcott's play *Pantomime* (1978). Set in the West Indies, the play has only two main characters: Harry Trewe, the English proprietor of a guest house, and Jackson Phillip, a kind of subordinate or servant from Trinidad. Harry has come up with an idea to attract guests to his small hotel; he has been rehearsing a kind of vaudeville dinner show, loosely based on Daniel Defoe's novel about an English castaway, *Robinson Crusoe* (1719). Although Harry assumes that he will play the role of Crusoe and Jackson the role of Friday, the cannibal whom Crusoe teaches to speak English, Jackson suggests a role reversal. The result is a kind of rewriting not only of Defoe's novel but also of the history of colonialism. In one scene, Jackson, in his role as cultural imperialist, begins to teach Harry, the subaltern, in the best tradition of Robinson Crusoe: by giving names to various objects in view. However, instead of naming the objects in English, Jackson uses a factitious quasi-African tongue. Thus, if only in microcosm, the power structure and authority of colonialism are subverted and transposed.

Other notable examples of postcolonial literature include *Wide Sargasso Sea* (1966) by Jean Rhys, in which the life of Bertha Rochester, a character in Charlotte Bronte's *Jane Eyre* (1847), is told as a kind of prequel, and the works of Gabriel García Márquez, V. S. Naipaul, and Salman Rushdie.

POSTMODERNISM

Postmodernism is a term offered by some literary historians to refer to the period from the mid 1970s to the present. Although it was originally employed to designate styles of post-World War II architecture, the word *postmodernism* is now widely used to define contemporary culture and technology, as well as art.

Broadly applied, postmodernism describes an age transformed by information technology, shaped by electronic images, and fascinated by popular culture.

Despite much discussion and debate about whether postmodernism is an extension of modernism or a radical alternative to it, most critics and theorists agree that postmodernist writers seem to favor the modernists' experiments with technique while rejecting their "elitism" or alienation from popular culture. In his essay entitled "Pluralism in Postmodern Perspective" (1986), Ihab Hassan delineates a catena (chain of connected subjects) of postmodern theory and experience. Among them he includes indeterminacy, fragmentation, decanonization, selflessness, the unrepresentable, hybridization, carnivalization, and participation.

In using the term *indeterminacy*, Hassan refers to the growth of relativism, the notion that truth is subject to time, place, and context. By *fragmentation*, he means the inability to understand or appreciate any process, idea, system, or institution as a unified or coherent whole. *Decanonization* suggests the loss of faith in cultural and political authority: the authority of political leaders, scientific experts, secular laws, or the doctrines of religion, to offer but a few examples. *Selflessness* belies the notion that an individual exists in a way that is knowable and stable: what one thinks about one's self is an illusion or misunderstanding that one believes in order to avoid fears of nothingness and chaos. The concept of *the unrepresentable* extends the modernist notion that the mysteries of life cannot be described or named but only suggested; in postmodern theory such mysteries as the presence of God or a natural order are treated as hopeless and hilarious fictions. *Hybridization* refers to the tendency of postmodern writings to violate the notion of discrete genres. Postmodern texts reject the notion of boundaries between high culture and popular culture: Shakespeare's tragedies may be linked and studied with televison situation comedies without any questions of appropriateness, taste, or qualitative judgment. *Carnivalization* suggests the postmodern tendency to revel in absurdity, travesty, grotesquerie, and parody. The need for *participation* in reading postmodern texts, as Hassan points out, is related to the indeterminacy of the text:

> Indeterminacy elicits participation; gaps must be filled. The postmodern text, verbal or nonverbal, invites performance: it wants to be written, revised, answered, acted out. . . . At its best, as Richard Poirier contends, the performing self expresses "an energy in motion, an energy with its own shape"; yet in its "self-discovering, self-watching, finally self-pleasuring response to . . . pressures and difficulties," that self may also veer toward solipcism, lapse into narcissism.

In other words, in participating in or performing them, one may tend to revise postmodern texts into mere reflections of one's own needs or concerns.

Thomas Pynchon's *The Crying of Lot 49* (1966) is a work of prose fiction that embodies many of these postmodern qualities. In one episode of the novel, the protagonist, Oedipa Maas, a beautiful young woman whose recently deceased lover, Peirce Inverarity, has left her an enormous estate to manage, meets with Inverarity's lawyer, Metzger, who was formerly a child film star working under the name of Baby Igor. During the course of their meeting in

Oedipa's motel room, the two of them notice that one of Baby Igor's films, in which he plays a boy who accompanies his father on military missions in a miniature submarine, is showing on television.

> Oedipa refilled her wine glass. They lay now, staring at the screen, flanks just lightly touching. There came from the TV set a terrific explosion. "Mines!" cried Metzger, covering his head and rolling away from her. "Daddy," blubbered Metzger in the tube, "I'm scared." The inside of the midget sub was chaotic, the dog galloping to and fro scattering saliva that mingled with the spray from a leak in the bulkhead, which the father was now plugging with his shirt. "One thing we can do," announced the father, "go to the bottom, try to get under the net."
>
> "Ridiculous," said Metzger. "They'd built a gate in it, so German U-boats could get through to attack the British fleet. All our E class subs simply used that gate."
>
> "How do you know that?"
>
> "Wasn't I there?"
>
> "But," began Oedipa, then saw how they were suddenly out of wine.

In particular, this passage offers examples of indeterminacy and selflessness in the ambiguity between Metzger the character in the novel and Metzger/Baby Igor the character in the film; so much so that Metzger the character in the novel not only reacts to the faked explosion in the film but also insists on his personal knowledge of the tactics in the real war that the film fictionally depicts. This indeterminacy suggests a confusion between reality and "reelity," between natural existence and existence in film or fiction, which raises the question of whether or not all notions of existence are merely types of fictions. The hybridization of genres is manifest in Pynchon's parody of a B-movie war film within a scene that parodies a popular fiction depiction of a one-night stand in a motel. The confusion of roles and selves continues as Metzger explains the similarities between lawyers and actors:

> "A cash nexus," brooded Oedipa, "you and Perry Mason, two of a kind, it's all you know about, you shysters."
>
> "But our beauty lies," explained Metzger, "in this extended capacity for convolution. A lawyer in a courtroom, in front of any jury, becomes an actor, right? Raymond Burr is an actor, impersonating a lawyer, who in front of a jury becomes an actor. Me, I'm a former actor who became a lawyer. They've done the pilot film of a TV series, in fact, based loosely on my career, starring my friend Manny Di Presso, a one-time lawyer who quit his firm to become an actor. Who in this pilot plays me, an actor become a lawyer reverting periodically to being an actor. The film is in an air-conditioned vault at one of the Hollywood studios, light can't fatigue it; it can be repeated endlessly."

All of this is offered in the spirit of carnivalization; the text itself revels in the absurdity of the endless repetition of personas playing the roles of personas who play the roles of personas, and so on.

Examples of postmodern films include *The Terminator* (James Cameron, 1984), *Blade Runner* (Ridley Scott, 1982), *Natural Born Killers* (Oliver Stone, 1995), and *Fargo* (Joel Coen, 1996). See **MODERNISM** and **PARODY**.

PROTAGONIST

The term *protagonist* is commonly used to refer to the hero or heroine in a story, poem, novel, play, or film. However, the word derives from the Greek *protagonistes*, meaning "the first actor"; a protagonist may be the main character without proving to be a hero or a heroine. Protagonist also contains the root word *agon*, which means "contest." At the most basic level, works of literature often involve a contest between protagonist and antagonist.

In many cases, the protagonist is best described as the character around whom the plot is centered. The narrator of F. Scott Fitzgerald's *The Great Gatsby* (1925), for instance, goes to great lengths to identify Jay Gatsby as the protagonist of the novel, even though he is not a classic hero:

> Only Gatsby, the man who gives his name to this book, was exempt from my reaction—Gatsby, who represented everything for which I have an unaffected scorn. If personality is an unbroken series of successful gestures, then there was something gorgeous about him, some heightened sensitivity to the promises of life, as if he were related to one of those intricate machines that register earthquakes ten thousand miles away. This responsiveness had nothing to do with that flabby impressionability which is dignified under the name of "creative temperament"—it was an extraordinary gift for hope, a romantic readiness such as I have never found in any other person and which it is not likely I shall ever find again. No—Gatsby turned out all right at the end. . . .

The narrator explains that, despite his imperfections, Gatsby is worthy of attention and consideration because of his unique personality and "gift for hope." The rest of the novel serves in part to justify Gatsby's status as protagonist: he "turned out all right at the end."

Kate Chopin's *The Awakening* (1899) offers an example of a protagonist introduced by a third-person narrator:

> Edna Pontellier could not have told why, wishing to go to the beach with Robert, she should in the first place have declined, and in the second place have followed in obedience to one of the two contradictory impulses which impelled her.
>
> A certain light was beginning to dawn dimly within her,—the light which, showing the way, forbids it.
>
> At that early period it served but to bewilder her. It moved her to dreams, to thoughtfulness, to the shadowy anguish which had overcome her the midnight when she had abandoned herself to tears.

In short, Mrs. Pontellier was beginning to realize her position in the universe as a human being, and to recognize her relations as an individual to the world within and about her.

The attention that the narrator gives to Mrs. Pontellier's thoughts and feelings, as well as the suggestion of moving beyond the "early period" of her life, helps one to identify her as the protagonist of the novel. In this case, the *agon*, or contest, takes place, at least in part, between "the two contradictory impulses which impelled her." See **ANTAGONIST**.

PSYCHOANALYTIC THEORY AND CRITICISM

The term *psychoanalytic criticism* is used to describe the application of psychoanalytic theory to the interpretation of a text. The most influential psychoanalytic theories in literary criticism have been those propounded by Sigmund Freud, Carl Jung, Jacques Lacan, and their disciples.

Freudian Theory

Freudian theories are based on the notion that the motivations for human behavior arise from the unconscious mind more than conscious and rational thought. In his writings and lectures, Freud describes three psychic zones: the **id**, the **ego**, and the **superego**. He associates the id with "the pleasure principle," since this part of the human psyche is devoted to satisfying primal desires. The id is largely unconscious, completely amoral, predominantly irrational, and often self-destructive. However, Freud also thinks of the id as the source of creativity and vital energy. The ego, by contrast, is associated with "the reality principle," since this zone of the psyche comprises most of the conscious mind and operates upon the dictates of reason. Freud characterizes the ego as a regulating agent of the id and as a mediator between the conscious and the unconscious. The superego is associated with "the morality principle" and that which we commonly think of as conscience. Although it is predominantly unconscious, the superego also serves to regulate the desires of the id.

According to Freud, in normal psychic development the more dangerous or socially unacceptable urges of the id are censored and repressed by the ego and superego. Repression involves a kind of unconscious for getting or avoidance of primitive and infantile desires. Perhaps the most familiar example is described by Freud as the **Oedipus complex**, which in the classic instance involves the desire of a male child to obtain the exclusive love of his mother by killing his father. Although these unacceptable desires are repressed, they sometimes manage to express themselves through dreams or fantasies, both of which Freud associates with literature. Freud's experience suggested to him that these repressed feelings or urges are presented through symbols and displacements that disguise the objects of desire in forms that are more acceptable and less threatening. These symbols manage to elude the censorship of the ego and the superego; thus, they provide clues or signs at the conscious level of unconscious desires.

Freudian psychoanalytic criticism originated with Freud himself, who wrote books and essays on works such as Shakespeare's *Hamlet* and the novels of Fyodor Dostoevsky. Following his example, Freudian critics have offered psychoanalytical readings of literary works. Some attempt to psychoanalyze the author's unconscious revelations; others psychoanalyze the responses of readers; and still others psychoanalyze the work and its characters. Perhaps the most basic procedure of the last type of reading is to look for symbols and complexes that express psychological states or repressions. In Guy de Maupassant's story "In the Moonlight" (1884), for instance, the protagonist is a middle-aged priest who reveals his repressed sexuality when he learns that his favorite niece is engaged to be married:

> All day long he remained silent, swollen with anger and with rage. To his priestly zeal against the mighty power of love was added the moral indignation of a father, of a teacher, of a keeper of souls, who has been deceived, robbed, played with by a child. He felt the egotistical sorrow that parents feel when their daughter announces that she has chosen a husband without them and in spite of their advice.
>
> After his dinner he tried to read a little, but he could not attune himself to it and he grew angrier and angrier. When it struck ten he took his cane, a formidable oaken club which he always carried when he had to go out at night to visit the sick. Smilingly he regarded the enormous cudgel, holding it in his solid, countryman's fist and cutting threatening circles with it in the air. Then suddenly he raised it and, grinding his teeth, he brought it down upon a chair, the back of which, split in two, fell heavily to the ground.

The sexual nature of his reaction is suggested not only by the phrase "swollen with anger" but also by "the enormous cudgel," an obvious phallic symbol (representation of the male sexual organ), with which he vents his rage. In other words, the priest's repressed sexual feelings present themselves in symbolic ways that are permitted by the censoring zones of the ego and superego.

Jungian Theory

The Swiss psychoanalyst Carl Jung, one of Freud's most gifted students, expanded his teacher's idea of the individual unconscious to a notion of a "collective unconscious." According to Jung, all peoples in all cultures possess and respond to inherited images and mythic processes generally described as archetypes. Jung also propounded a theory of the process of psychic individuation, by which men and women may achieve a healthy psychological maturity. The three archetypes involved in this process are the persona, the anima, and the shadow. The persona is the side of our personality that we present to the world; the shadow is our secret self, whose desires we seek to hide; the anima is a kind of mediator between the persona and the shadow. In Jung's theory, psychic individuation may be achieved only when the persona, with the aid of the anima, confronts and accepts the presence of the shadow. The Biblical story of man's fall from grace, for all its tragic implications, may be understood from a Jungian perspective as a mythic rendering of the process of individuation. Adam represents the persona, the seemingly perfect and obedient creature of God who, through the mediation of the anima, Eve, confronts the shadow, Satan, and recognizes his desire to partake of the tree of knowledge of good and evil. Indeed, considered as an archetypal structure, the story personifies the need to recognize and accept both the admirable and sordid sides of one's psychic makeup. Failure to do so results in a kind of neurosis, in which one projects onto others one's own capacity for good or evil.

Lacanian Theory

The French psychoanalyst Jacques Lacan re-examines Freud's theories through the prism of language. According to Lacan, the stages of a child's psychological development are threefold. In the imaginary stage, the child experiences a sense of wholeness and unity, as typified by the satisfaction of all his needs by the mother, that is shattered through his recognition of individuality and separateness in the mirror stage. Lacan employs the plausible scene of a child observing its image in a mirror to express the idea of his first recognition of "the other." The image the child sees, while ostensibly himself, is not identical to himself, and thus the child experiences for the first time the fragmentation of the human condition. Indeed, through this glimpse of "the other," the child begins to become aware of his separation from everyone and everything. The third stage, which Lacan calls the symbolic, is associated with the acquisition of language. In the imaginary stage, the child has no need of formal language since his needs are satisfied without his asking and because he has no awareness of otherness. After undergoing the mirror stage, the child is forced to enter the symbolic world of language by Oedipal conflict, for which Lacan uses the French phrase "le nom/non du père," meaning both the name of the father and the no of the father. This phrase suggests how the father's coming between the child and his mother forces the child to recognize separation and to employ language to distinguish between itself and others. The child uses language to name those objects .and people that were once part of himself and wholly unified. Since they are no longer a part of him (or he of them), he knows them only symbolically, through the symbols of language.

Since Lacan associates the symbolic sphere of language with the father, some of the feminists who have been influenced by his work have theorized that the pre-Oedipal imaginary is a feminine alternative to the patriarchal world of language. Feminist Julia Kristeva has called this pre-symbolic state the "semiotic register"; moreover, she has theorized that it may suggest an alternative way of knowing and communicating known to mothers and children before the introduction of language. See **ARCHETYPE**, **FEMINIST CRITICISM**, and **OEDIPUS/ELECTRA COMPLEX**.

PUN

A pun is a play on words that sound the same (or at least similar) but have different meanings. For instance, in Act 1, scene 2, of *Hamlet* (1601), Shakespeare employs two puns in Hamlet's response to Claudius's expression of paternal concern for his grieving nephew/stepson:

KING: . . . But now, my cousin Hamlet, and my son—

HAMLET: [Aside] A little more than kin, and less than kind.

KING: How is it that the clouds still hang on you?

HAMLET: Not so, my lord; I am too much in the sun.

In his aside, Hamlet plays on the differences between *kin* (blood relations) and *kind* (sympathetic): Claudius has become more than an uncle, but he is, in reality, less than sympathetic to Hamlet's feelings. Hamlet's reply to Claudius's question plays on the words *sun/son*. Hamlet sees too clearly what has happened, and he understands the situation differently because he is the actual son of the dead king and the nominal son of the new king, Claudius. In other words, he is saying that he is too much the son as son-in-law.

While puns may be used to make the reader aware of serious or painfully ironic truths, they may also be employed purely for the sake of wit. The chapter of Lewis Carroll's *Alice's Adventures in Wonderland* (1865) entitled "The Mock Turtle's Story" offers a number of silly but amusing puns. The following dialogue occurs as Alice and the Mock Turtle are comparing the curricula at their respective schools:

"I couldn't afford to learn it," said the Mock Turtle, with a sigh. "I only took the regular course."

"What was that?" inquired Alice.

"Reeling and Writhing, of course, to begin with," the Mock Turtle replied; "and then the different branches of Arithmetic—Ambition, Distraction, Uglification, and Derision. . . ."

Alice did not feel encouraged to ask any more questions about it: so she turned to the Mock Turtle, and said, "What else had you to learn?"

"Well, there was Mystery," the Mock Turtle replied, counting off the subjects on his flappers,—"Mystery, ancient and modern, with Seaography: then Drawling—the Drawling-master was an old conger-eel, that used to come once a week: he taught us Drawling, Stretching, and Fainting in Coils."

"What was that like?" said Alice.

"Well I can't show it you, myself," the Mock Turtle said: "I'm too stiff. And the Gryphon never learnt it."

"Hadn't time," said the Gryphon: "I went to the Classical master, though. He was an old crab, he was."

"I never went to him," the Mock Turtle said with a sigh. "He taught Laughing and Grief, they used to say. . . ."

"And how many hours a day did you do lessons?" said Alice, in a hurry to change the subject.

"Ten hours the first day," said the Mock Turtle: "nine the next, and so on."

"What a curious plan!" exclaimed Alice.

"That's the reason they're called lessons," the Gryphon remarked: "because they lessen from day to day."

Some of the puns in this passage are similar in sound: Reeling and Writhing for Reading and Writing; Laughing and Grief for Latin and Greek; Drawling and Stretching for Drawing and Sketching. Others are delightfully absurd plays: Uglification for Multiplication; Fainting in Coils for Painting in Oils. The only perfect puns are those of lesson/ lessen and crab (crustacean/grouch).

Q

QUATRAIN

A quatrain is a four-line stanza of poetry. Several types of quatrains may be distinguished by their line lengths and rhyme schemes: **ballad stanzas**, **Heroic quatrains**, and **unrhymed quatrains**, among others.

The **ballad stanza** usually consists of alternating lines of iambic **tetrameter** and iambic **trimeter**, with an *abab* or an *abcb* rhyme scheme. An excerpt from Samuel Taylor Coleridge's "The Rime of the Ancient Mariner" (1798) will serve as an example of the latter rhyme scheme:

> He holds him with his glittering eye—
> The Wedding Guest stood still,
> And listens like a three years' child:
> The Mariner hath his will.
>
> The Wedding Guest sat on a stone:
> He cannot choose but hear;
> And thus spake on that ancient man,
> The bright-eyed Mariner.

Heroic quatrain consists of four lines of iambic **pentameter** with an *abab* rhyme scheme. The opening lines of Thomas Gray's "Elegy Written in a Country Church-Yard" (1751) offer an example:

> The curfew tolls the knell of parting day,
>   The lowing herd wind slowly o'er the lea,
> The plowman homeward plods his weary way,
>   And leaves the world to darkness and to me.
>
> Now fades the glimmering landscape on the sight,
>   And all the air a solemn stillness holds,
> Save where the beetle wheels his droning flight,
>   And drowsy tinklings lull the distant folds;

Unrhymed quatrains include any unrhymed verses that present themselves in four-line stanzas. An excerpt from Imamu Amiri Baraka's "KA 'BA" (1967) offers an example:

> A closed window looks down
> on a dirty courtyard, and black people
> call across or scream across or walk across
> defying physics in the stream of their will.
>
> Our world is full of sound
> Our world is more lovely than anyone's
> tho we suffer, and kill each other
> and sometimes fail to walk the air.

Although he breaks his lines into groups of four, Baraka (also known as LeRoi Jones) eschews the use of rhymes, perhaps because he believes rhyming inappropriate to the subject matter. Many modern and contemporary poets consider rhymed quatrains to be artificial and restrictive. See **BALLAD**, **METER**, and **RHYME**.

QUEER THEORY AND GAY AND LESBIAN STUDIES

Although it has pejorative connotations, some scholars and theorists of gay and lesbian studies have adopted the word *queer* to describe the "otherness" of homosexuality, which has conventionally been considered suspiciously different from the cultural norm of heterosexuality. *Queer theory* is a general term used to delineate a broad range of issues relating to genders, desires, and embodiments that problematize or resist heterocentrism (the presentation of heterosexuality as natural and dominant). As an approach to literature, queer theory refers to a way of reading employed in gay and lesbian studies that explores not only works of literature written by homosexuals but also writings that are in any sense expressive of homosexual desire or repression.

In Western literature, one of the earliest and most famous expressions of homosexual desire is the poetry of Sappho, a Greek lyric poet of the seventh century B.C., who lived on the isle of Lesbos, from which the word *lesbian* derives. Although what remains of Sappho's poetry exists in fragments, the lesbian themes are clear. In one of a series of poems addressed to a girl named Atthis, Sappho writes:

> It was you, Atthis, who said
>
> "Sappho, if you will not get
> up and let us look at you
> I shall never love you again!
>
> "Get up, unleash your suppleness,
> lift off your Chian nightdress
> and, like a lily leaning into
>
> "a spring, bathe in the water.
> Cleis is bringing your best
> purple frock and the yellow

"tunic down from the clothes chest;
you will have a cloak thrown over
you and flowers crowning your hair". . .
                (trans. Mary Barnard)

Other expressions of homosexual desire in literature are less direct. For instance, many scholars of American literature suspect that in the eleventh section of *Song of Myself* Walt Whitman's description of a young woman's thoughts upon seeing young men bathing naked is, at least in part, an expression of the author's desires:

Twenty-eight young men bathe by the shore,
Twenty-eight young men and all so friendly;
Twenty-eight years of womanly life and all so lonesome.

She owns the fine house by the rise of the bank,
She hides handsome and richly drest aft the blinds of the window.

Which of the young men does she like the best?
Ah the homeliest of them is beautiful to her.
Where are you off to, lady? For I see you,
You splash in the water there, yet stay stock still in your room.

Dancing and laughing along the beach came the twenty-ninth bather,
The rest did not see her, but she saw them and loved them.

The beards of the young men glisten'd with wet, it ran from their long hair,
Little streams pass's over their bodies.

An unseen hand also pass'd over their bodies,
It descended tremblingly from their temples and ribs.

The young men float on their backs, their white bellies bulge to the sun,
    they do
    not ask who seizes fast to them.
They do not know who puffs and declines with pendant and bending arch,
They do not think whom they souse with spray.

Other works of interest to gay and lesbian studies include George Etherege's *The Man of Mode* and other Restoration comedies, E. M. Forster's *Maurice*, and the poetry of Langston Hughes, Allen Ginsburg, and Adrienne Rich, many of which are anthologized in *The Lesbian and Gay Studies Reader*, edited by Henry Abelove, Michele Aina Barale, and David Halperin.

Adrienne Rich's *On Lies, Secrets, and Silence* (1979), Annmarie Jagose's *Queer Theory: An Introduction* (1996), Eve Kosofsky Sedgwick's *Between Men: English Literature and Male Homosexual Desire* (1985), Judith Butler's *Bodies that Matter* (1993), and Gregory Woods's *A History of Gay Literature: The Male Tradition* (1998) are among the growing number of critical works relating to queer theory and gay and lesbian studies. Eve Kosofsky Sedgwick's *Epistemology of the Closet* (1990), for example, examines the ways in which homosexuality is figured in Herman Melville's *Billy Budd*, Oscar Wilde's *The Picture of Dorian Gray*, and Henry James's "The Beast in the Jungle." See **DECONSTRUCTION**.

R

READER-RESPONSE CRITICISM

Reader-response is a term employed to describe a wide variety of attempts to discover the effects of literature on readers. Long-standing questions about the roles and the competence of readers in the process of interpreting literature came to a head in the early 1970s when Stanley Fish, one of the proponents of reader-response theory, challenged the authority of one of the principal doctrines of **New Criticism**: namely, the "**affective fallacy**," which dismisses the notion that literature may be judged on the basis of its emotional effects on a reader and implies that interpretation should be left to those who are competent readers. Fish challenges both notions by suggesting that all readings are in some sense misreadings and that to focus on the text alone, thereby ignoring the roles of readers, is to misunderstand the process of reading.

In his book entitled *Is There a Text in This Class?* (1980), Fish alludes to a passage from Milton's "L'Allegro" (1645):

> And, if I give thee honour due,
> Mirth, admit me of thy crew,
> To live with her, and live with thee
> In unreproved pleasures free;
> To hear the lark begin his flight,
> And, singing, startle the dull night,
> From his watch-tower in the skies,
> Till the dappled dawn doth rise;
> Then to come, in spite of sorrow,
> And at my window bid good morrow,
> Through the sweet-briar or the vine,
> Or the twisted eglantine. . . .

Fish quotes a series of letters written in 1934 to the *Times Literary Supplement*, all of which seek to explain who or what the speaker in the poem implies when he wishes "to come, in spite of sorrow, / And at my window bid good morrow." In the course of several weeks, subscribers to the *Supplement* offered cases for "Mirth," the "lark," the "dappled dawn," and even the speaker himself. One of Fish's principal implications in reporting this controversy is that not all ambiguities of reading can be or need be resolved by an authoritarian critic. Indeed, Fish, as a postmodernist, welcomes the very insolubility of the question:

> Rosamund Tuve has written that the pleasures enumerated in "L'Allegro" all have "the flat absence of any relation to responsibility which we sometimes call innocence." What I am suggesting is that the experience of reading the poem is itself such a pleasure, involving just that absence; for at no point are we held responsible for an action or an image beyond the moment of its fleeting appearance in a line or a couplet.

In addition to problematizing the authority of critical interpretations, Fish questions the notion of the reader as an individual subject. In response, he proposes the concept of "interpretive communities": that is to say, readers make texts meaningful according to the reading strategies they have been influenced to use by formal education and other processes of socialization. Thus, meaning becomes a product of the cultural context of an interpretive community as much as the text itself. In a similar vein, Norman Holland has examined the psychological context of reader-response, and Jane Tompkins has explored the gender context of interpretive communities. See **AFFECTIVE FALLACY, INTERPRETATION/MEANING, NEW CRITICISM/FORMALISM,** and **POSTMODERNISM.**

REALISM

Literary critics employ the term *realism* to describe an approach to literature that seeks to represent human experience as realistically and truthfully as possible. For literary historians, realism may be understood in part as a reaction by English, French, and American novelists in the second half of the nineteenth century against the romanticism and sentimentality that flourished in the novels of the first half of that century.

In his "Preface to *The American*" (1909), Henry James distinguishes between realistic and romantic approaches to literature:

> The real represents to my perception the things we cannot possibly *not* know, sooner or later, in one way or another. . . . The romantic stands, on the other hand, for the things that, with all the facilities in the world, all the wealth and all the courage and all the wit and all the adventure, we never *can* directly know; things that can reach us only through the beautiful circuit and subterfuge of our thought and our desire.

As James suggests, the novelist committed to realism focuses on that part of existence that humans can know directly, materially, and pragmatically. Later in the same preface, James goes on to explain the realist's contract with his or her audience: "There is our general sense of the way things happen—it abides with us indefeasibly, as readers of fiction, from the moment we demand that our fiction shall be intelligible; and there is our particular sense of the way they don't happen, which is liable to wake up unless reflexion and criticism, in us, have been skillfully and successfully drugged." Thus, novelists in the realist tradition seek to represent "the ways things happen" by means of **mimesis**: that is, imitation of the actual.

Whereas romantic novels often deal with "the beautiful circuit and subterfuge of our thought and desire," the novels of the realists in the late nineteenth century often focus on the commonplace and the ordinary. In the opening chapter of Book Two of *Adam Bede* (1859), the English novelist George Eliot (Mary Ann Evans) describes this predilection:

> So I am content to tell my simple story, without trying to make things seem better than they were; dreading nothing, indeed, but falsity, which, in spite of one's best efforts, there is reason to dread. . . .
>
> It is for this rare, precious quality of truthfulness that I delight in many Dutch paintings which lofty-minded people despise. I find a delicious sympathy in these faithful pictures of a monotonous homely existence, which has been the fate of so many more among my fellow-mortals than a life of pomp or of absolute indigence, of tragic suffering or of world-stirring actions. I turn, without shrinking, from cloud-borne angels, from prophets, sibyls, and heroic warriors, to an old woman bending over her flower-pot, or eating her solitary dinner, while the noonday light, softened perhaps by a screen of leaves, falls on her mob-cap, and just touches the rim of her spinning-wheel, and her stone jug, and all those cheap common things which are the precious necessities of life to her. . . .

As Eliot's descriptions suggest, the typical (though by no means the exclusive) subjects of the realists are those associated with working-class and middle-class life, rather than those associated with the rich and famous or the poor and oppressed.

Several of the late nineteenth-century realists openly satirized the conventions of romantic and sentimental fiction. Mark Twain, for instance, lampoons the falseness and lack of verisimilitude of sentimental fiction in "The Story of the Bad Little Boy" (1867):

> Once there was a bad little boy whose name was Jim—though, if you will notice, you will find that bad little boys are nearly always called James in your Sunday-school books. It was strange, but still it was true, that this one was called Jim.
>
> He didn't have a sick mother, either—a sick mother who was pious and had the consumption, and would be glad to lie down in the grave and be at rest but for the strong love she bore her boy, and the anxiety she felt that the world might be harsh and cold toward him when she was gone. Most bad boys in the Sunday books are named James, and have

sick mothers, who teach them to say, "Now, I lay me down," etc., and sing them to sleep with sweet plaintive voices, and then kiss them good-night, and kneel down by the bedside and weep. But it was different with this fellow. He was named Jim, and there wasn't anything the matter with his mother—no consumption, nor anything of that kind. She was rather stout than otherwise, and she was not pious; moreover, she was not anxious on Jim's account. She said if he were to break his neck it wouldn't be much loss. She always spanked Jim to sleep, and she never kissed him goodnight; on the contrary, she boxed his ears when she was ready to leave him.

Throughout this passage, Twain deliberately plays on the difference between "the way things happen" in actuality and the idealistic desires represented in sentimental fictions.

In addition to Eliot, James, and Twain, notable realists of the nineteenth century include the American novelist William Dean Howells and the French writer Honoré de Balzac. See **MIMESIS** and **NATURALISM**.

REFRAIN

A refrain consists of the repetition of a line or part of a line, usually at the end of each stanza or section of a poem. Refrains are often used in songs; Shakespeare's song entitled "Winter" from *Love's Labour's Lost* (1595) offers an example:

When icicles hang by the wall,
    And Dick the shepherd blows his nail,
And Tom bears logs into the hall,
    And milk comes frozen home in pail,
When blood is nipped and ways be foul,
Then nightly sings the staring owl,
    "Tu-whit, tu-who!"
A merry note,
While greasy Joan doth keel the pot.

When all aloud the wind doth blow,
    And coughing drowns the parson's saw,
And birds sit brooding in the snow,
    And Marian's nose looks red and raw,
When roasted crabs hiss in the bowl,
Then nightly sings the staring owl,
    "Tu-whit, tu-who!"
A merry note,
While greasy Joan doth keel the pot. (5.2.912-929)

In a song, a refrain often serves as a chorus during which several voices may join in the singing.

In special forms of poetry such as the **villanelle**, refrains are mandatory because the pattern of the poem calls for repetition of lines. Dylan Thomas's "Do not go gentle into that good night" (1952) provides an example:

Do not go gentle into that good night,
Old age should burn and rave at close of day;
Rage, rage against the dying of the light.

Though wise men at their end know dark is right,
Because their words had forked no lightning they
Do not go gentle into that good night.

Good men, the last wave by, crying how bright
Their frail deeds might have danced in a green bay,
Rage, rage against the dying of the light.

Wild men who caught and sang the sun in flight,
And learn, too late, they grieved it on its way
Do not go gentle into that good night.

Grave men, near death, who see with blinding sight
Blind eyes could blaze like meteors and be gay,
Rage, rage against the dying of the light.

And you, my father, there on the sad height,
Curse, bless me now with your fierce tears, I pray.
Do not go gentle into that good night.
Rage, rage against the dying of the light.

In this villanelle, line 1 is repeated in its entirety in lines 6, 12, and 18; likewise, line 3 is repeated fully in lines 9, 15, and 19. In all, eight of the nineteen lines belong to the refrains, making the poem hauntingly repetitive.

Refrains are also common in work songs; Langston Hughes's "ShareCroppers" (1942) offers an example:

Just a herd of Negroes
Driven to the field,
Plowing, planting, hoeing,
To make the cotton yield.

When the cotton's picked
And the work is done
Boss man takes the money
And we get none,

Leaves us hungry, ragged
As we were before
Year by year goes by
And we are nothing more

Than a herd of Negroes
Driven to the field—
Plowing life away
To make the cotton yield.

In the nineteenth century, songs such as this were sung by Negro slaves, as well as railroad and mine workers; the refrains often served the purpose of timing repetitive tasks or movements. See **CHORUS**.

RENAISSANCE PERIOD (IN ENGLISH LITERATURE)

The term *renaissance* is French for "rebirth" and refers to the period distinguishing the change from the medieval to the modern in European history. The Renaissance or early modern period encompasses several shorter periods including the early Tudor age, the Elizabethan age, the Jacobean age, and the Caroline and Commonwealth periods. The early Tudor age (1500-1557) is characterized by the rediscovery of classical literature and ideas and the reformation of the English Church. Writers from this period include poets Sir Thomas Wyatt and Henry Howard, Earl of Surrey, and prose writer Sir Thomas More. The Elizabethan age encompasses the reign of Elizabeth I (1558-1600). Major developments took place in English commerce and naval power, and nationalism surged, especially after the defeat of the Spanish Armada in 1588. The age encompasses such writers as Sir Philip Sidney, Edmund Spenser, Christopher Marlowe, William Shakespeare, and Ben Jonson. A representative work from the period is Shakespeare's *Richard III* (1597). In Act I, scene I, Richard, Duke of Gloucester, enters alone:

> Now is the winter of our discontent
> Made glorious summer by this sun of York;
> And all the clouds low'r'd upon our house
> In the deep bosom of the ocean buried.
> Now are our brows bound with victorious wreaths,
> Our bruised arms hung up for monuments,
> Our stern alarums chang'd to merry meetings,
> Our dreadful marches to delightful measures.
> Grim-visag'd War hath smooth'd his wrinkled front;
> And now, in stead of mounting barbed steeds
> To fright the souls of fearful adversaries,
> He capers nimbly in a lady's chamber
> To the lascivious pleasing of a lute.

Richard laments the peace and pleasure of the present age and determines to cause trouble in the kingdom. The play is set during the War of the Roses in the fourteenth century but also reflects on the violent struggle for the monarchy during the Renaissance period. The blank verse (unrhymed iambic pentameter) of Shakespeare's works conveys a conversational tone as Richard speaks to the audience. Anaphora (the repetition of the same phrase) gives the rhythmic effect of chanting in the speech. Through this speech, Shakespeare reveals Richard's character: he is a man of intelligence, imagination, and sardonic wit. The passage begins with seasonal metaphors, which convey correspondences between natural processes and human affairs, then shifts to an altering personification of "War" that is wittily conveyed both by diction and consonance. That Richard loathes the change from "dreadful marches to delightful measures" becomes clear as he describes "Grim-visag'd War" capering "to the lascivious pleasing of a lute."

The Jacobean Age covers the reign of James I (1603-1625) and includes the writings of John Donne, the King James translation of the Bible, Shakespeare's great tragedies, and the revenge tragedies of George Chapman and John Webster. The Caroline period refers to the reign of Charles I (1625-1649) and the time of the English Civil War. Supporters of the king (Cavaliers) battled with supporters of Parliament (Roundheads). Writers of this time include the Cavalier poets (Robert Herrick, Richard Lovelace, and John Suckling) and Richard Burton. The Civil War culminated with the beheading of Charles I in 1649, and Parliament then ruled England under the Puritan leader Oliver Cromwell, who died in 1658. The Puritan Interregnum or Commonwealth period extends from the death of Charles I to the restoration of Charles II in 1660. During the Commonwealth period, theaters were closed by the Puritans for moral and religious reasons, and drama disappeared temporarily. Major writers during the Commonwealth period include the metaphysical poets Andrew Marvell, Henry Vaughan, and Abraham Cowley and prose writers Thomas Hobbes and Jeremy Taylor.

Marvell's "An Horatian Ode Upon Cromwell's Return from Ireland" (1650) is a representative work of the Puritan Interregnum:

> The forward youth that would appear
> Must now forsake his muses dear,
> Nor in the shadows sing
> His numbers languishing.
> 'Tis time to leave the books in dust,
> And oil the unused armour's rust;
> Removing from the wall
> The corslet of the hall.
> So restless Cromwell could not cease
> In the inglorious arts of peace.

In this ode, Marvell offers a panegyric about Cromwell, but his tone is at times tentative and even skeptical about the new ruler. Marvell's skepticism is evident in the ambiguity of some of his expressions: the term *forward* means ambitious, but it can also refer to presumptuous or aggressive behavior. See **AMBIGUITY**, **ODE**.

RESTORATION PERIOD (IN ENGLISH LITERATURE)

The Restoration period extends from 1660 until 1700. The name of the period derives from the restoration of the Stuart line of the English monarchy. It encompasses the reign of Charles II (1660-1685), the Glorious Revolution of

1688, and the reign of the Protestant monarchs William and Mary of Orange (1688-1702). Neoclassicism began to predominate, especially in the work of John Dryden. Neoclassicist authors, such as Dryden, espoused the qualities associated with ancient Greek and Roman cultures, namely balance, reason, unity, and clarity. Other major writers of the period include John Milton, whose **epic** poem *Paradise Lost* was published in 1667, and John Bunyan, whose moral **allegory** *The Pilgrim's Progress*, was published between 1678 and 1684. In drama, the period is characterized by a major backlash against the austerity and gravity of the Commonwealth period. The theaters were revitalized after being banned during the Puritan Interregnum. Drama flourished, especially the **comedy of manners**. Major playwrights include William Congreve, Aphra Behn, George Etherege, and William Wycherly. Many plays depicted the wit, bawdiness, cynicism, and amorality of life in the court in London. Some contemporary commentators vilified the Restoration playwrights for their immorality, but others viewed them as serious social critics. A passage from Wycherly's *The Country Wife* (1675) exemplifies both the bawdiness of the play and its satirical qualities:

SQUEAMISH: Do not approach us!

  DAINTY: You herd with the wits, you are obscenity all over!

SQUEAMISH: And I would as soon look upon a picture of Adam and Eve, without fig leaves, as any of you, if I could help it, therefore keep off, and do not make us sick. (Act 2, scene 1, (2.1.432-436))

Mrs. Squeamish and Mrs. Dainty pretend to be prudish and honorable in their morals but prove to be lecherous and dishonorable in the course of the play. The drama uses irony and word play to expose the hypocrisy and falsity of high society.

In *The Rover* (1677), Aphra Behn satirizes marriages arranged for monetary gain or social status and shows an ideal union between the witty Hellena and the roving gallant Willmore. After Willmore proposes to his beloved, Hellena jokingly requests his name:

WILLMORE: I am called Robert the Constant.

  HELLENA: A very fine name! Pray, was it your faulkner [keeper of hawks] or butler that christened you? Do they not use to whistle when they call you?

WILLMORE: I hope you have a better, that a man may name without crossing himself—you are so merry with mine.

  HELLENA: I am called Hellena the Inconstant.

The couple exchanges ironic repartees: Willmore has a roving eye for women and has until now proven inconstant, whereas Hellena's love for Willmore has always been constant. The wit and teasing humor of the like-minded couple bode well for a marriage. See **ALLEGORY, CLASSICISM, COMEDY OF MANNERS**, and **EPIC**.

RHETORIC/RHETORICAL SCHEMES

The word *rhetoric* may be used to designate both the art of persuasive speaking and the science of composition. As Edward P. f. Corbett explains in his *Classical Rhetoric for the Modern Student* (1965), for the ancients, rhetoric was a matter of oral persuasion. The *Rhetoric* of Aristotle (384-322 B.C.) offers a response to the objections of Plato (c. 428-348 B.C.), who argues that a speaker's rhetoric is admirable only so far as it is an expression of truth. Aristotle's *Rhetoric* focuses on ways of inventing arguments that seek to discover the truth and appeal to reason, emotion, and ethics. Thus, for Aristotle, the rhetorician must employ logical arguments, recognize the nature of his or her audience, and maintain an ethical stance.

The works of the Latin scholar Cicero (106-43 B.C.) insist that the orator must possess great and wide learning, as well as a talent for invention and persuasion. Drawing on the work of Cicero, Quintilian (c. 35-100 A.D.) designated rhetoric as having five elements: *inventio, dispositio, elocutio, memoria,* and *pronuntiatio. Inventio* is a Latin word for *invention.* In preparing an oration or a persuasive essay, the speaker or writer must search for suitable arguments that appeal to an audience ethically, emotionally, and/or logically. *Dispositio* is Latin for *arrangement.* For an argument to be persuasive, it must be organized effectively. In the classic tradition, the orator begins with an introduction of theme or thesis; moves on to exposition or narrative, which serves to explain the particular instance or case in question; provides an overview of the main points; argues for one side of the question or issue; and then refutes the other side of the argument. *Elocutio* is a Latin word for *style:* matters of diction (word choice) and syntax (word order). *Memoria* is Latin for *memory.* In the ancient world, speeches were memorized. Since we have managed over time to develop technology that stores information, memorization has seemingly become less necessary, although it is still useful. *Pronuntiatio* is the Latin word for *delivery:* the use of voice and gestures in speech; the management of tone in writing.

Rhetorical schemes may be employed as stylistic means to express or enhance persuasive arguments. Some of the basic schemes of construction are parallelism, antithesis, anaphora, chiasmus, and climax.

Parallelism

Parallelism is a means of arranging a series of related words, phrases, or clauses. A passage from Franklin D. Roosevelt's second inaugural address (1937) demonstrates the parallel arrangement of words: "I see one-third of a nation ill-housed, ill-clad, ill-nourished." As this example manifests, parallelism is an effective means of creating emphasis through similarity. An excerpt from Abraham Lincoln's second inaugural address (1865) offers an example of parallel phrases:

> With malice toward none; with charity for all; with firmness in the
> right, as God gives us to see the right, let us strive on to finish the work
> we are in: to bind up the nation's wounds, to care for him who shall

have borne the battle, and for his widow and his orphan, to do all
which may achieve and cherish a just and lasting peace among ourselves,
and with all nations.

Both the phrases "With malice . . . with charity . . . with firmness . . ." and "to
bind . . . to care . . . to do . . ." are parallel syntactically and grammatically. In
one of his speeches, Winston Churchill describes a political opponent as

> one of those orators of whom it was well said, "Before they get up, they
> do not know what they are going to say; when they are speaking,
> they do not know what they are saying; and when they have sat down,
> they do not know what they have said." (1912)

This excerpt offers an example of parallel (complex) sentences.

Antithesis

Antithesis is the juxtaposition of phrases, clauses, or sentences with other similarly structured sentences or parts of sentences to which they are opposed in content or meaning. The term derives from a Greek construction meaning "set in
opposition." In a 1962 edition of the *New York Journal-American*, Martin Luther
King was quoted as saying, "I want to be the white man's brother, not his
brother-in-law." The structure of the two subject complements "the white
man's brother, not his brother-in-law" is similar, but the second complement is
set in opposition to the first. A passage from Mary Wollstonecraft's *A Vindication
of the Rights of Woman* (1792) provides an example of a series of complex sentences constructed on the principle of antithesis:

> One cause of this barren blooming I attribute to a false system of edu-
> cation, gathered from the books written on this subject by men who,
> considering females rather as women than human creatures, have been
> more anxious to make them alluring mistresses than affectionate wives
> and rational mothers; and the understanding of the sex has been so
> bubbled by this specious homage, that the civilized women of the
> present century, with a few exceptions, are only anxious to inspire love,
> when they ought to cherish a nobler ambition, and by their abilities and
> virtues exact respect.

Wollstonecraft employs antithesis to contrast the lower ambitions pursued by most
women of her age with "a nobler ambition" enabling them to "exact respect."

Anaphora

Anaphora is a scheme of repetition in which the same word or group of words is
used to begin successive clauses or sentences. Walt Whitman employs anaphora in
his poetry to achieve the rhythmic effect of chanting or singing in a free verse poem.
The following passage from "Song of Myself" (1855) offers a number of examples:

> I think I could turn and live with animals, they are so placid and self-
>   contained,

I stand and look at them long and long.
They do not sweat and whine about their condition,
They do not lie awake in the dark and weep for their sins.
They do not make me sick discussing their duty to God,
Not one is dissatisfied, not one is demented with the mania of owning
    things,
Not one kneels to another, nor to his kind that lived thousands of years ago,
Not one is respectable or unhappy over the whole earth.

This same scheme of repetition is picked up by Anne Sexton in her poem entitled "In Celebration of My Uterus" (1969):

Sweet weight,
in celebration of the woman I am
let me carry a ten-foot scarf,
let me drum for the nineteen-years-olds,
let me carry bowls for the offering
(if that is my part)
Let me study the cardiovascular tissue,
let me examine the angular distance of meteors,
let me suck on the stems of flowers
(if that is my part)

Chiasmus

Chiasmus is a rhetorical scheme through which balance is achieved by reversing
the syntax of the first part in the second part. At its simplest, chiasmus takes the
form of a line such as "A wit with dunces and a dunce with wit" from Alexander
Pope's *The Dunciad* (1742). Emily Dickinson employs chiasmus to witty effect in
her poem "Much Madness is divinest Sense" (1890):

Much Madness is divinest Sense—
To a discerning Eye—
Much Sense—the starkest Madness—

Chiasmus is particularly effective in creating irony through the reversal of
accepted truths or familiar ideas.

Climax

Climax is a rhetorical scheme in which words and phrases are arranged to suggest an order of rising importance or magnitude. An excerpt from John F.
Kennedy's "Inaugural Address" (1961) offers an illustration:

All this will not be finished in the first hundred days. Nor will it be
finished in the first thousand days, nor in the life of this administration,
nor even perhaps in our lifetime on this planet. But let us begin.

Climax can be used, as in this example, to great dramatic effect in both writing and speaking.

RHYME

Critics and commentators commonly use the word *rhyme* to identify repetitions of similar sounds that are sustained through two or more lines of verse. One function of rhyme is to help readers respond both aurally and emotionally to the lines. When one sound is already echoing in a reader's consciousness and the poem reinforces that sound with a similar one, readers may derive not only pleasure or displeasure but also a sense of form and coherence, or lack of the same. Not all associated sounds are pleasurable, nor should they be, since poets often attempt to find rhymes that produce sounds or effects capable of eliciting particular emotional and intellectual responses. Rhymes may be recognized in three ways: according to sound, position, or syllable.

Rhyme and Sound

The most familiar type of rhyming is achieved with full rhymes. A **full rhyme** is defined as two or more words that have the same vowel sound followed by the same consonants in their last stressed syllables. The following lines from W. H. Auden's "In Memory of W. B. Yeats" (1940) offer examples:

> In the nightmare of the dark
> All of the dogs of Europe bark,
> And the living nations wait,
> Each sequestered in its hate. . . .

The pairs "dark"/"bark" and "wait"/"hate" have the same vowel sounds followed by the same consonants in the last stressed syllables. Full rhymes such as these tend to confer a sense of closure because of the emphasis they receive when they are spoken aloud.

Approximate rhymes include imperfect (half or slant) rhymes and alliterative rhymes. Imperfect rhymes share similar vowel and consonant sounds. An excerpt from Diane Ackerman's "Sweep Me Through Your Many-Chambered Heart" (1978) provides illustrations of these rhymes:

> Sweep me through your many-chambered heart
> if you like, or leave me here, flushed
> amid the sap-ooze and blossom: one more dish
> in the banquet called April, or think me hard-
> won all your days full of women. . . .

The pairs "heart"/"hard" and "flushed"/"dish" are imperfect because they share similar but not identical terminal consonant sounds. Imperfect rhymes are less appealing to the ear than full rhymes and may be used to suggest uneasiness or dissatisfaction.

Alliterative rhymes have identical initial consonant sounds, but the succeeding sounds may vary. Emily Dickinson's "It was not Death, for I stood up" (1891) offers an example:

> It was not Frost, for on my Flesh
> I felt Siroccos—crawl—
> Nor Fire—for just my Marble feet
> Could keep a Chancel, cool. . . .

The pairs "flesh"/"feet" and "crawl"/"cool" are alliterative rhymes; indeed, Dickinson employs this kind of consonance throughout the stanza: "frost"/ "flesh" and "fire"/"feet."

Identical rhymes occur whenever the entire final stressed syllables produce exactly the same sound. In many cases, this kind of rhyming involves the repetition of the same words. The following lines from T. S. Eliot's "The Love Song of J. Alfred Prufrock" (1917) provide an illustration of identical rhyme:

> There will be time, there will be time
> To prepare a face to meet the faces that you meet. . .

The repetition of "time" and "meet" expresses feelings of ennui and despair.

Rhyme and Position

The two principal classifications of rhymes by position are end rhymes and internal rhymes. **End rhymes** occur when the last words of two lines rhyme, whether the rhymes are full or approximate. The opening lines of Gwendolyn Brooks's "First Fight. Then Fiddle" (1949) are not only full in sound but terminal in position:

> First fight. Then fiddle. Ply the slipping string
> With feathery sorcery; muzzle the note
> With hurting love; the music that they wrote
> Bewitch, bewilder. Qualify to sing . . .

The pairs "string"/"sing" and "note"/"wrote" form full end rhymes.

The other principal type of rhyme according to position is **internal rhyme**. When two or more words in a single line rhyme with each other, whether fully or approximately, the rhyme is internal. Edgar Allan Poe's "The Raven" (1845) is famous for its internal rhyming:

> And the Raven, never flitting, still is sitting, still is sitting
> On the pallid bust of Pallas just above my chamber door;
> And his eyes have all the seeming of a demon's that is dreaming,
> And the lamp-light o'er him streaming throws his shadow on
>   the floor;
> And my soul from out that shadow that lies floating on the floor
>   Shall be lifted—nevermore!

Internal rhymes such as "flitting" and "seeming" rhyme with the end rhymes "sitting" and "dreaming."

Rhyme and Syllable

With **masculine rhymes**, the similarity of sound is found only in the final stressed syllable. The following lines from Derek Walcott's "Europa" (1976) employ masculine rhymes:

> Both would have kept their proper distance still,
> if the chaste moon hadn't swiftly drawn the drapes
> of a dark cloud, coupling their shapes.

The rhyme of "drapes" and "shapes" comes in the final stressed syllable of the words; therefore, this is a masculine rhyme.

Feminine rhymes, by contrast, consist of an accented syllable followed by one or more unaccented syllables. The fourth section of Wallace Stevens's "Peter Quince at the Clavier" (1923) offers a number of illustrations:

> The body dies; the body's beauty lives.
> So evenings die, in their green going,
> A wave, interminably flowing.
> So gardens die, their meek breath scenting
> The cowl of winter, done repenting.
> So maidens die, to auroral
> Celebration of a maiden's choral.

The pairs "going"/"flowing"; "scenting"/"repenting"; and "auroral"/ "choral" are feminine rhymes since the last syllable in each word is unstressed. Feminine rhymes are effective in producing light or tragicomic tones. See **ALLITERATION** and **CONSONANT SOUNDS**.

RHYTHM

In discussing poetry, critics use the word *rhythm* to describe recurring patterns of stress, quantity, and pitch. Of these, rhythms created by patterns of stressed and unstressed syllables are the most easily and commonly understood. The standard units of rhythm in English are **duple** or **two-syllable rhythms**—iambic and trochaic—and **triple** or **three-syllable rhythms**—dactyls and anapests.

The following line from Wallace Stevens's "Peter Quince at the Clavier" (1923) is an example of an iambic rhythm: "The body dies; the body's beauty lives."

```
    u   /   u   /     u   /   u   /    u   /
The bod / y dies; / the bod / y's beaut / y lives.
```

The duple rhythm forms the pattern of an unstressed syllable followed by a stressed syllable. This is, therefore, a **rising rhythm**, since the pattern of emphasis moves from low to high.

The following line from Emily Dickinson's "There's a certain Slant of light" (1890) offers an example of a trochaic rhythm: "None may teach it—Any—."

```
     /     u     /  u     /     u
None may / teach it— / Any—
```

This duple rhythm forms the pattern of a stressed syllable followed by an unstressed syllable. This is, therefore, a **falling rhythm**, since the pattern of emphasis moves from high to low.

The following line from Lord Byron's "The Destruction of Sennacherib" (1815) offers an example of an **anapestic rhythm**: "With the dew on his brow, and the rust on his mail."

```
 u   u   /    u   u   /      u   u  /    u   u   /
With the dew / on his brow, / and the rust / on his mail
```

This triple rhythm forms the pattern of two unstressed syllables followed by one stressed syllable. This is, therefore, a rising rhythm.

The following line from Thomas Hardy's "The Voice" (1914) offers an example of a **dactylic rhythm**: "Woman much missed, how you call to me, call to me."

```
  /    u   u     /    u    u   / u   u    /  u  u
Woman much / missed, how you / call to me, / call to me
```

This triple rhythm forms the pattern of one stressed syllable followed by two unstressed syllables. This is, therefore, a falling rhythm.

The **sprung rhythm** of Gerard Manley Hopkins's poetry is marked by an unpredictable number of stressed syllables. Each foot begins with a strongly stressed syllable, which may be followed by another stressed syllable or a number of unstressed syllables. The following lines from Hopkins's "God's Grandeur" (1918) serve as an example:

```
   u     /    u   / /      / u     /      /     /
And / though the / last lights / off the / black / West / went /
  /     /   u u u    /      /      / u       /
Oh, / morning at the / brown brink / eastward, / springs. . . .
```

This technique allows Hopkins to create a syncopated rhythm that places heavy emphasis on words and sounds. See **METER**.

ROMANCE

The word *romance* was originally used to describe medieval narratives of knights and other heroes whose deeds were courtly and chivalric. Early romances include *Sir Gawain and the Green Knight* (1375) and *Sir Orfeo* (early fourteenth century). These early verse romances often blended elements of magic and morality. Revived interest in the medieval romance inspired such writers as Sir Walter Scott (*Marmion*, 1808) and John Keats ("The Eve of St. Agnes," 1820) at the beginning of the nineteenth century. In the modern era, however, the term has also been used mainly to distinguish two kinds of prose fiction: a novel, which is more nearly based on observation of life, and a romance, which is more often the product of fancy than observation.

In "The Custom-House," which serves as an introduction to *The Scarlet Letter* (1850), Nathaniel Hawthorne seeks to define a romance by describing the conditions that he finds most conducive to writing one:

> Moonlight, in a familiar room, falling so white upon a carpet, and showing all its figures so distinctly,—making every object so minutely visible, yet so unlike a morning or noontide visibility,—is a medium the most suitable for a romance-writer to get acquainted with his illusive guests. There is the little domestic scenery of the well-known apartment; the chairs, with each its separate individuality; the centre table, sustaining a work-basket, a volume or two, and an extinguished lamp; the sofa; the book-case; the picture on the wall;—all these details, so completely seen, are so spiritualized by the unusual light, that they seem to lose their actual substance, and become things of intellect. Nothing is too small or too trifling to undergo this change, and acquire dignity thereby. A child's shoe; the doll seated in her little wicker carriage, the hobby-horse;—whatever, in a word, has been used or played with, during the day, is now invested with a quality of strangeness and remoteness, though still almost as vividly present as by daylight. Thus, therefore, the floor of our familiar room has become a neutral territory, somewhere between the real world and fairy-land, where the Actual and the Imaginary may meet, and each imbue itself with the nature of the other.

In other words, if a novel may be said to concern itself primarily with the real or actual world as observed by the light of day, a romance may be thought to present a mixture of reality and fantasy, or "the Actual and the Imaginary," as observed by the light of the moon.

Emily Bronte's *Wuthering Heights* (1848) offers an example. In the course of the work, Bronte describes a supernatural love between Cathy and Heathcliff, who, though separated by marriages to others and by Cathy's death, nevertheless seem capable of communicating with each other. In the beginning of the story, which is told in retrospect, Lockwood, one of the narrators, reports his visit to the home of the aging Heathcliff, where he experiences a kind of half-dream in which he hears a weeping child trying to enter his room. Terrified, he screams in alarm, whereupon Heathcliff rushes in to discover what is the matter. Having learned from Lockwood of the strange voice, Heathcliff asks him to leave the room:

> I obeyed, so far as to quit the chamber; when, ignorant where the narrow lobbies led, I stood still, and was witness, involuntarily, to a piece of superstition on the part of my landlord, which belied, oddly, his apparent sense.

He got onto the bed, and wrenched open the lattice, bursting, as he pulled at it, into an uncontrollable passion of tears.

"Come in! come in!" he sobbed. "Cathy, do come. Oh do—once more! Oh! my heart's darling! hear me this time—Catherine, at last!"

The spectre showed a spectre's ordinary caprice; it gave no sign of being; but the snow and wind whirled wildly through, even reaching my station, and blowing out the light.

In this way, the apparently realistic narrative offered by Lockwood is tinged with the fantastic. Although Lockwood does not yet accept the possibility of this supernatural communication, the idea is strongly suggested by both Heathcliff's actions and the force of the wind through the window. This suggestion of the imaginary merging with the actual is one of the main elements of romance in Bronte's book.

Contemporary examples of this subgenre include Daphne du Maurier's *Rebecca* (1938) and contemporary Harlequin romances, which combine elements of mystery and adventure with a formulaic relationship between an innocent young heroine and a handsome, experienced older man. See **COURTLY LOVE** and **GOTHIC**.

ROMANTICISM

In a historical sense, Romanticism was a movement in philosophy, political theory, and the arts that developed in France and Germany in the latter half of the eighteenth century and flourished in England through to the first quarter of the nineteenth century. The most prominent historical event associated with Romanticism was the French Revolution (1789-1799), which for many presaged the end of aristocratic rule and hereditary social divisions in Europe. Romantic thinkers asserted the potential of men and women to be limited neither by nature nor by tradition.

In literary history, the term *Romanticism* is most commonly associated with the work of several English authors of the late eighteenth and early nineteenth centuries: William Blake, William Wordsworth, Samuel Taylor Coleridge, Percy Bysshe Shelley, Lord Byron, Mary Shelley, and John Keats, among others. Although their poetry differs in many ways, the English Romantic poets have often been grouped by critics such as Rene Wellek according to their similarities with one another and their differences from the Neoclassicists. Speaking of the broader Romantic movement, Wellek writes in "The Concept of Romanticism in Literary History" (1963),

we find throughout Europe the same conceptions of poetry and of the workings and nature of the poetic imagination, the same conception of nature and its relation to man, and basically the same poetic style, with a use of imagery, symbolism, and myth which is clearly distinct from that of eighteenth-century Neoclassicism.

Indeed, Romanticism is often associated with the primacy of imagination, the worship of nature, and the use of natural imagery and symbolism in mythmaking.

The Romantic Imagination

In many ways, the English Romantic poets sought to restore not only imaginative elements but also emotional qualities to English poetry, which had been dominated by the rationalism and intellectualism of Neoclassical authors for most of the eighteenth century. In his Preface to the Second Edition of the *Lyrical Ballads* (1800), Wordsworth wrote that "poetry is the spontaneous overflow of powerful feelings." For many of the English Romantics, these powerful feelings came as a result of a sympathetic imagination, what Keats described in a letter (December 17, 1817) as a "Negative Capability": "that is when man is capable of being in uncertainties, Mysteries, doubts, without any irritable reaching after fact & reason." A passage from Keats's "Ode to a Nightingale" (1820) suggests both this negative capability and the emotions that accompany it. In the poem, the speaker addresses a nightingale, whose song beckons him to "leave the world unseen, / And with thee fade away into the forest dim." At one point in the poem, the speaker seems nearly to merge his identity with the nightingale:

> Away! away! for I will fly to thee,
>   Not charioted by Bacchus and his pards,
> But on the viewless wings of Poesy,
>   Though the dull brain perplexes and retards:
> Already with thee! tender is the night,
>   And haply the Queen-Moon is on her throne,
>   Cluster'd around by all her starry Fays;
>   But here there is no light,
> Save what from heaven is with the breezes blown
>   Through verduous glooms and winding mossy ways.

By reaching out sympathetically to the nightingale, the speaker seems capable of imaginatively experiencing the nightingale's world and existence, if only temporarily.

The Romantics and Nature

The English Romantics often employed descriptions of natural landscapes, objects, and processes to express emotional states. William Wordsworth's "I Wandered Lonely as a Cloud" (1804) offers an example:

> I wandered lonely as a cloud
> That floats on high o'er vales and hills,
> When all at once I saw a crowd,
> A host, of golden daffodils;
> Beside the lake, beneath the trees,
> Fluttering and dancing in the breeze.

Although in one sense the poet would seem to derive pleasure from the daffodils, in another sense he seems to project his pleasure onto them; thus, he describes the flowers as dancing, as though they were capable of feeling and expressing joy:

> The waves beside them danced; but they
> Out-did the sparkling waves in glee:
> A poet could not but be gay,
> In such a jocund company: I gazed—and gazed—but little thought
> What wealth the show to me had brought:
>
> For oft, when on my couch I lie
> In vacant or in pensive mood,
> They flash upon that inward eye
> Which is the bliss of solitude;
> And then my heart with pleasure fills,
> And dances with the daffodils.

The poet's mood is inspired by the natural scene, but he also seems to exploit the natural landscape in retrospect to alter his mood. In this way, nature serves as a means of self-expression, but what is expressed often betokens self-absorption.

Romantic Imagery and Symbolism

In expressing their relation to the natural world, the English Romantics prized particularity of description. They did not attempt to explain natural processes and characteristics in scientific ways; rather, they sought to be specific in a way that demonstrated their sympathy with nature. One means of expressing this sympathy is to present a multisensory experience. Keats's "Ode to a Nightingale" (1820) provides an example:

> I cannot see what flowers are at my feet,
>   Nor what soft incense hangs upon the boughs,
> But, in embalmed darkness, guess each sweet
>   Wherewith the seasonable month endows
> The grass, the thicket, and the fruit-tree wild;
>   White hawthorn, and the pastoral eglantine;
>   Fast fading violets cover'd up in leaves;
>   And mid-May's eldest child,
> The coming musk-rose, full of dewy wine,
>   The murmurous haunt of flies on summer eves.

All the senses are represented and intermixed in this passage: "soft incense" (tactile and olfactory); "embalmed darkness" (tactile and visual); "musk-rose, full of dewy wine" (olfactory and palatal); "murmurous haunt of flies" (auditory and tactile).

The Romantic use of **symbol** is often highly subjective and personal; however, certain recurring metaphors in English Romantic poetry achieve the status of symbol. As M. H. Abrams has explained in "The Correspondent Breeze: A Romantic Metaphor" (1984), they are particularly fond of making "symbolic equations between breeze, breath, and soul, respiration and inspiration, the reanimation of nature and of the spirit." Shelley's "Ode to the West Wind" (1819) offers several illustrations:

> O wild West Wind, thou breath of Autumn's being,
> Thou, from whose unseen presence the leaves dead
> Are driven, like ghosts from an enchanter fleeing,
>
> Yellow, and black, and pale, and hectic red,
> Pestilence-stricken multitudes: O thou,
> Who chariotest to their dark wintry bed
>
> The winged seeds, where they lie cold and low,
> Each like a corpse within its grave, until
> Thine azure sister of the Spring shall blow
>
> Her clarion o'er the dreaming earth, and fill
> (Driving sweet buds like flocks to feed in air)
> With living hues and odours plain and hill:
>
> Wild Spirit, which art moving everywhere;
> Destroyer and preserver; hear, oh hear!

In these lines, the wind becomes symbolic both of a necessarily destructive force (in autumn) and a force of revival (in spring): "Destroyer and preserver." See **EPIPHANY**, **CLASSICISM**, **SYMBOL**, and **SYNESTHESIA**.

S

SATIRE

A satire is a literary work that seeks to criticize and correct the behavior of human beings and their institutions by means of humor, wit, and ridicule. Literary critics familiar with classical forms of satire generally recognize two main types: **direct** (or **formal**) **satire** and **indirect satire**.

Direct satire is marked by the author's use of the first person in his or her address to readers. Some direct satires take the attitude of **Horatian satires**, named after the Roman poet Horace (first century B.C.), whose work sought to correct human behavior through gentle humor. Examples of Horatian satire include Joseph Addison's essays for *The Spectator*. In *The Spectator* of May 10, 1711, for instance, Addison makes fun of his contemporaries' desire to embrace and indulge in one of the latest literary fashions: namely, the figure-poem or *carmen figuratum*, in which the poet shapes the lines of the poem to form a picture that suggests the poem's subject (e.g., Herbert's "Easter Wings" [1633]). Calling this kind of verse an example of false wit, Addison offers some humorous speculations about the absurd ends to which this trend might lead:

> I have communicated this Thought to a young Poetical Lover of my
> Acquaintance, who intends to present his Mistress with a Copy of Verses
> made in the Shape of her Fan; and if he tells me true, has already finished
> the three first Sticks of it. He has likewise promised me to get the Measure
> of his Mistress's Marriage-Finger, with a Design to make a Posie in the
> Fashion of a Ring which shall exactly fit it. It is so very easy to enlarge
> upon a good Hint, that I do not question but my ingenious Readers will
> apply what I have said to many other Particulars; and that we shall see the
> Town filled in a very little Time with Poetical Tippets [little capes],
> Handkerchiefs, Snuff-Boxes, and the like Female Ornaments.

Addison's mild satire seeks to correct his society's inclination to prefer style over substance, or as he puts it himself in commenting on a poem shaped like an egg, "the Author seems to have been more intent upon the Figure of his Poem, than upon the sense of it."

By contrast, **Juvenalian satire**, named after the Roman poet Juvenal (first century A.D.), is more aggressive in its ridicule and unforgiving in its moral judgment. This is the mode engaged by Jonathan Swift in "A Modest Proposal for preventing the Children of poor People in Ireland, from being a Burthen to their Parents or the Country; and for making them beneficial to the Publick" (1729). As a way of ridiculing the public-policy planners of his day, Swift proposes to provide for these poor children "in such a manner [that], as, instead of being a Charge upon their Parents, or the Parish, or wanting Food and Raiment for the rest of their Lives, they shall, on the contrary, contribute to the feeding and partly to the Cloathing of many thousands." Having explained the problem, he presents his solution:

> I shall now therefore humbly propose my own thoughts, which I hope will not be lyable to the least Objection.
>
> I have been assured by a very knowing American of my acquaintance in London, that a young healthy Child well nursed is at a year old a most delicious, nourishing, and wholesome Food, whether stewed, roasted, baked, or boyled, and I make not doubt that it will equally serve in a Fricasie, or Ragout.

By offering this monstrous suggestion in a language and tone of calm reason, Swift ridicules the mentality of the public officials or policy advisors whose mathematical approach to problems excludes human feeling or concern. Juvenalian satire rarely excuses the object of ridicule by letting up on the scourge of contempt as does Horatian satire.

Of the many kinds of indirect satire, the most celebrated is **Menippean satire**, named after the Greek Cynic philosopher Menippus (third century B.C.). This tradition of satire often mixes prose and verse, and it is typically marked by a contentious and often ridiculous debate taking place at a convention, a banquet, or a party. An excerpt from Lewis Carroll's chapter of *Alice's Adventures in Wonderland* (1865) entitled "A Mad Tea Party," which begins with a description of a table set for tea and a March Hare, a Hatter, and a sleeping Dormouse sitting at it, will serve as an illustration. Upon taking her place at the table, Alice becomes involved in an absurd conversation characterized by silly arguments over nothing at all:

> The Hatter opened his eyes very wide . . . but all he said was "Why is a raven like a writing-desk?"
>
> "Come, we shall have some fun now!" thought Alice. "I'm glad they've begun asking riddles—I believe I can guess that," she added aloud.
>
> "Do you mean that you think you can find out the answer to it?" said the March Hare.
>
> "Exactly so," said Alice.
>
> "Then you should say what you mean," the March Hare went on.
>
> "I do," Alice hastily replied; "at least—at least I mean what I say— that's the same thing, you know."
>
> "Not the same thing a bit!" said the Hatter. "Why, you might just as well say that 'I see what I eat' is the same thing as 'I eat what I see'!"

"You might just as well say," added the March Hare, "that 'I like what I get' is the same thing as 'I get what I like'!"

"You might just as well say," added the Dormouse, which seemed to be talking in its sleep, "that 'I breathe when I sleep' is the same thing as 'I sleep when I breathe'!"

"It *is* the same thing with you," said the Hatter, and here the conversation dropped, and the party sat silent for a minute, while Alice thought over all she could remember about ravens and writing-desks, which wasn't much.

This rambling conversation among eccentric guests satirizes in particular the mindset of those who spend all their intellect arguing over semantics (the meaning of words) and pedantry (e.g., irrelevant questions of grammar and syntax) instead of addressing the substance or point of a discussion.

Another name for Menippean satire, offered by Northrop Frye, is *anatomy*; Frye gives it this name because Menippean satirists delight in poking fun at those who boast only systemized knowledge and spout long lists of facts and trivia. Gabriel García Márquez picks up on this latter aspect of Menippean satire in his story entitled "Big Mama's Funeral" (1961). Realizing that she is about to die, Big Mama, the matriarchal ruler of the fictional Kingdom of Macondo, satisfies her ego by listing both her material possessions and the immaterial accomplishments of her administration, which take the form of an absurd anatomy:

> . . . Big Mama raised herself up on her monumental buttocks, and in a domineering and sincere voice, lost in her memories, dictated to the notary this list of her invisible estate:
>
> The wealth of the subsoil, the territorial waters, the colors of the flag, national sovereignty, the traditional parties, the rights of man, civil rights, the nation's leadership, the right of appeal, Congressional hearings, letters of recommendation, historical records, free elections, beauty queens, transcendental speeches, huge demonstrations, distinguished young ladies, proper gentlemen, punctilious military men, His Illustrious Eminence, the Supreme Court, goods whose importation was forbidden, liberal ladies, the meat problem, the purity of language, setting a good example, the free but responsible press, the Athens of South America, public opinion, the lessons of democracy, Christian morality, the shortage of foreign exchange, the right of asylum, the Communist menace, the ship of state, the high cost of living, republican traditions, the underprivileged classes, statements of political support.
>
> She didn't manage to finish. The laborious enumeration cut off her last breath. Drowning in the pandemonium of abstract formulas which for two centuries had constituted the moral justification of the family's power, Big Mama emitted a loud belch and expired.

By making this list consist largely of trite phrases, political platitudes, trivialities, and concepts cut off from any meaningful contexts, García Márquez satirizes the blatant chicanery and unwavering self-absorption of political despots. See **PARODY**.

SEMIOTICS/SEMIOLOGY

The words *semiotics* and *semiology* both derive from the Greek *semeion*, meaning "sign." Each may be used to designate a scientific study of signs, whether they be oral, written, musical, gestural, or pictorial signs. For literary theorists, however, the most significant branch of semiology has been the study of oral and written language: linguistics.

Peirce and Representation

Semiotics is a word used by American philosopher C. S. Peirce (1839-1914) to denote his study of the ways in which signs are representative and meaningful (semantics); the ways in which they can be organized (syntax); and the ways in which they may be interpreted in context (pragmatic logic). Through his investigations, Peirce decided that signs are used to represent objects in three ways, which he called iconic, symbolic, and indexical. **Iconic representations** are based on resemblance; thus, portraits, landscape paintings, mimicry, and sound effects are all examples of icons, since they seek to imitate. **Symbolic representations**, such as languages, are not based on resemblance. They proceed from a social contract or cultural agreement; thus, for example, we agree to call a large plant with a trunk, branches, and leaves a tree so that we can communicate with other English-speaking members of our society. Written language is symbolic as well; thus, we can write the word *tree* to symbolize a large plant with a trunk, branches, and leaves. **Indexical representations** are based on cause and effect. For instance, upon seeing smoke, we infer that it is the effect of a particular cause: namely, fire. Detectives often work with indexical representations: footprints, fingerprints, and traces of blood are all indicative of the persons who caused them to be left at the scene of a crime.

Saussure and Sign

The other major influence on twentieth-century studies of signs is the Swiss linguist Ferdinand de Saussure, who called the discipline *semiology*. In his *Course in General Linguistics* (1916), Saussure insists on a dichotomy between **parole**, an individual speech act, and **langue**, a whole system of language. Many linguists before and after Saussure have focused their attention on parole (or speech). For instance, they study the ways in which words are articulated by means of breathing, using one's lips and tongue, and voicing (or not voicing) sounds in the larynx. Other linguists have been interested principally in a **paradigmatic** study of speech, a type of linguistic history of etymology (the origins and developments of words) and changes in spelling and pronunciation over the course of time. By contrast, Saussure seeks to make a **syntagmatic** study of langue, in which he considers the whole system of language at a given time.

In order to clarify his discussion of semiology, Saussure begins by examining the relationship between the basic elements of a sign, as well as the relationship between the sign and its referent. The **sign** consists of a **signifier**—a speech

sound (e.g., a spoken word, such as *love, democracy*, or *tree*) or a graphic representation (e.g., a written representation of each of these sounds)—and a **signified**—
a concept, idea, or mental image (e.g., a concept of love, an idea of democracy, a
mental image of what a tree looks like). Of greatest importance to contemporary
theory is Saussure's claim that the relationship between these two, signifier and
signifed, is not only symbolic but arbitrary; that is to say, we have no compelling
reason to use the word *tree*, for instance, to refer to the concept of a large plant
with a trunk, branches, and leaves. Moreover, if the relationship between the
signifier and the signified is arbitrary, so is the relationship between the whole
sign (both the word and the concept) and the **referent** (the actual object itself).
Indeed, the relation between a word and the object to which it refers is always
unstable and problematic. For instance, the word *tree* is used to refer to objects
that are very different from one another: maple trees, palm trees, spruce trees,
not to mention shoe trees, hat trees, tree toads, and tree diagrams. In addition,
we know that other languages use different words to refer to a large plant with a
trunk, branches, and leaves: *arbre* in French, *arbol* in Spanish, and *Baum* in German, to name but a few. None of these signs is more or less correct than others;
instead their differences simply exemplify Saussure's point that langue, the whole
system of language, is an abstract construct with arbitrary rules and conventions
that we must follow nevertheless if we wish to communicate.

Saussure's other influential principle is that if the relationship between signifiers
and signifieds—spoken (or written) words and the concepts traditionally linked
with them—is arbitrary, and if the relationship between signs and referents—the
compound of words/concepts and the objects with which they are commonly
associated—-is arbitrary, then signifiers, signifieds, and signs have no positive meaning in and of themselves. We call certain concepts of a large plant with a trunk,
branches, and leaves *trees* because that is the convention in English, not because
the sound of the word *tree* or the letters used to write *tree* are inseparably or indis-
putably linked with this concept. Moreover, we associate this compound of the
word *tree* and of the concept *tree* with an actual large plant with a trunk, branches,
and leaves because that is what we are obliged to do in order to speak and think like
others in our linguistic group, not because the sign *tree* is inextricably or absolutely
identical with the object to which we refer. Yet although the sign *tree* does not
really mean anything, except in these wholly arbitrary and conventional senses, it
is meaningful to the system of language in its negative relation or difference; that
is to say, *tree* is meaningful in our system of language because it is not any other
word: *bee, sea, free, agree, dog, cat, house, democracy, love*, and all the rest.

The idea of studying language as a system of laws and relations proved to
be profoundly influential upon structuralist approaches to literature and many
other disciplines. The notion of the arbitrary relation between signifier and signified, as well as the insistence that signs are meaningful only in the negative
relation of difference, is one of the first principles of poststructural and deconstructive theories. See **DECONSTRUCTION** and **STRUCTURALISM/
POSTSTRUCTURALISM**.

SETTING

Literary critics and commentators generally use the word *setting* to designate the time and place in which the action of a narrative occurs. The term is also employed by some to include the situation or context of a work of literature: historical setting, social setting, cultural setting, and so on. Settings may be both physical and metaphorical. The setting of Sam Shepard's play entitled *Fool for Love* (1983), for instance, is explicitly physical:

> SCENE: Stark, low-rent motel room off the edge of the Mojave Desert. Faded green plaster walls. Dark brown linoleum floor. No rugs. Cast iron four poster single bed, slightly off center favoring stage right, set horizontally to audience. Bed covered with blue chenille bedspread. Metal table with well-worn yellow Formica top. . . .

The opening stage directions for Beth Henley's *Crimes of the Heart* (1979) are explicit about both place and time:

> THE SETTING
>
> The setting of the entire play is the kitchen in the Magrath sisters' house in Hazlehurst, Mississippi, a small southern town. The old-fashioned kitchen is unusually spacious, but there is a lived-in, cluttered look about it. There are four different entrances and exits to the kitchen: the back door; the door leading to the dining room and the front door of the house; a door leading to the downstairs bedroom; and a staircase leading to the upstairs room. There is a table near the center of the room, and a cot has been set up in one of the corners.
>
> THE TIME
>
> In the fall; five years after Hurricane Camille.

The "cluttered look" of the house seems to symbolize the psychological clutter of the troubled minds of the three sisters. Moreover, the smalltown setting and description of the "lived-in" kitchen reinforce the idea of the confined existence of the eldest sister, Lenny.

The following passage, describing the principal setting of Emily Bronte's *Wuthering Heights* (1847), seems to be both physical and symbolic:

> Wuthering Heights is the name of Mr. Heathcliff's dwelling, "wuthering" being a significant provincial adjective, descriptive of the atmospheric tumult to which its station is exposed in stormy weather. Pure, bracing ventilation they must have up there at all times, indeed: one may guess the power of the north wind, blowing over the edge, by the excessive slant of a few stunted firs at the end of the house; and by a range of gaunt thorns all stretching their limbs one way, as if craving of the alms of the sun.

This description of setting may be understood to be metaphorical in its suggestion that it is not only the landscape that has suffered through storms and become stunted in growth, but also the characters of the novel. They, too, live gauntly, stretching forth their souls "as if craving the alms of the sun."

SIMILE

A simile is a direct comparison using "like" or "as" to coordinate the tenor, or object of comparison, and the vehicle, or means of comparison. A passage from Robert Frost's "Birches" (1916) offers an example of a simile using "like" to coordinate a comparison:

> You may see their trunks arching in the woods
> Years afterwards, trailing their leaves on the ground
> Like girls on hands and knees that throw their hair
> Before them over their heads to dry in the sun.

In this simile, arching birch trees are presented as the tenor, and girls on hands and knees drying their hair serve as the vehicle. The simile seeks to compare their appearance.

Archibald MacLeish's poem "Ars Poetica" (1926) employs a number of similes using "as" to coordinate comparisons:

> A poem should be palpable and mute
> As a globed fruit,
>
> Dumb
> As old medallions to the thumb,
>
> Silent as the sleeve-worn stone
> Of casement ledges where the moss has grown—

In each of these similes, "poem" serves as the tenor. The vehicles include "globed fruit"; "old medallions"; and "sleeve-worn stone / Of casement ledges where moss has grown." In each case, the simile seeks to compare the desired muteness of a poem to the silence of a concrete object.

Similes are commonly employed in prose as well as poetry. A passage from Sandra Cisneros's "One Holy Night" (1988) offers two illustrations:

> Rachel says that love is like a big black piano being pushed off the top
> of a three-story building and you're waiting on the bottom to catch it.
> But Lourdes says it's not that way at all. It's like a top, like all the colors
> in the world are spinning so fast they're not colors anymore and all
> that's left is the white hum.

The tenor of both similes is "love"; the vehicles are "a big black piano" and "a top." The first simile compares being in love to waiting to catch a piano falling off the top of a building. The second compares the experience of love to a spinning top whose colors are blurred into "the white hum" of a perfectly centered velocity. See **METAPHOR**.

SOLILOQUY

A soliloquy is commonly defined as a speech intended to be delivered on stage by a solitary character, in which the character reveals his or her nature, thoughts, and motives. However, soliloquies are sometimes given while other characters stand at the back of the stage. In any event, soliloquies are not part of the dialogue; they represent the inner workings of the characters' minds, often taking the form of silent thought and self-debate.

Shakespeare's *Romeo and Juliet* (1595) offers an example of a soliloquy:

> Juliet: Gallop apace, you fiery-footed steeds,
> Towards Phoebus' lodging; such a waggoner
> As Phaeton would whip you to the west,
> And bring in cloudy night immediately.
> Spread thy close curtain, love-performing night,
> That runaway's eyes may wink, and Romeo
> Leap to these arms, untalk'd of and unseen! (3.2.1-7)

The two lovers are limited in expressing their feelings to others because of their need for secrecy. Therefore, we come to learn of Juliet's youthful impatience for the embrace of Romeo through a soliloquy.

Peter Shaffer's *Equus* (1973) offers a contemporary instance of a soliloquy when Alan Strang comments on his horse-god, Equus, and his psychiatrist, Dr. Dysart:

> (ALAN) Now he's gone off to rest, leaving me alone with Equus. I can hear the creature's voice. It's calling me out of the black cave of the Psyche. I shove in my dim little torch, and there he stands—waiting for me. He raises his matted head. He opens his great square teeth, and says—(Mocking.) "Why? . . . Why—ultimately—Me? . . . Do you really imagine you can account for ME? Totally, infallibly, inevitably account for Me? . . . Poor Doctor Dysart!"

In this soliloquy, Alan reveals to the audience what he cannot or will not reveal to Doctor Dysart: his worship of Equus and the state of his mind. Since Alan does not always communicate fully with the other characters, we must rely in part on these soliloquies to understand him. See **ASIDE** and **DRAMATIC MONOLOGUE**.

SONNET

The classic sonnet is a poem composed of fourteen (or, more rarely, sixteen) lines of **iambic pentameter** with some form of alternating end rhyme and a turning point that divides the poem into two parts. The structure of a sonnet allows it to present a theme, situation, or problem and then seek to resolve the theme or problem, or to comment on the situation.

The two basic types of sonnets are the Petrarchan (Italian) sonnet and the Shakespearean (English) sonnet. The **Petrarchan sonnet** consists of an octave (eight lines before the turn) and a sestet (six lines after the turn). The octave consists of two quatrains, four lines each, having a rhyme scheme of *abba abba*. The sestet may vary in rhyme scheme. The common variations are *cdc dcd; cde cde; cde ced; cdd cee*. Robert Frost's "Design" (1936) is an example of a Petrarchan sonnet:

> I found a dimpled spider, fat and white,
> On a white heal-all, holding up a moth
> Like a white piece of rigid satin cloth—
> Assorted characters of death and blight
> Mixed ready to begin the morning right,
> Like the ingredients of a witches' broth—
> A snow-drop spider, a flower like a froth,
> And dead wings carried like a paper kite.
> What had that flower to do with being white,
> The wayside blue and innocent heal-all?
> What brought the kindred spider to that height,
> Then steered the white moth thither in the night?
> What but design of darkness to appall ?—
> If design govern in a thing so small.

The octave and sestet are made evident by the use of a single period at the end of the first part, as well as the space between the two sections of the poem. The octave describes the situation: the speaker's coming across a white spider holding up a white moth upon a white flower. The sestet comments on the situation by asking a series of questions. The rhyme scheme of the octave is the standard *abba abba·*, the sestet, however, presents a somewhat unusual variation: *bcb bcc*.

The **Shakespearean** or **English sonnet** consists of three quatrains (four lines each) and a rhyming couplet (two lines). The turn in a Shakespearean sonnet occurs at the end of the third quatrain. In the English sonnet, the theme (situation or problem) is presented in the course of the first twelve lines; the resolution comes in the last two lines of the rhyming couplet. Shakespeare's "Sonnet LXXIII" (1609) offers an example:

> That time of year thou mayst in me behold
> When yellow leaves, or none, or few, do hang
> Upon those boughs which shake against the cold,
> Bare ruined choirs, where late the sweet birds sang.
> In me thou see'st the twilight of such day
> As after sunset fadeth in the west,
> Which by and by black night doth take away,
> Death's second self, that seals up all in rest.
> In me thou see'st the glowing of such fire
> That on the ashes of his youth doth lie,

As the death bed whereon it must expire,
Consumed with that which it was nourished by.
This thou perceiv'st, which makes thy love more strong,
To love that well which thou must leave ere long.

The beginning of each of the three quatrains is marked by the variations of the formula "thou mayst in me behold," and the end of each is punctuated by a full stop. Moreover, each quatrain is dominated by a controlling metaphor: time of year, time of day, time before a fire burns out. These first twelve lines present the problem of growing old and realizing how little time one has left. The couplet comments on this problem by suggesting a certain irony: the less time one has to live, the more precious life seems. The rhyme scheme of this sonnet is the classic *abab cdcd efef gg*.

Carmen Tafolla's "Chispa, the Pachuco Sonnet" (1992) is a contemporary example of an English sonnet:

When stubborn Chispa takes cowhead and tripe,
And makes of it a feast that thirty years
Will turn into expensive fare and ripe
To whims elite from poverty's arrears,
And ese vato glides, his pose the deer's,
But head held back at angle to the sun,
The slant of pyramids his body hears.
The Aztec thus danced too, same angle done.
Another's gesture comes from Babylon.
The word from Africa transforms, survives.
The song of China lingers on the tongue.
Posed also to the sun, Quetzalcoatl smiles.
Chispaseed, the spirit never dies, the flame
of centuries' sabor is carried on, the same.

The first twelve lines of this sonnet offer examples in support of the theme, which is aptly summarized in the couplet: the savor of life— whether it be for food, poetry, art, dance, language, or song—never dies out of the human spirit. The rhyme scheme of this sonnet—*abab bcbc cdcd ee*—is a variation on the standard Shakespearean scheme. See **METER**.

STREAM OF CONSCIOUSNESS

William James first used the phrase *stream of consciousness* in *Principles of Psychology* (1890) to describe the ebb and flow of thoughts of the waking mind. In literary criticism, the terms *stream of consciousness* and *interior monologue* are both used to describe narrative techniques that present multileveled flows of rational and irrational thoughts and impressions uninhibited by grammar, syntax, and logical transitions. Stream of consciousness narratives may be categorized according to two types: **indirect** and **direct interior monologue**.

James Joyce's novel *Ulysses* (1922) offers many examples of stream of consciousness narration. In the Calypso chapter, for instance, the protagonist (Leopold Bloom), having left his wife in bed, slips into a stream of consciousness as he goes to buy his breakfast. While observing the everyday matters of weather, traffic, and local (Dublin) landmarks, he thinks of his wife (Molly), his father-in-law (Tweedy), their experiences in Gibraltar, and the funeral he shall attend later in the day:

> No. She didn't want anything. He heard then a warm heavy sigh, softer, as she turned over and the loose brass quoits on the bedstead jingled. Must get those settled really. Pity. All the way from Gibraltar. Forgotten any little Spanish she knew. Wonder what his father gave for it. Old style. Ah yes! of course. Bought it at the governor's auction. Got a short knock. Hard as nails at a bargain old Tweedy. Yes sir. At Plevna that was. I rose from the ranks, sir, and I'm proud of it. Still he had brains enough to make that corner in stamps. Now that was farseeing.
>
> ★ ★ ★ ★ ★ ★ ★ ★ ★ ★
>
> He crossed to the bright side, avoiding the loose cellarflap of number seventy five. The sun was nearing the steeple of George's church. Be a warm day, I fancy. Specially in these black clothes feel it more. Black conducts, reflects, (refracts, is it?), the heat. But I couldn't go in that light suit. Make a picnic of it. His eyelids sank quietly often as he walked in happy warmth. Boland's breadvan delivering trays of our daily but she prefers yesterday's loaves turnover crisp crowns hot. Makes you feel young. . . .

This passage is an indirect interior monologue; the narrator occasionally interrupts the flow of thoughts and impressions: "He crossed to the bright side . . ." and "His eyelids sank quietly . . ."

In *The Sound and the Fury* (1929), William Faulkner uses direct interior monologue, which issues directly from an identifiable character source, to present the flow of consciousness of a young man who is contemplating suicide:

> Then the curtains breathing out of the dark upon my face, leaving the breathing upon my face. A quarter hour yet. And then I'll not be. The peacefullest words. Peacefullest words. *Non fui. Sum. Non sum.* Somewhere I heard bells once. Mississippi or Massachusetts. I was. I am not. Massachusetts or Mississippi. Shreve has bottle in his trunk. *Aren't you even going to open it* Mr and Mrs Jason Richard Compson announce the *Three Times. Days. Aren't you even going to open it* marriage of their daughter Candace *that liquor teaches you to confuse the means with the end.* I am. Drink. I was not.

The content of the passage is a mixture of consecutive thoughts in the present interrupted by associations with works of literature, Latin phrases, past experiences, snatches of conversation, recollections of sounds and speeches, and vague musings.

In *Beloved* (1987), Toni Morrison employs a direct interior monologue to present the consciousness of a character who has been imbued with the racial memories of African slaves chained to and packed in the hulls of ships crossing the Atlantic Ocean:

> All of it is now it is always now there will never be a time when I am not crouching and watching others who are crouching too I am always crouching the man on my face is death his face is not mine his mouth smells sweet but his eyes are locked some who eat nasty themselves I do not eat the men without skin bring us their morning water to drink we have none at night I cannot see the dead man on my face daylight comes through the cracks and I can see his locked eyes I am not big small rats do not wait for us to sleep someone is thrashing but there is not room to do it in if we had more drink we could make tears

In this passage, the narrator presents a series of images, sometimes unconnected by transitions, that float in time. As does Faulkner, Morrison eschews the use of punctuation to suggest the random selection of images and recollections.

STRUCTURALISM/POSTSTRUCTURALISM

The term *structuralism* is commonly used to describe theoretical approaches that study language and literature as systems having operational structures or codes: that is to say, recognizable patterns and parts. The term *structuralist* may also be applied to contemporaneous approaches to a number of other disciplines, especially anthropology. *Poststructuralism* is a term that describes a number of approaches to language, literature, and culture, all of which question and critique the validity and authority of structural analyses.

Structural Approaches to Language and Literature

The concept of structuralism developed from the approaches to the study of language (linguistics) invented by Ferdinand de Saussure and C. S. Peirce (see **Semiotics**). Unlike linguists before them, who studied the history and development of language (a diachronic view), Saussure and Peirce sought to discover the rules and relations governing the language of a particular time and place (a synchronic view). This structural approach to linguistics, seeing language as a complete and formal system, enabled them to treat language as a science with identifiable tendencies and forms. Formal studies of language seek to analyze the composition and behavior of words (**morphology**). Likewise, these structural analyses work to discover common patterns or structures of phrases, clauses, and sentences (**syntax**).

For literary theorists and critics, such formal approaches to morphology and syntax suggested that whole narratives might be analyzed to discover, for instance, generic characters and basic patterns of plot. Thus, the study of literature could be treated as a science. One of the important innovators and practitioners in this development was the Russian scholar Roman Jakobson, who is often credited with giving meaning and currency to structural approaches to literature, as well as other disciplines. In his writings, Jakobson insists that the proper study of the literary critics is "literariness": that is, the recurring structures and patterns of literary language and literary productions. This call for attention to matters of form led some critics to focus on literature as a system separated from other cultural processes (see **New Criticism**).

In his *Morphology of the Folktale* (1970), Vladimir Propp analyzes the structure of Russian fairy tales and demonstrates that they have a similar narrative syntax. He offers a list of thirty-one narrative sequences or "functions" that are common to fairy tales of various cultures, beginning with "one of the members of a family absents himself [or herself] from home" and ending with "the hero [or heroine] is married and ascends the throne." Thus, for instance, "Jack and the Beanstalk" begins with Jack's taking a cow to a marketplace. Likewise, "Snow White" begins with the heroine's abandonment in a forest. According to Propp, functions two and three are "an interdiction [a command or request] is addressed to the hero" and "the interdiction is violated." In "Jack and the Beanstalk," Jack is instructed to trade the cow for money or food, but he decides to trade it for some magic beans. Functions five, six, and seven are described by Propp as "the villain receives information about his [or her] victim," "the villain attempts to deceive his [or her] victim in order to take possession of him [or her] or of his [or her] belongings," and "the victim submits to deception and thereby unwillingly helps his [or her] enemy." In "Snow White," the evil stepmother receives information about Snow White by means of her magic mirror; she then deceives Snow White into eating the poisoned apple; at last, Snow White agrees to eat the poisoned apple and falls into the wicked stepmother's control. Although not all fairy tales partake of each of the thirty-one functions, Propp claims that they do follow a clearly structured sequence of events.

In *S/Z* (trans. 1974), Roland Barthes asserts that classic or "readerly" fiction may be understood according to five basic codes: the proairetic code of actions (plot); the hermeneutic code of puzzles (suspense); the semic code (character and setting); the cultural code (general knowledge); and the symbolic code (theme). In his book-length structural analysis, Barthes divides Honoré de Balzac's story "Sarassine" into 561 lexies (or units of meaning) that readers understand as belonging to one or more of the five codes. The story begins with the narrator's description of a scene, in which he contrasts a wintry landscape outside with a high-spirited party inside:

> I was deep in one of those daydreams which overtake even the shallowest of men, in the midst of the most tumultuous parties. Midnight had just sounded from the clock of the Elysée-Bourbon. Seated in a window recess and hidden behind the sinuous folds of a silk curtain, I could contemplate at my leisure the garden of the mansion where I was spending the evening. The trees, partially covered with snow, stood out dimly against the grayish background of a cloudy sky, barely

whitened by the moon. Seen amid these fantastic surroundings, they vaguely resembled ghosts half out of their shrouds, a gigantic representation of the famous Dance of the Dead. Then, turning in the other direction, I could admire the Dance of the Living! a splendid salon decorated in silver and gold, with glittering chandeliers, sparkling with candles.

Discussing the second of the lexies ("I was deep in one of those daydreams"), Barthes notes that the implied structure of the whole passage indicates that "there will be nothing wayward about the daydream introduced here: it will be solidly constructed along the most familiar rhetorical lines, in a series of antitheses: garden and salon, life and death, cold and heat, outside and interior. The lexia lays the groundwork, in introductory form, for a vast symbolic structure." The symbolic codes (or themes) of the story, in other words, are structured in the form of binary oppositions.

The Move from Structuralism to Poststructuralism

Although in many ways Barthes's approach adheres to the principles of structuralism, it also represents the growing shift from structuralism to poststructuralism that developed in the latter half of the twentieth century. Having written a book entitled *The Elements of Semiology* (1964), Barthes was aware of both the uses and limitations of structural linguistics. For, as he and others understood, one of the principal concepts of Saussurean linguistics is that the relationship between words and their meanings is arbitrary; that is to say, words are not meaningful in and of themselves but only in so far as they are different from other words. If the relationships between the basic elements of linguistic systems are arbitrary, then it followed for Barthes and others that the entire concept of a logically structured language was arbitrary as well. Moreover, they recognized that structuralist critiques of literature often relied on the recognition and ordering of binary oppositions—light/darkness, rational/irrational, man/woman, for instance—that involved arbitrary judgments and preferences: rational thought is superior to irrational thought, much as light is preferable to darkness; likewise, the rational logic of man is superior to the irrational feelings of woman.

Through the very process of constructing their own analyses, a number of structuralists grew increasingly cognizant of the ways in which structural theories of language and literature "deconstructed" themselves when examined in regard to their arbitrary foundations and binary logic (see **Deconstruction**). In short, as Jonathan Culler explains in *On Deconstruction: Theory and Criticism after Structuralism* (1982), structuralism gave way to poststructuralism because of a loss of faith in the logic of rational systems:

If we identify deconstruction as a leading form of post-structuralism and thus oppose it to structuralism, we may reach the conclusions outlined by J. Hillis Miller . . . [that] deconstruction arrives in the wake of structuralism to frustrate its systematic projects. The scientific ambitions of structuralists are exposed as impossible dreams by deconstructive analyses, which put in question the binary oppositions through which structuralists describe and master cultural productions. Deconstruction shatters their "faith in reason" by revealing the uncanny irrationality of texts and their ability to confute or subvert every system or position they are thought to manifest. Deconstruction, by these lights, reveals the impossibility of any science of literature and returns critical inquiry to the task of interpretation.

As Culler suggests, poststructuralism proceeds from a radical skepticism about the ability of literature to present and sustain rational, ordered, and logical systems, since, like language itself, literature is grounded in arbitrary concepts. Poststructuralist theories and practices have encouraged and supported a number of contemporary approaches to literature and culture: deconstruction, Lacanian and post-Lacanian psychoanalysis, feminist theories, and cultural studies. See **CULTURAL CRITICISM, DECONSTRUCTION, FAIRY TALE, FEMINIST CRITICISM, NEW CRITICISM/ FORMALISM, PSYCHOANALYTIC THEORY AND CRITICISM,** and **SEMIOTICS/ SEMIOLOGY**.

SUBLIME

The word/term *sublime* may be used to describe religious awe, boundlessness, natural grandeur, and potent emotion. In "On the Sublime" (first-century A.D.), Longinus describes the magnificence and vastness of stars in the skies, of mountains, of volcanoes, and of the ocean as foundations of the sublime. The sublime was of special interest in the eighteenth century. In *Philosophical Inquiry into the Origin of Our Ideas of the Sublime and Beautiful* (1757), Edmund Burke highlights the significance of terror. Burke views the sublime as different from beauty. He connects darkness, solitude, infinity, and power with the sublime and light, smallness, smoothness, and delicacy with beauty. A cult of the sublime developed in the second half of the eighteenth century. Burke's ideas became fashionable and influenced such works as the poems of Thomas Gray and William Collins and the Gothic novel. In *Critique of Judgment* (1790), Kant amplifies the concept of the sublime and defines it as "what is absolutely great." For Kant, sublimity takes place when the faculties are inadequate to assimilate prodigious natural wonders and art of great magnitude. The observer of such greatness must set in motion a more elevated mental ability to fathom and penetrate such marvels. In Ann Radcliffe's *The Italian* (1796), Ellena contemplates the surroundings near her prison:

> She ascended the winding steps hastily, and found they led only to a door, opening into a small room, where nothing remarkable appeared, till she approached the windows, and beheld thence an horizon, and a landscape spread below, whose grandeur awakened all her heart. The consciousness of her prison was lost, while her eyes ranged over the

wide and freely-sublime scene without. She perceived that this chamber was within a small turret, projecting from an angle of the convent over the walls, and suspended, as in air, above the vast precipices of granite, that formed part of the mountain. These precipices were broken into cliffs, which in some places, impended far above their base, and in others, rose, in nearly-perpendicular lines, to the walls of the monastery, which they supported. Ellena, with a dreadful pleasure, looked down them, shagged as they were with larch, and frequently darkened by lines of gigantic pines bending along the rocky ledges, till her eye rested on the thick chestnut woods that extended over their winding base, and which, softening to the plains, seemed to form a gradation between the variegated cultivation there, and the awful wildness of the rocks above.

Ellena transmutes her fear into an acute apprehension of the magnificence of the awe-inspiring scenery. She dwells on the sublimity of the mountains and activates a higher mental faculty to absorb "with a dreadful pleasure" all of the "awful wildness of the rocks." See **GOTHIC**.

SYMBOL

The word *symbol* derives from the Greek verb *sumballein*, meaning "to throw together, compare." Literary critics and commentators commonly employ the term to designate an object or a process that not only serves as an image itself but also refers to a concept or abstract idea that is important to the theme of the work.

In literary criticism, symbolic comparisons are generally considered to be more open to interpretation and various in meaning, whereas allegorical comparisons (or emblems) are often prescribed and more particular. In Kate Chopin's *The Awakening* (1899), for instance, the process of learning how to swim takes on a symbolic significance for the protagonist, Edna Pontellier:

Edna had attempted all summer to learn to swim. She had received instructions from both the men and women; in some instances from the children. Robert had pursued a system of lessons almost daily; and he was nearly at the point of discouragement in realizing the futility of his efforts. A certain ungovernable dread hung about her when in the water, unless there was a hand near by that might reach out and reassure her.

But that night she was like the little tottering, stumbling, clutching child, who of a sudden realizes its powers, and walks for the first time alone, boldly and with over-confidence. She could have shouted for joy. She did shout for joy, as with a sweeping stroke or two she lifted her body to the surface of the water.

A feeling of exultation overtook her, as if some power of significant import had been given her soul. She grew daring and reckless, overestimating her strength. She wanted to swim far out, where no woman had swum before.

Edna's hardwon success in learning how to swim may be read as a symbol of her quest for independence, confidence, and self-sufficiency. The act of swimming is itself an image of physical achievement. But, in addition, Edna feels "as if some power of significant import had been given her soul." Thus, although the significance of this symbolic process is not fixed, her swimming may be interpreted as symbolic of the idea of feeling powerful and self-reliant.

A symbol may be associated with only one referent, as is a street sign forbidding a left turn or another warning of a school-crossing. In literature, however, most symbols are multivalent. In Nathaniel Hawthorne's *The Scarlet Letter* (1850), for instance, the letter takes on a number of competing significances. At the beginning of the novel, the protagonist, Hester Prynne, is forced to wear the scarlet letter upon her breast as an emblem of her sin: A for Adultery. In the course of the tale, however, the symbolic meaning of the letter seems to change. In discussing Hester's ministry to the poor and the sick, the narrator recognizes this alteration of the letter's signification:

> There glimmered the embroidered letter, with comfort in its unearthly ray. Elsewhere the token of sin, it was the taper of the sick-chamber. It had even thrown its gleam, in the sufferer's hard extremity, across the verge of time. It had shown him where to set his foot, while the light of earth was fast becoming dim, and ere the light of futurity could reach him. . . . Her breast, with its badge of shame, was but the softer pillow for the head that needed one. She was self-ordained a Sister of Mercy; or, we may rather say, the world's heavy hand had so ordained her, when neither the world nor she looked forward to this result. The letter was the symbol of her calling. Such helpfulness was found in her;—so much power to do, and power to sympathize,—that many people refused to interpret the scarlet A by its original signification. They said that it meant Able, so strong was Hester Prynne with a woman's strength.

Thus, the palpable image of the scarlet letter symbolizes first the concept of her sin and later the idea of her strength.

In some cases, the reference or meaning of literary symbols is deliberately indeterminate. In Denise Chavez's story "Willow Game" (1986), for example, the narrator describes three trees that were significant to her as a child. She then recalls how each of the trees changed. The last of them, a willow tree, began to die after a neighbor's oldest son, Ricky, cut off its branches:

> It was not long after Ricky's emerging manhood that the Willow began to ail, even as I watched it. I knew it was hurting. The tree began to look bare. The limbs were lifeless, in anguish, and there was no discernible reason. The solid, green rooms of our child's play collapsed, the passageways became cavernous hallways, the rivers of grass died and there was not shade. The tree was dying. . . .
>
> It wasn't until years later (although the knowledge was there, admitted, seen) that my mother told me that one day she went outside

to see Ricky standing on a ladder under our Willow. He had a pair of scissors in his hands and was cutting whole branches off the tree and throwing them to one side. Mother said, "What are you doing, Ricky?" He replied, "I'm cutting the tree." "Do you realize that you're killing it?" she responded calmly. It is here that the interpretation breaks down, where the photographs fade into grey wash, and I momentarily forget what Ricky's reply was, that day, so many years ago, as the limbs of our willow fell about him, cascading tears, willow reminders past the face of my mother who stood solemnly and without horror.

Although the mutilation and death of the tree seem to suggest the passing of youth and innocence, the tree's symbolism remains deliberately vague and mysterious. See **ALLEGORY**.

SYNECDOCHE

Synecdoche is a Greek word that literally means "to take up with another." In literary criticism, the term describes a figure of speech in which a part of an object or a process is used to represent the whole. The following excerpt from T. S. Eliot's "Preludes" (1917) offers two examples:

> The morning comes to consciousness
> Of faint stale smells of beer
> From the sawdust-trampled street
> With all its muddy feet that press
> To early coffee-stands.
> With the other masquerades
> That time resumes,
> One thinks of all the hands
> That are raising dingy shades
> In a thousand furnished rooms.

Both the "muddy feet that press / To early coffee-stands" and "the hands / That are raising dingy shades" are synecdochal figures. The feet are representative parts of workers whose morning routine begins with a visit to the coffee shops. The hands are representative of the many apartment dwellers whose daily ritual is started by raising the shades on windows. Eliot seems to use synecdoche in these lines to emphasize both the anonymity of these commonplace people and their seemingly mechanical and repetitive actions, as though their feet and hands operated automatically. See **METONYMY**.

SYNESTHESIA

The word *synesthesia* literally means "sensations together." Literary critics and commentators use the term to refer to figures of speech or images that describe a particular sensory experience as though it were appreciated through one or more of the other senses. The first stanza of Emily Dickinson's poem "There's a certain Slant of light" (1890) offers an example:

> There's a certain Slant of light,
> Winter Afternoons—
> That oppresses like the Heft
> Of Cathedral Tunes—

The "Slant of light," which is normally experienced visually, is described in terms of the sense of touch and hearing. Moreover, the light is not compared to the auditory sense or sound "Of Cathedral Tunes" but to the tactile sense of their "Heft." Dickinson may well be using synesthesia to suggest that the "certain Slant of light, / Winter Afternoons" penetrates to and reverberates through the whole of her being: her muscles, nerves, and soul.

The following lines from Octavio Paz's poem "This Side" (1987) offer a more contemporary example:

> There is light. We neither see nor touch it.
> In its empty clarities rests
> what we touch and see.
> I see with my fingertips
> what my eyes touch. . . .
>   (trans. Eliot Weinberger)

As the speaker puts it, his tactile sense enables him to see, and his visual sense enables him to feel.

T

THEME

Critics and commentators commonly employ the term *theme* to designate any significant, recurring, or developed idea, concept, or argument in a work of literature. Some works present a central or dominant theme; others play with or interweave a number of related themes.

A theme may be overtly stated or subtly suggested. Charles Dickens's *Great Expectations* (1861) offers an example of the former. Near the middle of the novel, Pip, who is both the protagonist and the narrator, recollects both his snobbery toward his friend Joe and his attempts to rationalize his feelings:

> All other swindlers upon earth are nothing to the self-swindlers, and with such pretences did I cheat myself. Surely a curious thing. That I should innocently take a bad half-crown of somebody else's manufacture, is reasonable enough; but that I should knowingly reckon the spurious coin of my own make, as good money! An obliging stranger, under pretence of compactly folding up my bank-notes for security's sake, abstracts the notes and gives me nutshells; but what is his sleight of hand to mine, when I fold up my own nutshells and pass them on myself as notes.

Although Dickens employs the extended metaphor of forgery, the equation between "self-swindlers" and self-deceivers is clearly made. Thus, the theme of this passage is the concept of lying to or deceiving one's self.

In other works, the theme is implied or suggested rather than stated. Such is the case in Rita Dove's poem "The House Slave" (1980):

> The first horn lifts its arm over the dew-lit grass
> and in the slave quarters there is a rustling—
> children are bundled into aprons, cornbread
>
> and water gourds grabbed, a salt pork breakfast taken.
> I watch them driven into the vague before-dawn
> while their mistress sleeps like an ivory toothpick

and Massa dreams of asses, rum and slave-funk.
I cannot fall asleep again. At the second horn,
the whip curls across the backs of the laggards—

sometimes my sister's voice, unmistaken, among them.
"Oh! pray," she cries. "Oh! pray!" Those days
I lie on my cot, shivering in the early heat,

and as the fields unfold to whiteness,
and they spill like bees among the fat flowers,
I weep. It is not yet daylight.

Although the stated subject of this poem is slavery, two of the unstated but significant themes are the concepts of sympathy and guilt: the speaker's sympathy for the field slaves and her feelings of guilt about the plight of her sister.

TONE

Tone is a term used to describe an author's attitude toward a reader, although some commentators use the term interchangeably with *mood*, which in the strictest sense refers to the author's attitude toward the subject of the work. The distinction is not always clear because tone and mood are often intermixed; that is to say, the author's attitude toward the subject may influence or color his or her attitude toward the reader.

In prose fiction, authors may reveal their attitudes directly through intrusive narration. Henry Fielding's *Tom Jones* (1749) offers a number of passages that indicate a tone of firm but kindly moral instruction:

> To say the truth, want of compassion is not to be numbered among our
> general faults. The black ingredient which fouls our disposition is envy.
> Hence our eye is seldom, I am afraid, turned upward to those who are
> manifestly greater, better, wiser, or happier than ourselves, without
> some degree of malignity; while we commonly look downwards on the
> mean and miserable, with insufficient benevolence and pity. In fact, I
> have remarked, that most of the defects which have discovered them-
> selves in the friendships within my observation, have arisen from envy
> only; a hellish vice; and yet one from which I have known very few
> absolutely exempt. But enough of a subject which, if pursued, would
> lead me too far.

Fielding's tone is both paternal and authoritative, but it does not come across as sanctimonious or intolerant.

Wilfred Owen's poem *"Dulce Et Decorum Est"* (1920), which takes its title from an ode by Horace ("Sweet and fitting it is to die for one's country") and repeats the allusion fully in the last two lines of the poem, offers an example of authorial tone in a work overtly addressed to a reader or listener. Having described the horrors of trench warfare in the First World War, including the description of a comrade who chokes to death during exposure to mustard gas, Owen finishes with a direct appeal to his reader:

> If in some smothering dreams you too could pace
> Behind the wagon that we flung him in,
> And watch the white eyes writhing in his face,
> His hanging face, like a devil's sick on sin;
> If you could hear, at every jolt, the blood
> Come gargling from the froth-corrupted lungs,
> Obscene as cancer, bitter as the cud
> Of vile, incurable sores on innocent tongues, —
> My friend, you would not tell with such high zest
> To children ardent for some desperate glory,
> The old Lie: *Dulce et decorum est Pro patria mori.*

The tone of anger, bitterness, and accusation in this passage is betrayed through the graphic descriptions and use of harsh-sounding consonants: "If you could hear, at every jolt, the blood / Come gargling from the froth-corrupted lungs, / Obscene as cancer, bitter as the cud / Of vile, incurable sores on innocent tongues."

Emily Dickinson's poem "I'm Nobody! Who are you?" (1891) is an example of tone intermixed with **mood**:

> I'm Nobody! Who are you?
> Are you—Nobody—Too?
> Then there's a pair of us?
> Don't tell! they'd advertise—you know!
>
> How dreary—to be—Somebody!
> How public—like a Frog—
> To tell one's name—the livelong June—
> To an admiring Bog!

The speaker's attitude toward both her subject and her listener is one of wry and mocking humor. The first part of the poem takes up a conversational tone that suggests a certain lightness. The second part of the poem uses **anaphora** ("How dreary . . ."; "How public . . .") and **rhyme** ("Frog" and "Bog") to establish a gently satiric tone of superiority toward her subject. See **MOOD, RHETORIC/ RHETORICAL SCHEMES**, and **VOICE**.

TRAGEDY

The word *tragedy* derives from the Greek *tragoidia*, meaning "goat song." Whether this word alludes to a ceremony in which a goat was sacrificed, as some have speculated, or to a goat offered as a prize for the best performance, as others have proposed, is unclear. What does seem clear is that tragedy in the more modern sense of a drama depicting the downfall, suffering, or death of one or more characters began as a highly ritualized performance involving both song and dance.

The most important work on ancient Greek tragedies is Aristotle's *Poetics* (fourth century B.C.), which seeks to define the structure and purpose of tragedy.

In discussing the structure of tragedy, Aristotle is concerned primarily with plot. He asserts that tragic plots should have a clear beginning, middle, and end, and that the action should be ordered and continuous, proceeding from causal necessity. Aristotle contrasts this "**unity of action**" with episodic plots in which incidents occur without any probable sequence or cause. As to the purpose of tragedy, he insists that the events should inspire fear or pity, through which the members of the audience experience **catharsis**. The nature of this catharsis has long been the subject of debate. Some critics have described it as a type of purgation that restores the audience to a desired emotional balance. Others have associated catharsis with moral purification. And some commentators insist that catharsis serves a cognitive purpose, enabling the audience to achieve a greater clarity of intellect.

Aristotle goes on in his *Poetics* to discuss **simple and complex plots**. In the simple plot the change of fortune of the protagonist takes place "without Reversal of Situation and without Recognition," whereas in the complex plot, the change in fortune "is accompanied by such Reversal, or by Recognition, or by both." For Aristotle, a perfect tragedy, in order to inspire true fear or pity, should be constructed as a complex plot concerning a "highly renowned and prosperous" protagonist "whose misfortune is brought about not by vice or depravity, but by some error or frailty."

Sophocles's *Oedipus the King* (fourth century B.C.) provides an example of a tragedy that embodies Aristotle's unities and other virtues. In the beginning of the play, Oedipus, the king of Thebes and husband of Jocasta, learns from the Delphic Oracle that the plague visited upon his city is attributable to the unsolved murder of Laius, Oedipus's predecessor as king and Jocasta's former husband. Although he is warned by the blind seer Teiresias not to pursue the truth of the situation, Oedipus determines to find Laius's killer and bring him to justice. In the course of events, Oedipus learns that he himself killed Laius without knowing his victim's identity; moreover, Oedipus discovers that Laius was his father and that Jocasta is his mother. In recalling how he had attempted to avoid the fate predicted for him (to kill his father and marry his mother) by fleeing the city of his adoptive parents, Oedipus ponders a change in fortune clearly marked by both "Reversal of Situation" (**peripeteia**) and "Recognition" (**anagnorisis**). As Aristotle recommends, the *peripeteia*, meaning "to fall around," and the *anagnorisis*, meaning "to know again," coincide in this tragedy. Oedipus's fall occurs at the moment he achieves insight into his true identity. All that remains is the third part of the tragic plot: suffering. According to Aristotle, "the incident of suffering results from destructive or painful action such as death on the stage, scenes of very great pain, the infliction of wounds, and the like."

The nine tragedies of the playwright called Seneca (The Younger) proved to be the most influential of the Roman period. These Senecan tragedies, versions or imitations of earlier Greek tragedies, are notable for their recurring themes of revenge, as well as their descriptions of offstage bloodletting and murder. In addition, Seneca introduced supernatural elements such as ghosts. These themes and elements clearly influenced the work of Renaissance playwrights, particularly those of the Elizabethan age and the Jacobean period in England, such as Thomas Kyd's *The Spanish Tragedy* (1594), John Webster's *The White Devil* (1608), and William Shakespeare's *Titus Andronicus* (1594). Unlike Senecan tragedies, these *revenge tragedies* (or *tragedies of blood*, as they are sometimes called) dealt with themes of retribution using onstage depictions of violence and murder. Indeed, *Titus Andronicus* is infamous for its body count.

The most famous of revenge plays, Shakespeare's *Hamlet* (1601), draws upon several elements of Senecan tragedy. In Act 1, scene 5 of the play, the dialogue between Hamlet and the ghost of his late father (secretly murdered by Claudius, his brother) explicitly introduces the theme of revenge:

GHOST: Revenge his foul and most unnatural murder.

HAMLET: Murder!

GHOST: Murder most foul, as in the best it is,
But this most foul, strange, and unnatural.

HAMLET: Haste me to know't, that I wings as swift
As meditation, or the thoughts of love,
May sweep to my revenge.

The subplots of Fortinbras and Laertes seeking revenge for their father's death support and deepen the theme of retribution. In the end, the number of those killed on or offstage includes Polonius, Ophelia, Laertes, Gertrude, Claudius, and Hamlet himself. But more than merely a play about revenge and murder, Hamlet is a tragedy in the Aristotelian sense, for it presents the downfall of a worthy protagonist. As Horatio observes upon Hamlet's death, "Now cracks a noble heart. Good night, sweet prince / And flights of angels sing thee to thy rest!" (5.2.359–360).

The notion that a tragedy in the great tradition must enact the downfall of a great and noble protagonist has been increasingly challenged by modern drama and dramatists. Plays such as Henrik Ibsen's *A Doll's House* (1879), Eugene O'Neill's *Mourning Becomes Electra* (1931), Tennessee William's *A Streetcar Named Desire* (1947), and Arthur Miller's *Death of a Salesman* (1947) present protagonists who are more antiheroic than heroic and often far from being noble born. Moreover, the downfalls of these protagonists are more often psychological, involving inexorable revelations of their many and complex frailties rather than a single tragic flaw. Nevertheless, the plays often accord to and argue for a type of tragic dignity in their characters. As Willy Loman's wife, Linda, explains to her son Biff in Act 1 of *Death of a Salesman*:

I don't say he's a great man. Willy Loman never made a lot of money.
His name was never in the paper. He's not the finest character that ever
lived. But he's a human being, and a terrible thing is happening to him.

So attention must be paid. He's not to be allowed to fall into his grave like an old dog. Attention, attention must be finally paid to such a person.

Linda's argument would seem to be Arthur Miller's as well: that the suffering and death of a "low man" can be a tragedy. See **DRAMA**, **PROTAGONIST**, and **RENAISSANCE**.

TRANSCENDENTALISM

Although the term *transcendental* was first used in a philosophical sense by the German philosopher Immanuel Kant, transcendentalism as a school of thought and a literary movement is most closely associated with a group of American thinkers and writers who formed The Transcendental Club in Boston in the 1830s. The members of this club and their followers—Ralph Waldo Emerson, Henry David Thoreau, Bronson Alcott, and Margaret Fuller, among others— thought of transcendentalism as a philosophy whereby one would seek to transcend the mere physical world of the senses and elevate one's soul to a higher moral or spiritual plane. In many ways, American Transcendentalism was a loose collection of beliefs against the conventions of late eighteenth- and early nineteenth-century American religious, economic, and philosophical thought: a lingering Calvinist theology with its emphasis on God's sovereignty; rampant materialism and burgeoning industrialization; and Lockean empiricism, which held that human knowledge is limited to that which can be known through the senses. Drawing on the philosophy of Plato (who insisted that reality existed in the realm of ideas rather than in the physical world), the prose and poetry of English Romantic poet Samuel Taylor Coleridge (who touted the power of reason as an imaginative faculty above mere understanding), and Eastern religions (which vaunted the spiritual above the material), the transcendentalists proclaimed the primacy of the human soul.

In his essay entitled "Nature" (1836), Emerson contradicts the notion of God as an absolutely sovereign and distant deity by describing an ecstatic experience of the divine in nature:

Standing on the bare ground,—my head bathed by the blithe air, and uplifted into infinite space,—all mean egotism vanishes. I become a transparent eyeball; I am nothing; I see all; the currents of the Universal Being circulate through me; I am part or particle of God.

As this passage suggests, American transcendentalists tended toward pantheism: the belief that God is universally manifested throughout nature but is best understood as a transcendent reality that can only be reached through spiritual contemplation. In order to attain this transcendent reality, as Emerson argues in "Nature," one must learn to appreciate objects, elements, and forces in the natural world as more than mere commodities:

When we speak of nature in this manner, we have a distinct but most poetical sense in the mind. We mean the integrity of impression made by manifold natural objects. It is this that distinguishes the stick of timber of the wood-cutter from the tree of the poet. The charming landscape which I saw this morning, is indubitably made up of some twenty or thirty farms. Miller owns this field, Locke that, and Manning the woodland beyond. But none of them owns the landscape. There is a property in the horizon which no man has but he whose eye can integrate all the parts, that is, the poet. This is the best part of these men's farms, yet to this their warranty-deeds give no title.

At the level of commodity, man sees a discontinuous landscape of discrete properties to be bought, owned, or sold. But the man who looks with the eye of the poet, using what Coleridge called imagination and Emerson calls reason, is capable of appreciating the organic unity of the landscape at an aesthetic level (as beautiful). Beyond this level, Emerson believes, there are ever higher "platform[s] of experience" at which to appreciate nature; indeed, at the level of spiritual contemplation, man may come to see nature as a manifestation of the perfect idea of divine order and reason. In describing both the aesthetic and spiritual levels of appreciating nature, Emerson contradicts Lockean empiricism by declaring that man has an intuitive faculty that can do more than merely record sensory impressions. (It is likely no coincidence that one of the individualized fields Emerson mentions is owned by a man named Locke).

As a metaphor for these always expanding platforms of experience, Emerson employs the graphic representation of concentric circles and the description of ripples in a pool of water. As he explains in his essay entitled "Circles,"

> The eye is the first circle; the horizon which it forms is the second; and throughout nature this primary figure is repeated without end. It is the highest emblem in the cipher of the world. St. Augustine described the nature of God as a circle whose center is everywhere and its circumference nowhere.

Besides Emerson's essays and poems, the other major expression of American Transcendentalism is Henry David Thoreau's *Walden* (1854), in which he describes the transcendent ideas and experiences he contemplated and met with during more than two years of living alone in the woods near Concord, Massachusetts. See **AMERICAN LITERARY PERIODS**, **PLATONIC**, and **ROMANTICISM**.

TYPOLOGY

The word *typology* derives from the Greek *typos*, meaning "a mark or a blow, a figure or outline." In this sense, a type may be understood as a kind of **archetype** or original to be repeated or copied. Typology, or the study of types, began as a means of interpreting the Bible. Early Biblical scholars interpreted both the Old and New Testaments as a history of salvation, in which a person, an object, or an event in the Old Testament symbolizes another to come in the New

Testament. In its earliest form, typological interpretation found correspondences between types or originals in the Old Testament that prefigure characters and events in the New Testament, and antitypes that are the ultimate events in the New Testament that are foreshadowed in the Old Testament. These antitypes are nearly always associated with the coming of Jesus as the Messiah and events surrounding his life, crucifixion, and ascension to heaven. For example, according to typological interpretation, the story of Jonah and the whale prefigures the death and resurrection of Christ. Jonah's time in the belly of the whale symbolically rehearses Christ's suffering and death on the cross. The whale's releasing of Jonah from its belly symbolically prefigures Christ's emerging from his tomb and ascending to heaven. For typologists, such correspondences were not imagined or read into the Bible. The types and antitypes were meant by God to be recognized and understood, so that readers of the Bible could become more fully aware of God's intentions. Most familiarly, the analogies between type and antitype signified a paradigm or repeated example of God's testing the faith of Biblical characters through suffering. Those whose faith enabled them to endure suffering were rewarded through God's grace with eternal salvation.

Although typology as a means of Christian interpretation and expression soon gave way to allegory, it experienced a renaissance after the Reformation when Protestant sects began to conceive of analogies between their experiences and those of Biblical figures. This new version of typology is particularly noticeable in the writings of the Separatists and the Puritans who colonized New England in the seventeenth century. For example, in his journal entitled *Of Plymouth Plantation*, William Bradford implicitly compares the sufferings of the Separatists who sailed on the Mayflower and landed in Massachusetts to the plight of the Israelites in the Old Testament:

> So many, therefore, of these professors as saw the evil of these things in these parts, and whose hearts the Lord had touched with heavenly zeal for His truth, they shook off this yoke of antichristian bondage, and as the Lord's free people joined themselves (by a covenant of the Lord) into a church estate, in the fellowship of the gospel, to walk in all His ways made known, or to be made known unto them, according to their best endeavours, whatsoever it should cost them, the Lord assisting them.

As suggested by the phrases "yoke . . . of bondage" and "covenant of the Lord," in this analogy the type is the Israelites of Exodus, and the antitype is God's new chosen people: the pilgrims who made their exodus to the New World. In a latter passage about their landing at Plymouth, Bradford explicitly alludes to Mount Pisgah, the mountain from which Moses viewed the Promised Land.

A different kind of typology, one in which natural objects or processes are the types for moral lessons or spiritual truths, is exemplified by a passage from John Winthrop's *History of New England:*

> At Watertown there was (in view of divers witnesses) a great combat between a mouse and a snake, and after a long fight, the mouse

prevailed and killed the snake. The pastor of Boston, Mr. Wilson, a very sincere, holy man, hearing of it, gave this interpretation: that the snake was the devil; the mouse was a poor contemptible people, which God had brought hither, which should overcome Satan here, and dispossess him of his kingdom.

In typological interpretation, the type is the combat between creatures in the physical world of nature (the mouse and the snake) and the antitypes are the struggles between forces of good and evil in the metaphysical world of spirit (the Puritans in New England and Satan). This kind of typology gave rise to a variety of writings—religious tracts, sermons, poems, and essays—in which the authors sought to "spiritualize" nature and common occupations, such as farming and husbandry. Edward Taylor's poem "Upon a Wasp Chilled with Cold," in which he describes a wasp extending its appendages to warm them in the sun, offers an example of this spiritualizing of nature. Seeing and recognizing the wasp's example, Taylor realizes he should spiritually warm himself in the radiance of God's grace.

Jonathan Edwards's *Images and Shadows of Divine Things*—a collection of preliminary notes, observations, and reflections edited into book form much later by Perry Miller—offers perhaps the ultimate example of early American typological interpretation. In his third image, for instance, Edwards sees roses as types that embody the meaning of Christian suffering and salvation:

> Roses grow upon briars, which is to signify that all temporal sweets are mixed with bitter. But what seems more especially to be meant by it is that pure happiness, the crown of glory, is to be come at in no other way than by bearing Christ's cross, by a life of mortification, self-denial, and labor, and bearing all things for Christ. The rose, that is chief of all flowers, is the last thing that comes out. The briary, prickly bush grows before that; the end and crown of all is the beautiful fragrant tree.

For Edwards, roses are types created by God to show forth that just as the "briary, prickly bush" grows before the flowers bloom, so those who seek salvation must know "a life of mortification, self-denial, and labor" before they receive the "crown" of God's grace in heaven. See **ALLEGORY**, **ANALOGY**, **ARCHETYPE**, and **TROPE**.

U

UNDERSTATEMENT

Understatement is a general term for figures of speech that represent a matter or a case at less than its full force of truth. Two Greek words that have been associated with understatement are *meiosis*, which derives from a verb meaning "to diminish," and *litotes*, which means "simplicity." In many ways, understatement is the opposite of exaggeration or hyperbole, which seeks to make a matter or case larger and more grandiose than it is.

A simple example of *meiosis* might be to say of the Arctic Circle that "it is a little chilly there in winter." Oscar Wilde employs *meiosis* in his play *The Importance of Being Earnest* (1895) when one of his characters remarks to another who has pronounced himself an orphan, "To lose one parent, Mr. Worthing, may be regarded as a misfortune; to lose both looks like carelessness." *Litotes* usually involves understatement through a form of negation: "my dachshund's legs are not the longest I've seen on a dog." The last line of Robert Frost's "Birches" (1916) offers an example of *litotes:*

> I'd like to go by climbing a birch tree,
> And climb black branches up a snow-white trunk
> Toward heaven, till the tree could bear no more,
> But dipped its top and set me down again.
> That should be good both going and coming back.
> One could do worse than be a swinger of birches.

The speaker contemplates climbing trees and swinging down to the earth from their uppermost branches as a metaphor for spiritual renewal. See **HYPERBOLE**.

UTOPIA/DYSTOPIA

The word **Utopia** is a pun on the Greek words *eutopia*, meaning "good place," and *outopia*, meaning "no-place." The English word was invented by Sir Thomas More, who wrote a book of the same title in 1516, in which he describes his idea of a perfect political state. The earliest work describing a Utopia is Plato's *Republic* (fourth century B.C.). In this work, Socrates describes an ideal state in which the needs of justice, commerce, and education are served by a class of guardians. In Book III, for instance, Socrates outlines the conditions and training required to ensure that these guardians would serve the republic and not themselves:

> Then besides that education, it is only common sense to say that the dwellings and other belongings provided for them must be such as will neither make them less perfect Guardians nor encourage them to mal-treat their fellow citizens.
> True.
> With that end in view, let us consider how they should live and be housed. First, none of them must possess any private property beyond the bare necessities. Next, no one is to have any dwelling or store-house that is not open for all to enter at will. Their food, in the quantities required by men of temperance and courage who are in training for war, they will receive from the other citizens as the wages of their guardianship, fixed so that there shall be just enough for the year with nothing over; and they will have meals in common and all live together like soldiers in a camp. Gold and silver, we shall tell them, they will not need. . . . They alone of all the citizens are forbidden to touch and handle silver or gold, or to come under the same roof with them, or wear them as ornaments, or drink from vessels made of them. This manner of life will be their salva-tion and make them the saviours of the commonwealth.

Other literary Utopias include William Morris's *News From Nowhere* (1891), H. G. Wells's *A Modern Utopia* (1905), and Charlotte Perkins Gilman's *Herland* (1915). In *Herland*, Gilman offers a vision of a feminist-socialist Utopia:

> Such high ideals as [these women] had! Beauty, Health, Strength, Intellect, Goodness—for these they prayed and worked.
> They had no enemies; they themselves were all sisters and friends. The land was fair before them, and a great future began to form itself in their minds.
> The religion they had to begin with was much like that of old Greece—a number of gods and goddesses; but they lost all interest in deities of war and plunder, and gradually focused on their Mother Goddess altogether. Then, as they grew more intelligent, this had turned into a sort of Maternal Pantheism.
> Here was Mother Earth bearing fruit. All that they ate was fruit of motherhood, from seed or egg or their product. By motherhood they were born and by motherhood they lived—life was, to them, just the long cycle of motherhood.

Gilman imagines a world without war, where women have created an entirely new system of social roles based on a "practically universal affection, rising to exquisite and unbroken friendships."

In contrast, **dystopia** is a Greek word meaning "bad place." As a literary term, it is used to describe a work of literature that projects a future world, state, or situation in which the human condition is wholly degraded. George Orwell's novel *1984*, which was published in 1948, depicts a world that is divided into three totalitarian states that are constantly at war. The condition of the protagonist, Winston Smith, is characterized by the passage that introduces him:

> The hallway smelt of boiled cabbage and old rag mats. At one end of it a colored poster, too large for indoor display, had been tacked to the wall. It depicted simply an enormous face, more than a meter wide: the face of a man of about forty-five, with a heavy black mustache and ruggedly handsome features. Winston made for the stairs. It was no use trying the lift. Even at the best of times it was seldom working, and at present the electric current was cut off during daylight hours. It was part of the economy drive in preparation for Hate Week. The flat was seven flights up, and Winston, who was thirty-nine, and had a varicose ulcer above his right ankle, went slowly, resting several times on the way. On each landing, opposite the lift shaft, the poster with the enormous face gazed from the wall. It was one of those pictures which are so contrived that the eyes follow you when you move. BIG BROTHER IS WATCHING YOU, the caption beneath it read.

As this passage suggests, Smith lives in an environment of material and economic decay; he is himself physically and spiritually deteriorated. Moreover, the totalitarian rule of Big Brother has reduced the citizens of Oceania to a state of paranoid fear, blind obedience, and utter dependence.

Aldous Huxley's *Brave New World* (1932) depicts a different kind of dystopia in which science and technology are deployed to control human beings, not through fear but by conditioning them to accept an existence of mindless pleasure and obedience. In the beginning of the novel, Huxley describes a laboratory in which the citizens of this new world are hatched from incubators:

> Bent over their instruments, three hundred Fertilizers were plunged, as the Director of Hatcheries and Conditioning entered the room, in the scarcely breathing silence, the absent-minded soliloquizing hum or whistle, of absorbed concentration. A troop of newly arrived students, very young, pink and callow, followed nervously, rather abjectly, at the Director's heels. Each of them carried a note-book, in which, whenever the great man spoke, he desperately scribbled . . .
>
> "Just to give you a general idea," he would explain to them. For of course some sort of general idea they must have, if they were to do their work intelligently—though as little of one, if they were to be good and happy members of society, as possible.

Dystopias usually express concern or fear about a potentially dreadful future. A number of post-World War II films, such as *Planet of the Apes* (Franklin J. Schaffner, 1968) and *Terminator* (James Cameron, 1984), project the state of the world following a series of cataclysmic or nuclear wars. Other dystopias express anxiety over the effects of advances in biotechnology, depletion of natural resources, or growing lawlessness among modern societies. Literary dystopias developing out of these concerns include Ursula K. Leguin's *The Left Hand of Darkness* (1969) and Margaret Atwood's *The Handmaid's Tale* (1986). Film dystopias include *Mad Max* (George Miller, 1979), *Blade Runner* (Ridley Scott, 1982), and *The Crow* (Alex Proyas, 1994).

V

VICTORIAN PERIOD (IN ENGLISH LITERATURE)

The Victorian period encompasses the reign of Queen Victoria from 1837 to 1901. During this era, many works were written in response to the events of the time. The era was one of prodigious disruption, reform, and transition in many areas of life including law, science, religion, medicine, economics, and philosophy. Technological changes, including the advent of railways, the telegraph, and steamships, transformed the country. Some writers ratified the changes of the time, but others sharply denounced them.

In the poetry of the period, Romantic characteristics were still evident, but many writers reacted to changes of the time period or looked back with nostalgia to the remote past. Poets from this period include Alfred Lord Tennyson, Robert Browning, Elizabeth Barrett Browning, Matthew Arnold, and Algernon Charles Swinburne. Tennyson, in particular, represents the mindset of many individuals of his generation in his mid-century poem *In Memoriam* (1850). In this work, Tennyson laments the death of his close friend Arthur Hallam. The death of his friend leads to reflections on religious faith and immortality. In the face of new scientific discoveries, the speaker in the poem at times almost succumbs to despair and fear of the loss of a benevolent God:

> O, yet we trust that somehow good
> Will be the final goal of ill,
> To pangs of nature, sins of will,
> Defects of doubt, and taints of blood;
>
> That nothing walks with aimless feet,
> That not one life shall be destroyed,
> Or cast as rubbish to the void,
> When God hath made the pile complete;
>
> That not a worm is cloven in vain,
> That not a moth with vain desire
> Is shrivell'd in a fruitless fire,
> Or but subserves another's gain.

Behold, we know not anything;
I can but trust that good shall fall
At last—far off—at last to all,
And every winter change to spring.

So runs my dream; but what am I?
An infant crying in the night;
An infant crying for the light.
And with no language but a cry. (Lyric LIV)

The speaker meditates on the logical evidence against the notion of immortality. Brutal natural laws such as the extinction of species clash with the viewpoint that God is munificent. As a result, the speaker trusts in benevolent nature but feels like an "infant crying in the night."

The Victorian era is well known for its prose, both nonfiction and fiction. Nonfiction prose writers include Thomas Carlyle, Matthew Arnold, John Henry Newman, John Ruskin, and Walter Pater. Fiction writers include Charles Dickens, William Thackeray, the Brontes, George Eliot (Mary Ann Evans), Anthony Trollope, and Thomas Hardy. In *Bleak House* (1854), Dickens opens with a description of the streets of London:

Fog everywhere. Fog up the river, where it flows among green aits and meadows; fog down the river, where it rolls defiled among the tiers of shipping, and the waterside pollutions of a great (and dirty) city. Fog on the Essex marshes, fog on the Kentish heights. Fog creeping in the cabooses of collier-brigs; fog lying out on the yards, and hovering in the rigging of great ships; fog drooping on the gunwales of barges and small boats. Fog in the eyes and throats of ancient Greenwich pensioners, wheezing by the firesides of their wards; fog in the stem and bowl of the afternoon pipe of the wrathful skipper, down in his close cabin; fog cruelly pinching the toes and fingers of his shivering 'prentice boy on deck. . . . The raw afternoon is rawest, and the dense fog is densest, and the muddy streets are muddiest, near that leaden-headed old obstruc-tion, appropriate ornament for the threshold of a leaden-headed old corporation: Temple Bar. And hard by the Temple Bar, in Lincoln's Inn Hall, at the very heart of the fog, sits the Lord High Chancellor in his High Court of Chancery.

Dickens criticizes the corruption of the city with his symbolic description of the fog, smoke, and mud of the city streets. The description suggests that responsi-bility is being evaded by those in authority (especially in the courts of law), and that the lives of rich and poor are tainted in such a pestilent environment. Dick-ens's use of **anaphora** (repetition of words and phrases at the beginning of sen-tences) emphasizes through sound the overwhelming nature of this moral corruption. The passage comes to a climax with a description of the "High Court of Chancery," which, Dickens implies, is the center and the seat of this corruption.

VOICE

Voice is a term used by some critics to discuss a discernible authorial presence, even in works in which the author is not the narrator or speaker. Jane Austen's *Pride and Prejudice* (1813) offers an example of a direct authorial voice from the beginning:

> It is a truth universally acknowledged, that a single man in possession of a good fortune, must be in want of a wife.
>
> However little known the feelings or views of such a man may be on his first entering a neighbourhood, this truth is so well fixed in the minds of the surrounding families, that he is considered as the rightful property of some one or other of their daughters.

In this and many other passages in the novel, the author's voice becomes appreciable through **tone**, her attitude toward her readers, and her **mood**, her attitude toward her subject. In this case, the authorial voice is humorously ironic in tone and gently satiric in mood.

Charlotte Bronte's *Jane Eyre* (1847) provides an instance of authorial voice making itself apparent through a first-person narrator. Although the story of a young woman seeking to find her role and purpose in life is told by the protagonist (Jane Eyre) herself, Bronte's voice emerges in passages such as the following:

> Nobody knows how many rebellions ferment in the masses of life which people earth. Women are supposed to be very calm generally: but women feel just as men feel; they need exercise for their faculties, and a field for their efforts as much as their brothers do; they suffer from too rigid a restraint, too absolute a stagnation, precisely as men would suffer; and it is narrow-minded in their more privileged fellow creatures to say that they ought to confine themselves to making puddings and knitting stockings, to playing on the piano and embroidering bags. It is thoughtless to condemn them, or laugh at them, if they seek to do more or learn more than custom has pronounced necessary to their sex.

Although these words are spoken by Jane, the very nature of the passage, which is more discourse or commentary than storytelling, betrays an authorial presence.

In modern and contemporary literature, the use of voice is often more subtle, as in V. S. Naipaul's description of his protagonist in the story "My Aunt Gold Teeth" (1967):

> She ate little and prayed much. Her family being Hindu, and her husband being a pundit, she, too, was an orthodox Hindu. Of Hinduism she knew little apart from the ceremonies and the taboos, and this was enough for her. Gold Teeth saw God as a Power, and religious ritual as a means of impressing that Power for great practical good, her good.

Authorial voice is discernible in the phrase "and this was enough for her" and in the added commentary of "her good." The use of voice enables the author to establish a certain ironic distance between himself and the protagonist; it also serves to betray his attitude toward her. See **MOOD** and **TONE**.

PART II

✳

Strategies for Writing Essays about Literature

Introduction

"Strategies for Writing Essays about Literature" is designed to assist students in writing analytical and research essays on literature. We have included six sample student essays with our annotations. The first deals with mood and images in Rita Dove's "Silos" (1989). The second discusses irony and point of view in Kate Chopin's "The Story of an Hour" (1894). The third is a research paper on the Cinderella motif in Jane Austen's *Pride and Prejudice* (1813). The fourth compares novels by Mark Twain and J. M. Barrie. The fifth compares a film version to an original text. The sixth compares Shakespeare's *Hamlet* (1601) to Arthur Miller's *Death of A Salesman* (1949). Our annotations provide advice on organizing and developing content (use of evidence, convincing conclusions) and techniques for improving presentation (transitions, quoting material).

While we fully recognize that no single prototype for writing an effective literary essay exists, we illustrate methods and strategies that have proved successful for many of our own students. We provide a background narrative to each essay, describing challenges faced by student writers in composing their essays and strategies for solving them. The background essays are intended as brief case studies on the process of writing a literary essay from start to finish. The essays highlight terms used in *A Contemporary Guide to Literary Terms*. All terms discussed in the first part of the book appear in boldface in the sample essays to emphasize their importance. In addition, "Strategies for Writing Essays About Literature" includes sections on Advice for Essay Examinations, Avoiding Plagiarism, and A Brief Guide to Documenting Sources.

Background Narrative on "Mood and Images in Rita Dove's 'Silos'"

CHOOSING A SUBJECT

Rhonda Martinez experienced frustrations common to most college student writers before embarking on her first literary paper in an introduction to literature course. The assignment appeared straightforward enough: "Select a poem, preferably one not covered in course lectures, and write a three- to four-page essay on theme and technique (form, meter, rhyme, punctuation, imagery, tone, mood, alliteration, and so on) in the work. Be sure to offer direct quotations to illustrate and support your arguments." Faced with such an infinite choice, she found it difficult to make a decision. After reading several poems in the literature anthology, she selected three possibilities. Any of the alternatives might have worked for her; however, she chose a poem whose subject matter she had experienced first-hand. Rita Dove's "Silos" offers perspectives on an urban landscape dominated by cylindrical silos: the student came from a large city whose chief industry was agricultural products, so she certainly understood the subject.

PREPARING TO WRITE AND ORGANIZING MATERIAL

Knowing the time constraints placed on her by other college courses and a part-time job, this student wisely left herself enough time to write a rough draft, a second draft, and a final revision. After encountering severe writer's block, she reviewed the entries for specific literary terms (**imagery, mood, metaphor, and diction**) in *A Contemporary Guide to Literary Terms*. This reviewing process served as a trigger to her thinking and informed her reading. She detected images and layers of metaphor she had not noticed on her first reading of the selected poem. Because it was necessary to clarify the meaning of the poem, she realized she would have to make a case in defense of her argument. With this resolve in mind, she carefully reread the poem several times (twice aloud to herself) and started to list the key images and terms she planned to discuss.

Organizing the document posed another challenge. At first, she considered discussing all of the images and then the special features she had noticed in the poem. But the plan for the essay seemed fragmented and chaotic. After some reflection, she decided that a more effective strategy would be to consider the elements in each of the four short sections of the poem on a line-by-line basis. She began to draft the essay.

DRAFTING AND REVISING THE ESSAY

Rhonda completed the draft, took a break, and then returned to her essay after several hours so she could review her material with a fresh perspective. The essay was certainly "rough," but she still had time to refine it. Many words and phrases were overused in the essay, so she searched for synonyms in a thesaurus to ensure greater variety. Recognizing the importance of precise terms and lucid definitions, she decided to look up the original meaning and evolution of the word *silo* in the dictionary; this search yielded a useful insight, which she elected to use in her conclusion. She continued to revise the document by rereading the poem and adding more analysis of details she had not previously remarked on.

After leaving the document overnight, she prepared to work on the final revised draft. The spell checker served as a starting point. Then she worked on eliminating poorly introduced sentences (for instance, those beginning with "there was" and "it is") and on strengthening her general style of presentation. A particular piece of advice was dredged up in her memory: after circling all forms of the verb *to be,* she went back over the essay and substituted strong verbs. For example, she substituted "a bird that symbolizes" for "a bird that is symbolic of." After working for several hours on her presentation, Rhonda noted that her essay was not only more convincing but also more concise. She left the title of the essay until last. By now the topic was clear cut, and the title was easy to devise. Before printing a final draft, she ensured that the paper conformed to MLA format. She then proofread the document, reading the last paragraph first and then moving backward through the essay toward the beginning. This proofreading technique made her examine the material in a new way; she found it easier to detect flaws and minor errors.

Silos

RITA DOVE

Like martial swans in spring paraded against the city sky's
shabby blue, they were always too white and
suddenly there.

They were never fingers, never xylophones, although once
a stranger said they put him in mind of Pan's pipes   5
and all the lost songs of Greece. But to the townspeople
they were like cigarettes, the smell chewy and bitter
like a field shorn of milkweed, or beer brewing, or
a fingernail scorched over a flame.

No, no, exclaimed the children. They're a fresh packet of chalk,   10
dreading math work.

They were masculine toys. They were tall wishes. They
were the ribs of the modern world.

Sample Essay

Rhonda Martinez
English 101
Dr. G. Hudson
28 January 2003

Mood and Images
in Rita Dove's "Silos"

Ⓐ

Ⓑ   The setting of Rita Dove's "Silos" (1989) is a surreal urban landscape predominated by cylindrical silos (receptacles for grain or fodder) that reek of bitter
Ⓒ odors. Although the mood of the poem may seem pessimistic or discordant at first, the poet's use of **imagery**, layers of **metaphor**, pace, and **diction** eventually
Ⓓ produces a distinctly different impression. Dove expresses an ambivalent attitude by using varying points of view to create a multilayered or relativist perspective of the silos.   1

Ⓔ   "Silos" begins with a **simile**: "Like martial swans in spring paraded against the city sky's / shabby blue, they were always too white and / suddenly there"
Ⓕ (1–3). Words and phrases such as "martial," "shabby," and "too white" may foster a negative impression of the appearance of the silos in the landscape. But the negative connotations of these terms are offset by the reference to spring, a time associated with regeneration and fresh beginnings, and by the image of the swan, a bird that symbolizes transformation and metamorphosis (as in the familiar story in which an ugly duckling turns into a graceful swan). In addition, the use of **enjambement** in lines 2 and 3 of this first section of the poem—"and / suddenly there"—
Ⓖ underscores the notion of change and renewal. The abrupt phrase stands out visually and aurally, emphasizing the sudden apparition of the bright silos against the blue sky.   2

Ⓗ   The second section of "Silos" indicates what the silos cannot be described as and introduces the remark of a stranger: "They were never fingers, never
Ⓘ xylophones, although once / a stranger said they put him in mind of Pan's pipes
Ⓙ and all the lost songs of Greece" (4–6). While the reference to "lost songs" may manifest an elegiac mood, the allusion to Pan, the Greek god of feasts and merrymaking, creates a note of exuberance. The stranger's allusion to the Greek myth of Pan elevates the silos to a god-like status; however, the poet seems to be

---

Ⓐ Title indicates author and work and orients reader to subject.

Ⓑ Introduction mentions author, work, and date early on.

Ⓒ Author introduces reader to material she will cover in the essay.

Ⓓ Thesis is clearly set out in final statement of the introduction. This is the point the author intends to prove in the essay.

Ⓔ Paper offers a line-by-line analysis of the poem starting with the opening section.

Ⓕ The author fairly considers both sides of the issue but starts to marshal evidence in favor of her argument.

Ⓖ Brief quotations are used effectively as evidence and are followed by detailed comments and interpretation.

Ⓗ Transition sentence—the essay continues its line-by-line analysis.

Ⓘ Line numbers are used for all quotations. Slash marks are used to show line endings in poems.

Ⓙ Author provides detailed commentary on and analysis of quotations to strengthen the case she is making in the paper.

concerned about creating a more personal, down-to-earth myth for the city's inhabitants. The poem is a journey into the town's history; it probes communal memories and presents the multifarious perspectives of a group of townspeople. The inhabitants of the city differ greatly from the outsider in their opinion of the silos:

Ⓚ
    ... But to the townspeople
they were like cigarettes, the smell chewy and bitter
like a field shorn of milkweed, or
beer brewing, or
a fingernail scorched over a flame.
(6-9)
                               3

Ⓛ
    In contrast to the scholarly stranger, who associates the silos with Pan's pipes, the townspeople react to the silos in a more visceral way, noting how the silos assault their senses and inward feelings with their cigarette-like appearance and their "chewy and bitter" odor like that of "a fingernail scorched over a fire." Dove highlights these visceral reactions by her use of concrete diction: "a field shorn of milkweed, or beer brewing." With this use of language, she makes the silos seem more comforting and familiar sights, a vital part of the landscape, rather than objects rising above the people. Moreover, the poem generates a strong sense of the extended community of the town in the description of the reactions of the group to the silos.
                               4

Ⓜ
    In the third section, the poem continues to describe the reaction of the group to the silos, this time that of the youngest generation: "No, no, exclaimed the children. They're a fresh packet of chalk, / dreading math work" (10–11). The children of the townspeople bring the silos down to earth once again by comparing them to new sticks of chalk. This is a comforting association but one not necessarily relished by the children since it reminds them of regimented schoolwork. The free verse form of the poem with its natural, conversational rhythms ("No, no, exclaimed the children. They're a fresh packet of chalk") also reinforces the idea that the silos have taken on the aspect of the familiar for the townspeople, despite their initial abrupt and "martial" appearance.
                               5

    The final lines provide a range of perspectives on the silos: "They were masculine toys. They were tall wishes. They / were the ribs of the modern world"

Ⓝ
(12–13). These lines are forceful in their use of **anaphora** ("They were ..."; "They were ..."; "They were ..."), which provides a rhythmic effect of chanting at the finale of the poem. The townspeople have become like a chorus, offering weighty pronouncements. The richness of viewpoints is all-encompassing. The silos are "masculine toys," invoking the phallic symbolism of the cylindrical structures. They are "tall wishes," invoking the notion of humanity's quest to harvest and contain the natural environment. They are "the ribs of the modern world," a metonymic figure, invoking the idea that the silos have human attributes.
                               6

Ⓚ Long quotations of four or more lines are set off from the main body of the essay text.
Ⓛ Author closely examines the poet's language and literary techniques to give force to her argument in the essay.
Ⓜ Transition sentence.
Ⓝ Author uses ellipses to indicate missing words or phrases.

◎   The **mood** of the poem becomes clearer if the reader considers the etymology of the word *silo*, which derives from the Old English verb *sawan* meaning "to sow." In other words, Dove intentionally sows a multitude of lyrical images and constructions of the silos, from their initial warlike appearance to their representation of the aspirations of modern humanity. Ultimately, the silos take on a mysterious, fertile, and ambivalent quality, full of complexity and vitality. The poem itself becomes like a receptacle or silo, containing a rich storehouse of meanings.   7

Ⓟ **Works Cited**

American Heritage Dictionary of the English Language. 3rd ed. Boston: Houghton, 1992. Print.

Poulin, A., ed. *Contemporary American Poetry.* 6th ed. Boston: Houghton, 1996. Print.

◎ Conclusion returns to thesis but also adds a new insight to give the ending more punch. The validity of the argument is clearly highlighted.

Ⓟ A "Works Cited" section is included for all sources.

Background Narrative on "Point of View and Irony in Chopin's 'The Story of an Hour'"

SELECTION OF A TOPIC

The second major writing assignment in English 101: Introduction to Literature called for an essay on short prose fiction. From among five paper topics, Gary Crawford chose to write on the following:

> 4. Discuss Chopin's use of narrative point of view to create dramatic irony in "The Story of an Hour." Start by offering a thesis statement, clarifying sentences, and a statement of organization in the first paragraph; then introduce each point, offer direct quotations to illustrate the point, and provide analysis of the illustration to develop and explain the point.

Gary selected this topic for several reasons: first of all, he understood the story; second, the instructor's lectures and handouts on narrative point of view and irony had made sense to him; third, he knew he could find specific quotations to illustrate his points. In short, although he liked some of James Joyce's and Flannery O'Connor's stories better, he felt more confident writing about Chopin's work because he believed he could handle the topic.

PRELIMINARY WORK

Gary began by rereading the handouts on narrative point of view and irony. He reminded himself that third-person narratives are either omniscient or limited.

According to the handout, "An omniscient third-person narrator knows everything about characters' actions, thoughts, and feelings, whereas a limited third-person narrator tends to focus attention on the perceptions, thoughts, and feelings of a single character."

Looking specifically for quotations to use in illustrating narrative point of view, Gary reread the story. He had marked a few passages during the class discussion of the text, but this time he found many more and better examples. Moreover, he was reminded by his class notes that the instructor had mentioned that the story begins and ends with an omniscient narrator, but that it employs a limited narrator in the middle. He underlined words and phrases that seemed to him particularly indicative of omniscient or of limited points of view. In doing so, he noticed that the shifts in point of view coincided with the protagonist's going in and out of her room. These were logical points of transition in the story's plot.

The irony of the final line was a topic of discussion in the class meeting on Chopin's work. Gary began to think about why the conclusion was ironic and for whom. He consulted the handout on irony again and focused on the section concerning dramatic irony. According to the handout, dramatic irony occurs when "the reader shares with the narrator (or authorial voice) knowledge of a situation or intention unknown to one or more of the characters." Gary decided that the knowledge the narrator and the reader share in the story concerns Mrs. Mallard's true feelings about her husband's death. He looked for passages in the middle section that helped to set up the irony of the final line.

STARTING THE ESSAY: ORGANIZATION

In writing the first essay, Gary had wasted several hours trying to perfect his introductory paragraph. This time he followed his instructor's advice: "Write the middle or body of your essay first because you don't know where you are going until you have been there." He opened a file on his computer and typed the passages he had decided to quote (starting with the beginning of the story and moving paragraph by paragraph to the end). Then he inserted a rough introduction before each of the quotations and a few lines of analysis or explanation after.

Having determined the basic content of the body of his essay, Gary turned to his introductory paragraph. He played around with several thesis statements before settling on one that stated the main points of the essay concisely. Then he wrote a clarifying sentence to explain the thesis statement. The statement of organization, however, proved more difficult. In reviewing the body of his essay, he recognized that his quotations and analysis could be divided into three parts: a discussion of the beginning of the story, with its omniscient narrator; a discussion of the middle of the story, with its limited narrator; and a discussion of the conclusion, with its return to an omniscient point of view. He wrote two sentences previewing this organization.

SECOND DRAFT

Having left his rough draft alone for a few days, Gary returned to it and began to revise his essay. He remembered that his first essay had been criticized for lack of development. The instructor had advised him to offer analysis of quotations by explaining how they illustrated the point he was trying to make. The student imagined that he was explaining the meaning of each quotation to the class. As he revised each paragraph, he read it carefully to himself to be certain the sentences made sense and followed logically.

When finished with the body and introduction, Gary moved to the conclusion. He reminded himself of his thesis statement and realized that he had not explained how the irony of the story revealed the theme. He thought of rewriting the introduction, but then he decided to discuss the theme in his conclusion, since the irony was most obvious at the end of the story. This strategy would allow him to return to the thesis without merely reiterating his introduction. In this way, he would make his conclusion stronger and less repetitive. He had unwittingly saved his most important point for last.

FINAL TOUCHES

Taking his instructor's advice, Gary read his essay aloud, noting any sentences that sounded awkward or seemed unclear. On his first paper, he had failed to use effective transitions between paragraphs. He focused his attention on connecting points by reminding his reader of what had been discussed in the previous paragraph and relating that argument to his introduction of new material in the next paragraph.

Gary had also experienced problems with weak diction, especially in his choice of verbs. He tried to use more active verbs, replace *is* and *have* with more specific verbs, and to avoid the multiple repetition of verbs such as *state* and *show*. Before printing, Gary consulted a sample essay the instructor had copied for the class. In reviewing the sample, he discovered that he had mispunctuated his quotations and had forgotten to offer a title at the beginning and a "Work Cited" entry at the end. In his title, he included the author's name, the title of the story, and a brief description of the main points of the essay. He placed the story's title in quotation marks. He inserted a "Work Cited" entry using standard MLA form. Then, having entered the necessary information in the top left-hand corner of the first page, and having created a header with his last name and a page number at the top right-hand corner of each page, he highlighted the entire document below the title and double spaced it.

For the final touch, he ran a spell check and then checked the essay himself for typographical errors and missing words or sentences.

The Story of an Hour

KATE CHOPIN (1851–1904)

Knowing that Mrs. Mallard was afflicted with a heart trouble, great care was taken to break to her as gently as possible the news of her husband's death.

It was her sister Josephine who told her, in broken sentences; veiled hints that revealed in half-concealing. Her husband's friend Richards was there, too, near her. It was he who had been in the newspaper office when intelligence of the railroad disaster was received, with Brently Mallard's name leading the list of "killed." He had only taken the time to assure himself of its truth by a second telegram, and had hastened to forestall any less careful, less tender friend in bearing the sad message.

She did not hear the story as many women have heard the same, with a paralyzed inability to accept its significance. She wept at once, with sudden, wild abandonment, in her sister's arms. When the storm of grief had spent itself she went away to her room alone. She would have no one follow her.

There stood, facing the open window, a comfortable, roomy armchair. Into this she sank, pressed down by a physical exhaustion that haunted her body and seemed to reach into her soul.

She could see in the open square before her house the tops of trees that were all aquiver with the new spring life. The delicious breath of rain was in the air. In the street below a peddler was crying his wares. The notes of a distant song which some one was singing reached her faintly, and countless sparrows were twittering in the eaves.

There were patches of blue sky showing here and there through the clouds that had met and piled one above the other in the west facing her window.

She sat with her head thrown back upon the cushion of the chair, quite motionless, except when a sob came up into her throat and shook her, as a child who has cried itself to sleep continues to sob in its dreams.

She was young, with a fair, calm face, whose lines bespoke repression and even a certain strength. But now there was a dull stare in her eyes, whose gaze was fixed away off yonder on one of those patches of blue sky. It was not a glance of reflection, but rather indicated a suspension of intelligent thought.

There was something coming to her and she was waiting for it, fearfully. What was it? She did not know; it was too subtle and elusive to name. But she felt it, creeping out of the sky, reaching toward her through the sounds, the scents, the color that filled the air.

Now her bosom rose and fell tumultuously. She was beginning to recognize this thing that was approaching to possess her, and she was striving to beat it back with her will—as powerless as her two white slender hands would have been.

When she abandoned herself, a little whispered word escaped her slightly parted lips. She said it over and over under her breath: "Free, free, free!" The vacant stare and the look of terror that had followed it went from her eyes. They stayed keen and bright. Her pulses beat fast, and the coursing blood warmed and relaxed every inch of her body.

She did not stop to ask if it were or were not a monstrous joy that held her. A clear and exalted perception enabled her to dismiss the suggestion as trivial.

She knew that she would weep again when she saw the kind, tender hands folded in death; the face that had never looked save with love upon her, fixed and gray and dead. But she saw beyond that bitter moment a long procession of years to come that would belong to her absolutely. And she opened and spread her arms out to them in welcome.

There would be no one to live for her during those coming years; she would live for herself. There would be no powerful will bending hers in that blind persistence with which men and women believe they have a right to impose a private will upon a fellow-creature. A kind intention or a cruel intention made the act seem no less a crime as she looked upon it in that brief moment of illumination.

And yet she had loved him—sometimes. Often she had not. What did it matter! What could love, the unsolved mystery, count for in face of this possession of self-assertion which she suddenly recognized as the strongest impulse of her being!

"Free! Body and soul free!" she kept whispering.

Josephine was kneeling before the closed door with her lips to the keyhole, imploring for admission. "Louise, open the door! I beg; open the door—you will make yourself ill. What are you doing, Louise? For heaven's sake open the door."

"Go away. I am not making myself ill." No; she was drinking in a very elixir of life through that open window.

Her fancy was running riot along those days ahead of her. Spring days, and summer days, and all sorts of days that would be her own. She breathed a quick prayer that life might be long. It was only yesterday she had thought with a shudder that life might be long.

She rose at length and opened the door to her sister's importunities. There was a feverish triumph in her eyes, and she carried herself unwittingly like a goddess of Victory. She clasped her sister's waist, and together they descended the stairs. Richards stood waiting for them at the bottom.

Someone was opening the front door with a latchkey. It was Brently Mallard who entered, a little travel-stained, composedly carrying his grip-sack and umbrella. He had been far from the scene of the accident, and did not even know there had been one. He stood amazed at Josephine's piercing cry; at Richards' quick motion to screen him from the view of his wife.

But Richards was too late.

When the doctors came they said she had died of heart disease—of joy that kills.

Sample Essay

Gary Crawford
English 101
Dr. Barton
March 4, 2003

Ⓐ   Point of View and Irony
                    in Chopin's "The Story of an Hour"

Ⓑ   In "The Story of an Hour" (1894), Kate Chopin creates and emphasizes the
      theme through her use of **narrative point of view** and **irony**. By shifting
      between omniscient and limited points of view, Chopin reveals both the **irony** of
Ⓒ   the protagonist's fate and the theme of the story. The story consists of three parts:
      exposition, body, and conclusion. The beginning and end of the story, both of
      which are presented by an omniscient narrator, serve as a frame for the middle of
      the story, in which the point of view is limited.   1
Ⓓ   In the exposition, Chopin employs an omniscient narrator, whose immediate
      concern is to reveal the mentality and motives of those attending Mrs. Mallard: 2

Ⓔ   Knowing that Mrs. Mallard was afflicted with a heart trouble, great care was taken
          to break to her as gently as possible the news of her husband's death.   3
                  It was her sister Josephine who told her, in broken sentences; veiled hints
          that revealed in half-concealing. Her husband's friend Richards was there, too,
          near her. It was he who had been in the newspaper office when the intelligence
          of the railroad disaster was received, with Brently Mallard's name heading the
          list of "killed." He had only taken time to assure himself of its truth by a second
          telegram, and had hastened to forestall any less careful, less tender friend in
Ⓕ   bearing the sad message. (12)   4

          The narration is omniscient in the sense that the narrator offers insights as to
Ⓖ   whereabouts, actions, and intentions of at least two separate characters, Josephine
      and Richards, as well as Mrs. Mallard's "heart trouble" and "the list of 'killed'"
      issued by the newspaper office.   5
Ⓗ   The omniscient narration of the exposition gives way to a more nearly limited
      point of view employed in the body, to which Chopin makes transition in the
      space of two short paragraphs: 6

Ⓐ Title clearly indicates author, work and subject to be covered.
Ⓑ Opening indicates author, title, and date of work to be discussed. The thesis is estab-
    lished in the first two sentences.
Ⓒ Final sentences of introduction elaborate on the thesis and forecast the three-pronged
    organization of the essay.
Ⓓ Transition. Author discusses story section-by-section, starting with exposition.
Ⓔ Long passages of more than four lines are set off from the main body of the essay.
Ⓕ Provide page numbers after quoted material.
Ⓖ Development and analysis. Author explains his use of a particular term and uses
    phrases from the quoted material to reinforce his point.
Ⓗ Transition sentence. Connects paragraphs by reminding readers what has been
    discussed in the previous paragraph and introducing the subject of the next one.

When the storm of grief had spent itself she went away to her room alone. She would have no one follow her. 7

There stood, facing the open window, a comfortable, roomy armchair. Into this she sank, pressed down by a physical exhaustion that haunted her body and seemed to reach into her soul. (13) 8

Ⓘ   The narration shifts from the public world of the others in attendance to the private sphere of Mrs. Mallard. This change is signaled by Mrs. Mallard's going "away to her room alone." Although Mrs. Mallard "would have no one follow her," the narrator follows her, in a sense, and focuses on her exclusively. 9

Ⓙ   In this middle section, which begins as Mrs. Mallard sinks into an armchair before an open window, the limited narration allows readers privileged access to the protagonist's intimate thoughts and feelings. Indeed, the narrator proceeds to describe a kind of dream, during which Mrs. Mallard's "gaze was fixed away off yonder on one of those patches of blue sky. It was not a glance of reflection, but

Ⓚ   rather indicated a suspension of intelligent thought" (13). 10

Ⓛ   In the course of her dream, Mrs. Mallard experiences an **epiphany**, a moment of sudden insight into herself and her new circumstances: 11

There was something coming to her and she was waiting for it, fearfully. What was it? She did not know; it was too subtle and elusive to name. But she felt it, creeping out of the sky, reaching toward her through the sounds, the scents, the color that filled the air. 12

Now her bosom rose and fell tumultuously. She was beginning to recognize this thing that was approaching to possess her, and she was striving to beat it back with her will—as powerless as her two white slender hands would have been. 13

When she abandoned herself, a little whispered word escaped her slightly parted lips. She said it over and over again under her breath: "Free, free, free!" The vacant stare and the look of terror that had followed it went from her eyes. They stayed keen and bright. Her pulses beat fast, and the coursing blood warmed and relaxed every inch of her body. (13) 14

Ⓜ   In these paragraphs, the limited narration reveals at least two ironies: the first is that, far from feeling devastated by the loss of her husband, Mrs. Mallard actually experiences a sense of relief; and the second is that, far from proving incapable of bearing the strain of emotion, Mrs. Mallard's heart seems to improve. The narrator, who is keyed into Mrs. Mallard's body and soul, describes "her pulses beating fast"

Ⓝ   and "her coursing blood warm[ing] . . . every inch of her body." 15

Ⓘ Author again uses evidence from quoted passage to develop forceful points in favor of his argument.

Ⓙ Transition sentence. Author moves to second part of the argument.

Ⓚ In-text quotation with punctuation after parentheses.

Ⓛ Author clarifies meaning of a term to elucidate further his comment.

Ⓜ Development and analysis. Author draws inferences based on evidence in the paragraphs and clearly explains how the author uses the literary technique to build particular effects.

Ⓝ Ellipsis used to signify missing words.

◎   The revelations of the limited narration in the body of the story, or dream sequence, also set up the ultimate irony of the conclusion. Having gained privileged access to the protagonist's feelings, readers of the story are prepared to understand her reaction to the events that follow. Chopin modulates the point of view from limited to omniscient in the passage describing Mrs. Mallard's emergence from her room: 16

> She rose at length and opened the door to her sister's importunities. There was a feverish triumph in her eyes, and she carried herself unwittingly like a goddess of Victory. She clasped her sister's waist, and together they descended the stairs. Richards stood waiting for them at the bottom.   17
>
> Someone was opening the front door with a latchkey. It was Brently Mallard who entered, a little travel-stained, composedly carrying his grip-sack and umbrella. He had been far from the scene of the accident, and did not even know there had been one. He stood amazed at Josephine's piercing cry; at Richards' quick motion to screen him from the view of his wife. (14)   18

The shift from limited to omniscient narrative becomes clear with the narrator's moving from the consciousness of Mrs. Mallard to the description of Brently Mallard's appearance, ignorance of the accident, and reaction to Josephine's "piercing cry." The action is no longer seen exclusively from the protagonist's private view; the narrative reports the awareness of the other characters.   19

This change in point of view is significant because it makes readers aware of a

ⓟ **dramatic irony:** namely, that they have acquired information unavailable to the characters in the story, except for Mrs. Mallard. Thus, readers may recognize that the final paragraph of the story reflects a misunderstanding of the protagonist's feelings: 20

> When the doctors came they said she had died of heart disease—of joy that kills. (14) 21

The **dramatic irony** of this final statement depends on readers' knowledge of the joy that Mrs. Mallard experiences in recognizing her newfound freedom. The other characters and the doctors misinterpret the cause of her death as proceeding from Mrs. Mallard's "joy" upon learning that her husband had not been killed. In these closing lines, the theme of the story becomes clear: Mrs. Mallard's "heart

ⓠ trouble" is not so much physical as spiritual or emotional. She feels trapped in a marriage that limits her freedom. Chopin's skillful manipulation of narrative point of view sets up the conclusion, making it both ironic and poignant.   22

ⓡ ## Work Cited

Chopin, Kate. "The Story of an Hour." Rpt. in Bernard A. Prabeck, Helen Ellis, and Hartley Pfeil, eds. *Exploring Literature Through Reading and Writing.* Boston: Houghton, 1982. Print.

◎ Transition. Author deals with third part of argument.

ⓟ Conclusion returns to thesis (but does not merely repeat introduction) and deals with the ending of the story.

ⓠ Author ends by making a specific point about the theme of the work and adding the incisive insight into the effects of the finale of the short story.

ⓡ "Work Cited" section includes source for text used in essay.

Background Narrative on "The Cinderella Motif in Austen's *Pride and Prejudice*"

SELECTING AND NARROWING A SUBJECT

Amanda Miller took time choosing the subject for her research paper because she wanted to deal with an area that she found interesting. She considered examining the handling of the heroine in the novel, but this subject seemed too broad. She was also struck by the author's moral tone, but this was a subject more suited to a long essay than to a five- to six-page research paper. Nonetheless, she kept these thoughts in mind as she reviewed her lecture notes on *Pride and Prejudice*. In one of the lectures, the professor had discussed the fairy tale elements operating in many eighteenth-century English novels. After viewing the 1940 film version and the 1995 television series of the work, Amanda became even more aware of the strong Cinderella motif operating in *Pride and Prejudice*. She then devised a plan for a paper in which she could incorporate the handling of the heroine and the author's moral tone by focusing on the Cinderella motif. After outlining her own thoughts on the subject, Amanda visited the university library to discover what research was available on the subject.

DETERMINING CREDIBILITY AND APPROPRIATENESS OF SECONDARY SOURCES

Amanda used a two-pronged strategy in determining the secondary sources for her paper. First, she began her search in the reference section of the library by consulting the most recent annotated bibliography on Austen secondary sources. The annotations helped her to narrow her search to seven works dealing specifically with the Cinderella motif in Austen's works. Second, she consulted the online library database. After she keyed in "Fairy Tales" for the subject, numerous works appeared on the screen. She then narrowed the search by limiting it to "Cinderella," which substantially decreased the number of texts. By this time, Amanda had gathered the titles of ten secondary sources she wished to consider. After collecting the materials, Amanda began to read the portions of the works dealing with her proposed subject.

The major criterion Amanda used in initially determining the appropriateness of her secondary sources was currency; she elected to consult works written in the past ten years. But she did not limit herself to these works. Several of them made detailed references to older critical texts, that seemed influential and useful. She determined to consider these works as well. After a while, she noticed that the commentators seemed to belong in either one critical camp or in another, and she therefore started to list some of their major arguments and to choose appropriate quotations epitomizing their views. She also noticed that her own conclusions about the Cinderella motif in Austen were quite different from those of certain literary critics but similar to those of others. With this information in mind, she resolved to offer a summary of the critical controversy on her subject at the onset of the paper and then to argue her own case, pointing out where her argument differed from and shared similarities with the critics. Her paper was now beginning to take shape.

CHOOSING ORGANIZATION STRATEGIES

Amanda was familiar with a number of organization strategies that she had already used in other papers: comparison/contrast; explication; analysis; argument. She considered the different methods and decided that most of them could be used effectively. In the first part of the essay, she offered a synthesis of the viewpoints of other commentators. She compared and contrasted their opinions by offering first one set of opinions then the other. This comparative section provided a context for her own argument.

This student used the organization strategy of analysis after the opening section. She dealt with each component of the argument she had sketched out in the introduction, so the essay consisted structurally of four components (in addition to the introductory section). In each case, she used the strategy of argument; that is to say, she made a major point and then she supported it with evidence directly from the text or with the comment of a literary critic. In dealing with quoted materials, Amanda incorporated the strategy of explication; that is to say, she developed the meaning or implication of a point.

REFINING THE INTRODUCTION AND CONCLUSION

Having written the body of her essay, Amanda was in a good position to see how she should refine the introduction to the essay. After her general points about the critical controversy, she added a polished thesis statement and clarifying sentences; she then honed her description of the sections of the essay in a statement of organization, which served as a kind of preliminary map of the structure of the essay.

Amanda concluded the essay with one of her strongest and most encompassing points, which she had deliberately saved for the end. She provided a quotation that epitomized the issue at hand; she then developed the argument in this quotation by offering her own refinements. In addition, she elected to discuss the finale of the text in her own conclusion, thereby providing a strong sense of closure.

Sample Essay

Amanda Miller
English 475
Dr. Hudson
10 January 2003

Ⓐ
The Cinderella Motif in Jane
Austen's Pride and Prejudice

As do many of Jane Austen's novels, *Pride and Prejudice* (1813) offers a variation on the Cinderella story. The novel tells the story of a small-town girl who eventually marries a good man, and it ends with the heroines, Elizabeth and Jane,

Ⓑ achieving or exceeding their dreams of love. Although it was widely accepted and enjoyed in Austen's day, the Cinderella motif has long been a subject of controversy with educators and experts in child development. In the twentieth century, psychologists have argued over whether the story of Cinderella is beneficial or harmful to children, and some feminists have objected to the message it sends. These controversies provide a context for viewing Austen's use of the fairy tale in her novel: that is, as both an object of **satire** and a means of moral instruction. In *Pride and Prejudice,* the Cinderella motif functions to highlight the

Ⓒ individual characteristics of Elizabeth Bennet and her relation to her "Prince"; the qualities of Jane Bennet and her interaction with her fairy godmother; and Elizabeth's relations with other members of her family. Austen also **parodies** (or offers a witty imitation of) the ending of the Cinderella story to present a serious moral point.   1

Many variants of the Cinderella tale exist; the most famous is that of Charles Perrault, *Stories or Tales of Past Times* (1697), which was published in English in 1729. Perrault presents a shy, docile Cinderella who requires the help of a fairy godmother to overcome her wicked stepmother and stepsisters and who wins the love of her prince through her beauty and modesty alone. Although children of the eighteenth century enjoyed this fairy story, educational authorities such as Sarah

---

Ⓐ Title orients reader to the subject of the essay and the author and title of the work.

Ⓑ Author provides a context for her argument by summarizing the views of other commentators on the subject.

Ⓒ Author highlights her own argument in the paper and presents the structure and components of her essay.

Ⓓ Trimmer warned parents of the dangers of permitting their children to read such tales. In her opinion, Cinderella "paints some of the worst passions that can enter into the human breast, and of which little children should, if possible, be entirely ignorant; such as envy, jealousy, a dislike of stepmothers and half sisters, vanity, a love of dress, etc." (qtd. in Lurie 14). Even Perrault expressed doubt about the point of Cinderella, although he added two unconvincing morals to the tale. In the first, he indicated that the story proves that Cinderella won the prince because of her charm and grace. In the second, he noted that the tale demonstrates that a person cannot succeed without
Ⓔ a fairy godmother to display his or her merit (Barchilon 89-91).   2

Unlike Trimmer and Perrault, psychologist Bruno Bettelheim claims that fairy tales such as Cinderella offer benefits and contribute to the emotional health of children by helping them adapt to the outside world: 3

Ⓕ   One of the greatest merits of "Cinderella" is that, irrespective of the magic help Cinderella receives, the child understands that essentially it is through her own efforts, and because of the person she is, that Cinderella is able to transcend magnificently her degraded state, despite what appear as insurmountable obstacles. It gives the child confidence that the same will be true for him.... (243)   4

Ⓖ Bettelheim argues that the story of Cinderella presents each of the stages in personality development necessary to achieve self-fulfillment. In Bettelheim's opinion, this tale helps to relieve a child's anxiety about life. But clearly the degree of intended moral instruction in a fairy tale such as Cinderella seems suspect.   5
Ⓗ   In *Pride and Prejudice,* Austen does use the fairy tale motif for a moral purpose. But she employs it to demonstrate on the one hand that fantasies such as Cinderella are built on superficial notions of beauty, charm, and passion, and that unions built on principles of virtue and sense are preferable. On the other hand, the fantasy ending of the fairy tale is still imposed, but only after the characters have gone through a suitable period of growth and enlightenment. In this way, Austen satirizes the Cinderella motif by altering some of its conventions. In other words, she seeks to criticize and correct the Cinderella paradigm by means of humor and mild ridicule.   6
Ⓘ   Drawing on **feminist** critical theory, Mei Huang offers analysis of patriarchal practices and observes that the Cinderella story in many English novels is "a narrative about female desire and ambition" (67). This is certainly the case in *Pride and Prejudice* where Elizabeth and Jane pursue and attain their dreams. But
Ⓙ they are not mere "gold-diggers" looking for rich, handsome men to marry. In the case of Elizabeth, she is far from being impressed by Darcy's attentions at first. Darcy is like a prince: he is handsome, noble, and in possession of a magnificent

---

Ⓓ Author quotes a passage quoted by a critic and gives appropriate credit.
Ⓔ Author provides citation for paraphrased material.
Ⓕ Both sides of the issue are fairly presented using direct quotations from the sources to support the arguments.
Ⓖ Author provides analysis of the remarks of the commentator.
Ⓗ Author reiterates her argument in the paper and starts to build her case using evidence from the text.
Ⓘ Author uses secondary sources in support of her own points but also qualifies them to highlight the originality of her argument.
Ⓙ Author deals with first component of the argument set out in the introduction— Elizabeth's characteristics and interaction with Darcy.

estate in the north of England. After he snubs her and her family, Elizabeth stubbornly believes him to be incorrigibly proud and snobbish. Priding herself on her superior ability to judge others, she is also appalled by his discouragement of Bingley's courting of her sister and his alleged ill-treatment of Wickham. But after she reads Darcy's letter and visits his estate, she realizes that he is kindly and humane, and that she has overestimated her ability to judge. The housekeeper at Pemberley praises Darcy for his kindness and generosity, and Elizabeth's opinion of her suitor changes greatly: 7

Ⓚ   As a brother, a landlord, a master, she considered how many people's happiness were in his guardianship!—How much of pleasure or pain it was in his power to bestow!—How much of good or evil must be done by him! Every idea that had been brought forward by the housekeeper was favorable to his character, and as she stood before the canvas, on which he was represented, and fixed his eyes upon herself, she thought of his regard with a deeper sentiment of gratitude than it had ever raised before; she remembered its warmth, and softened its impropriety of expression. (272)   8

Ⓛ   The relationship of Elizabeth and Darcy is certainly not one of love at first sight. Unlike the fairy tale, their feelings take time to develop. Elizabeth modifies her view as she gazes at Darcy's portrait and reflects on the servant's words. The idea begins to dawn on her that he might have the qualities she desires in a husband. In the course of the novel, Austen stresses that both Elizabeth and Darcy must change their views. Elizabeth tests her prince and discovers his worth, just as he discovers hers. Far from being the passive Cinderella figure of Perrault's fairy tale, Elizabeth is active and resourceful and ensures her prince's foot fits the slipper, just as he must prove worthy of her (Hudson 105).   9

Ⓜ   Jane Bennet, on the other hand, bears a much closer resemblance to the meek, self-effacing, obliging heroine of the Perrault fairy tale. Elizabeth even says to Jane that she is "too good. Your sweetness and disinterestedness are really angelic. I do not know what to say to you…. *You* wish to think all the world respectable"
Ⓝ   (134–135). But when Elizabeth is troubled, she turns to her sister "of whose rectitude and delicacy she was sure her opinion could never be shaken" (128). Like the figure in the tale, Jane must endure the cold, arrogant behavior of the Bingley sisters, but eventually her charm and sweetness win out. Jane also resembles the Cinderella figure of the fairy tale in that she needs help. D. W. Harding argues that Austen's novels are about the "Cinderella theme with the fairy godmother
Ⓞ   omitted" (173). But on the contrary, Elizabeth functions as Jane's fairy godmother in *Pride and Prejudice* in that she reprimands Darcy for his interference and urges him

---

Ⓚ Long quotations from primary and secondary sources are indented to set them off from the main body of the paper.
Ⓛ Author provides analysis of the quotation, explaining and demonstrating how it helps to make her claim in the paper more convincing.
Ⓜ Author deals with second component of her argument—Jane's characteristics and her fairy godmother.
Ⓝ Short quotations are incorporated in the body of the text followed by the page number in parentheses.
Ⓞ Author uses and refutes the view of a commentator to strengthen the validity of her argument.

to promote Bingley's suit, enlightening him to the advantages of the match. Moreover, with the assistance of Darcy, she helps to alleviate the threat to her sister's fortunes (and her own) created by Lydia's rashness in eloping with Wickham. In this way, Elizabeth enables Jane to marry her prince by sense and moral guidance rather than the agency of magic. In Austen's fiction, loyal sisters and brother-like heroes contribute to the education and in forming the prospects of Cinderella figures like Jane (Hudson 118).   10

Ⓟ   Allusions to the Cinderella story are particularly evident in *Pride and Prejudice* in the presentation of family relations. Elizabeth possesses intelligence and discrimination, qualities lacking in other members of her family. Her situation is like that of the fairy tale character. Like Cinderella with her stepmother, she has to endure her mother's jealousy and unkindness. In addition, her sisters humiliate and embarrass her, both intentionally and unintentionally. At the Netherfield ball, Elizabeth endures a mass of humiliations, ranging from her mother's insulting remarks to Darcy to Mary's atrocious "entertainment," and from her father's heavy-

Ⓠ handed halting of her sister's playing to Lydia's boisterous and vulgar behavior. And Lydia's foolishness only increases over time owing to her mother's indulgence and father's nonchalance, for she disgraces her family by eloping with the villainous Wickham. Elizabeth also endures the insults of snobbish Lady Catherine de Bourgh, who criticizes her family and accuses Elizabeth of polluting the "shades of Pemberley" in her desire to marry her nephew. In the 1940 film version of *Pride and Prejudice,* director Robert Z. Leonard transforms Lady Catherine into a fairy godmother figure, who helps to unite Darcy and Elizabeth. But in the text, despite all her problems, Elizabeth survives and even manages to assist her family using her judgment and wit to guide her. Her qualities of character therefore benefit her and other members of her family.   11

Ⓡ   Like the heroine of the fairy tale, Elizabeth triumphs at the end of the novel, but the moral point is more explicit in *Pride and Prejudice* than in Perrault's tale. For Elizabeth earns her success because of her characteristics and ethical appeal. She has evolved as a person, learning to be more tolerant and less inclined to judge by appearance or hearsay (as in the case of both Darcy and Wickham). She helps her older sister, and she is loyal and useful to other members of her family, in spite of their shortcomings. Her assistance continues to her family even after her marriage. As the wife of a wealthy man and mistress of a powerful estate, she will be able to help Kitty and Mary, and she even provides monetary assistance for Lydia. Moreover, it appears that she will be an excellent mentor to Darcy's shy sister Georgiana.   12

      Some feminist critics have asserted that Austen's *Pride and Prejudice* eventually confirms the very messages it seems to mock in the beginning: 13

Ⓟ Author deals with the third component of her argument set out in the introduction—
   Elizabeth's relations with other members of her family.
Ⓠ Author paraphrases episodes and incidents from the text in support of her claim.
Ⓡ Author handles the fourth component of the argument set out in the introduction—
   Austen's parody of the ending of the Cinderella story to present a moral point.

Ⓢ   The famous beginning . . . opens with an ironical recapitulation of the dearest scheme of Mrs. Bennet: "It is a truth universally acknowledged that a single man in possession of a good fortune must be in want of a wife" (51). But the brilliant marriage contract that her smart Elizabeth strikes in the end outshines Mrs. Bennet's wildest plotting. Perhaps the old convention, however abused and deteriorated, still contains too much truth, literarily and literally, to be completely dispensed with. Perhaps in the old Cinderella story there is still space for a heroine to work out her self-fulfillment, no matter how qualified. (Huang 104)   14

Ⓣ   The convention, even though it is "abused" and reworked in Austen's novel, can happen in real life, and the heroine can achieve self-fulfillment. But the ending of *Pride and Prejudice* is not merely a romantic story of two people. Austen emphasizes this idea in Elizabeth's comments on her gratitude to Darcy: "he was the person, to whom the whole family was indebted for the first of benefits, and whom she regarded with an interest, if not quite so tender, at least as reasonable and just, as what Jane felt for Bingley" (334). In other words, unlike the fairy tale that focuses on the wedded happiness of the prince and Cinderella at the finale, in *Pride and Prejudice,* the happiness, interdependence, and continuing development of an entire community of individuals is highlighted. In this way, the novel offers an example of **intertextuality**; that is to say, Austen's *Pride and Prejudice* continually refers to and relies on knowledge of another text—the story of Cinderella. The interweaving of these two stories allows the reader to compare and contrast Austen's vision of relationships between men and women with that presented in Cinderella.   15

Ⓤ **Works Cited**

Austen, Jane. *Pride and Prejudice*. London: Oxford UP, 1985. Print.

Bettelheim, Bruno. *The Uses of Enchantment: The Meaning and Importance of Fairy Tales*. New York: Knopf, 1976. Print.

Barchilon, Jacques. *The Authentic Mother Goose Fairy Tales and Nursery Rhymes*. Denver: Alan Swallow, 1960. Print.

Harding, D. W. " Regulated Hatred: An Aspect of the Work of Jane Austen." *Jane Austen: A Collection of Critical Essays*. Ed. Ian Watt. Englewood Cliffs: Prentice, 1963. 166–179. Print.

Huang, Mei. *Transforming the Cinderella Dream*. New Brunswick: Rutgers UP, 1990. Print.

Hudson, Glenda. *Sibling Love and Incest in Jane Austen's Fiction*. London: Macmillan, 1992; paperback, 1999. Print.

Lurie, Alison. *Don't Tell the Grown-Ups: Subversive Children's Literature*. Boston: Little, 1990. Print.

Pride and Prejudice. Dir. Robert Z. Leonard. Perf. Greer Garson and Laurence Olivier. MGM, 1940. Film.

Ⓢ Author uses quotation from a secondary source in support of her point but stresses the originality of her own argument.

Ⓣ Author concentrates on the ending of the text in her conclusion.

Ⓤ "Works Cited" includes bibliographical references for all primary and secondary sources used in the paper.

Background Narrative on "Excursions into Neverland: The Importance of the Edenic World in *Peter and Wendy* and *The Adventures of Tom Sawyer*"

CHOOSING A SUBJECT

Ellen Shoffner carefully perused the list of possible subjects for the course paper in her nineteenth-century children's literature course. She chose to write on the following:

> 6. Compare the importance and role of the Edenic world in at least two
> works of nineteenth-century children's literature. What similarities do
> you detect between the fantasy worlds in the texts? Are there any major
> differences? How and why, in each case, is the location significant?

She selected this subject because she found it appealing and had already highlighted specific passages dealing with this topic in several novels. Almost all of the works of literature in the course handled the subject, but Ellen chose to compare two novels (J. M. Barrie's *Peter and Wendy* and Mark Twain's *The Adventures of Tom Sawyer*) with satirical qualities that show how reality intrudes on the Edenic world of childhood.

ORGANIZING THE COMPARATIVE ESSAY

Once she had chosen her subject, Ellen turned to the entry on "Utopia/Dystopia" in *A Contemporary Guide to Literary Terms* to find precise terminology for her essay. She began to list quotations related to her subject and to group them according to similarities and differences. Her list grew long, and she became concerned as to how she should organize her material. Should she deal with Barrie's *Peter and Wendy* in the first half of her paper and then with Twain's *The Adventures of Tom Sawyer* in the second half, as seemed most obvious? Ellen noticed that this strategy of comparison seemed to create almost two separate essays. Was there a more effective way of making comparisons between the novels? She consulted her professor during office hours and was advised to use a point by point strategy of comparison. With this strategy, she would establish a point of comparison between the works of literature and then compare and contrast them side by side within a series of paragraphs.

WRITING THE ESSAY

Ellen made the three major comparisons between the two novels and began to organize the structure of her paper using the more effective point-by-point organization technique. First, she compared the physical characteristics of the settings in the two novels and demonstrated how the intrusion of reality reveals how the Edenic world is both attractive and repelling. Second, she compared forms of shelter in both novels, and how they become inadequate for the children. Third, she compared the significance of food in the two novels, and how the yearning and guilt associated with it culminates in the children's desire to return home. Since the essay frequently turned from one point of comparison to another, Ellen realized the need to use strong transitions (phrases such as "however," "similarly," "by way of contrast," "in addition to," "a further example of," etc.) to reinforce the structure of her argument. She concluded her essay by effectively comparing the endings of the two novels and commenting on how the children in both *Peter and Wendy* and in *The Adventures of Tom Sawyer* gain an understanding of home and experience a desire to return to society.

Sample Essay

Ellen L. Shoffner
May 30, 2002
English 475: Nineteenth-Century Children's Literature
Dr. Hudson

Ⓐ   Excursions into Neverland:
            The Importance of the Edenic World in
         Peter and Wendy and *The Adventures of Tom Sawyer*

The experience of the Edenic world is an important part of the character
development of the children in *Peter and Wendy* (1911) and in *The Adventures of
Tom Sawyer* (1876). In these satirical texts, children experience their imaginations
unfettered by repressive aspects of society such as government, money, education,
Ⓑ or religion. Free of parental control, they make their own rules in a **Utopia** or
"good place" where harmony, innocence, and a sense of escape prevail—seemingly
forever. Eventually reality intrudes upon Utopia, presenting itself in the form of a
storm, threatening adults, or simply as guilt or longing. The intrusion of reality
reveals the physical characteristics of these Edenic worlds as both attractive and
repelling, and the shelter and food in these worlds as equally satisfying and
problematic. The result is that the children gain an understanding of the significance
Ⓒ of home and experience a desire to return to society.   1

        The physical characteristics of Neverland and Jackson's Island are initially
attractive. Neverland is "snug and most compact" and "not in the least alarming"
Ⓓ (Barrie 74). On Jackson's Island there is "a delicious sense of repose and peace ... a
deep pervading calm and silence" (Twain 88). Tom and his friends enjoy "snug
nooks carpeted with grass and jeweled with flowers" (90). The equivalent for
Wendy and her brothers is the mermaids' lagoon, a pool of "vivid colours" where
"mermaids come up ... to play with their bubbles" (Barrie 140). In both texts the
Ⓔ natural world appears idyllic and benign. On Neverland "turtles [bury] their eggs
in the sand," and a "flamingo" and a "wolf with her whelps" coexist peacefully
(Barrie 105). On Jackson's Island nature reposes in a great "meditation" (Twain 88).
The presence of creatures is described in a paragraph of parataxis: a "green worm"
incorporates Tom into his morning routine and the worm's procession is followed
by a string of ants, ladybugs, a catbird, a squirrel, a fox, and butterflies (88). Twain's
compounding of the abundance of nature before Tom's eyes—"Life manifested
itself"—indicates a oneness between the boy and the natural world (88). A sense of
creation and harmony prevails.   2

        However, just as imagination has a dark side, these islands have their repelling
characteristics. At night Neverland's "unexplored patches" are full of "black
shadows" and "the roar of beasts" (Barrie 106). In Peter's absence "things are

Ⓐ The title clearly indicates the topic of the paper and indicates the texts to be covered
    in the essay.
Ⓑ Author uses terms from *A Contemporary Guide to Literary Terms* throughout the essay to
    add precision to her argument.
Ⓒ Thesis is clearly set out in introductory paragraph.
Ⓓ Citations are provided for each author along with page numbers.
Ⓔ Author makes comparisons on a point-by-point basis, dealing first with one text and
    then comparing it to the other.

usually quiet on the island" but with Peter present "the whole island [is] seething
Ⓕ with life" (112). The choice of the word "seething" lends an ominous undercurrent
to the "life" of the island—a foreshadowing of dangers to come. At the "turn of the
moon" the pleasant lagoon becomes "dangerous for mortals" and the mermaids
"utter strange wailing cries" (140). The presence of the mysterious is felt as
"shivers" and "shadows [which steal] across the water, turning it cold" (142). The
lagoon becomes a "formidable and unfriendly place" for the children, the
Ⓖ "unknown . . . [is] stalking toward them" (142). The **symbolism** refers to an
abstract idea significant for the theme of the work. In this case, the symbolism of
shadow and night as harbingers of evil is as prevalent in the fantasy world as it is in
the world of reality. The Edenic world cannot hold fear at bay.   3

Ⓗ   Similarly, Jackson's Island turns foreboding as a storm approaches. There is a
"brooding oppressiveness in the air" and a "solemn hush" falls upon the boys
(Twain 104). As in *Peter and Wendy,* the sense is that something is *coming to get them.*
When the storm hits the island the terrified boys "[stumble] over roots and among
vines in the dark" trying to escape the torrent (Twain 104). The storm "seemed
likely to tear the island to pieces, burn it up, drown it to the treetops, blow it
away" (105). An overriding sense of pending annihilation pervades these scenes.
While the storm leaves the boys on Jackson's Island feeling "awed" and "thankful"
(105) to have avoided catastrophe, Peter Pan faces possible annihilation "with a
smile on his face" thinking that "To die will be an awfully big adventure" (Barrie
152). Peter's cavalier attitude can be attributed to his immortality, but Tom, Joe,
and Huck are not protected by a similar fantasy and must eventually reconcile
Ⓘ themselves to the possibility of death.   4

The shelters of Neverland and Jackson's Island hold equally compelling
pleasures and challenges. On Neverland the children's house resembles an animal
burrow; it is underground, and accessible only through "hollow trees." The cave-
like home is "one large room . . . with a floor in which you could dig" and an
"enormous fire-place" (Barrie 133–134). On Jackson's Island the boys make their
camp "twenty or thirty steps within the somber depths of the forest" (Twain 85).
They "stretch themselves out on the grass" and sleep together in the open air (85).
The simplicity and closeness to the earth of these shelters reflects the desire for
Ⓙ connection to the earth, freedom from the constraints of domestic order, and the
importance of relationship over comfort or appearances.   5

Unfortunately, these forms of shelter become insufficient for the children
when the violence of nature or the threat of enemies intrudes. When the storm hits
Jackson's Island the boys run for their only man-made source of protection—the
"tent" of sailcloth—yet they are stripped of even this simple connection to the
outside world (140). Similarly, the sanctity of the underground shelter on
Neverland is violated when Hook is able to drop poison into a medicine cup that is
"standing on a ledge within easy reach of the pirate" (Barrie 182). Regardless of

---

Ⓕ Author offers specific commentary on author's use of words in quotations.
Ⓖ Term is defined in *A Contemporary Guide.*
Ⓗ Author uses transitions (similarly, however, etc.) effectively to show links between
ideas and to reinforce the structure of the paper.
Ⓘ Author effectively makes contrasts between the two texts she is discussing.
Ⓙ Author uses a combination of short and longer quotations from the texts to support
her points.

isolation or seclusion, these Edenic worlds remain susceptible to dark storms and
the evil influences of the adult world.   6

Ultimately, existence on these Edenic islands depends upon the availability of
food. Tom Sawyer and his friends initially provide food for themselves by stealing it
from home. They arrive on the island with "boiled ham," a "side of bacon" and a
chunk of stolen fire (Twain 83). Although the island easily provides them with a
"feast" of turtle eggs and a fine catch of fish, they are bothered by the idea that
"taking bacon and hams . . . was plain simple *stealing*—and there was a command
against that in the Bible" (87.9). The joy of eating freshly caught fish is tempered
by the guilt of eating food "sullied with the crime of stealing" (87). Reality, in the
Ⓚ form of guilt, encroaches upon the **Utopia**.   7

The abundance of food on Neverland vacillates according to Peter's whim and
imagination. Sometimes the children have "to make-believe that they [have] had
their dinners" while at other times food is plentiful, although its source is unknown
(Barrie 128). The children occasionally eat "roasted bread-fruit, yams . . . and
bananas," but they never know "whether there [will] be a real meal or just a make-
believe" (135). On both of these islands, obtaining food is shadowed by
uncertainty. The longing and guilt associated with food is part of the scenario of
Ⓛ dystopia occurring on the islands that culminates in the children's desire to return
home.   8

Intrusions of reality in the form of storms, dangerous adults, guilty feelings,
and the need for shelter and food merge into "homesickness" and "melancholy"
(Twain 100) for Tom and his friends and a "dread" of being barred from return for
Wendy and her brothers (Barrie 167). The significance of their excursions lies in
the fact that they have experienced freedom, innocence, fear, and growth on their
own terms, outside the bonds of society, but are willing to return. Society has
something to offer them. Children who previously delighted in escape and "soared
out . . . into the night" return to the solidity of home (Barrie 212). Having twice
Ⓜ crossed the liminal threshold, they are ready to incorporate the adult world into
their child world—in their return is the implied acceptance of growing up.   9

Ⓝ Works Cited

Barrie, J.M. *Peter and Wendy*. Oxford: Oxford University Press, 1991. Print.

Twain, Mark. *The Adventures of Tom Sawyer*. New York: Penguin, 1997. Print.

Ⓚ Author reinforces her thesis made in the introduction concerning the intrusion of reality on Utopia in the two texts.
Ⓛ Author continues to make point-by-point comparisons throughout the paper. In this
   case, she compares the children's situations on the islands they visit in the two texts.
Ⓜ Author makes a concluding comparison between the two texts and supports her major
   argument in the paper with more quotations from the text.
Ⓝ Author includes a complete list of works cited at the end of the document.

＊

Background Narrative on "Love and Money in Jane Austen's *Sense* and *Sensibility*: A Comparison of Novel and Film"

CHOOSING A SUBJECT

Nora Traut chose to compare Ang Lee's film version of Jane Austen's *Sense and Sensibility* to the original novel for the major project in a course on women in literature and film. She selected this novel because she had enjoyed reading Austen's novels in several of her university courses. In addition, she chose the Ang Lee film version because she had already viewed it and noticed significant differences between the text and film worthy of discussion in a course paper.

COMPARING THE FILM VERSION AND THE ORIGINAL TEXT

Once she had chosen her subject, Nora perused several entries in *A Contemporary Guide to Literary Terms* to find specific terms and examples for feminist criticism and film editing for her analysis. She reviewed the film version of *Sense and Sensibility* and noted where there were similarities and differences between the film and novel. The major question she wanted to consider throughout her paper was whether the feminist concerns in the novel received equal emphasis in the film version, or if they were obscured in any way. She considered technical elements of the novel (including plot, character, point of view, mood, and setting), and how they transferred to the film. She also reflected on whether the film dealt with the same themes as the text. Nora quoted specific passages from the novel and described scenes from the film in order to illustrate similarities and differences.

In organizing the paper, Nora used a point-by-point comparative strategy. In other words, she examined an issue or element in the novel and then noted how the handling of that issue or element was similar or different in the film. Since the essay frequently turned from one point of comparison to another, Nora realized the need to use strong transitions (phrases such as *however, similarly, nevertheless, not only,* etc.) to reinforce the structure of her argument. She con cluded her essay by effectively comparing the ending of the novel with the finale of the film to give a strong sense of closure to the paper.

Sample Paper

Nora E. Traut
English 373
Dr. Glenda Hudson
November 13, 2003

Love and Money in Jane Austen's *Sense and Sensibility:*
A Comparison of Novel and Film

Jane Austen's novel *Sense and Sensibility* (1811) intermingles love and money so that they are inseparable. Love is forbidden or made difficult where there is no money, and, conversely, love is unnecessary when sufficient funds fill its void. Through her use of **satire**, Austen seeks to criticize and correct the behavior of her

Ⓐ society using humor, wit, and **irony** (Barton/Hudson 176). Under the direction of Ang Lee, the 1995 film *Sense and Sensibility* exposes some of the negative impact on women because of male-dominated tradition, but it fails to expose fully the insensitivity toward and among women that results from their subservience to men. It also fails to show the solidarity of women who struggle through their difficult situations, or the fierce rivalry and insincerity of those who try to succeed at any

Ⓑ cost.   1

Ⓒ A significant practice in feminist criticism is raising awareness of the ways in which women are oppressed or marginalized (Barton/Hudson 71). In *Sense and Sensibility,* the Dashwood women are confined to their situation by traditions and attitudes whereby wealth is controlled by men and reserved for their male descendants. Henry Dashwood would like to break from this mold and bequeath a comfortable legacy upon his wife and daughters, but his uncle, who sees no harm in his own male-centered actions, thwarts his wishes. Lack of concern for women's welfare is exemplified by the thoughtless way he overlooks ten years of consistent care and attention from his nephew's wife and three daughters. He changes his will

Ⓐ Author paraphrases a definition of a term from *A Contemporary Guide to Literary Terms* to reinforce her argument.
Ⓑ Author begins to makes comparisons between the text and film in the opening paragraph and points out how the film differs from the novel.
Ⓒ Author paraphrases a definition from *A Contemporary Guide to Literary Terms* to reinforce the point she is trying to make.

to benefit a male toddler who wins his heart through its "imperfect articulation," selfishness, "cunning tricks, and a great deal of noise" (2). Unable to earn their living, as society does not allow women the occupational opportunities afforded to men, the Dashwood women are now quite helpless. By leaving out this change in the uncle's will, Ang Lee's film omits Austen's emphasis on the tenuousness of

Ⓓ women's fate.   2

The lack of wealth, which causes the Dashwood women's confinement, leaves them at the mercy of others to bring them into social circles; therefore, Mrs. Jennings invites them to London. She feels a responsibility for the young Dashwood women, and although most of her "well-meant but ill-judged attentions" (164) miss their mark, she tries in her own ineffectual way to help them. She shows her concern for Mariamie after learning of Willoughby's engagement by futilely enticing her with "a variety of sweetmeats and olives, and a good fire" (165). With more compassion than understanding, she consoles Marianne by saying, "[H]e is not the only young man in the world worth having; and with your pretty

Ⓔ face you will never [lack] admirers" (164). Marianne is not comforted by Mrs. Jennings's condolences and is blind to her love and concern. Later, Mrs. Jennings's compassion is exhibited (without comic effect) through her support of Elinor and Marianne during the latter's illness. After Marianne recovers from her malady, she looks at her previous actions toward others in a different light. She recognizes her self-centeredness and can now appreciate "the unceasing kindness of Mrs. Jennings" (300) and especially the love and support she has received from Elinor. This realization of female solidarity and support brings Marianne to rational behavior and prompts her to repent for her prior abandonment to her own sensibilities.   3

In the film, however, the female solidarity is diminished and Mrs. Jennings remains merely a comical figure when director Ang Lee leaves her behind in

Ⓕ London and has Elinor (Emma Thompson) request Colonel Brandon's (Alan Rickman) assistance in returning to Barton. By making the colonel be the only friend who stays with Elinor during Marianne's (Kate Winslet) near-fatal infection, Colonel Brandon becomes a savior-figure who supports the tragedy-stricken women when all others leave. As a result, the genuine motherly concern of Mrs. Jennings is never exposed. Marianne's subsequent love for the colonel, therefore, results from her dependence on him rather than from rational realization of his worth. Lee does not afford Marianne the emotional maturation that Austen endowed upon her. The Marianne of the film remains childishly dependent.   4

Ⓖ   Not only does Lee diminish female solidarity and emotional growth, but he also downplays feminine resourcefulness. In her novel, Jane Austen exposes some women's callous pursuit of wealth by showing Lucy's shrewdness as she manipulates her way through social barriers. Although she is low in worth on the "marriage market," she comes "well provided with admiration" (107), which she uses to her

---

Ⓓ Author reinforces the argument set out in the introduction.

Ⓔ Author uses a combination of short and long quotations from the text to support her points.

Ⓕ Author again makes a point-by-point comparison between the novel and film version and highlights the differences between the two forms.

Ⓖ Author effectively uses transitions at the beginning of paragraphs to reinforce the structure of her argument.

own advantage. She flatters anyone necessary to achieve her goal of a comfortable marriage. When the family inheritance is transferred from Edward to Robert, Lucy accordingly transfers her affection from the elder to the younger, and now wealthier, brother. Robert's excessive vanity leaves him easy prey for her flattery. In a society that limits a woman's ability to make her own way in the world, Lucy must resort to her own limited resources. She relies on her wealth of cunning and "unceasing attention to self-interest" (327). Although she may not approve, Austen uses Lucy as a depiction of the inventiveness of desperate women.   5

Ⓗ   In the film, however, Lee diminishes Lucy's desperate pursuit of financial stability by softening her mercenary tendencies. He downplays Lucy's cunning by implying a mutual attraction when Robert keeps his arms around a willing Lucy at a ball and asks permission to escort her home. This change diminishes her cold-hearted quest for wealth and weakens her self-reliant and resourceful character. In the text, her lack of honor and dignity supplies the **irony** in the liberating consequences of her behavior; her disregard for Edward's (Hugh Grant) feelings gives him the greatest happiness by allowing him to marry for love.   6

Nevertheless, love is not all that is required for happiness. Austen understands the importance of financial self-sufficiency. At the close of Lee's film, Colonel Brandon gleefully throws handfuls of coins into the air after his wedding, emphasizing that the Dashwoods' money problems are over and making the colonel look like the savior of them all. In contrast, Jane Austen makes it clear that although money has a great deal to do with happiness, Elinor and Edward are not completely dependent on the colonel and his gift of the living at Delaford. Austen gives them far more money than Lee does in his film, and she endows them with a better understanding of their need for it: "[N]either of them were quite enough in love to think that three hundred and fifty pounds a year would supply them with the comforts of life" (321). Only by Edward's reinstating himself in his mother's good graces and thus being assured of "an income quite sufficient to their wants" (326) are they free to marry. Jane Austen comprehends money's very important

Ⓘ   place in the world, but she ridicules the priority that is placed on it. In his film, Ang Lee ignores Elinor and Edward's natural dependence on it, and plays up the romance between them with no practical consideration for their financial needs beyond those scantily met by Colonel Brandon's offer of the living at Delaford. Thus Colonel Brandon is again transformed into a savior-figure for both the Dashwood women and Edward.   7

Society's traditional male dominance serves to keep women subservient. Women can offer aid to each other through female solidarity, as Mrs. Jennings tries to do, and through sibling solidarity, like Elinor and Marianne; however, not all women share this bond of comradeship. Ironically, most of Marianne's and Elinor's problems have arisen through the actions of other women. Miss Smith disinherits Willoughby for his dishonorable behavior toward Eliza, which spurs him to dishonor his love of Marianne and marry for wealth. Fanny refuses to share the uncle's inheritance that should have gone to Mrs. Dashwood and her daughters; then she considers Elinor financially unfit to marry her brother. She and

---

Ⓗ Author makes another point of comparison between the novel and film version.
Ⓘ Author offers interpretation of quotations provided in the paper and continues to make comparisons between the novel and film.

Mrs. Ferrars see Elinor, and later, Lucy, as rivals to their pile of gold that they ferociously protect. Ironically, it is this very action of financial exclusion that solves Elinor's problems. Through his disinheritance, Edward is simultaneously freed of his mother's manipulation and an unwanted fiancee. Through Lucy's manipulation of the situation, Edward is free to marry for love. Jane Austen's *Sense and Sensibility* is full of ironies, and the most satisfying one in her work that centers on money's influence is the happiness that befalls those who are least influenced by it.   8

The **irony** continues to this day as her tale has been changed to appeal to modern society. In other words, the result of circumstances in the film is the
ⓙ opposite of what might be expected. It is ironic that a film that keeps women reliant on men both financially and emotionally would successfully appeal to a society that purports to esteem a self-reliant woman. Lee's downplaying of financial concerns may be in accord with our society's outward expression that wealth can't buy happiness, but it falls short of the materialistic reality that sends parents to the workplace and children to day care centers. The success of this film may imply a societal attraction to traditional values.   9

Works Cited

Austen, Jane. *Sense and Sensibility*. 1811. New York: Bantam Books, 1983. Film.

Barton, Edwin, and Glenda Hudson. *A Contemporary Guide to Literary Terms*. Boston: Houghton Mifflin, 1997. Print.

Sense and Sensibility. Dir. Ang Lee. Perf. Emma Thompson and Hugh Grant. Columbia, 1995. Print.

ⓙ Author paraphrases a definition from *A Contemporary Guide to Literary Terms* to support her comparison between text and film.

A Student Essay that Compares and Contrasts Two Dramas

One final student essay serves to illustrate how to compare and contrast two literary works; it also shows how to quote, lineate, and cite works of drama.

Eduardo Martinez
English 1B
Dr. Edwin Barton
April 30, 2010

High and Low Tragedy:
Shakespeare's *Hamlet* and Miller's *Death of a Salesman*

William Shakespeare's *Hamlet* (1603) is a high tragedy in the sense that it follows many of the traditions of ancient Greek tragedies and Senecan tragedies of the Roman period, dramas that are "notable for their recurring themes of revenge, as well as their descriptions of off-stage bloodletting and murder . . . [and] supernatural elements such as ghosts" (Barton and Hudson 222). But, above all, Hamlet is a high tragedy "in the Aristotelian sense" because it "presents the downfall of a worthy protagonist" (Barton and Hudson 222). Arthur Miller's *Death of a Salesman* (1949), on the other hand, is a low tragedy because it does not present the decline or fall of a noble hero; in fact, the protagonist of Miller's play is Willy Loman, whose last name suggests that he is a "low man," not a man of greatness who possesses a noble mind and heart. In an essay entitled "Tragedy and the Common Man" (1949), Miller argues that "the common man is as apt a subject for tragedy in its highest sense as kings were" (Miller). Nevertheless, the differences in plot, diction, and tone between Shakespeare's tragedy and Miller's tragedy are significant.

Near the end of Act 3, scene 1 of Hamlet, Ophelia expresses her sorrow about Hamlet's "madness" by saying,

> O, what a noble mind is here o'erthrown!
> The courtier's, soldier's, scholar's, eye, tongue, sword,
> Th' expectancy and rose of the fair state,
> The glass of fashion and the mould of form,
> Ⓐ   Th' observed of all observers, quite quite down! (3.1.146–150)

First of all, Ophelia describes Hamlet's mind as "noble." Then she goes on to list his fields of accomplishment as political, military, and scholarly, using the metonymy of "eye, tongue, sword" to stand for these fields. She also says that Hamlet is the "glass" or mirror and the "mould" or model that everyone looks to for inspiration. For Ophelia, the worst part of this tragedy is that Hamlet has fallen "quite quite down" from a great height. It is this downfall that leads her to say at the end of her speech, "O, woe is me / T' have seen what I have seen, see what I
Ⓑ see!" (3.1.156–157).
Ⓒ   By contrast, in the first act of *Death of a Salesman*, Willy appears to be losing his mind since he is speaking as though he is living in the past when his son Biff was young and full of promise. When Biff criticizes his father, Linda, Willy's wife, remarks, ". . . . He's the dearest man in the world to me, and I won't have anyone making him feel unwanted and low and blue," to which Biff replies, "He's got no character." Angered by Biff's claim, Linda says:

> . . . . I don't say he's a great man. Willy Loman never made a lot of money. His name was never in the paper. He's not the finest character that ever lived. But he's a human being, and a terrible thing is happening to him. So attention must be paid. He's not to be allowed to fall into his grave like an old dog.
> Ⓓ   Attention, attention must finally be paid to such a person.

Ⓔ   When Linda admits in her speech in Act One that her husband is not "a great man" and that he is not "the finest character that ever lived," she is using diction

---

Ⓐ For block quotations of plays written in verse, use the same lineation (line beginnings and endings) as in the original text.

Ⓑ After quotation from a play with acts, scenes, and line numbers, use Arabic numerals and place periods after act and scene numbers.

Ⓒ Use transitions that indicate points of comparison or contrast to clarify meaning for the reader.

Ⓓ For plays that are written in prose rather than verse, use paragraph form for block quotations.

Ⓔ For plays that do not have scenes and line numbers, introduce quotation by indicating which act it is from.

that is markedly different from that used by Ophelia. Instead of using figures of speech that indicate Willy's excellence, she uses the pathetic simile "to fall in his grave like an old dog" in her plea for "attention . . . to such a person" as her husband. Thus, the tone of her speech is more desperate than poignant.

Both protagonists think about committing suicide, but again the diction and tone, as well as the reasons associated with their contemplations, are remarkably different. In his most famous soliloquy, Hamlet ponders,

> To be, or not to be, that is the question:
> Whether 'tis nobler in the mind to suffer
> The slings and arrows of outrageous fortune,
> Or to take arms against a sea of troubles,
> And by opposing end them . . . (3.1.56–60)

Hamlet uses metaphors to describe his situation; he is being assaulted as though in a battle by "slings and arrows of outrageous fortune." He wonders whether he should "suffer" his fate or "take arms against a sea of troubles, / And by opposing end them." The metaphor comparing his fortune to "a sea of troubles" suggests how awesome and seemingly unstoppable his troubles are. In any case, Hamlet's ultimate concern is which choice is "nobler in the mind." On the other hand, Willy Loman's troubles, which he at first seeks to end by asphyxiation and latter accomplishes by smashing his car, seem almost trivial by comparison. In Act One, for instance, Willy wonders why he is increasingly unsuccessful as a salesman:

> I'm fat. I'm very foolish to look at, Linda. I didn't tell you, but Christmas time I happened to be calling on F. H. Stewarts, and a salesman I know, as I was going to see the buyer I heard him say something about—walrus. And I—I cracked him right across the face. I won't take that. I simply will not take that. But they do laugh at me. I know that.

Willy's outrageous fortune, in this case, is that he has to endure insults about his looks. Instead of contemplating whether or not it is nobler "to take arms," Willy hits the man who insulted him "right across the face" because he "simply will not take that." Nevertheless, he knows that he is "very foolish to look at" and that "they laugh at [him]." Willy is concerned here largely with appearances, whereas Hamlet is concerned, as he puts it in another speech, not with what "seems" but with what "is." Willy's pride rises when someone says he looks like a "walrus," but this is nothing like the "sea of troubles" that Hamlet faces, which is far from laughable.

In fact, no one laughs at Hamlet or insults him except Hamlet himself, and even Claudius the king fears and respects him. In the denouement of the play, both Horatio, Hamlet's only true friend, and Fortinbras, the prince of an enemy country, pay tribute to him. When Hamlet dies, Horatio says,

> Now cracks a noble heart. Good night, sweet prince,
> And flights of angels sing thee to thy rest! (5.2.344–345)

The phrase "noble heart" echoes Ophelia's "noble mind" in Act 3 and fits very well with the remarks of Fortinbras at the very end of the play:

> Let four captains
> Bear Hamlet like a soldier to the stage,

> For he was likely, had he been put on,
> To have proved most royal . . . (5.2.380–383)

Fortinbras means that Hamlet would have "proved most royal" because he would have been a noble king and a noble soldier. At the end of *Death of a Salesman*, after Biff remarks that his father "didn't know who he was," Willy's younger son, Happy, replies that "Willy Loman did not die in vain":

> He had a good dream. It's the only dream you can have—to come out number-one man. He fought it out here, and this is where I'm gonna win it for him. (Act 2)

The stage directions indicate that Biff gives "a hopeless glance at HAPPY" and turns to go. There is no consensus that Willy was a noble man or even that his dream "to come out number-one man" was a good or worthy dream. Happy's insistence that his father "did not die in vain" seems more like emotional bluster than truth. In short, Willy's death may be worthy of "attention," but it is nothing like the tragedy of Hamlet's passing.

Works Cited

Barton, Edwin J. and Glenda A. Hudson. A *Contemporary Guide to Literary Terms*, 2*ⁿᵈ* ed. Boston: Houghton Mifflin Company, 2004. Print.

Miller, Arthur. *Death of a Salesman*. Rpt. in *The Norton Anthology of American Literature*, 5*ᵗʰ* ed. *Vol. 2*. Eds. Nina Baym et al. New York: W. W. Norton & Company, 1979. 1917–1985. Print.

⒡ _____. "Tragedy and the Common Man." From *The Theater Essays of Arthur Miller*. New York: Viking Press, 1978. 3–7. In **theliterarylink.com.** 24 April 2010. Online.

Shakespeare, William. *The Tragical History of Hamlet Prince of Denmark*. Ed. A. R. Branmuller. New York: Penguin Putnam, Inc., 2001. Print.

⒡ See the section entitled "A Brief to Documenting Sources" for examples of works cited entries for online sources.

Final Tips

ADVICE FOR ESSAY EXAMINATIONS

In preparing for essay examinations, students should try to anticipate the nature of the questions and start to consider suitable examples to use in support of the case they are making in their responses. Students should also reread texts and go over passages highlighted in lectures and discussions. Writing a series of explanatory sentences for each important passage will help the student prepare to analyze quotations.

Read through the entire examination carefully to plan time for completing the test efficiently. Try to jot down a scratch outline before writing to help with organization. In most cases, instructors do not want plot summary. Use plot summary only to set up the context of specific examples or quotations. Do not make nebulous generalizations or unsubstantiated pronouncements. Whenever possible, refer directly to the text to demonstrate or exemplify a comment or remark. Students should develop their essays by explaining precisely how the quotations or examples serve to illustrate the points they are trying to make.

Correct interpretation of examination questions is crucial. Students should understand the meanings of the following terms:

- **Define** means describe the essential characteristics or features (or clarify the exact meaning) of a term, passage, or text.
- **Criticize** means offer commentary on or interpretation of a text.
- **Explicate** means explain the meaning or implication of a passage or text.
- **Compare/contrast** means find similarities and differences between passages or texts.
- **Outline** means provide an overview of the predominant ideas in a text.

Above all, students should be aware of the importance of asking their instructors questions about the nature of the examinations.

AVOIDING PLAGIARISM

Most colleges and universities offer clear statements of policy and guidelines concerning plagiarism. As explained in the statement on "Academic Integrity" for the California State University, Bakersfield 2009–2011 Catalog, for instance, "Plagiarism is a specific form of academic dishonesty (cheating) which consists of the misuse of published or unpublished works of another by claiming them as one's own. Plagiarism may consist of handing in someone else's work as one's own, copying or purchasing a pre-written composition and claiming it as one's own, using paragraphs, sentences, phrases, words or ideas written by another without giving appropriate citation, or using data and/or statistics compiled by another without giving appropriate citation.

In order to avoid plagiarism, students must learn to recognize improper ways of borrowing words and ideas from another. A passage from John Conder's *Naturalism in American Fiction* (1984) will serve as an example:

> The interchapters of Steinbeck's novel (*The Grapes of Wrath*) create a network of interlocking determinisms through their emphasis on the operations of abstract, impersonal forces in the lives of the Oklahomans. Chapter is especially effective both in capturing the poignancy of the human situation created by such forces and in pointing to the kind of deterministic force underlying the others in the novel. In one fleeting episode a nameless Oklahoman who threatens the driver of a bulldozer leveling his house is told that armed resistance is futile, for the driver acts in service of the bank, and "the bank gets orders from the East." The Oklahoman cries, "But where does it stop? Who can we shoot?" "I don't know," the driver replies. "Maybe there's nobody to shoot. Maybe the thing isn't men at all. Maybe . . . the property's doing it" (52). Or at least the bank, the monster requiring "profits all the time" in order to live and dwarfing in size and power even the owner men, who feel "caught in something larger than themselves" (44, 42).
> The vision that appears here has a name: economic determinism (143).

What follows is an illegal paraphrase of Conder's ideas and expression; the offending words and phrases are marked in boldface:

> The chapters of Steinbeck's *Grapes of Wrath* that do not focus on the actions of the Joad family serve to **create a network of interlocking determinisms**. These chapters emphasize **the operations of impersonal forces** in the lives of the migrants. When a farmer whose house is going to be bulldozed asks the driver whom he should shoot, the driver responds that **he acts in the service of the bank**, and "the bank gets orders from the East." He goes on to say that "Maybe there's nobody to shoot." In this way, the driver implies that the whole situation is a kind of **economic determinism**.

The writer of this illegal paraphrase is obliged to credit and cite his or her source by acknowledging the source in the body of the passage, by placing quotation marks around the direct quotations, and by citing the page numbers of the quotations from both Conder's book and *The Grapes of Wrath*. Finally, the student must offer works cited entries for both sources at the end of his or her essay. The following changes show how a student can meet his or her obligations to borrowed material:

> In *Naturalism in American Fiction* (1984), John Conder asserts that the chapters of Steinbeck's *Grapes of Wrath* that do not focus on the actions of the Joads serve to "create a network of interlocking determinisms" (142). He goes on to state that these chapters emphasize "the operations of abstract, impersonal forces in the lives of the Oklahomans" (Conder 142). As an example of this situation, Conder cites the scene in which a farmer whose house is going to be bulldozed asks the driver whom he should shoot. The driver explains that he works for the bank and that "the bank gets orders from the East." He goes on to say that "Maybe there's nobody to shoot" (qtd. in Conder 142–143). Conder comments that this entire scene represents a kind of "economic determinism" (143).

This passage gives credit to Conder and cites quotations accurately. However, some instructors might note that the student relies too heavily on Conder's ideas. Thus, giving proper credit to sources may help students see where they need to develop their own ideas and offer their own analyses.

The following is a works cited list for this portion of the appendices:

Works Cited

Statement on "Academic Integrity." California State University, Bakersfield 2009–2011 Catalog.

Conder, John. *Naturalism in American Fiction*. Lexington, KY: U of Kentucky P, 1984.

A BRIEF GUIDE TO DOCUMENTING SOURCES

Quotations

Most students of literature will need to quote primary sources (novels, stories, poems, plays), and some will be expected to quote secondary sources (biographies, letters, authors' essays, as well as scholars' books and essays offering critical analyses of literature). The guidelines for citing and documenting sources in essays about literature have been set by the Modern Language Association (MLA). This style of documentation employs parenthetical citations after quotations; that is to say, the crucial bibliographic information is placed in parentheses at the end of the quotation or paraphrase.

The standard means of quoting a primary source consists of placing the author's last name and the page number of the quotation in parentheses.

> "The Story of an Hour" concludes with an ironic statement: "When the doctors came they said she had died of heart disease—of joy that kills" (Chopin 14).

In this type of "in-text" quotation, the parenthetical citation is placed after the close of quotation marks but before the punctuation mark. A more straightforward way to quote a primary source is to introduce the author and the title of the work to be quoted.

> Kate Chopin's "The Story of an Hour" concludes with an ironic statement: "When the doctors came they said she had died of heart disease—of joy that kills" (14).

Because the author's name has been mentioned in the introduction to the quotation, the parenthetical citation offers only the page number. Likewise, in essays that use quotations from only one source, parenthetical citations need cite only the page number.

Longer quotations of more than two or three sentences should be set off from the text by means of ten-spaced indentation (fifteen for the beginning of a paragraph) from the left margin. These "block quotations" require different punctuation:

> In the exposition of "The Story of an Hour," Chopin employs an omniscient narrator, whose immediate concern is to reveal the mentality and motives of those attending Mrs. Mallard:
>
>> Knowing that Mrs. Mallard was afflicted with a heart trouble, great care was taken to break to her as gently as possible the news of her husband's death.
>>
>> It was her sister Josephine who told her, in broken sentences; veiled hints that revealed in half-concealing. Her husband's friend Richards was there, too, near her. It was he who had been in the newspaper office when the intelligence of the railroad disaster was received, with Brently Mallard's name heading the list of "killed." He had only taken time to assure himself of its truth by a second telegram, and had hastened to forestall any less careful, less tender friend in bearing the sad message. (12–13)

Block quotations are double-spaced. They do not require quotation marks; the indentation of the left margin indicates that the passage is quoted. Moreover, the parenthetical citation is placed after the punctuation mark, unlike the "in-text" quotation. Because this passage is quoted from two consecutive pages, the citation notes both of them.

"In-text" quotations of poems differ from excerpted passages of stories and novels in two ways: lines of poetry are separated by slash marks, and they are identified with line numbers rather than page numbers.

> Rita Dove's "Silos" begins with a simile: "Like martial swans in spring paraded against the city sky's / shabby blue, they were always too white and / suddenly there" (1–3).

The slash marks indicate where the lines end in the poem. The line numbers are indicated in parentheses.

Longer passages of more than two or three lines should be offered in block quotations. Block quotations of poetry differ from those of prose in one very significant detail: block quotations of poetry must reflect the lineation (line breaks) of verse:

> Rita Dove's "Silos" begins with a series of similes and negated similes:
>
>> Like martial swans in spring paraded against the city sky's shabby blue, they were always too white and suddenly there.
>>
>> They were never fingers, never xylophones, although once a stranger said they put him in mind of Pan's pipes and all the lost songs of Greece . . . (1–6)

The lines end precisely as they do in the book of poetry or the anthology of literature from which they have been quoted. The ellipsis at the end of the quotation indicates some words that have been omitted from the quotation. If only some words in the middle of a sentence have been omitted, use . . . to indicate the omission. If you omit a sentence in the quotation, use . . . to indicate the omission. If you omit some words at the end of a sentence, use . . . to indicate the omission. Note that ellipsis is represented by three spaced points; any additional punctuation should be separated by one space. Use ellipsis sparingly.

Quotations of lines from a play that is divided into acts, scenes, and lines require a different form of citation.

> For much of the play, Othello makes the mistake of trusting Iago. For instance, he seeks and accepts Iago's advice concerning Cassio:
>
>> And, for I know thou'rt full of love and honesty
>> And weigh'st words before thou giv'st them breath,
>> Therefore these stops of thine fright me the more . . . (3.3.118–120)

If the lines are offered in verse, the quotation must reflect the exact line breaks. The parenthetical citation gives the act, scene, and line numbers, separated by periods.

The guidelines for quoting secondary sources (most often critical essays) are the same as those for quoting stories and novels. If the author's name is mentioned in the introduction to the quotation, the parenthetical citation need include only the page number(s).

> According to Bettelheim, the story of Cinderella is beneficial to a child because "it gives the child confidence" (90).

Otherwise, the author's last name appears along with the page number(s).

Some feminist critics have asserted that Austen's *Pride and Prejudice* eventually confirms the very messages it seems to mock in the beginning:

> The famous beginning . . . opens with an ironical recapitulation of the dearest scheme of Mrs. Bennet: "It is a truth universally acknowledged that a single man in possession of a good fortune must be in want of a wife" (51). But the brilliant marriage contract that her smart Elizabeth strikes in the end outshines Mrs. Bennet's wildest plotting. Perhaps the old convention, however abused and deteriorated, still contains too much truth, literarily and literally, to be completely dispensed with. (Huang 104)

For electronic or non-print sources, offer sufficient information in the in-text citation to enable a reader to locate the source in the list of works cited. Some electronic sources, such as web pages, do not always indicate a specific author and may not have page numbers. If the author's name is available, offer the author's name in parenthesis as usual, followed by page numbers, if available. If the author's name is not given and there are no formal page numbers, simply place the title of electronic or non-print source (or a reasonable abbreviation of the title) in parenthesis after the quotation or paraphrase.

Works Cited Entries

At the end of an essay, the student must provide a list of works cited. The entries on this list offer bibliographic information about the quoted sources. The sources are listed in alphabetic order, according to the last names of the authors. The general format consists of providing the author's name, the title of the work, and information about the publication. The first line of the entry begins flush with the left margin; all succeeding lines should be indented five spaces. The whole list should be double-spaced; additional spaces between entries are unnecessary. The samples below cover the types of sources students are most likely to use for essays of literary analysis. For more complete coverage of MLA style, readers should consult the *MLA Handbook for Writers of Research Papers,* Eighth Edition, by Joseph Gibaldi.

The increasing use of online sources for both critical and research essays necessitates some words of caution. First, students should be careful to evaluate electronic sources to make certain that they are reputable and scholarly. Second, students should consult the most recent MLA handbook or a serviceable writer's handbook for citation formats. With the various kinds of sources now available, the formats have become too numerous to reproduce here. But, as a general rule, the citation should include (1) the author or editor of the site or page, if available, (2) the title of the site or page, (3) the date of posting, (4) the institution or organization associated with the site or page, if available, and (5) the date the site or page was accessed by the student.

Book by a Single Author

Harveit, Lars. *Workings of the Picaresque in the British Novel.* Atlantic Highlands, NJ: Humanities, 1987. Print.

Morrison, Toni. *Beloved.* New York: Knopf, 1987. Print.

Book by Two or Three Authors

Barton, Edwin, and Glenda Hudson. *A Contemporary Guide to Literary Terms*. Boston: Houghton, 1997. Print.

Draback, Bernard A., Helen E. Ellis, and Hartley A. Pfeil. *Exploring Literature Through Reading and Writing*. Boston: Houghton, 1982. Print.

Poem, Story, or Essay Collected in an Anthology

Dove, Rita. "Silos." *Contemporary American Poetry*. 6th ed. Ed. A. Poulin, Jr. Boston: Houghton, 1996. 113. Print.

Kelly, Gary. "Jane Austen, Romantic Feminism, and Civil Society." *Jane Austen and Discourses of Feminism*. Ed. Devoney Looser. New York: St. Martin's, 1995. 19–34. Print.

Novel or Play Collected in an Anthology

Hansberry, Lorraine. *A Raisin in the Sun. The Heath Guide to Literature*. 3rd ed. Ed. David Bergman and Daniel Mark Epstein. Boston: Heath, 1992. 1369–1426. Print.

Introduction, Preface, Foreword, or Afterword

Daiches, David. Introduction. *Wuthering Heights*. By Emily Bronte. New York: Penguin, 1965. 7–25. Print.

Article in Journal with Continuous Pagination

Shroeder, Natalie E., and Ronald A. Schroeder. "Betsy Trotwood and Jane Murdstone: Dickensian Doubles." *Studies in the Novel* 21 (1989): 268–78. Print.

Article in Journal without Continuous Pagination

McDowell, Deborah E. "New Directions for Black Feminist Criticism." *Black American Literature Forum* 14.4 (Winter 1980): 25–46. Print.

Article in Online Database

McLeod, Deborah. "Disturbing the Silence: Sound Imagery in Conrad's *The Secret Agent*." *Journal of Modern Literature* 33.1 (Fall 2009): 117–131. 10 June 2010. Web.

Film

Sense and Sensibility. Dir. Ang Lee. Perf. Emma Thompson and Hugh Grant. Columbia, 1995. Film.

GRAMMAR, PUNCTUATION, AND STYLE

Grammar: Common Problems

Fragments. Incomplete sentences are among the most common and most serious errors in English composition. In order to be complete, a sentence must have both a subject and a verb, and the sentence must be able to stand on its own grammatically and as a complete thought.

1. Be careful about starting a sentence with the relative pronouns *who, whom, which,* and *that.*

   Fragment (see italics): In the third act, Hamlet has an opportunity to kill Claudius. *Which is what the ghost of his father has urged him to do.*

   Complete Sentence: In the third act, Hamlet has an opportunity to kill Claudius, which is what the ghost of his father has urged him to do.

2. Be careful about starting a sentence with a present participle (modifier ending with -ing).

   Fragment (see italics): In the graveyard scene, Laertes leaps into Ophelia's grave. *Showing the strength of his love for his sister.*

   Complete Sentence: In the graveyard scene, Laertes leaps into Ophelia's grave, showing the strength of his love for his sister.

3. Be careful about using a present participle as a main verb.

   Fragment (see italics): With the play within the play, Hamlet confirms that Claudius is a murderer. *The king's reaction revealing his guilty conscience.*

   Complete Sentence (see italics): With the play within the play, Hamlet confirms that Claudius is a murderer. *The king's reaction reveals his guilty conscience.*

Agreement Errors. These most commonly occur when subjects and verbs do not agree in number or when pronouns do not agree with their antecedents (words to which they refer).

1. Do not confuse the object of a preposition with the subject of the sentence.

   Lack of Agreement (see italics): By the end of the play, the audience realizes that at least one of the *characters are* liars.

   Agreement (see italics): By the end of the play, the audience realizes that at least *one* of the characters *is* a liar.

2. If the object of a preposition is followed by a relative pronoun *(who, whom, which, that),* the object of the preposition determines whether the verb is singular or plural.

   Lack of Agreement (see italics): He is *one* of the characters who *is* a liar.

   Agreement (see italics): He is one of the *characters who are* liars.

3. When the subject is compound and uses "or" or "nor," the subject nearer to the verb determines whether the verb is singular or plural.

    Lack of Agreement (see italics): Neither *Hamlet* nor the other members of the royal family *emerges* from the final scene alive.

    Agreement (see italics): Neither Hamlet nor the other *members* of the royal family emerge from the final scene alive.

4. A pronoun must agree in number (singular or plural) with its antecedent.

    Lack of Agreement (see italics): Each *one* of the characters has *their* own motives.

    Agreement (see italics): Each one of the characters has *his* or *her* own motive.

    Lack of Agreement (see italics): *Everybody* has *their* own ways of reading a poem.

    Agreement (see italics): *Everybody* has *his* or *her* own way of reading a poem.

Punctuation: Common Problems

Comma Usage

1. Use a comma after an introductory prepositional phrase.

    Comma: In the beginning of the play, the characters are introduced in rapid succession.

2. Use a comma in a complex sentence when the subordinate clause comes first.

    Comma: Although Hamlet is not by nature a violent man, he contemplates the murder of Claudius.

3. Use a comma to separate the independent clauses connected by a coordinating conjunction in a compound sentence.

    Comma: Hamlet has recently lost his father, and Fortinbras has recently lost his.

4. Do not use a comma before the coordinating conjunction in a compound predicate.

    No Comma: Ophelia loves Hamlet but obeys her father's wishes.

Semicolon Usage

1. Use a semicolon between two closely related, independent clauses without a coordinating conjunction to connect them. Do not use a comma.

    Semicolon: Laertes leaps into his sister's grave, Hamlet leaps in to challenge him.

2. Use a semicolon between two independent clauses connected by a conjunctive adverb *[therefore, nevertheless, otherwise,* and many others).

    Semicolon: Hamlet loves his mother dearly; nevertheless, he cannot forgive her for marrying Claudius so quickly after his father's death.

Colon Usage

1.   Use a colon after a complete sentence that introduces a list, an example, or a fragmentary description.

   Colon: Hamlet's situation is mirrored by two other characters' situations: those of Fortinbras and Laertes.

2.   Do not use a colon after a fragment.

   Incorrect Use of Colon: The characters whose situations mirror Hamlet's are: Fortinbras and Laertes.

Style

Avoiding Personal Pronouns

1.   Avoid using first- and second-person pronouns: *I, me, my, you, your.*

   Poor: I think Claudius is a sympathetic antagonist in places.

   Better: Claudius is a sympathetic antagonist in places.

   Poor: As you can see, Ophelia is mad.

   Better: Ophelia is mad.

Introducing Quotations by Providing a Context

1.   Quotations must be properly introduced by providing a context: either where they appear in the work or what they contribute to the argument of the work.

   Poor: Shakespeare says, "My mistress' eyes are nothing like the sun; / Coral is far more red than her lips' red" (1–2).

   Better: Shakespeare begins the sonnet by contradicting the exaggerated conceits of Petrarchan sonnets: "My mistress' eyes are nothing like the sun; / Coral is far more red than her lips' red" (1–2).

   Poor: Shakespeare writes "[t]hat music hath a far more pleasing sound" (10).

   Better: Remarking on his mistress's voice, Shakespeare declares "[t]hat music hath a far more pleasing sound" (10).

   Poor: "To love that well which thou must leave ere long" (14) means that the speaker has learned to appreciate life as his death nears.

   Better: The speaker has learned to appreciate life as his death nears and urges his friend "[t]o love that well which thou must leave ere long" (14).

Index of Authors and Works

Index of Terms

Boldface numbers indicate definitions

Acknowledgments

Pages 2–3: From "Bantams in Pine-Woods," from *The Collected Poems of Wallace Stevens* by Wallace Stevens, copyright 1954 by Wallace Stevens and renewed 1982 by Holly Stevens. Used by permission of Alfred A. Knopf, a division of Random House, Inc., and Faber &. Faber, Ltd.

Page 8: From "Sunday Morning," from *The Collected Poems of Wallace Stevens* by Wallace Stevens, copyright 1954 by Wallace Stevens and renewed 1982 by Holly Stevens. Used by permission of Alfred A. Knopf, a division of Random House, Inc., and Faber & Faber, Ltd.

Page 8: From "Lost Sister," reprinted by permission of Yale University Press.

Page 9: From "Dream Deferred," from *The Collected Poems of Langston Hughes* by Langston Hughes, copyright © 1994 by The Estate of Langston Hughes. Used by permission of Alfred A. Knopf, a division of Random House, Inc.

Pages 18–19: From G. Blakemore Evans, *The Riverside Shakespeare,* first edition. Reprinted by permission of the Houghton Mifflin Company.

Page 23: From *Amadeus* by Peter Shaffer. Copyright © 1980 by Peter Shaffer. Reprinted by permission of HarperCollins Publishers, Inc.

Page 26: From "Sylvester's Dying Bed," from *The Collected Poems of Langston Hughes* by Langston Hughes, copyright © 1994 by The Estate of Langston Hughes. Used by permission of Alfred A. Knopf, a division of Random House, Inc.

Page 27: Reprinted by permission of the publishers and the Trustees of Amherst College from *The Poems of Emily Dickinson,* Thomas H. Johnson, ed., Cambridge, Mass.: The Belknap Press of Harvard University Press. Copyright © 1951, 1955, 1979 by the President and Fellows of Harvard College.

Pages 29–30: From G. Blakemore Evans, *The Riverside Shakespeare,* first edition. Reprinted by permission of the Houghton Mifflin Company.

Page 30: Excerpt from "Poem," from *The Complete Poems: 1927–1979* by Elizabeth Bishop. Copyright © 1979, 1983 by Alice Helen Methfessel. Reprinted by permission of Farrar, Straus and Giroux, LLC.

Pages 34–35: From "Jacklight," copyright © 1984 by Louise Erdrich, reprinted with the permission of The Wylie Agency, Inc.

Page 35: Reprinted by permission of the publishers and the Trustees of Amherst College from *The Poems of Emily Dickinson,* Thomas H. Johnson, ed., Cambridge, Mass.: The Belknap Press of Harvard University Press. Copyright © 1951, 1955, 1979 by the President and Fellows of Harvard College.

Page 37: From "Never May the Fruit Be Plucked" by Edna St. Vincent Millay, 1923 from *Collected Poems,* 1967. Reprinted courtesy of The Edna St. Vincent Millay Society.

Pages 38–39: From *Death of a Salesman* by Arthur Miller, copyright 1949, renewed © 1977 by Arthur Miller. Used by permission of Viking Penguin, a division of Penguin Group (USA) Inc.

Page 40: From G. Blakemore Evans, *The Riverside Shakespeare,* first edition. Reprinted by permission of the Houghton Mifflin Company.

Pages 43–44: From G. Blakemore Evans, *The Riverside Shakespeare,* first edition. Reprinted by permission of the Houghton Mifflin Company.

Page 45: Reprinted by permission of the publishers and the Trustees of Amherst College from *The Poems of Emily Dickinson,* Thomas H. Johnson, ed., Cambridge, Mass.: The Belknap Press of Harvard University Press. Copyright © 1951, 1955, 1979 by the President and Fellows of Harvard College.

Page 46: From *Petrarch: Selected Poems,* translated into English by Anthony Mortimer. Copyright © 1977 by The University of Alabama Press. Used by permission of the publisher.

Pages 47–48: From "History," from *New and Selected Poems* by Gary Soto.

Copyright © 1995. Used with permission of Chronicle Books, LLC, San Francisco. Visit ChronicleBooks.com.

Page 49: Reprinted with the permission of Scribner, an imprint of Simon & Schuster Adult Publishing Group, from *The Collected. Works of W.B. Yeats, Volume One: The Poems, Revised,* edited by Richard J. Finneran. Copyright © 1928 by The Macmillan Company; copyright renewed © 1956 by Georgie Yeats.

Page 49: From "A Sea-Chantey," from *Collected Poems: 1948–1984* by Derek Walcott. Copyright © 1986 by Derek Walcott. Reprinted by permission of Farrar, Straus and Giroux, LLC and Faber & Faber, Ltd.

Page 50: Excerpts from "Digging" from *Poems: 1965–1975* by Seamus Heaney. Copyright © 1980 by Seamus Heaney. Reprinted by permission of Farrar, Straus and Giroux, LLC and Faber & Faber, Ltd.

Page 51: From "The Apotheosis of Major Doe," from *Mandela's Earth and Other Poems* by Wole Soyinlca, copyright © 1988 by Wole Soyinka. Used by permission of Random House, Inc.

Pages 55–56: Reprinted by permission of the publishers and the Trustees of Amherst College from *The Poems of Emily Dickinson,* Thomas H. Johnson, ed., Cambridge, Mass.: The Belknap Press of Harvard University Press. Copyright © 1951, 1955, 1979 by the President and Fellows of Harvard College.

Page 58: From *The Homecoming* by Harold Pinter. Copyright © 1965 by Harold Pinter. Used by permission of Grove/Atlantic, Inc.

Page 63: From "Windigo," copyright © 1984 by Louise Erdrich, reprinted with the permission of The Wylie Agency, Inc.

Page 69: From "Elegy," from *Collected Poems: 1948–1984* by Derek Walcott. Copyright © 1986 by Derek Walcott. Reprinted by permission of Farrar, Straus and Giroux, LLC and Faber &. Faber, Ltd.

Page 72: From "Epitaph for an Old Woman," by Octavio Paz, translated by Eliot Weinberger, from *Collected Poems 1957–1987,* copyright © 1986 by Octavio Paz and Eliot Weinberger. Reprinted by permission of New Directions Publishing Corp.

Page 73: "A Pig's Eye View of Literature: The Lives and Times of John Keats, Percy Bysshe Shelley and George Gordon Noel, Lord Byron," from *The Portable Dorothy Parker* by Dorothy Parker, edited by Marion Meade, copyright © 1928, renewed © 1956 by Dorothy Parker; copyright © 1973, 2006 by The National Assoc. for the Advancement of Colored People. Used by permission of Viking Penguin, a division of Penguin Group (USA) Inc.

Page 76: "Vision," from *She Had Some Horses* by Joy Harjo, Copyright © 1982 by Joy Harjo. Used by permission of the publisher, Thunder's Mouth Press.

Page 83: From *On Lies, Secrets, and Silence: Selected Prose: 1966–1978* (New York: Norton, 1979). Used by permission of W.W. Norton &. Company, Inc.

Pages 83–84: "My Papa's Waltz," copyright 1942 by Hearst Magazine, Inc., from *The Collected Poems of Theodore Roethke* by Theodore Rothke. Used by permission of Doubleday, a division of Random House, Inc. and Faber & Faber, Ltd.

Page 90: From *Death of a Salesman* by Arthur Miller, copyright 1949, renewed © 1977 by Arthur Miller. Used by permission of Viking Penguin, a division of Penguin Group (USA) Inc.

Pages 91–92: From G. Blalcemore Evans, *The Riverside Shakespeare,* first edition. Reprinted by permission of the Houghton Mifflin Company.

Pages 92–93: From "Crab," by Kamau Brathwaite. Reprinted by permission of Kamau Brathwaite.

Page 103: From "The Love Song of J. Alfred Prufroclc," by T.S. Eliot, reprinted by permission of Faber &. Faber, Ltd.

Page 112: Reprinted by permission of the publishers and the Trustees of Amherst College from *The Poems of Emily Dickinson,* Thomas H. Johnson, ed., Cambridge, Mass.: The Belknap Press of Harvard University Press. Copyright © 1951, 1955, 1979 by the President and Fellows of Harvard College.

Pages 112–113: From "The Love Song of J. Alfred Prufroclc," by T.S. Eliot, reprinted by permission of Faber & Faber, Ltd.

Page 113: From "The Fist," from *Collected Poems: 1948–1984* by Derek Walcott. Copyright © 1986 by Derek Walcott. Reprinted by permission of Farrar, Straus and Giroux, LLC and Faber & Faber, Ltd.

Pages 116–117: From "Poppa Chicken" by Margaret Walker, 1989, from *This is My Century: New and Collected Poems* by Margaret Walker Alexander. Reprinted by permission of The University of Georgia Press.

Page 117: From *Getting Home Alive* by Aurora Levins Morales (Ann Arbor, Michigan: Firebrand Books, 1986], Copyright © 1986 by Aurora Levins Morales and Rosario Morales.

Page 121: Excerpt from *The Joker of Seville* by Derek Walcott. Copyright © 1978 Derek Walcott. Reprinted by permission of Farrar, Straus and Giroux, LLC.

Pages 125–126: Lines from the first of the *Pisan Cantos,* by Ezra Pound, from *The Cantos of Ezra Pound,* copyright © 1934, 1937, 1940, 1948, 1956, 1959, 1962, 1963, 1966, and 1968 by Ezra Pound. Reprinted by permission of New Directions Publishing Corp. and Faber & Faber, Ltd.

Page 139: From "Preludes," by T.S. Eliot, reprinted by permission of Faber & Faber, Ltd.

Pages 141–142: "Encounter," from *Hard Labor* by Cesare Paves, translated by William Arrowsmith, copyright © 1976 by William Arrowsmith. *Lavorare Stanca* Copyright 1943 by Giulio Einaudi editore, Torino. Used by permission of Viking Penguin, a division of Penguin Group (USA) Inc.

Pages 142–143: "Daddy," from *Ariel* by Sylvia Plath. Copyright © 1963 by Ted Hughes. Reprinted by permission of HarperCollins Publishers, Inc.

Page 145: Excerpts from "Digging" and "Elegy for a Still-Born Child" from *Poems: 1965–1975* by Seamus Heaney. Copyright © 1980 by Seamus Heaney. Reprinted by permission of Farrar, Straus and Giroux, LLC and Faber & Faber, Ltd.

Page 154: Lines from "A Country Walk" by Thomas Kinsella from *Poems 1956–1973.* Reprinted by permission of the author.

Page 156: "The Death of the Ball Turret Gunner," from *The Complete Poems* by Randall Jarrell. Copyright © 1969, renewed 1997 by Mary Von S. Jarrell. Reprinted by permission of Farrar, Straus and Giroux, LLC and Faber &. Faber, Ltd.

Page 156: From "The Crazy Woman" by Gwendolyn Brooks, from *Blacks* by Gwendolyn Brooks. ©1991. Published by Third World Press, Chicago, 1991.

Page 157: From "After Twenty Years" by Fadwa Tuquan. Copyright © 1979 by Fadwa Tuquan. Reprinted by permission.

Pages 161–162: From G. Blakemore Evans, *The Riverside Shakespeare,* first edition. Reprinted by permission of the Houghton Mifflin Company.

Page 174: "KA 'BA," reprinted by permission of Sterling Lord Literistic, Inc. Copyright by Amiri Baraka.

Pages 174–175: From *Sappho: A New Translation,* translated by Mary Barnard. Copyright © 1958 The Regents of the University of California. Copyright renewed by Mary Barnard. Used with the permission of The University of California Press.

Page 180: "Do not go gentle into that good night," by Dylan Thomas, from *The Poems of Dylan Thomas,* copyright © 1952 by Dylan Thomas. Reprinted by permission of New Directions Publishing Corp.

Pages 180–181: From "Share-Croppers," from *The Collected Poems of Langston Hughes* by Langston Hughes, copyright © 1994 by The Estate of Langston Hughes. Used by permission of Alfred A. Knopf, a division of Random House, Inc.

Page 186: Excerpt from "In Celebration of My Uterus," from *Love Poems* by Anne Sexton. Copyright © 1967, 1968, 1969 by Anne Sexton. Reprinted by permission of Houghton Mifflin Company Sterling Lord Literistic, Inc. All rights reserved.

Pages 188: Reprinted by permission of the publishers and the Trustees of Amherst College from *The Poems of Emily Dickinson,* Thomas H. Johnson, ed., Cambridge, Mass.: The Belknap Press of Harvard University Press. Copyright © 1951, 1955, 1979 by the President and Fellows of Harvard College.